Mission as Integrated Witness

Mission as Integrated Witness

A Missional Reading of the Foot-Washing Narrative (John 13:1–38)

JAE-SUK LEE

WIPF & STOCK · Eugene, Oregon

MISSION AS INTEGRATED WITNESS
A Missional Reading of the Foot-Washing Narrative (John 13:1–38)

Copyright © 2021 Jae-Suk Lee. All rights reserved. Except for brief quotations in critical publications or reviews, no part of this book may be reproduced in any manner without prior written permission from the publisher. Write: Permissions, Wipf and Stock Publishers, 199 W. 8th Ave., Suite 3, Eugene, OR 97401.

Wipf & Stock
An Imprint of Wipf and Stock Publishers
199 W. 8th Ave., Suite 3
Eugene, OR 97401

www.wipfandstock.com

PAPERBACK ISBN: 978-1-7252-9754-8
HARDCOVER ISBN: 978-1-7252-9755-5
EBOOK ISBN: 978-1-7252-9756-2

05/17/21

To my wife, Esther Eun-Sook Han, whose beautiful nature is an ever-present witness of Jesus's sacrificial love and service in humility

Contents

Preface	ix
Acknowledgments	xiii
List of Abbreviations	xv
Introduction	1
1 | Preliminary Considerations on Missional Hermeneutics for John's Gospel	4
2 | Mission as Integrated Witness in John's Gospel	41
3 | Understanding the Foot-Washing Narrative in Light of Mission as Integrated Witness	101
4 | Missional Implications of John's Gospel for the Future of the Evangelical Mission	148
Conclusion	192
Bibliography	195
Author Index	211
Subject Index	215
Ancient Document Index	225

Preface

FOR THE STUDY, I was initially interested in these questions arising from my own experience. What is a mission? What does the Bible tell us about its meaning and significance? As a Korean Presbyterian Church (Hapdong) missionary, I worked in Mindanao, the Philippines from 2005 to 2014. My missionary commitment was to obey Jesus's Great Commission to go and make disciples (Matt 28:19–20). In the mission field, I went house-to-house in order to evangelize people, with the aim of disciple-making and church-planting. In this work, I was most influenced by the Lausanne Covenant (1974) and my denominational understanding of mission. Evangelism was the priority. Of course, I believed that assuming social responsibilities was a way for Christians to participate in the reign of God. Yet, according to the principle of separation between church and state that was generally accepted by Korean churches, my fellow missionaries and I hesitated to engage in sociopolitical activities in the mission field. Instead, we assumed that the transformation of society could happen through the disciple-making of people. Therefore, we concentrated only on evangelism for conversion, soul-salvation, disciple-making, church-planting, and church-growth. My missiological reading of the Bible focused on Jesus's Great Commission given to his disciples. In proof-texting, I interpreted the Bible to justify my missionary works and reinforce evangelism, which aims at the proclamation of the gospel, making-discipleship, church planting, and social services.

As time went by, however, a serious question occurred to me about this missionary focus: "Are we missionaries living as Jesus's disciples in this land?" Despite our passion for and commitment to such diverse missionary activities, in actuality the people seemed not to think of us as Jesus's genuine disciples, but rather simply as rich missionaries or teachers. Besides, many people of different religions in the region distrusted Christians because their lives did not match the message they delivered. One day, when

I visited a Muslim village, an Arabic teacher there mocked the Christian life, pointing out that Christians lived lives of denial, corruption, sexual disorder, violence, and falsehood, which did not correspond with the lofty faith and doctrine they confessed with their lips. In this way, the life of many Christians disrupted the execution of Jesus's Great Commission. This unfortunate reality seriously challenged my previous notion of mission and its effectiveness.

Eventually, I came back to the essential question of what mission is. I wanted to hear what the Bible says about the mission. Until recently, scholars have largely done two kinds of missional hermeneutics. *Firstly*, a missional reading is to interpret the whole Bible through a metanarrative theme. George F. Vicedom, Johannes Blauw, Richard Bauckham, and Christopher J. H. Wright propose that missional reading premises a conceptual framework of coherently reading the Old and New Testaments. Their methodology is 'biblical-theological interpretation.'[1] While some scholars separate the Old Testament from the New Testament,[2] they read the Old and New Testament in a single book from a missionary or missional perspective. Their missional reading aims to understand God's mission and his people's mission through the entire Bible. *Secondly*, David Bosch, James V. Brownson, and Johannes Nissen emphasize the diversity of each biblical text, which reflects the unique mission paradigm of the individual recipient community in their context.[3] To put it in a nutshell, although admitting that the Bible deals with one subject within the theological structure, I argue that the biblical authors would write their theological understanding of God's mission. They narrate their theological interpretation of historical events in the form of a story and narratives.[4] Therefore, for me, a missional hermeneutic should primarily begin with a literary-exegetical interpretation of the text. In addition, the missional hermeneutic aims to hold a dialogue between texts and today's Christian readers. For the dialogue with Evangelicals, I paid attention to Lausanne conferences.

Above all, at the 2010 Cape Town Congress, John's Gospel was used to provide a theological basis for God's mission as "his sending act" (John 20:21). Emphasizing that the world is the object of his great love, though fallen away from God, the Cape Town Congress appeals that mission began

---

1. Vicedom, *Mission of God*, 52; Blauw, *Missionary Nature*, 72; Bauckham, *Bible and Mission*, 11; Wright, *Mission of God*, 118; cf. Köstenberger and O'Brien, *Salvation*, 19–20; Redford, *Missiological Hermeneutics*, 12.

2. Kaiser Jr., *Mission* (2012), Nissen, *New Testament* (2007) and so forth.

3. Bosch, *Transforming Mission*, 20–25, 57–124; Brownson, *Speaking the Truth*, 39; Nissen, *New Testament*, 21–97.

4. Enns, *Inspiration and Incarnation*, 117; Anderson, *Understanding*, 24–27.

with his love (3:16). This shows that John's Gospel was used as the primary fundamental and central biblical text in the 2010 conference, after the 'sending language' (17:18; 20:21) was interpreted in the frame of Jesus's Great Commission at the 1974 Lausanne Conference. Evangelicals' reading of John may explain the justification for the engagement of the church and Christians in both preaching the gospel for the conversion of unbelievers and being committed to social responsibilities. However, John talks about Jesus and his disciples' mission, in an integrated sense. John spotlights proclamation and witness in life. Jesus was sent to preach the word of God, and to make people believe the word and get eternal life. The purpose of the disciples' sentness, too, is to proclaim Jesus and his teachings. At the same time, just as Jesus shows the Father in his life, so should the disciples bear witness to Jesus through their daily lives in love and service (John 14:9; 13:35). Andreas J. Köstenberger examines John's 'sending language' through semantic studies.[5] He highlights both evangelism and discipleship.[6] Jesus's sending of the disciples presupposes that their discipleship practices "humble servant spirit (cf. 13:1–15), mutual love (cf. 13:35; 15:13), and unity (cf. 17:21, 23, 25)."[7] Surely, as Köstenberger's observation is to hear John's voice, missional reading should observe what the text said and is saying. John does not describe love and service as a motive for evangelism and social service. Instead, he argues that Jesus and the disciples' lives are witnesses, which should not be separated from evangelism. I ensure that this Johannine mission concept can exert developmental influence on today's evangelicals, who aspire toward evangelism and social responsibilities.

---

5. Köstenberger, *Missions of Jesus*, 2–3.
6. Köstenberger, *Missions of Jesus*, 177n129.
7. Köstenberger, *Missions of Jesus*, 211.

Acknowledgments

WHILE STUDYING AT FULLER Theological Seminary, I have experienced God's amazing providence. He has finished the good work he began. I acknowledge that I couldn't complete my race without his grace and help. God gave me a great mentor who is a good teacher and friend. I give thanks to Dr. Keon-Sang An for guiding me from the beginning to the end of my journey into this field. He is a model for life-witness that I want to write about in this paper. Dr. An was willing to devote his time and finances to my growth and ongoing formation of spirituality, personality, and academic achievements. Under his supervision, my writing took a turn for the better and became richer.

I would like to thank Dr. Christopher M. Blumhofer and Dr. Kirsteen Kim. Studying with Dr. Blumhofer, I acquired the methodology of the study of the Gospel and the Bible. Through his insight and comments, he allowed me to focus on the biblical text. Dr. Kim has had a decisive influence on my understanding of mission history and evangelicals' mission. I will not forget her generous, and at the same time sharp, guidance. Also, I want to thank Dr. Dean Deppe. He did not hesitate to read my dissertation or to critique it. His questions and comments will be very helpful in developing my idea. My thankful heart is given to Sister Ariana and Sister Judy, who worked hard to edit my paper.

I thank Dr. Timothy Ki-ho Park. He gave me several scholarships and encouraged me to study. If he hadn't sponsored me, I wouldn't have begun studying. I also express my thanks to Dr. Rev. Keun-Soo Kim, Dr. Rev. Ikbong Jang, Sister Sungeun Kim, Hanwool Church (Bundang, Korea), Hanultari Presbyterian Church (LA, USA), and supporters in Korea. They served my family and me with great love. Finally, I sincerely thank my lovely wife Eun-Sook and two sons Hyunbin and Hyunwoo. While I was studying here, they became strength and motivation to me. I will never forget my beloved daughter, Hyunji, who rests in God's bosom.

List of Abbreviations

CTC	Cape Town Commitment 2010
ESV	English Standard Version
LC	Lausanne Covenant 1974
LOP	Lausanne Occasional Paper
LXX	Septuagint
MM	Manila Manifesto 1989
MT	Masoret Text
NA28	Novum Testamentum Graece
TDNT	Theological Dictionary of the New Testament
1QS	1QCommunity Rule
4QFlor	4Q Florilegium (4Q174)
4Q285	4Q Serekh Milhuamah
m. Sukkah	Mishnah Sukkah
1 Macc	1 Maccabees
2. Macc	2 Maccabees
T. Abr	Testament of Abraham (2–3 Apocalypse of Baruch)
Jos. Asen	Joseph and Aseneth
Mishnah Ber	Mishnah Berakhot
Tob	Tobit
Spec. Leg	*De Specialibus Legibus*

Leg. Ad Gaium   *Legatio ad Gaium*

Introduction

This study aims to examine the missional implications of Jesus's foot-washing narrative (John 13:1–38) for today's evangelicals' mission. For his recipient community, John refers to an integrated witness as the mission of evangelism and life-witness in the mutual indwelling relationship between God, Jesus, and the disciples. In particular, the foot-washing narrative signifies life-witness and evangelism as the disciples' mission for both the faith community and the world. So far, Johannine scholars have interpreted the foot-washing narrative in various aspects: an example of humility or hospitality;[1] a symbol of the Eucharist[2] and baptism;[3] a symbol of the forgiveness of sin through Jesus's redemptive death;[4] an anticipation of persecution from the unbelieving Jews;[5] and an ethical interpretation.[6] Only some scholars have attempted to interpret the foot-washing narrative from the missional perspective.[7] In this investigation, I will literarily exegetically deal with John's use of sending language and formulae, which present Jesus and his disciples' integrated witness as mission. I point out that the foot-washing narrative also connotes the mission concept. Furthermore, I propose the missional

---

1. Barrett, *Gospel according to St. John*, 437; Hultgren, "Johannine Footwashing," 539–46; Keener, *Gospel of John*, 901–14.

2. Maynard, "Role of Peter," 534–35.

3. Brown, *John I–XII*, 566–68; Paschal, "Sacramental Symbolism," 151–76; Dodd, *Interpretation*, 401–3.

4. Beasley-Murray, *John*, 234; Thompson, *John*, 282.

5. Weiss, "Footwashing," 298–325.

6. Schnackenburg, *Gospel according to St John*, 3:12, 23; Thompson, "His Own Received Him Not," 258; Köstenberger, "John," 485; Thomas, *Footwashing*, 87.

7. Weiss, "Footwashing," 321; Lombard and Oliver, "Working Supper," 361; Okure, *Mission*, 196–97; Gorman, *Abide and Go*, 88.

meaning of the foot-washing narrative to today's evangelical readers in order to build their communities as a missional community.

In chapter 1, I define a missional hermeneutic for John's Gospel and its two interpretative methods: (1) literary-exegetical interpretation and (2) theological interpretation. The former is to examine the concept of mission spoken by the author in a literary and semantic world. The latter interpretation is to understand the biblical text from the author's theological perspective and today's reader's theological perspective. Next, I briefly look into the recent discussions on mission in John's Gospel.

In chapter 2, I explore John's Gospel from a literary-exegetical interpretive point of view. My focus is on how John talks about mission in his literary and semantic world. The author uses the term "send" in the whole Gospel. This observation attempts to comprehend mission by interpreting what John says about God's sending of the Son and Jesus's sending of the Holy Spirit and the disciples (John 17:18; 20:21). John's sending language and formulae show that the author is beginning and completing God's mission, centered on the sentness and witness of both Jesus and the disciples in the unity-relationship, or mutual indwelling. In Jesus's mission, God not only discloses himself through Jesus's life, identity, and works but also fulfills salvation for the world. Above all, God reveals his nature (love and humble service) in Jesus's daily life among people and sacrificial death on the cross. Conversely, Jesus bears witness to God in and through his life and works. At the same time, his testimony of God is never separated from the completion of mission as a specific task for the salvation of the world. Jesus's mission is passed on to his disciples. They are sent to testify to the triune God both through their lives (and identity) and through preaching and teaching the gospel. In the Gospel, Jesus and the disciples' mission are life-witness and evangelism in the integrated sense.

In chapter 3, I deal with Jesus's foot-washing narrative literarily and exegetically. Jesus presents the completion of his mission and its meanings. Then, he interprets his symbolic act for the disciples' mission. They have to continually bear witness to Jesus after he came back to the Father (13:1, 35). Through the frame of "as . . ., so . . ." and sending language (13:16, 20), John shares that the disciples must be sent to both the faith community and the world to live a life of witness, and testify to Jesus (13:20, 35 with 1:14, 18; 17:18; 20:21). Their lives and proclamation are rooted in sacrificial love and humble service, which are embodied in his forgiving the betrayal of disciples, the world, and enemies by washing them, and, ultimately, in Jesus's sacrificial death. They must live Jesus's life in the faith community and, at the same time, in the world. Their lives are the witness of life, showing that they are Jesus's disciples (13:35, 36; 17:23). The disciples continue to do the work of evangelism under Jesus's command to lead the world to forgiveness, faith, and eternal life in the light and the truth (13:16; 15:27; 17:20; 20:23).

In chapter 4, I concentrate on what missional implications John gives today's evangelicals for their mission, who follow Lausanne conferences. First of all, I investigate contemporary evangelicals' definitions of mission. They held three international conferences (1974, 1989, 2010), and showed a gradual transformation in the concept of mission. In the 1974 Lausanne Congress, evangelicals talked about evangelism and social participation in the frame of dichotomy. They asserted mission as evangelism. Later, in 1989 and 2010, evangelicals developed a holistic or integral understanding of mission as evangelism and witness of life. But in the 2010s, some evangelicals criticized Cape Town's agreement. They insist on mission as evangelism in contrast to a holistic mission.

Finally, I propose that John's foot-washing narrative gives missional implications and insights into their debate. John alludes to mission as an integrated witness of life-witness and evangelism in the unity-relationship with God. Three conferences have interpreted God's sending act in terms of Jesus's Great Commission. However, as some scholars have shown recently, when John narrates Jesus's and the disciples' sentness, the author does not separate their life-witness from evangelism. As Jesus is in oneness with the Father, so also are they united with Jesus in the sharing of life, identity, and works with the sender in mutual indwelling. John emphasizes that the incarnate Jesus is abiding in the midst of them through the Holy Spirit. Therefore, John's missional implications such as evangelism, love, and humble service, as shown by Jesus's foot-washing narrative, should not be missed by the evangelicals living today. They are the "sent" incarnational, consecrating, and hermeneutical community of an integrated witness, in which the incarnate Jesus is abiding.

1

Preliminary Considerations on Missional Hermeneutics for John's Gospel

THIS CHAPTER AIMS TO both define a missional hermeneutical approach to reading John's Gospel, and to observe, in advance, the scholarly understanding of the Johannine mission and foot-washing narrative. Until recently, reading the Bible from a missional perspective has taken a variety of approaches. The first has been to interpret the Bible in order to provide proof for mission movements or to find biblical foundations for mission. The second has been an attempt to read either the entire Bible or individual biblical texts as a larger subject, or as the metanarrative of God's mission.[1] By evaluating these two approaches, I will delineate a missional hermeneutic for reading the Gospel of John. Finally, I will briefly discuss recent studies surrounding the Johannine mission and explain what further study is needed. In discussions with scholars, I will also look at the important missional elements in Jesus's foot-washing narrative.

---

1. The *missio Dei* is defined as God's sending act from his person that discloses himself and saves the world (Latin verb *mitto*, to send) (Bauckham, *Bible and Mission*, 94; Wright, *Mission of God*, 202–10). In John's Gospel, the *missio Dei* points to God sending the Son into the world to reveal himself and save humanity (John 1:14, 18; 3:16–21; 8:28; 9:4; 14:10; 16:32; 17:18; 20:21). Then, the Son sends his disciples, with the Holy Spirit, for witness to God and the execution of his salvation (1:33; 3:4–11; 7:37–39; 13:15, 34–35; 15:26–27; 16:7–11; 20:22–23) (Bauckham, *Bible and Mission*, 10).

APPROACHES TO THE CHRISTIAN USE OF THE BIBLE FOR MISSION

Modern Christians have been engaged in interpreting the Bible through the lens of mission by way of three approaches: (1) proof-texting of the Bible for mission, (2) biblical foundations for mission, and (3) missional hermeneutics. These methods are associated with the questions of today's readers: (1) will readers read the Bible verses as justification for missionary activities and strategies? (2) will readers read the entire Bible, or just an individual text, in order to find the theological meaning and implications of mission? and (3) will the Bible be read within the readers' context?

Proof-Texting Method

Since the days of cross-cultural missionary movements, the proof-texting method has been useful in both motivating and justifying Christian missions on the basis of Jesus's Great Commission (Matt 28:19–20; Mark 16:15; Luke 24:46–48; John 20:21): "go" or "send" and "make disciples of all nations" (Matt 28:19–20; John 20:21).

Prior to the Edinburgh Missionary Conference of 1910, Christian mission was involved in expanding the movement around the world. Gustav Warneck (1703–1791) and William Carey (1761–1834) suggest that the goal should be to save the heathens, according to the Bible (Matt 28:18–20; Mark 16:15; Luke 24:46–48; John 20:21; Acts 1:8; 4:15; 22:21; 26:16–18). They acknowledge that a missionary movement took place between primitive and modern church history in which Christians were sent far away so that unbelievers could be converted to Christ. The primary mission here focused on the pagan conversion to Christ from sin and idolatry.[2] Warneck and Carey's reading was restricted to a proof-texting of the Bible under the motto "go and make disciples" (Matt 28:19–20).[3]

At the Edinburgh Missionary Conference, participants expounded two aspects of Christian mission. The first intensified the mission movement concerning the "Student Volunteer Movement (Foreign Mission): World Evangelization of Our Generation," in which participants explained the successful expansion of Christianity across the world (Committee II).[4] The conference focused on the issue of delivering Christian messages

---

2. Carey, *Enquiry*, 68.
3. Warneck, *Protestant Missions*, 1–2; Moule, *Charles Simeon*, 18.
4. Van Gelder, *Missional Church*, 18.

to the non-Christian world, especially the "west to the rest."[5] The second aspect was motivated by the recognition of the challenge of Christian mission among non-Christian societies (Commissions I and IV).[6] In order to motivate and justify Christian mission as the "urgent evangelization of the region," mission leaders highlighted Jesus's Great Commission.[7] Their Bible reading is the proof-text, or selective approach, needed to provide relevance for the missionary movements and activities of Gentile nations. They believed that proclamation, witness, and teaching were the missional activities of Jesus and the disciples.

After the Edinburgh meeting in 1910, John R. Mott published the book *The Evangelization of the World in this Generation*, in which he clarifies his central ideas of world evangelization and missionary work.[8] Mott and his contemporary Christians maintain that the Bible is God's revelation. Based on that idea, they tried to obey Jesus's Great Commission. Mott underscores the biblical message that people can be saved from "the power of sin and its penalty," and also claims that the Bible deals with God's will for the salvation of all nations and races (Mark 16:15; Luke 24:46, 47; Matt 28:19, 20; Acts 1:8).[9]

In short, the proof-texting method used by Warneck, Carey, Warneck, Moule, and Mott justifies why they should preach the gospel. In spite of the biblical texts characterizing their various missiological concepts from a literary contextual point of view, proof-texting the Bible for overseas missions aimed at the salvation of souls also reveals common facts. Various writings, such as the Synoptics, the Gospel of John, Paul's letters, and those from others, make it clear to the witnesses of the gospel that Jesus and the disciples were sent ("send" [ἀποστέλλω, 1 Cor 1:17; John 20:21; Acts 28:28 or πέμπω, Phil 2:19; John 20:21; Acts 19:31]). Jesus is sent to fulfill God's salvation, and his disciples are sent to share in his mandate (Matt 28:19–20; Mark 16:15, 20; Luke 24:47–48 [Acts 1:8]; John 20:21, 30–31; Rom 1:1, 15; 1 Pet 1:12). Their primary mission is to make people believe in the gospel (Luke 26:17 [for Paul], Acts 13:26; 28:28; Rev 1:9).[10] For this reason, the proof-texting method emphasizes that all early church communities are fundamentally commanded to send, proclaiming faith in the gospel.[11]

---

5. Stanley, *World Missionary Conference*, 5.
6. Stanley, *World Missionary Conference*, 121–30.
7. McGavran, "What Is Mission," 19.
8. Mott, *Evangelization of the World*, vii–viii.
9. Mott, *Evangelization of the World*, 18, 20, 23.
10. Köstenberger, *Missions of Jesus*, 14.
11. Bosch, *Witness to the World*, 14.

Biblical Foundations of Mission

In observing the historical contexts and activities of the early church and Israel, scholars work to find the biblical foundations for contemporary churches' mission by questioning the missionary movements of historical Israel and the early churches.

On the one hand, some scholars have limited the initiative of missionary movements to the intertestamental period (from Malachi to John the Baptist) and the New Testament era. According to Joachim Jeremias, "Israel was not a missionary people" until Israel undertook a religious mission to convert Gentiles to Judaism after the Maccabean era.[12] For Jeremias, mission indicates the early church's proclamation of the gospel to all nations (Mark 13:10; 14:9; Matt 26:13; Acts 10:1—11:18, 20; Gal 2:7; Rev 14:6–7). The terms "send" (Gal 2:9) and "missionary commission" support the church's cross-cultural mission (Matt 28:18–20; 1 Tim 3:16).[13]

Jeremias's reading of the New Testament centers around Jesus's kingdom movement and the sending of harvesters to the world (1 Tim 6:3; 2 Tim 1:10), and determines the theoretical and practical aspects of the direction, goals, and nature of Christian mission. The exalted Jesus commanded his disciples to gather God's eschatological people among the Jews, and to also go further to the Gentiles. His observations provide the biblical basis for the harvest of the church's mission.[14]

David Bosch's view is similar to Jeremias's, also arguing that the Synoptic Gospel portrays the various missions of the recipient community. Bosch's critical approach is carried out by historical criticism, so he stresses the activities of missionary, witness, and evangelism in the sending formula.[15] Like Jeremias, Bosch does not deal with the Old Testament, but sees that YHWH did not send his servants to convert Gentiles across geographical, religious, and social boundaries.[16] Of course, Bosch acknowledges the essential role of the Old Testament in the New Testament's mission. However, his main opinion is still that the Old Testament participated in revealing God and his dynamic actions for Israel without mentioning that Israel was sent to the nation under missionary orders.[17] Instead, Bosch asserts that the New Testament books reflect the unique contextual issues of each recipient

---

12. Jeremias, *Jesus' Promise*, 11.
13. Jeremias, *Jesus' Promise*, 19–25.
14. Cf. Hahn, *Mission*, 16, 137, 140, 142, 146–47.
15. Bosch, *Witness*, 14.
16. Bosch, *Witness*, 43.
17. Bosch, *Witness*, 17–19.

community, and the writers of the books realign Jesus's events and teachings in association with their readers' situations by employing topographical, theological, and symbolic terms and framework.[18]

Bosch's observations note that the early churches of the New Testament showed a unique mission paradigm within their historical contexts, and he provides a biblical-theological basis for the missions of today's churches within their new paradigms. Bosch's various mission paradigms led to the discovery of the content and models of mission pursued by the early church in the worlds of politics, economy, religion, and Jewish and Greek cultures.[19] They are presented on a biblical basis for the argument that, in modern times, the mission of the church should be evangelistically centered in terms of the achievement of eschatological salvation, or that various forms of mission should coexist in the new paradigm.[20]

On the other hand, attempts have been made to observe Israel's mission in the Old Testament through the critical and exegetical methodology.[21] Carroll Stuhlmueller demonstrates in *The Biblical Foundations for Mission* (1983) that the Old Testament reflects the theological concepts of mission such as Israel's acculturation in the secular realm, ongoing individual and social reformation through prophetic challenges, and universal salvation of other nations.[22] In particular, Stuhlmueller emphasizes that the Old Testament deals with the centripetal-centrifugal concept of mission on the stages of "secular liberation," "secular celebration," and "liturgical celebration" for the church's mission for the marginalized and the oppressed.[23] As the coauthor of the book, Donald Senior continues to look into the New Testament. He characterizes the church's universal mission in light of the missionary movement of the early faith-communities.[24] The church's missionary nature and responsibility are rooted in the fulfillment of the cosmic salvation expressed throughout Scripture.[25] Ultimately, the important attempt of Senior and Stuhlmueller is to read the entire Bible critically exegetically as a way of obtaining theological implications for the church's world mission.[26]

---

18. Bosch, *Transforming Mission*, 20–25, 57–124; Brownson, *Speaking the Truth*, 39; Nissen, *New Testament*, 21–97.

19. Hengel, *Judaism and Hellenism*, 210–37; Brownson, *Speaking the Truth*, 2.

20. Dodd, *Interpretation*, 223–26.

21. Senior and Stuhlmueller, *Biblical Foundations*, 5n3, 6n4.

22. Senior and Stuhlmueller, *Biblical Foundations*, 315.

23. Senior and Stuhlmueller, *Biblical Foundations*, 15.

24. Senior and Stuhlmueller, *Biblical Foundations*, 98–107, 110–36, 249–53, 261–62, 276–77, 288–94.

25. Senior and Stuhlmueller, *Biblical Foundations*, 98–105, 199–203, 260–64.

26. Senior and Stuhlmueller, *Biblical Foundations*, 241–43, 276, 292–94, 310, 315–48.

In short, from the historical-critical and exegetical methods, scholars have investigated the early churches' mission activities and the development of mission paradigms within their historical situations.[27] Their discussions have played an important role in providing a biblical basis for Christian missionary activities in a variety of contexts by examining how each book of the Bible speaks of mission in the context of life.[28]

Missional Hermeneutics

Differently than the above-stated scholars' perspective on the activities of the early church and Israel, another hermeneutical way of reading the entire Bible is through a biblical-theological reflection, in which readers interpret how the mission of God and his people is explained from both a theological and a narrative perspective.

First, since the advent of the *missio Dei* theory in the 1950s, scholars have discovered both the theological meaning of mission, and the meaning for today's Christian mission. Their approach draws attention to reading the entire Bible from a theological perspective. George F. Vicedom argues, from the *missio Dei* perspective, that God's salvation expands from particularism to universalism, starting with Jesus Christ.[29] His argument is an observational understanding of God's redemptive history from an eschatological perspective. This eschatological view emerges from Johannes Blauw, who assumes that his views are rooted in God's eschatological salvation activity.[30] Blauw emphasizes the continuity of the Old and New Testaments, arguing that God's mission is to bring salvation to the world by moving from Israel to every nation in redemptive history. Blauw distinguishes the concept of centripetal mission from centrifugal mission as follows: the former is defined as the missional function of Israel, which indicates Israel's response to God's actions, while, in contrast, the latter refers to missionary activity as "an act of going out for proclamation among the nations."[31] YHWH's servant will realize this in the sense of God's eschatological promise and fulfillment (Isa 42:4).[32]

---

27. Osborne, *Hermeneutical Spiral*, 6; Wright, *Victory of God*, 174; Nissen, *New Testament*, 13–16.
28. Brownson, *Speaking the Truth*, 2.
29. Vicedom, *Mission of God*, 52.
30. Blauw, *Missionary Nature*, 72.
31. Blauw, *Missionary Nature*, 34.
32. Blauw, *Missionary Nature*, 34–43.

Blauw and Vicedom contribute to the missional reading of the Bible in two ways. *Firstly*, they read God's mission as the fulfillment of his eschatological salvation for all nations. This framework is a change between particularism and universalism. They also employ a biblical hermeneutical methodology in the scheme of *Heilsgeschichte*. Oscar Cullmann highlights the redemptive history in terms of a continuous timeline and process in the past, the present, and the future.[33] This present time as the "new age" is parenthesized by "this age" and "the coming age,"[34] the so-called eschatological framework of "already" and "not yet."[35] Reading the Bible from the redemptive history perspective tries to understand the whole Bible from both the standpoint of the Old Testament promises, and the fulfillment of the New Testament. This reading serves to emphasize to the church that the act of mission is located in the realization of God's great redemption. *Secondly*, Blauw proposes another mission definition—a centripetal aspect—while Vicedom subordinates the concept of conversion to a church-centered mission. According to Vicedom, the mission of the church is to proclaim the message of salvation to the state, inviting it to her.[36] In particular, Blauw's missional reading of the Old Testament influences modern theologians and scholars who construe the entire Bible from a centripetal point of view.

Second, from a metanarrative perspective, missional hermeneutics emphasizes that the whole Bible speaks about God's mission. Of course, not every story in the text deals directly with mission. As a result, readers try to study the missiological meaning and significance within the literary context. Therefore, although readers look at the Bible from the narrative perspective, they still presuppose a theological reflection.

A representative scholar, Christopher J. H. Wright, develops missional hermeneutics based on the framework of biblical-theological interpretation. He has published writings such as "Mission as a Matrix for Hermeneutics and Biblical Theology" (2004), *The Mission of God: Unlocking the Bible's Grand Narrative* (2006), *The Mission of God's People: A Biblical Theology of the Church's Mission* (2010), and "Reading the Old Testament Missionally" (2016). In these texts, Wright's overall timeline considers the entire Bible as the larger subject of the metanarrative of the mission of God and his people. For Wright, mission is key to biblical interpretation, which can encompass various themes of the texts:

---

33. Cullmann, *Christ and Time*, 8, 115.
34. Cullmann, *Christ and Time*, 13–17; specifically, see chap. 5.
35. Cullmann, *Christ and Time*, 121–74.
36. Vicedom, *Mission of God*, 103.

> All the great sections of the canon of Scripture, all the great episodes of the Bible story, all the great doctrines of the biblical faith, cohere around the Bible's central character—the living God and his grand plan and purpose for the whole of creation. The mission of God is what unifies the Bible from creation to new creation.[37]

Wright shines a light on God's true identity in creative and missional work, noting that YHWH's mission and Jesus's mission are constantly linked. In other words, YHWH's missional character and role are repeated in the mission of Jesus, the Holy Spirit, and his church.[38] While some scholars highlight the concept of mission by proclaiming the gospel to unbelievers, Wright maintains the "holistic mission" paradigm. This paradigm involves the concept of holiness (Lev 19:2, "I will be holy"), taking into account the ethical life (righteousness and justice) of God's people based on covenant.[39] This ethical life (sanctification) plays a decisive role in bridging the Old and New Testaments. According to Wright, "mission is not just something we do (though it certainly includes that)," but is also "the sense of being something" in terms of God's holy people. He connects the concept of "missional" with the covenant concept in the essential framework of the "just" (righteous) sociopolitical society.[40]

Wright is indebted to Richard Bauckham, who uses the term "*missionary* hermeneutic" in his book *Bible and Mission: Christian Witness in a Postmodern World*.[41] In this book, Bauckham develops his lecture delivered in Cambridge in 1999 under the title of "Mission as Hermeneutic for Scriptural Interpretation."[42] He divides the *missionary* hermeneutic into two narrative hermeneutics:

> A canonical hermeneutic, that is, a way of reading the Bible as a whole . . . a narrative hermeneutic, one which recognizes how the Bible as a whole tells a story, in some sense a single story, an overall narrative encompassing, of course, many other stories and including many forms of non-narrative literature within it, but constituting in its overall direction a metanarrative, a narrative about the whole of reality that elucidates the meaning of the whole of reality. A narrative hermeneutic recognizes the way

---

37. Wright, *Mission of God*, 17.
38. Wright, *Mission of God's People*, 210–21.
39. Wright, *Mission of God's People*, 124.
40. Wright, *Mission of God*, 296.
41. Wright, *Mission of God*, 64.
42. Bauckham, *Bible and Mission*, 11.

narrative creates its own world in front of the text and so interprets our world for us.[43]

Here, Wright strongly agrees with Bauckham's concept of "overall direction" as the "missionary direction," which enables a coherent reading of the (canonical) biblical themes and motifs of the whole Bible from the perspective of God's mission.[44] Although Bauckham humbly acknowledges that "mission itself is not the comprehensive subject of the whole Bible," he agrees that Scripture should be read from a canonical-narrative perspective of Scriptures as a whole story, or a metanarrative about all reality, for the Bible narrates God's narrative identity.[45] To be sure, Wright and Bauckham's missional hermeneutics approach contributes to the development of reading the Bible in a large narrative structure.[46]

In short, the biblical-theological approach premises that the Old and New Testaments are one book, whose authors narrate the concept of God's mission and his people's participation.[47] Subsequently, the missional hermeneutics regards mission as "a major key that unlocks the whole grand narrative of the canon of Scripture."[48]

Critical Evaluation of Recent Proposals regarding Missional Hermeneutics

First of all, the missional hermeneutics as a biblical-theological interpretation allows us to discuss mission in the area of biblical interpretation by overcoming the problem of the proof-texting approach and the historical-critical approach. Although a proof text strengthens how Christians can devote themselves to the church mission movement, its critical problem is a hermeneutical presupposition: "the authors do not consider theological coherence nor contextual backgrounds, but just strengthen dogmatic arguments."[49] Meanwhile, as the historical-critical and exegetical methods are involved with the historicity of individual texts or textual sources, the method helps readers to understand the historical background of the text

---

43. Bauckham, *Bible and Mission*, 11–12.
44. Wright, *Mission of God*, 29, 64; Bauckham, *Bible and Mission*, 92–94.
45. Wright, *Mission of God*, 28.
46. Cf. Wright, *Justification*, 34; Hunsberger, "Proposals," 309–21.
47. Cf. Köstenberger and Swain, *Father, Son, and Spirit*, 20; Osborne, *Hermeneutical Spiral*, 10; Brownson, *Speaking the Truth*, 39.
48. Wright, *Mission of God*, 17.
49. Allen and Swain, "In Defense of Proof-Texting," 589–606.

Preliminary Considerations on Missional Hermeneutics for John's Gospel   13

and the original author or first readers' intention. However, such an approach tends to miss "the organic progress of God's revelation in its historic continuity and multiformity."[50] Consequently, these hermeneutical approaches are likely to overlook the theological and literary messages of what the biblical texts say about the nature and character of mission in the historical process of God's mission.[51]

Yet, the missional hermeneutics premises a conceptual framework for consistently reading the Old and New Testaments. Specifically, Christopher J. H. Wright's main approach is titled "biblical-theological."[52] This biblical-theological discussion allows us to consider the hermeneutics of

---

50. Vos, *Biblical Theology*, 15, 20.

51. For example, in the literary-theological world of Matthew, Jesus's Great Commission is not simply confined to going and making disciples. Its passage must be construed in light of Jesus's eschatological rulership (Hagner, *Matthew 1–13*, 77). Jesus sends his disciples to all nations (Matt 24:14 with Mark 16:15; Luke 24:47–49; John 20:21, 22) to live the disciples' lives in their social location as the place of the triune God's presence (*Immanuel*, Matt 1:23 and 28:20). If anyone understands that the Matthean accounts signify the mission of going and making disciples in the form of authority and commandment or responsibility, a person does not consider the entire theology of Matthew. The author emphasizes the missional ethical life of Jesus's disciples in his kingdom. To be sure, their missional lives are realized in the form of sending out and the accomplishment of individual or collective task(s) for the fulfillment of God's salvation history. The risen Jesus sent his disciples into the world (Osborne, *Resurrection Narratives*, 91). He showed examples and taught the gospel of the kingdom (Matt 5–8) through discourses like many parables (13:1–52; chs. 18–20; 24:29—25:46) (Davies, *Sermon*, 455–57). In other words, those whom Jesus sends into the world must let the disciples keep (τηρεῖν in 19:17 [keep the Ten Commandments]) what he taught, as they are resembling the perfect life and identity of God the Father (5:48; cf. 5:38–42; 7:1, 3–5, 12; 21:1–8, 9–14; 18:12–35; 22:34–40) under the authority of Jesus (28:18) (Krentz, "Missionary Matthew," 30). The sent disciples into a society must reflect the ongoing relationship with Jesus (28:20) (Warren, *Matthew*, 73, 74; Overman, *Matthew's Gospel*, 125, 130, 134; Howell, *Matthew's Inclusive Story*, 255). This commission may challenge and encourage the faith community to live the life of Jesus's disciples under the Father's love and care for their missional context (Matt 10:28–31 and 6:25–34; 7:7–11) (Cranfield and Stanton, *Matthew*, 2:201–2; cf. Luz, "Final Judgment," 274–75; Davies and Allison, *Matthew*, 326; Warren, *Matthew*, 279, 445; Turner, *Matthew*, 178). Therefore, those who are sent by Jesus must be disciples who first keep Jesus's words under his authority and live a perfect life ("as the Father," Matt 5:48) that also serves the marginalized (25:34–46). They must also make people into Jesus's disciples and live a disciple's life until his second coming (28:20) in God's salvation-history (Luke 24:47–49). God accomplishes salvation by sending his Son Jesus according to his eschatological promise (Rom 1:1–3). Eventually, as proof-texting tends to pay attention to the dogmatic message of the text, this could ignore the diverse contextual (theological) interpretations of Scripture from both the biblical authors and current Christian readers (Vanhoozer, *Drama of Doctrine*, 27–272).

52. Wright, "Matrix," 132; *Mission of God*, 118; cf. Goheen, "Critical Examination," 230; Ladd, *New Testament*, 20.

understanding the Bible in pictures like the Great Creation and Covenants. N. T. Wright suggests that the Old and New Testaments should be read as the big picture of the "creation and covenant," pointing out that the entire Bible is a "great story of creation and covenant" that describes the relationship between Christ and the kingdom of God from both a covenantal and an eschatological perspective.[53] He argues that Paul also interprets the Bible as a story that reaches the climax of the Christ-event.[54] As with N. T. Wright's understanding, Christopher Wright's missional hermeneutics provides an important example of a biblical-theological consideration by studying how the Bible consists of a large theological world in which God's mission is embodied.

On the other hand, Christopher Wright's first significant contribution is to read the whole Bible within the missiological framework, beyond seeking historical precedents or biblical proofs for modern Christian mission. In general, the problem of hermeneutics through the lens of mission has a tendency either to impose modern mission concepts on the Bible, or to oversimplify the rich missional meanings of the biblical texts.[55] The fundamental cause of this problem is a lack of literary analysis, which results in the imposition of the concept of mission upon the Bible.[56] Through a biblical-theological approach, Wright examines the missiological meaning of metanarrative in its various literary and theological contexts. In his canonical reading of the Bible, Wright seeks to answer the contextual issues of Christian social participation.

Subsequently, Wright's contribution to missional hermeneutics examines the significant theological themes in the Bible's literary context, and reconsiders them in a missiological sense for current Christians. This has significantly contributed to the development of missional hermeneutics in a "missiological framework of biblical theology."[57]

On the other hand, a limitation of Wright's biblical theological approach in *The Mission of God* is that he is not able to apply his metanarrative frame to all biblical texts.[58] For instance, he excludes John from his study

---

53. Wright, *Justification*, 34; *Faithfulness of God*, 462–63.

54. Most biblical theologians agree with N. T. Wright in that, if the New and Old Testaments have any continuity, it is Jesus Christ as the fulfillment of God's promised salvation and new covenant. David L. Baker also argues that the continuity of Scriptures is confirmed in Jesus's personality and coming for the fulfillment of promise and new covenant and new creation (Baker, *Two Testaments*, 279–81).

55. Cf. Goheen, "Critical Examination," 234.

56. Glasser, *Announcing the Kingdom*, 11.

57. Wright, *Mission of God*, 31, 38.

58. Wright, *Mission of God*, 38.

because the Fourth Gospel does not deal with "the universality of God's promise to Abraham," and does not speak of the expansion of God's salvation into the world by the fulfillment of Abraham's blessing in terms of a "single narrative."[59] John, however, explains both God and the disciples of Jesus through the sending language, or through the term "witness" (John 3:32–33; 15:26–27 [3:16; 13:20; 17:18; 20:21]).[60] John speaks of mission within his literary-theological context, just as Matthew, Luke, and the letters of Paul each talk of God and his people within their own linguistic-literary structures. In this sense, the attempt to read the Gospel of John through the hermeneutical frame of Abrahamic blessing or command-obedience would impose the reader's own mission concept onto the Gospel.

Second, some scholars such as Michael J. Gorman, Joel B. Green, and Dean Flemming further the discussion of the diversity and unity of mission in that their hermeneutics observes how God's mission is theologically understood in individual texts. In studying the Pauline Epistles, Gorman, in his book *Becoming the Gospel*, pays attention to *missio Dei* and the engagement of churches with mission.[61] Gorman's missional hermeneutic attempts to find the implications of Paul's mission, and to then apply them to current situations. Basically, Gorman understands the missional concept in terms of "becoming like Christ by being in Christ."[62] This idea is bound with the nature of the church as "a living exegesis of the gospel of God."[63] He links the notion of becoming (e.g., faith, love, hope, peace, and justice of God) to being and doing as witnesses. His missional hermeneutics is associated with the theological interpretation of interpretive communities under the missional hermeneutical question: "How do we read Paul for what he says about *missio Dei* and about our participation in it?"[64] Gorman is engaged in the literary-theological methodology of missional hermeneutics, which deals with the Bible in terms of reading the narrative of mission. His concern is with how to read the Epistles of Paul, and he aptly demonstrates that the nature and function of God's mission are projected through Paul's life and the lives of his people. Joel B. Green and Dean Fleming examine the letters of James and Colossians, respectively, from a missional perspective. They underline the dyadic aspect of mission and missional.[65] Meanwhile, Flem-

---

59. Wright, *Mission of God*, 243n21, 515.
60. Schnelle, "Recent Views of John's Gospel," 352–59.
61. Gorman, *Becoming the Gospel*, 15.
62. Gorman, *Becoming the Gospel*, 32.
63. Gorman, *Becoming the Gospel*, 43.
64. Gorman, *Becoming the Gospel*, 51, 53, 58.
65. Green, "Reading James Missionally," 212.

ming emphasizes God's mission and its proclamation and embodiment in his people, as long as Flemming examines the methodology of a missional reading in the Epistle to the Colossians.[66] According to Flemming, mission necessarily entails "a witness of word" and "a witness of life" in missional contexts.[67] Neither Green nor Flemming repudiate the significance of the functional aspect of mission; however, they argue that mission should include the concept of "new Christian lifestyle," "reordering of life," or "integrated life."[68] This lifestyle is because God's missional and redemptive purpose creates a "mature and fruitful community" under Jesus's lordship, and an eschatological people who depend on God the Creator in the scheme of a new creation.[69]

The significant contribution of Gorman, Goheen, and Flemming is to investigate individual biblical text's unique missional meanings and implications. However, their methodology of theological interpretation in itself could be better if it is harmonized in its exegetically literarily examinations of the biblical texts. In my estimation, to interpret the author's missional concept, readers should deal with words in the semantic context, and at the same time, narratives and stories in a literary structure. If readers try to read the text in order to understand their mission, they might have a potentiality of imposing their language on the text according to interpreters' prejudice. Therefore, missional hermeneutics should include literary analysis and an exegetical-theological approach to individual texts, placing aside a biblical-theological approach of metanarrative to the whole Bible. Although we should acknowledge that the entire Bible speaks of God's mission as a unified theme, we also consent that each text reflects the readers' new context in which this mission is realized. Recognizing the diversity of each biblical text should first involve a study of its theology by analyzing the author's language and meanings in the literary world, taking into account the context of the first readers' lives implied by the text. Such a situation is reflected in the missional paradigm that emerges in the context of books.[70] The theological ideas spoken through the author's literary structure contain the notion of God and his people's mission. In this sense, to read the Gospel of John missionally, hermeneutics must observe John's language and literary world in order to discover the implications for readers.

66. Flemming, "Missional Reading of Colossians," 222.
67. Flemming, "Missional Reading of Colossians," 231.
68. Flemming, "Missional Reading of Colossians," 231.
69. Flemming, "Missional Reading of Colossians," 230; Green, "Reading James Missionally," 202, 205.
70. Bosch, "Towards a Hermeneutic," 76; *Transforming Mission*, 21, 34, 185.

METHODOLOGICAL CHARACTERISTICS OF MISSIONAL HERMENEUTICS

Missional hermeneutics comprehends the mission of God and his people in both the past and present contexts. Readers observe the nature of mission, its biblical-theological ideas, and the paradigm of the first readers' contextualized mission. At the same time, they can reinterpret such biblical elements in the context of their lives in order to participate in God's ongoing mission.[71] Thus, missional hermeneutics is necessarily based on biblical hermeneutics.[72] The term *hermeneutics* entails the derivation of the Greek *hermeneutikos* ("interpreting"). It not only interprets the original meaning of the text, but also what it means to me, and to us. In other words, biblical hermeneutics aims to fill in the gap between the contexts of the biblical text and of modern Christian readers.[73] Therefore, I propose that a missional hermeneutic is engaged in delving into the themes of the discourse in the text and giving those themes to today's Christians. They continue to discuss the themes within their community in order to participate in God's mission. Under this understanding of hermeneutics, we can consider two levels when interpreting the biblical text through the lens of mission: (1) "'within

---

71. Van Engen, *God's Missionary People*, 47–57; *Mission on the Way*, 97.

72. Silva, "Who Needs," 17; Wenham and Walton, *Exploring*, 92–102; Tate, *Biblical Interpretation*, 245–66. In general, hermeneutics is understood as the science and art of biblical interpretation. Modern hermeneutics began with the systematic hermeneutics of Fredrich Daniel Ernst Schleiermacher (Schleiermacher, *Hermeneutics and Criticism* [1998]; *Hermeneutics: The Handwritten Manuscripts* [1986]) and Wilhelm Dilthey (Dilthey, *Hermeneutics and the Study of History* [1996]) and philosophical hermeneutics of Martin Heidegger and Hans-Georg Gadamer in the twentieth century. Christopher J. H. Wright's hermeneutic methodology is placed on the line of Schleiermacher (Wright, *Mission of God's People*, 25). For further study, see Barton, *Biblical Interpretation* (1998). John Barton edited one book containing the biblical scholars' articles about a variety of biblical hermeneutic approaches. This book introduces eleven approaches: (1) historical-critical approaches ("historical interest," "genetic questions," "historical [diachronic] or original meaning of the texts for the first readers"); (2) literary readings ("typological understanding," "a theological and literary coherence between the books of the canon," "literary form of the Bible as a whole" [synchronic and diachronic]); (3) the social world (reconstruction of history and economic-socio-environmental contexts and "social organization and social setting" alongside "disciplines of sociology, archeology and anthropology"); (4) poststructuralist approaches ("new historicism and postmodernism," "mirror images of the readers"; (5) political readings; (6) feminist interpretation; (7) biblical studies and theoretical hermeneutics; (8) the Bible and Christian theology; (9) biblical study and linguistics; (10) aspects of the Jewish contribution to biblical hermeneutics; and (11) the Bible in literature and art. Most recently, Michael J. Gorman has developed the missional hermeneutic by studying the Pauline Epistles. See Gorman, *Becoming the Gospel*, 50–62.

73. Osborne, *Hermeneutical Spiral*, 5–7.

the text': mission as a literary plot, and (2) 'in front of the text': mission in the perception of the readers."[74]

In this respect, in order to read John's Gospel through the lens of mission, the characteristics of a missional hermeneutic should engage in both literary-exegetical and theological interpretations in the worlds of the text and of the readers.

Literary-Exegetical Interpretation

Missional hermeneutics is a literary and exegetical interpretation in the literary context of the text. Individual biblical texts explain the unique aspects of God's mission through the author's mission language and missional theme. The literary-exegetical interpretation aims to explore this mission language and missional meaning within the world of stories and narratives. The author describes theology using historical events and linguistic elements, and readers are interested in "what they (evangelists) have chosen to include (selectivity), and how they have ordered their material, and what plotlines they have inscribed the whole."[75] Green argues that reading the Bible begins with understanding the literary world.[76] While missional hermeneutics can potentially employ an historical-critical approach to the text, it primarily focuses on the author's literary context and theology in order to delineate missiological implications.[77]

I presume that John's missional perspective determines the technical words he uses to express ideas. Words generate meaning in sentences, phrases, and whole stories. For example, when John is characterized by sending languages (*apostellein* and *pempein*) in the literary world, he conceptualizes the various meanings of the language. However, from time to time, the criticism facing the literary-exegetical interpretation is that current readers try to justify meaning by putting the concept of mission into the Bible. If the Bible does not have the term *mission*, how can we understand that concept?

---

74. I basically agree that missional hermeneutics needs the "behind the text" study: the mission of the authors, editors, and communities. This investigation is helpful in understanding the original meaning of the author and the first readers. For this reason, Tim Carriker synthesizes three theologians' approaches (Darrell Guder's "behind the text," Wright's "within the text," and Michael Barram's "in front of the text") (Carriker, "Bible as Text," 29–42).

75. Osborne, *Hermeneutical Spiral*, 10.

76. Green, "Rethinking 'History,'" 161.

77. Cf. Hays, *Paul*, 154; Wright, *New Testament*, 8.

This raises doubts that interpreters tend to comprehend the text by imposing the meaning of the mission onto the book.[78]

Michael W. Stroope criticizes Christians who justify the concept of apostolic mission by examining the meaning of the semantic field.[79] As such methodologies attempt to observe biblical terms and phrases, some interpreters pay attention to the concept of the word *send*, along with related terms, in order to identify mission concepts among Christians today, although they tend to generalize the concept and apply it to the present Christian mission.[80] Stroope estimates that Köstenberger uses a semantic approach as justification for his mission. Köstenberger tries to observe general missiological phenomena by examining words and phrases, like sending terms and related expressions, in John's Gospel. However, Stroope criticizes Köstenberger for focusing on today's mission concepts rather than the word *mission*. Köstenberger's first step is to build a semantic field that verifies the definition of mission. What Stroope points out here is the prototype of Köstenberger's understanding of mission, which is a premise based on an understanding of the present Christian mission. He argues that Köstenberger ignores the inherent meaning of sending terms.[81]

However, my judgment is that, unlike Stroope's criticism, Köstenberger tries to observe the word *sending* language, and then pursues its meaning through semantic studies. His key research is an examination of the sending language in order to understand the mission of Jesus and his disciples.[82] Certainly, Köstenberger does not intend to impose the meaning of words, but instead uses the terms to discover meaning.[83]

Nonetheless, Stroope's critique is meaningful for missional hermeneutics. In the context where the term mission is absent, readers might

---

78. Keith Ferdinando claims that "the noun, mission, is not the biblical one, which makes it difficult to define on exegetical grounds" (Ferdinando, "Mission," 47). This major problem causes contemporary readers to confine the biblical word *apostellein* to the church's sending of missionaries to cross-cultural countries for making disciples and planting churches. Such an understanding results in the neglect of the diversity of mission (Ferdinando, "Mission," 47). This is a matter of the reduction of meanings. Ferdinando criticizes that mission is traditionally understood in view of the Greek word *apostellein* via the Latin *mitto*, so such a mission corresponds to the church's sending and making of disciples in the world. For Ferdinando, the concept of sending is too narrow, in spite of the fact that mission should be widely conceptualized (Ferdinando, "Mission," 47).

79. Stroope, *Transcending Mission*, 64, 70.

80. Stroope, *Transcending Mission*, 70.

81. Stroope, *Transcending Mission*, 64, 71.

82. Köstenberger, *Missions of Jesus*, 2–3.

83. Köstenberger, *Missions of Jesus*, 107.

unconsciously, or purposely, interpret the biblical text as a way of justifying their own mission(s). Therefore, we should seriously deliberate Stroope's question, noting that Köstenberger understands the words that John intended to speak by observing the language send. We must begin to read John missionally from the very point where the word *mission* is first used, which coincides with the verb *send*.[84] I presume that John describes the mission of Jesus and the disciples through the word *send*. Just as the Father sent the Son in John 17:18 and 20:21, the Son began the mission of God and his people by sending disciples. The word becomes clear in sentences and context. For example, although the Greek *apostellein* and *pempein* lexically mean "to send (someone) forth," "to send on service, with a commission" or "to send a message, to send word," their meaning(s) should also be considered within a context of words and in the literary context of the entire text.[85] As Osborne argues, the semantic field and context of words can decide their meanings.[86] Köstenberger agrees with these two scholars in that "context must be given priority" for "determining a term's meaning."[87] What these scholars say is an important part of hermeneutics. That is, hermeneutics determines the meaning of words within the literary structure of the whole text.[88] Accordingly, readers should observe sending language in terms of the logical relevance of paragraphs and stories.

---

84. With regard to the usage of sending language in the ancient Mediterranean world, Olga Spevak's analysis of two different meanings of the verb *mitto* are as follows: "(1) Caesar . . . statim nuntium in Bellovacos ad Marcum Caesar at once messenger-acc to Bellovaci to Marcus Crassum quaestorem mittit, cuius hiberna Crassus quaestor sends whose winter camp-nom aberant ab eo milia passuum XXV. Iubet . . . was about from him miles of paces 25 he orders 'Caesar . . . at once sends a messenger to the territory of the Bellovaci, to his quaestor Marcus Crassus, whose winter camp was about 25 miles away. He orders him . . .' (Caes. Gal. 5.46.1) (2) Helvetii . . . legatos ad eum mittunt. Cuius legationis Helvetii-nom envoys-acc to him send of this embassy Divico princeps fuit, qui . . . Divico-nom chief was who 'The Helvetii . . . send envoys to him. At the head of this embassy was Divico, who . . .' (Caes. Gal. 1.13.2)" (Spevak, *Constituent*, 132). The sending language in the passages shows the twofold meaning of both the unity between the sender and the sent, and the completion of the sent's task. These meanings are associated with Christian mission concept.

85. Cotterell and Turner, *Linguistics*, 82–97, 232; E. D. Hirsch Jr. emphasizes context as the key to determining "the guess of an interpreter" (Hirsch, *Validity*, 47–48). Language can have different meanings according to a semantic context (cf. Pagin and Pelletier, "Content," 33–44). James Barr encourages the semantic approach to Scripture, pointing out the interpretive danger of the lexicological study (Barr, *Semantics*, 233–34, 272). Barr critiques a biased interpretive problem of a word by neglecting the literary-theological world, or semantic context, constituting other words.

86. Osborne, *Hermeneutical Spiral*, 414.

87. Köstenberger, *Missions of Jesus*, 20.

88. Louw and Nida, *Greek-English Lexicon*, 15, 16.

In short, literary-exegetical interpretation concentrates on the semantic and literary structures, which is composed of various discourses and stories within the plot of the text. Readers should observe sending language in terms of the logical relatedness of paragraphs and narratives. Although sending language is dispersed throughout the text, the meaning of a word can be made clearer within the author's literary context; therefore, readers should consider the author's intention and purpose in order to exegetically explore the sending language found within the narratives and discourses of the text.

Theological Interpretation

A theological interpretation is divided into two aspects: the first is an author-centered interpretation, and the second is a reader-centered interpretation. The former tries to deal with the author's theology through a literary-exegetical interpretation discussed above, and requires the reader to explore the text through a neutral lens. The latter interprets the text through the readers' theological traditions and individual experiences. Readers naturally form hermeneutic frames while sharing the interpreted word in their faith community. It also serves as a theological frame to share with their community. Simultaneously, they tend to understand specific themes according to their interests and experiences in social activities.[89]

These two theological interpretations provide important tasks for missional hermeneutics. *Firstly*, readers should be able to understand the nature of mission by hearing what the text has to say about mission. *Secondly*, readers should seek the way of God's ongoing mission, along with their own participation.[90] In other words, missional hermeneutics pursues the readers' theological interpretation for their own community's "Rule of faith."[91] They may be allowed to revisit the text through the lens of their interested exegesis.

But these approaches are seemingly in conflict with one another. If the readers cannot escape their theological prejudices and hermeneutical frames, can they even interpret the author-centered theology? Meanwhile, if the readers interpret the text according to their own interests, how can they handle the uncontrollable tolerance of an interpreter's subjectivity, based on their own interests?[92]

---

89. Schneiders, "From Exegesis," 23–39; Silva, "Who Needs," 19–28; Kaiser, "Meaning," 31; Spinks, *Bible*, 6; Allison, "Theological Interpretation," 29.

90. Vanhoozer, "What Is Theological Interpretation," 14–15.

91. Allison, "Theological Interpretation of Scripture," 30–33.

92. Bultmann, "Exegesis," 294.

An Author-Centered Theological Interpretation

In modern times, the biggest issue discussed in hermeneutics is whether readers can understand the author's thinking within the text.

Jacques Derrida postulates that the text is not complete, but instead is open to diverse interpretations. He demurs to the objective reality or truth. In that case, the metanarrative is completely pessimistic.[93] Furthermore, according to him, the ultimate subject of interpretation must be turned over from the text to the readers so that they cannot universally interpret the text because of their different ways of thinking. Derrida's serious critique is supported by the argument that the author's philological limitation does not allow him or her to express his or her intention in words perfectly.[94] With regard to linguistic interpretation, meaning is dominated by a phonetic difference, rather than by a word itself.[95] In other cases, after completing a writing, the author does not stay in the world of the book. The subject of speaking is just language, but not the author. In this case, the text does not need to be deciphered because there is no speaker who signifies it.[96] As a result, interpretations have been engaged in dialoguing between the text and the contemporary world of readers, regardless of the author's original intention for the text. Readers bring their own specific questions to the text, attempting to receive answers from it. Through this, they might procure different meanings of the text according to their contextual lenses.

Obviously, not all readers can determine the single correct meaning of the biblical text. They might be open to perceiving the original authors' subconscious ideology because of the nature of language and the influence of cultural factors on interpretation. However, it cannot be said that the text has no specific meaning. The original author intended to deliver the messages to the original readers by describing them within the semantic and literary world. Conversely, readers are able to scrutinize the author's meaning by observing the narratives and story within the overall literary context. Readers endeavor to understand the text's meaning, although they cannot perfectly make sense of the text based on the historical contexts of the past, upon which the meaning of words depends.[97] As a result, theolog-

---

93. Derrida, *Of Grammatology*, 81, 158–59. Derrida objects to what Scripture tells about a metanarrative or the divine truth.

94. Tate, *Biblical Interpretation*, 5–8, 245–66.

95. See Saussure, *Course* (1959).

96. See Barthes, *Pleasure* (2009).

97. Gennari et al., "Context-Dependent Interpretation," 1278–79; William W. Klein warns against reading some biblical passage(s) in a normative perspective without context ("a text without a context may be a pretext") (Klein et al., *Introduction*, 299). He

ical interpretation focuses primarily on understanding certain key words, narratives, and discourses within the literary-theological context of the text, rather than reshaping the historical contexts.[98] Readers should hear what the text has to say. Their approach should examine the story and narratives in the text and the meanings of language for the unifying theme(s) in the semantic structure in order to lead their hermeneutical results into an agreed meaning.[99]

To put it briefly, readers humbly acknowledge that their interpretation cannot inevitably exclude hermeneutical prejudice and bias. Nevertheless, if they strive to exegetically read the text as well as they can, the readers might gather some of the meanings that the original author intended, based on the inspiration of the Holy Spirit.[100] I propose that missional hermeneutics should be based on the theological interpretation of the biblical text through the interpreter's attempt at exegesis.[101] Therefore, the first step of a missional hermeneutic is that readers should primarily be concerned with the exegesis of the semantic structure and literary context of the biblical writings, excluding prejudices as much as they possibly can.[102] The author's messages are incorporated into both story and narrative(s). The biblical authors tell about God, his works, and the community's faith and religious praxis through their worldview, or perspective, in both story and narratives.[103] These literary units consist of a whole literary-theological context. To interpret a narrative exegetically is to provide readers with the text's entire theology and central message.

---

criticizes the abuse of the Bible in terms of an "alleged interpretation," which may be the "pretext" or "invalid proof-texting" (Klein et al., *Introduction*, 299). Similarly, Charles Van Engen insists on "the Bible as tapestry, with the woof (horizontal threads) of various themes and motifs interwoven in the warp (vertical) of each historical context" (Van Engen, *Mission on the Way*, 41). As Van Engen argues, the Bible narrates God's historical missional activities as a tapestry. If the narratives and stories of the Bible are interwoven with various themes and contexts, mission can be observed in the use of biblical writers' storylines and their contextual descriptions. To me, Klein and Van Engen should be accepted in that scriptural texts describe God and his peoples' life in a specific situation. In other words, without contextual considerations, readers cannot appropriately read God's salvific-creating activity and people's participation, and those readers will not be able to understand the nature and character of mission. However, it is impossible for today's interpreters to reconstruct past events or understand the original situations of the first recipients.

98. Spinks, *Bible and the Crisis*, 7; Green, "Rethinking 'History,'" 161.
99. Black, *Linguistics*, 9–10.
100. Black, *Linguistics*, 11.
101. Spinks, *Bible*, 7; Allison, "Theological Interpretation," 29.
102. Bultmann, "Exegesis," 295; Black, *Linguistics*, 138–40.
103. Spinks, *Bible*, 8, 9.

A Reader-Centered Theological Interpretation

The Bible is the canonical book of God for the Christian faith community. To be sure, looking at an author's theology through literary-exegetical interpretation is an important goal of missional hermeneutics. However, it is also essential that the various missional meanings of the Bible are reinterpreted within the present context.[104] This interpretation does not merely link the text's "theological visions and practices" with the contextual topics of the current reader.[105] Instead, theological interpretation requires that communities read the Bible in the light of a particular situation.[106] Naturally, they try to read biblical texts through the lens of the presuppositions of faith, tradition, worldview, experience, and context (political, social, national, and so forth).[107] This theological interpretation is associated with biblical hermeneutics, which seeks to bridge the gap between the "strange world" of text and the world of the real reader.[108] This interpretation is not something an individual can do, as they are frequently exposed to subjective hermeneutic biases that are difficult to control. If an individual's theological interpretation is subordinate to "the uncontrollable tolerance of the interpreters' subjectivity based on their interests," the Bible will lose its place as the community's canonical book.[109] Therefore, theological interpretation depends on the hermeneutic framework of the faith community. Green states as follows:

> The texts that constitute the Bible were traditioned, written, and preserved by the same people of God now faced with the task of appropriating and embodying its message; this is the same community that received this collection of texts as canon; and this is the very community to which these texts were and are

---

104. Vanhoozer, *Drama*, 27–272.
105. Green, "Bible."
106. Hunsberger, "Proposals," 309–21.
107. Stanton, "Presuppositions," 60.
108. Beker, *New Testament*, 9; Green, "Bible."
109. Bultmann, "Exegesis," 294; The purpose of missional hermeneutics is to provide contemporary Christians with methods of perusing the canonical texts in light of the original context and meaning, and how to examine them in light of the new context for today's Christians' lives (Brownson, *Speaking the Truth*, 3). At first, Brownson's methodology revolves around the biblical texts, which constitute the traditional elements of the original gospel and the reshaping of Jesus's teaching and identity in light of their readers' new contexts. For Brownson, the reason biblical writers interweave the two elements is because the "religious logic and implicit assumptions" of biblical interpretation, the so-called "hermeneutical implications of the gospel" (Brownson, *Speaking the Truth*, 80), should have been applied to new contexts in history.

addressed. That is, we locate "the meaning" of Scripture not in the distant past in a far-away land, but in the community of God's people, past, present, and future.[110]

Green's argument is appropriate in that the faith communities have contextualized (or theologized) God's Word within a particular cultural context. *Firstly*, the biblical authors theologize the Word according to diverse theological frames, through which the various New Testament authors interpreted Scriptures in order to bear witness to Jesus Christ and his gospel.[111] At the same time, the authors reflected the unique contextual

---

110. Green, "Bible."

111. Enns, *Inspiration*, 132–63; N. T. Wright and Larry A. Hurtado assert that, in their context, the early Christian missionaries and church communities developed "christological monotheism" also called "binitarian" monotheism, which was that the earlier Christians tried to distinguish their own beliefs from others surrounding the Greco-Roman cultic (Wright, "Jesus and the Identity of God," 42–56; Hurtado, *Lord Jesus Christ*, 44, 111, 151–53). (1) In advocating the "pure monotheism" in Second Temple Judaism, Wright also admits that the plurality of divine realities emerges in scripture (Dan 7, Gen 1, Philo's the Similitudes of Enoch) and these passages are hard to interpret, even though it should be noted that these passages did not lead early Jewish Christians to abrogating an exclusive monotheism (Wright, *New Testament*, 258, 259). Wright claims that Jesus did not think of himself as God in the context of Jewish strong monotheism (Isa 40–55; Dan 6:4 "YHWH our God, YHWH is one!"), in opposition to Greco-Roman polytheism. He draws attention only to what the monotheistic God's uniqueness and personality were embodied in Jesus's humanity, the so-called "christological monotheism" (Wright, *New Testament*, 42–56). In other words, YHWH's divine identity presents within Jesus *Kyrios* (Phil 2:11) by way of "YHWH's Himself arriving in the person of the Messiah" (Wright, *Faithfulness of God*, 655), as he returns to Zion to fulfill his eschatological promise of Israel's recovery (Rom 14:11; Isa 45:23) (Wright, *Faithfulness of God*, 679, 1044, 1071). Wright argues that this belief originates from Jesus's apostles' "using God-language for Jesus" or "Jesus-language for the one God" (1 Cor 8:6): "He (Jesus) is not a semi-divine intermediate figure. He is the one in whom the identity of Israel's God is revealed, so that one cannot now speak of this God without thinking of Jesus, or of Jesus without thinking of the one God, the creator, Israel's God" (Wright, *Faithfulness of God*, 655, 666, 705). (2) Hurtado coins this term "binitarian" "to underscore the inclusion of Jesus with God as recipient of devotion" (Hurtado, "Binitarian Pattern," 30). Meanwhile, Hurtado proposes another factor of generating Christ-devotion. It is the religious-sociopolitical environment (Hurtado, *Lord Jesus Christ*, 74–77). He argues that early Christians confronted the Jewish political condemnation of Jesus. As a result, they needed to defend against Jews their polemic belief and shape the new form of Christ-devotion (e.g., Gal 1:13; 2:4–5, 11–14). Hurtado states as follows: "My research led me to judge that, although there were conceptual resources in ancient Jewish traditions that were likely drawn upon by earliest believers, there was not really a full analogy or precedent for the intensity and nature of the cultic expressions of devotion to Jesus. So, I concluded that, although it emerged initially in the variegated Roman-era Jewish tradition, early Jesus-devotion also comprised 'a somewhat distinctive mutation or innovation' in that historical context" (Hurtado, *One God*, 141, 144); Peter Enns and Howard I. Marshall uphold different approaches to

issues of their first readers or hearers by employing their own topographical, theological, and symbolic terms and frameworks.¹¹²

Secondly, church history shows that, just as the first readers understood the biblical texts as they were written in a particular context, so, too, have Christian readers and their communities read the texts in their context. Keon-Sang An investigates the example of a faith community's contextual interpretation in the Ethiopian situation.¹¹³ He argues that a contextual factor for the biblical hermeneutic, the so-called "social location" of faith communities, influences faith communities' interpretive practices, both individually and collectively.¹¹⁴ Following his observations, Christians should naturally consider the "social location of faith communities" as the goal of their community's Bible reading. This means that Christian communities have to illuminate their context and social cases as they question the texts. Concerning the hermeneutical role of Christian communities, Michael

---

the possibility of the biblical reinterpretation and re-adoption of the next generations of the early Christians. Enns argues that the Old Testament cannot be interpreted by the following generations of earlier Christians in the same way the apostles did. In this sense, Enns calls the scriptural interpretation methodology of the apostles, *apostolic hermeneutics* (Enns, *Inspiration*, 156–63). By contrast, while he agrees with Enns about Paul's hermeneutics that are centered on the new covenant "Jesus Christ as Lord and Savior," Marshall claims that, just as the early Christians used "a 'fixed tradition' or 'apostolic deposit' of doctrine (e.g., 1 Cor 12:3; 1 John 4:2–3)" or even Jesus's teachings according to the Holy Spirit, so, too, did the later Christians (Marshall, *Beyond the Bible*, 60, 64, 122).

112. Bosch, *Transforming Mission*, 20–25, 57–124; Brownson, *Speaking the Truth*, 39; Nissen, *New Testament*, 21–97; each biblical text contains a special theological contextual message, as the biblical authors deliver their messages differently depending on the situation. At the same time, though, the Bible is God's word as a divine revelation which penetrates the history of humanity, so it has unity. Accordingly, Christians readers take the twofold perspective on the Bible contingently and coherently. J. Christiaan Beker proposed the hermeneutical principle, the so-called "contingency-coherency scheme" (Beker, *New Testament*, 15). He notes as follows: "By coherence I mean the unchanging components of Paul's gospel, which contain the fundamental convictions of his gospel: Paul himself calls them 'the truth of the gospel' (Gal 2:5, 14), and threatens those who would pervert them with an apocalyptic curse (Gal 1:8, 9; cf. Phil 1:27; 2 Thess 1:8; 2:2). The term 'contingency' denotes the changing, situational part of the gospel, that is, the diversity and particularity of sociological, economical, and psychological factors that confront Paul in his churches and in his missionary work and to which he had to respond" (Beker, *Triumph of God*, 15–16). Paul was engaged in interplaying both continuity and discontinuity. To be sure, Paul's letters were accepted by Peter (2 Pet 3:15–16) as the revelatory messages for all the churches, in the same way as Peter's own letter. At the same time, the letters of Paul and Peter were written for recipients with ecclesial and sociopolitical issues (cf. 1 Cor 1:10–17; chs. 5–15).

113. An, *Ethiopian*, 47, 54.

114. An, *Ethiopian*, 60–61.

Barram spotlights the significant impact of a social location.[115] Christian communities should carry out the role of an "international hermeneutical community" by considering different contextual challenges.[116] The community of faith has to undertake the responsibility of the true bearer of mission in view of the church's essential missionary nature. Therefore, the hermeneutical communities of faith can develop contextual theology as a way of providing a theological framework for their members as they read Scriptures.[117] Christian readers share their experiences and the hermeneutical frame of their faith community. In listening to the story and narratives of the biblical author's theological frames, readers can re-consider missional language and implications of the text within the ideological framework of their community.

In short, missional hermeneutics should treat the text according to the symbiotic relationship between the text's theological world and the current readers' theological world. A theological interpretation is to explore the author's theological understanding of mission through literary-exegetical interpretation. At the same time, readers and their faith communities interpret the biblical text in light of their life's context in order to participate in God's ongoing mission. In this study, my reading of the Gospel will aim to give its missional implications to evangelicals for the ongoing discourse of their mission.

RECENT DISCUSSIONS ON MISSION IN JOHN'S GOSPEL

Scholars understand that John contains two concepts about mission: evangelism and the witness of life. *Firstly*, some scholars focus on mission languages and phrases of evangelism: "come and see" (1:39, 46), "harvest the crop for eternal life" (John 4:36), "testify" (1:32; 4:39; 21:24), "follow" (1:43; 8:12; 10:27; 13:36; 21:18–19) or "send" (17:18; 20:21). These words and phrases underline the semantic aspect and eschatological meaning, which conceptualize mission as evangelism for harvesting or ingathering.[118] However, they point out that the disciples' mission is not separated from discipleship. *Secondly*, some scholars demonstrate that the ultimate purpose of *missio Dei* is not merely restricted to evangelism, but also includes God's

---

115. Barram, "Bible," 44.

116. Bosch, *Transforming Mission*, 187.

117. Green, *Practicing Theological Interpretation*, 2–3.

118. Dodd, *Interpretation*, 9; Carson, *Gospel according to John*, 639–51; Thompson, *God of the Gospel*, 227; Brown, *John I-XII*, 440–41; Ferreira, *Johannine Ecclesiology*, 169–70, 196; Köstenberger, *Missions of Jesus*, 199, 218.

sharing of his life with humanity. They consent that mission originates in God's life and identity, and their primary concern is with how Christians can participate in the mission. This method is part of humanity's sharing with the divine life (Tom Clegg and Warren Bird [2001], R. Geoffrey Harris [2004], and Darrell L. Guder [2015], and Michael Gorman [2018]).[119] The way in which believers partake in the *missio Dei* is not just confined to evangelism, but also includes witness of life.

Among the scholars above, representatively, Köstenberger argues for a semantic interpretation around mission language, while Gorman has a theological understanding of mission that deals with the literary structure of the Gospels.

First, Köstenberger studies the Johannine mission from the semantic perspective. His salient argument is that the accounts of 17:18 and 20:21 play a role in the "universal hermeneutical key for mission in the Fourth Gospel" (cf. "Just as the Father sent me, I send you").[120] In linguistically investigating the terms *as* and *send* (or *descending* and *ascending*), Köstenberger engages with the theological and missiological question: "How are the missions of Jesus and of the disciples related?" He comprehends both the continuity and discontinuity of Jesus and his disciples' mission.[121]

Firstly, the Johannine Jesus's mission is not equivalent to that of the disciples, as his incarnation, divine signs, and salvific work are unique. He completes his mission through the "life-giving death."[122] Köstenberger also points out that Jesus's mission is interwoven with the messianic activities of God's redemptive history.[123] On the other hand, the mission of the disciples is continuous in the perspective of the eschatological messianic harvest.[124] The exalted Jesus sends the disciples to carry out his mission in the mutual relationship.[125] Thus, they are the "extension of forgiveness in Jesus's name to repentant sinners (cf. 20:23) and the proclamation of the gospel message (cf. 17:20)."[126]

---

119. Clegg and Bird, Harris, and Guder consent that John describes the *missio Dei* as God's loving act. His love is embodied in Jesus's sacrifice (Clegg and Bird, *Lost in America*, 20), which is "a self-giving love" (Harris, *Mission*, xi), in order to heal the nations and reconcile to all things (Guder, *Called to Witness*, 170–71).

120. Köstenberger, *Missions of Jesus*, 3.

121. Köstenberger, *Missions of Jesus*, 3–4.

122. Köstenberger, *Missions of Jesus*, 133.

123. Köstenberger, *Missions of Jesus*, 134.

124. Köstenberger, *Missions of Jesus*, 130–31.

125. Köstenberger, *Missions of Jesus*, 186–87, 210.

126. Köstenberger, *Missions of Jesus*, 212–20.

Secondly, discipleship is bound with evangelism.[127] Jesus's sending of the disciples presupposes that they are following him. That is, their discipleship practices "humble servant spirit (cf. 13:1–15), mutual love (cf. 13:35; 15:13), and unity (cf. 17:21, 23, 25)."[128]

In his study of the Johannine mission, Köstenberger clarifies the difference and continuity between the mission of Jesus and the disciples in the Gospel of John. He also observes that, when the disciples were sent to take over Jesus's mission, their primary mission was evangelism, such as "harvesting" (4:36–38), "greater works" (14:12), and "fruitbearing" (12:24; 15:8, 16).[129] Of course, Köstenberger also emphasizes the subject matter of following Jesus. He aptly explains the significance of discipleship for the disciples' testimony about the gospel (e.g., the "representational model").[130] In my opinion, these two mission concepts are found in two parts (chs. 1–12 and 13–21). The first focuses on Jesus's public ministry through the frame of "testimonies" and "harvesting."[131] John 1–12 highlights Jesus's, or others', witness and invitation to Jesus ("come and see"). Jesus openly talks about harvesting through a Samaritan woman's evangelism (4:36–38). John urges disciples to verbally testify to Jesus. Meanwhile, the second part pays attention to the faith community's life-witness without neglecting the importance of their evangelism (15:26–27; 17:20; 18:37). John articulates the phrase γνώσονται πάντες ὅτι ἐμοὶ μαθηταί ἐστε ("all people will know that you are my disciples"), ἵνα γνῷ ὁ κόσμος ("so that the world may know"), or ἵνα γινώσκῃ ὁ κόσμος ("so that the world may know") (13:35[15:8]; 14:31; 17:23). Chapter 13, verse 35 and 15:8 state that when disciples love one another, they will be Jesus's and will be known to the world. This is the consequence of the disciples' practice of sacrificial love as they live according to Jesus's model (13:15, 17). Chapter 14, verse 31 is relevant to Jesus's works to bear witness about the Father in mutual relationship of love, and although 17:23 emerges from his prayer form, it also points out that the disciples must reveal their intimate relationship with God in the world; through this relationship, their love is to bear witness to the invisible God.

Second, Gorman observes missional themes in the structure of the Gospel. John elucidates this binary mission concept in the literary structure of the whole Gospel. He analyzes the structure of the Gospel, suggesting the following outline:

127. Köstenberger, *Missions of Jesus*, 177n129.
128. Köstenberger, *Missions of Jesus*, 211.
129. Köstenberger, *Missions of Jesus*, 185.
130. Köstenberger, *Missions of Jesus*, 212–20.
131. Dodd, *Historical Tradition*, 31–49.

1. Opening: The Mission of God the Father and the Incarnation of the Son (1:1–18)

2. The Mission of the Father and the Son in Doing Signs and Giving Life (1:19—12:50)

3. The Mission of the Son in Death and the Future Mission of the Spirit-Empowered Disciples (13:1—19:42)

   a. The Mission Discourse and Prayer of Consecration and Commissioning (13:1—17:26)

   b. The Culmination and Completion of Jesus's Mission (18:1—19:42)

4. The Resurrection of the Son and the Mission of the Spirit-Empowered Disciples (20:1—21:25)[132]

Gorman continues to argue that John describes the central missional theme as "missional theosis" in the scheme of "participation" and "transformation," which are defined as participation in both God's continuous redemptive activity and his ontological life.[133] That is, both individual believers and a community might be involved in God's missional love, life, and activity through shalom (peace), which originates from the reconciliation between humanity and God through his forgiveness of sins.[134] Gorman characterizes Jesus's breathing into the disciples in the frame of the "new-creation and revivification."[135] Jesus's giving of the spirit proves that he gives life to them through forgiveness.[136] Just as Jesus did, so, too, should the disciples participate.

Essentially, Gorman agrees with R. Geoffrey Harris that John's mission concept is broader than the concept of spiritual salvation, for God takes care of the marginalized of the world.[137] While Gorman's definition of mission relates to the "comprehensive understanding of life," he, at the same time, does not neglect the role of the disciples as they gather and invite people to God's eternal life in both a particularized and a universal context.[138] Notably, Gorman prefers using the words *transformation* or *transformative*.[139] These terms are meant to be internally missional in the sense of the disciples'

---

132. Gorman, *Abide and Go*, 40.
133. Gorman, *Abide and Go*, 23, 25–26.
134. Gorman, *Abide and Go*, 27, 137.
135. Gorman, *Abide and Go*, 140.
136. Gorman, *Abide and Go*, 144.
137. Harris, *Mission*, 224, 228–29.
138. Gorman, *Abide and Go*, 55, 62, 65, 69.
139. Gorman, *Abide and Go*, 108.

participation in the divine life. The missional life and actions of these disciples are inseparable from abiding in God's abundant life and intimate covenant relationship.[140] Through "go" and "keep Jesus's word," their love and life flow externally into the world.[141] This is the purpose of Jesus's sentness, which bears witness of God to the world.[142]

In my estimation, Gorman supplies an important possibility of reading a narrative missionally in order to understand how the disciples might participate in the *missio Dei*. In particular, his understanding of mission is that humanity and the world share in God's life through forgiveness. In 20:23, John highlights that forgiveness is a very important missional theme. Jesus asks the disciples to participate in the forgiveness of sins, saying, "As the Father sent me, so also I send you" (20:21), and God's mission aims to "bring life to the world."[143] For this, the disciples can participate by inheriting Jesus's mission in terms of the forgiveness of sins (John 20:23).[144] John's unique use of the term "forgiveness" is associated with the phrases "takes away" the sin of the world and gives life to the world (1:29).[145] God's forgiveness enables the world, through Jesus's death, to participate in the mutual-relationship with God (3:16; 17:21).[146] For this purpose, the Father sent Jesus into the world (17:8), and Jesus commands the disciples to forgive the world's sins, urging them to undertake forgiveness toward the world.[147] John would demonstrate that Jesus's foot-washing narrative implies

---

140. Gorman, *Abide and Go*, 98, 99.

141. Gorman, *Abide and Go*, 94, 95, 122.

142. Gorman, *Abide and Go*, 123. Two aspects of John are emphasized: Jesus's Great Commission and his Great Commandment. Both of these are mission for a new community of faith that is created by Jesus's mission. Ross Hastings emphasizes John 20:21 as "the Greatest Commission" of "sending" and "bringing" (Hastings, *Missional God*, 15, 81). This Greatest Commission is different than Jesus's Great Command (Matt 28:19–20), as Hastings argues that the Johannine Great Commission is linked to God's creation command. He interprets John 20:19–23 in the frame of creation, redemption, and reconciliation (Hastings, *Missional God*, 156). This passage revolves around the birth of the community of *shalom* through Jesus's cross and imparting the Spirit after his resurrection (Hastings, *Missional God*, 21, 24). The new community's mission is to share *shalom* with the spoiled world and humanity by way of "the living and proclaiming of the gospel in its fullness" (Hastings, *Missional God*, 22, 33). It indicates reconciliation by way of forgiveness (Hastings, *Missional God*, 24, 25).

143. Thompson, *John*, 422.

144. Bauckham, *John*, 192–96; Coloe, "Sources," 77; "Welcome," 400–415; "Foot-washing," 392–94.

145. Thompson, *John*, 423.

146. Um, *Temple Christology*, 20.

147. Chennattu, *Johannine Discipleship*, 164–65.

forgiveness as an embodiment of sacrificial love and service through his death and glorification.

Both Köstenberger and Gorman understand John 13 missionally, noting that Jesus's foot washing implies the practice of the love and service of discipleship within the unity-relationship, or mutual indwelling. In comparing John 20:21 and 17:18, Köstenberger links the relationship of Jesus and the Father in love (13:34) and unity (17:11, 22–23) with the mission of the sent disciples, on the basis of interpretation of the proposition *kathos* ("just as"). However, these elements of mission (love and unity) are only an "initial appeal" for the world, and should be accompanied with the acts of "works" (14:12), "going" (15:16), "witnessing" (15:27), and "the verbal proclamation and exposition of the significance of Jesus's death and resurrection."[148] Moreover, Köstenberger contends that love is not for the world, but rather for Jesus and the members of the faith community (12:25–26; 13:1–3, 34, 35). Similarly, Gorman also highlights that the Johannine community's spirituality is the mutual indwelling of the disciples and the triune God that participates in the divine life, love, and life-giving. This relationship is founded on both their likeness to God and their becoming more and more like God. In John 15, the author describes that the unity of mission and spirituality is "*missio theosis*" in terms of dwelling (mutual indwelling) and go (witness) ("deification" or "divination").[149] In John 17, the disciples are enabled by the *Paracletos* to participate in Jesus's mission through the intimate relationship. In John 20, they expand shalom to the world. According to Gorman, Christian spirituality is the "lived experience of Christian belief, faith and discipleship, and of a transformative relationship with God."[150] Indeed, as these scholars observe, "relational unity" and "love" in the mutual indwelling relationship are meaningful missional metaphors in the context of John 13–17.[151] They understand that the account of Jesus's foot washing shows this well.

---

148. Köstenberger, *Missions of Jesus*, 190.

149. Gorman understands that John uses dwelling language in terms of the triune God's *perichoresis*. John develops the *perichoresis* concept in that Jesus and the disciples formulate God's indwelling place (the temple of God) (Gorman, *Abide and Go*, 72–73). They come from the Father and dwell within the mutual relation with him, which is intrinsically missional (Gorman, *Abide and Go*, 73).

150. Gorman, *Abide and Go*, 9.

151. While Gorman and others regard Jesus's discourses (chs. 13–17) as a literary unit (cf. Bennema, *Encountering Jesus*, 185–200), Mathew criticizes that such an analysis is engaged in the "christological features of Johannine discipleship" (Gorman, *Abide and Go*, 164). Of course, her point makes sense that Jesus's washing the disciples' feet and his discourses constitute a unit in the genre-structure of the "hour" and Judas's treachery between 13:1 and 17:26 (Gorman, *Abide and Go*, 154–56). However, Mathew

However, although Köstenberger and Gorman's interpretation of John's narratives is valid, relatively, little effort has been made to missionally read Jesus's foot-washing narrative in biblical scholarship. Typically, most biblical scholars have interpreted this narrative as follows:

First, some suggest an ecclesial, or sacramental interpretation. These interpretations consist of three groups. *Firstly*, William Whallon insists that the paschal lamb and the bread (Exod 12:8–17; Lev 23:5; Num 28:16) seemingly mean the body of Jesus accompanied by wine denotes his blood (John 19:33 and Exod 12:46).[152] *Secondly*, concerning the ceremony of the foot washing in terms of the Eucharist as a way of promoting the solidarity of the faith community, Erwin Fahlbusch argues that the ceremony fulfills Jesus's invitation to eat the living bread and drink his eternal blood (6:25–59).[153] *Thirdly*, Raymond E. Brown argues that this narrative consists of three parts: one, an introduction of the book of Glory; another Jesus's salvific death and baptismal symbolism; and the other, a lesson for practicing service toward one another. His postulation is that the second part does not result in the first edition of the gospel.[154] Although it is not convincing that Jesus's foot washing refers to the early church's sacramental implications, scholars basically agree with Brown's structural division of 13:1–11 and 13:12–20.[155] That is, those scholars concede to one narrative in two structures. The first part symbolizes Jesus's foot washing, and the second part gives the interpretation of his act for the disciples and the Johannine community's identity and life.

Second, the other interpretations are christological, eschatological, or ethical approaches. *Firstly*, Rudolf Schnackenburg argues that the interpretation of the Eucharist and baptism have nothing to do with each other in that the literary part is concerned with how "Jesus's death and his disciples' share

---

also argues that John 13–17 contains various genres as "a band of genres" for Jesus's message (Gorman, *Abide and Go*, 163). That is, the classification of a genre of discourse cannot be the criterion behind the theory that chapters 13 through 17 comprise a literary unit. That is why, for the determination of another literary unit, John forms the parallel structure of μετὰ τοῦτο (after this) or the syntactic structure of εἰς τέλος or τελειόω between 13:1, 2–5 (cf. v. 7, μετὰ ταῦτα) and 19:28 (Mathew, *Johannine Footwashing*, 164; cf. Barus, "John 2:12–25," 124–25). Mathew goes on to suggest another unit between chapters 13 and 20. She emphasizes sending language for Jesus as "the initiator of sending" under the Father's mission (13:20b; 15:26; 16:7; 20:21; cf. 4:38; 17:18) (Mathew, *Johannine Footwashing*, 217–18, 267–75). In particular, with regard to the latter, Craig S. Keener also strengthens Mathew's idea by noting "the sending of the Son is the heart of the Fourth Gospel's plot" (Keener, *Gospel of John*, 1204).

152. Whallon, "Pascha," 127.
153. Erwin, *Encyclopedia*, 60.
154. Brown, *John XIII–XXI*, 561–62.
155. Thompson, *John*, 281, 282; Morris, *Gospel according to John*, 611, 620; Lindars, *Gospel of John*, 452; Mathew, *Johannine Footwashing*, 140–46.

with his glory," while the latter part deals with Jesus's modeling action.[156] Marianne Meye Thompson follows Schnackenburg's observation that the structural interpretive matter is how the soteriological interpretation (13:6–11) links with the ethical interpretation (13:12–18).[157] Her focus is on the fact that the interpretation of Jesus's sacrificial death and forgiveness as the self-giving event is bound with his servant-service of sacrificial love and humility.[158] *Secondly*, Ingrid Rosa Kitzberger proposes various intertextual readings of John 13:1–20; 12:1–8; and Luke 7:36–50. She insists that these accounts reflect Jesus's teaching that "he has not come to be served but to serve and give life as a ransom for many (cf. Mark 10:45); he is like one who serves, and not like one who sits at the table (cf. Luke 22:27)."[159] She makes it clear that the foot-washing pericope includes a focus on the discipleship of loving service through humility. *Thirdly*, Alan R. Culpepper suggests that the story of the foot washing should be understood according to the new commandment (love) in terms of teaching the same meaning embodied through Jesus's crucifixion. Culpepper's idea is powerful because Jesus taught that his disciples should practice love and service, thereby externalizing Jesus's model (foot washing, sacrificial love, and death) for others to realize their discipleship (13:35).[160]

To be sure, Jesus's foot-washing narrative concentrates on his death and the disciples' lives.[161] This fact supports the second interpretation more than the first interpretation. Jesus's sacrificial and self-giving death is for the salvation of the world and at the same time, for the life-pattern of the faith community in the context.[162] For their lives, John probably highlights

---

156. Schnackenburg, *Gospel according to St John*, 3:12, 23.

157. Thompson, "His Own Received Him Not," 258.

158. Thompson, "His Own Received Him Not," 260–69.

159. Kitzberger, "Love and Footwashing," 205–6.

160. Culpepper, "Johannine Hypodeigma," 133–52.

161. Jesus's removal of his clothes (13:4 with 19:23) plays a crucial role in explaining the symbolism of the foot washing as a prediction of his crucifixion as a token of love that is based upon self-giving (Koester, *Symbolism*, 11, 116). That is, Jesus's death is the expression and completion of his love (Koester, *Symbolism*, 116).

162. As a sociocultural interpretation, Herold Weiss draws attention to the conflict between the Johannine community and the synagogue by interpreting ὥρα ("hour") to be the unbelieving Jews' persecuting moment of 16:2 and 4 with respect to the affliction of the Johannine community after Jesus departs to the Father (Weiss, "Footwashing," 306–8). Subsequently, he argues that the Johannine community construed the story of the foot washing in terms of an eschatological and pastoral meaning within the context of their martyrdom, regardless of the ceremonial or sacramental meaning (Weiss, "Footwashing," 325). Weiss's argument is congruent with Bultmann's rediscovery of the *Sitz im Leben* of the Johannine community (cf. Smith, *Composition and Order*, 238–49). Although Weiss's idea of martyrdom should be considered in terms of John's literary

Jesus's interpretation of his symbolic act. The early churches could easily understand his act through the diverse cultures of the Jewish, Greek, and Roman worlds, and then practice it (Rom 12:13; Heb 13:2; 1 Tim 3:2; Titus 1:8; 1 Pet 4:9).[163]

Yet, in my missional hermeneutical perspective, the second interpretation ought to move forward to understand the nature and role of Jesus's and the disciples' sentness as mission in the frame of "as . . ., so . . ." and sending (13:15, 16, 20; 17:18; 20:21). Maarten J. J. Menken pays attention to the literary structure of "as" in 20:19-23, which shows the relatedness of the mission of Jesus and disciples.[164] The relationship of the term *as* reflects the threefold unity: the Father and the Son, the Son and believers, and the Father and believers ("the Father is in me and I am in the Father," 10:38; 14:10-11, 20; 17:21-23). God initiated this unity-relationship as he gives life to people (6:37, 39; 10:28-29; 17:2, 6, 9-19; 18:9).[165] It is the expression of God's sacrificial love and the purpose of God's mission (3:16). The mutual loving service of the disciples generates unity in the community and the world (cf. foot washing, 13:1, 34; 14:21; 15:9, 12). This foot-washing act is the model and cause of the disciples' mission, meaning that the mission of Jesus and the disciples is a matter of life in the frame of the word *as* (13:15).[166] Their missional life becomes the tunnel that reveals the invisible God to the world (13:34-35).

Meanwhile, most recently, Bincy Mathew has appropriately examined the connections between the foot-washing narrative and Jesus's sending of his disciples in 20:19-23.[167] Additionally, Mathew emphasizes that the foot washing (13:1-20) is united with both the previous literary unit (chs. 11-12) and the later one (chs. 14-20 [21]).[168] She draws attention to the unity in structure and theme in a chiastic pattern. Although Mathew aptly understands the meaning of Jesus's missional act beyond the concept of

---

context (see the discussion of the missional interpretation of the foot washing in the chapter 3), it is appropriate that the Johannine community must have lived the life of Jesus's teaching in the world.

163. Hultgren, "Johannine Footwashing," 541-42; Thompson, *John*, 282; Thomas, *Footwashing*, 42, 57-60; Mathew, *Johannine Footwashing*, 69-127. Köstenberger argues that Jesus did not practice a rite, but rather exemplified loving service in humility (Gal 5:13; 6:2; Phil 2:6-8) (Köstenberger, "John," 485). This is because the foot washing in the Old Testament was exercised by slaves (Gen 18:4; 19:2; 24:32; 43:24; Judg 19:21; 1 Sam 25:41; cf. T. Abr 3:7-9, Jos. Asen 7:1).

164. Menken, *Studies*, 68.
165. Menken, *Studies*, 69.
166. Menken, *Studies*, 68.
167. Mathew, *Johannine Footwashing*, 267-75.
168. Mathew, *Johannine Footwashing*, 164.

imitation, her mission concept is that Christians should sacrificially love others in order to evangelize them.[169] In fact, she is concerned with examining the term *send* (*apostelo* and *pempo*) in order to achieve a task or mission.[170] She argues that Jesus's exemplary act is aimed at the disciples' imitation of him, and that he is represented with authority in the world through the agent-imagery.[171]

Mathew's missional understanding of the foot washing concludes that discipleship's loving practice leads unbelievers to faith in Jesus. Although she seems to be inclined toward the priority of evangelism, her observation of the narrative's missional frame will provide useful ideas for our study: the frame of sending and "as . . ., so . . ." (13:14–15, εἰ . . . ἐγὼ [if . . . I] . . . καὶ . . . ὑμεῖς [you also] . . . καθὼς ἐγὼ [just as I] . . . καὶ ὑμεῖς [you also] . . .).[172] For me, Jesus's foot-washing narrative symbolically anticipates his death, and also deals with its missional interpretation for the community's new lifestyle after his ascension. The mission of both Jesus and the Johannine context, as the dyadic witness during Jesus's physical absence, are remarkably described in the foot-washing narrative (13:1–38). My proposal is that, from a missional perspective, John describes the interpretation of Jesus's sacrificial death and resurrection for his community's life-witness and evangelism (13:15–16, 20, 34–36).

Firstly, John places Jesus's foot-washing narrative within the parenthetical structure of Jesus's death and glorification (chs. 13 and 21). Although, in general, John 13 is categorized as the farewell discourse (chs. 13–17), his foot washing primarily alludes to his death.[173]

    a. John's technical term *tithēmi* (John 13:4, "put" or "take off") clarifies the symbolic meaning of Jesus's death in the narrative, for this word is used to describe the good shepherd's sacrifice for his sheep (10:11, 15, 17, 18).[174]

    b. Considering that the foot washing is the sign of Jesus's death, this event underlines Jesus's sharing (*meros* 13:8) of life with his disciples.[175]

---

169. Mathew, *Johannine Footwashing*, 3.

170. Mathew, *Johannine Footwashing*, 270–72, 273.

171. Mathew, *Johannine Footwashing*, 271, 274, 330–34, 342–47, 362.

172. Mathew, *Johannine Footwashing*, 2018, 4.

173. Brown, *John XIII–XXI*, 597–601; Talbert, *Reading John*, 207–9; Moloney and Harrington, *Gospel of John*, 377–78; Coloe, *Dwelling*, 139–42; Bennema, *Encountering Jesus*, 185–200; Gorman, *Abide and Go*, 81.

174. Chennattu, *Johannine Discipleship*, 93.

175. Chennattu, *Johannine Discipleship*, 94–95.

c. When John interprets Jesus's act as a model or pattern for his community's life, he draws attention to Jesus's question: "Do you understand (γινώσκετε) what I have done to you?" (13:12). However, Jesus mentions, "What I am doing you do not understand now, but you will understand after these things" (13:7). These sentences make sense of the time interval; while in 13:7 John uses the future tense of γινώσκω ("you will understand after these things," γνώσῃ δὲ μετὰ ταῦτα), 13:12 employs the present tense of the verb. In comparison with 2:22 and 12:16, "after these things" mean Jesus's death and glorification in 13:7. After Jesus's sacrificial and exalted events, the disciples might understand Jesus's act through the frame of their sentness. Specifically, John parallels "Jesus's taking his garments" (ἔλαβεν τὰ ἱμάτια αὐτοῦ, 13:12) with "soldiers' taking his garments" (ἔλαβον τὰ ἱμάτια αὐτοῦ, 19:23). If this phrase foreshadowed Jesus's death, the disciples should have understood the meaning of his teaching and death.[176]

Secondly, Jesus establishes a community of humble loving service through his death, which is the community's interpretation in light of their context.[177] John highlights that the disciples should live the life set forth by Jesus's pattern (ὑπόδειγμα, 13:15), and that their lives are to be spent practicing Jesus's forgiveness, sacrificial love, and service.[178] These themes are not

---

176. Harris, "John," 343–44.

177. Chennattu, *Johannine Discipleship*, 160–61; their practice of love is their way of participating in "God's mission of bringing love, light, and life to the world" (Gorman, *Abide and Go*, 82).

178. Jesus's forgiveness, love, and service are the markers of the *new temple* (John 2:21). The functions of the temple in Jesus's day are (1) YHWH's dwelling-place, (2) the place of sacrifice, and (3) the temple's political significance (Wright, *Victory of God*, 406–12). Paul M. Hoskins senses that Jesus is the antitype of the temple in light of the typology "within the framework of salvation history and in works of prophecy like Isaiah and Ezekiel" (Hoskins, *Jesus*, 19) (cf. for an opposing position to the replacement of the temple of Jesus, see Lindars, *Gospel of John*, 144). He emphasizes that "the antitype does not merely recapitulate their type, but the movement from type to antitype is progressive in nature such that the antitype movement from type to antitype is progressive in nature such that the antitype surpasses the types" (Hoskins, *Jesus*, 185). John 1:14; 1:51; 2:18–22; and 4:20–24 strongly support Hoskins's argument that Jesus becomes the fulfillment or replacement of the temple by way of his being lifted up and his glorification (Isa 6:1–13; 60:7 [LXX], death, resurrection, and exaltation) (Hoskins, *Jesus*, 158; Kinzer, "Temple Christology," 447–64; Lieu, "Temple and Synagogue," 66, 67). Jesus is not only the new locus of God's presence, glory, and revelation, but his major role is also the completion of the temple's function through sacrificial death and resurrection (Wright, *Victory of God*, 405–12). The sacrificial ritual of the temple aims at forgiveness by washing away sins (Quarles, "New Perspective," 39–56; Wright, *Victory of God*, 409–11). However, John does not simply engage in the atoning function

separate, but rather organic. Jesus enacted these implications through his death. The terms "water" (13:5), "wash" (νίπτω, 13:8, 10, 14), and "hour" (13:1) are echoed in the first sign narrative ("water," ὕδωρ, 2:7, 9 [cf. 1:26; 3:22–23]; "purification," καθαρισμός, 2:6; "hour," ὥρα, 2:7, 9). These words symbolize Jesus's death (19:34, ὕδωρ) for the forgiveness of the world's sin (1:29). Along with his sacrificial death, Jesus practices a model of love and service in John 13–21, which includes the treacherous story of Judas Iscariot and Peter (13:36–38).[179] John confronts Jesus's washing with Judah's "lift[ing] up his heel" (13:2, 8–9 and 18, 21–30). In vv. 10 and 11, John shows that Jesus interweaves "not every one of you is clean" with "the one who was going to betray him." These expressions are antithetical to Jesus's declaration of "he now loved them to the very end" in 13:1 and 6:39.[180] Importantly, John explains that Jesus restores Peter and the other disciples, which presupposes his forgiveness of their betrayal (18:25–27 and 21:3). Therefore, the Son was crucified to take away the sin of the world, with his sacrifice implying forgiveness and life. What the Father sent the Son to give to the world was initiated by his sacrificial love. These themes appear throughout the discourse for his disciples after Jesus returns to the Father. However, these themes ultimately result in John and the community interpreting Jesus's life, teaching, and acts within their context. In particular, they had to interpret Jesus's foot washing and teaching ("you also ought to [ὀφείλετε] wash [νίπτειν] one another's feet [ἀλλήλων τοὺς πόδας]," 13:14), and then reconsider these implications. Therefore, John's interpretation of Jesus's symbolic act would form the faith and daily life of the disciples as "life-witness."[181]

In short, the sending language in 13:16, 20; 17:18; and 20:21 shapes a literary unit.[182] John demonstrates that the disciples interpreted Jesus's sal-

---

of the temple (Sanders, *Jewish Law*, 29). He instead illustrates the fulfillment of God's salvation (John 3:16) through prophets. That is, Jeremiah 31:34 and Ezekiel 16:63; 37:23–28 clarify that YHWH forgives the Israelites' sins and dwells in the midst of them as the everlasting sanctuary. John views Jesus's *new temple* figure as the witness of God's forgiveness through his presence (Thompson, *John*, 423). At the same time, he demonstrates that the disciples' mission is to participate in the *missio Dei* by Jesus, the *new temple*. Through both forgiveness and restoration, God's mission brings life into the world. This life reshapes the life-way and identity of both the world and humanity.

179. During Jesus's earthly ministry period, he practiced forgiveness, love, and service (John 4:15–18, 29; 5:1–14; 8:1–11).

180. In 13:1, the main verb is ἠγάπησεν (aorist, active, verb), while two participles are used: εἰδὼς and ἀγαπήσας, except for a verb ἦλθεν in the subordinate clause. The use of the main verb indicates that Jesus's love is the central theme of the foot-washing narrative (13:34–35).

181. Cf. Michaels, *Gospel of John*, 720; Beasley-Murray, *John*, 254; Brown, *John I–XII*, 541.

182. Coloe, "Sources," 73; Mathew, *Johannine Footwashing*, 164–65.

vific death and its meaning as a symbolic act for the life pattern and identity of the Johannine community.[183] His act is the fulfillment of purification, and an expression of sacrificial love and humble service that comes from the integrated, organic perspective of knowing and practice, which disciples today should continue to do in both their faith communities and the world. Finally, in chapters 2 and 3, I will attempt to understand the concept of mission that the narrative implies by the literary analysis and exegesis. Here, I will take a look at how the missional meaning of the whole Gospel of John is reflected in the narrative. Then, in chapter 4, I will consider what missional implications of John's Gospel, specially the foot-washing narrative, are for evangelicals who have participated in the Lausanne movements.[184]

SUMMARY

This chapter has the goal of looking into both (1) missional hermeneutical methods for the study of John's Gospel and (2) the current scholars' discussion surrounding the Johannine mission and Jesus's washing of the disciples' feet.

First, missional reading is based on missional hermeneutics. This hermeneutic has various methodologies: (1) a proof-texting method presents the basis of the missionary movement. Through their dogmatic understanding of the Bible, readers understand why the church should join in mission on Jesus's Great Commission; (2) through the historical-critical approach, the biblical foundation of mission investigates how the Old Testament shows Israel's contextualization, or how the early churches of the New Testament, according to Jesus's earthly mandate, did mission in each context; and (3) missional hermeneutics is a biblical-theological interpretation that reads the entire Bible narratively. Readers read the entire Bible and each biblical text in terms of the metanarrative of God and his people's mission.

Second, proof-texting and finding theological grounds are a great help in presenting the biblical bases for mission. However, they are limited in that readers might ignore the literary and theological, or contextual, aspects of the text. In this sense, missional hermeneutics helps readers understand the nature of mission and discover missional implications for contemporary Christians. Of course, the missional reading of the whole Bible also has the limitation of missing the diversity of individual texts. Likewise, a theological frame cannot be applied to all texts. For example, John's Gospel does not

---

183. Schnackenburg, *Gospel according to St John*, 3:7, 18–19.
184. Stott, *Christian Mission*, 26; Costas, *Christ Outside the Gate*, 6, 13–15.

contain the frame of the Abrahamic promises and fulfilment. For this reason, Christopher J. H. Wright excludes John from the mission of God.

Third, I examine two missional hermeneutic characteristics needed for the reading of John: (1) a missional hermeneutic should be based on literary-exegetical interpretation. As Stroope argues, the attempt to read the Bible through the lens of a modern Christian understanding of mission is to justify, or defend, their mission definition and activities. Stroope's argument is acceptable. Therefore, readers must try to read missional meanings and implications by exegeting biblical authors' language and theology in the literary context; and (2) a missional hermeneutic is theological interpretation. They ought to consider an author-centered theological interpretation through literary-exegetical interpretation. At the same time, it should be acknowledged that they are not free from their theological tradition and interests, which lead to various interpretations of the Bible. However, provided that the Bible is the Word of God given to the community of faith, this reader-centered theological interpretation must be within the hermeneutical function of the community. At times, the individual's uncontrollable subjectivity may be guided by the faith community.

Fourth, in scholars' recent discussion of the Johannine mission, they have recognized two mission concepts: (1) mission as evangelism: John speaks of eschatological harvest and ingathering of God's people; and (2) mission as life-witness: John does not distinguish between discipleship and mission. The second concept is understood by Jesus and his disciples in terms of "mutual indwelling," or "missional theosis," in terms of God's mission. The representative scholars who read John missionally are Köstenberger and Gorman. The former studies John's sending language through a semantic approach, explaining the discontinuity and continuity of Jesus and his disciples' mission, while the latter explains the theological significance of God's mission through literary structural analysis. As Stroope criticized, however, in terms of John's lack of the term mission, we need to look at how sending language is used missionally throughout John's entire context. Also, we do look at Jesus's foot washing in John 13 from a missional perspective.

In the following chapters, I will study (1) what the Johannine mission means in the formula of sending, (2) what the foot-washing narrative means and how its literary-exegetical interpretation is connected with a missional interpretation, and (3) what the missional implications of the foot washing are for today's evangelicals.

2

Mission as Integrated Witness in John's Gospel

THIS CHAPTER AIMS TO explore the mission of Jesus and his disciples as *integrated witness* through the missional structure of John's Gospel. In the literary structure of sending language and its formulae, Jesus bears witness to both the Father and his own mission. At the same time, Jesus sends the Holy Spirit and his disciples as witnesses to continue his mission (15:26-27; 20:21, 30-31; 21:24-25). In this study, I will focus on (1) John's missional structure, (2) the use of sending language and its formulae, (3) the nature of witness, (4) and the mission of Jesus and his disciples.

THE STRUCTURE OF THE GOSPEL

John narrates the mission of Jesus and the disciples throughout the structural aspect of the whole Gospel, which consists of two sections, chapters 1-12 and 13-21.[1] The first section engages with Jesus's signs and teachings within the

---

1. I presuppose that the Gospel is a book completed by editor(s) of the community that, even though they would reshape and reorganize materials, they maintained the witness of the Apostle John (21:24-25) (see Robinson, *Priority of John* [1985]). Therefore, this research regards John as the first writer; scholars have discussed the structure of the Gospel. C. H. Dodd, Raymond E. Brown, Marianne Meye Thompson, and J. B. Lightfoot agree the basic distinction of two structures or books: Dodd (1:1-51 Introduction; 2-12 Book of Signs; 13-20 Book of the Passion; 21:1-25 Epilogue),

sphere of his public ministry, while the second section shows the interpretation of Jesus's events and words for the disciples' mission within the context of his own mission's completion. My argument is that these two sections are linked under the sending theme (1:14; 17:18; 20:21). This theme talks about the *missio Dei*. By his sending of the Son, the Spirit, and the disciples, God accomplishes his mission of salvation and self-revelation. Ultimately, the purpose of God's mission is to make the world believe in God and Jesus so that it might receive eternal life (3:16-17; 12:44-45; 17:2-3, 20; 20:31).[2]

First, the entire Gospel deals with Jesus's and his disciples' mission as witness. Jesus witnesses to his identity and the Sender, and his purpose leads the world to faith.[3] However, while some believe in his sentness and testimonies, many others gradually react with hostility toward Jesus, and some try to kill him (5:16, 18, 19-32). This deepening of conflict ultimately brings readers to see the purpose of Jesus's death as the reason for his sentness (10:11; 11:50-52; 12:24). In chapter 13, when his hour to return to the

---

Brown (1:1-18 Prologue; 2-12 Book of Signs; 13-20 Book of Glory; 21:1-25 Epilogue), Thompson (1:1-18 Introduction to the Gospel; 1:19-12:50 Book of Signs: Jesus's Public Ministry; 13:1—21:22 Book of the Passion: Jesus's Last Words, Death, and Resurrection; 21:23-25 Epilogue), and Lightfoot 1:1-17 Introduction; 1:1-18 Doctrines of the Book; 1:19—2:11 Preparation for the Ministry; 2:12—12:50 Record of the Lord's Public Ministry; 13:1—20:31 Record of the Final Events; 21:1-25 Epilogue). Meanwhile, Craig L. Blomberg and J. Ramsey Michaels are involved with the thematic structure: Blomberg (1:1-51 Introductory Testimony; 2:1—11:57 Testimony of Signs and Discourses [2:1—11:57]; 12:1—20:31 Testimony of Death and Resurrection [12:1—20:31]; 21:1-25 Concluding Testimony [21:1-25]), Michaels (1:1-5 Preamble; 1:6—3:30 Testimony of John; 4:1—12:43 Jesus's Self-Revelation to the World; 13:1—16:33 Jesus's Self-Revelation to the Disciples; 18:1—21:25 Verification of Jesus's Self-Revelation). In contrast with the stated scholars, Merrill C. Tenney proposes the development theory of the narrative (Prologue [1:1-18], Period of Consideration [1:19—4:54], Period of Controversy [5:1—6:71], Period of Conflict [7:1—11:53], Period of Crisis [11:54—12:36a], Period of Conference [12:36b—17:26], Period of Consummation [18:1—20:31], and Epilogue [21:1-25]) (Brown, *John I-XII*, cxxxviii-cxxxix; Thompson, *John*, 16-17; Dodd, *Interpretation*, 289-444; Tenney, *John*, 36-45; Lightfoot, *St. John's Gospel*, 11-26; Blomberg, *Jesus and the Gospels*, 184-86; Michaels, *Gospel of John*, 30-37).

2. The term "belief" is John's central theme (2:23; 3:18; 4:39; 5:24, 38; 6:47; 8:30, 31; 12:44; 14:1, 11; 19:35; 20:8, 29). It appears in John's sending structure (Lightfoot, *St. John's Gospel*, 23-26).

3. William Loader sorts out John's understandings in the following ways: (1) the Son comes from the Father, (2) The Father has sent the Son, (3) The Father has authorized the Son, (4) The Son makes the Father known, (5) Jesus is the Son and God is the Father, and (6) The Son returns to the Father (Loader, *Christology*, 29). Loader's observation reflects that John's Christology is interwoven with the *missio Dei*, which means that God's self-manifestation and salvation comes through Jesus's sentness. Jesus came into the world to identify himself as the Son. John spells out the fact that God the Father sent Jesus and reveals himself in Jesus and through his works. Besides, the Father saves the world by washing people's sins with Jesus's blood and water (19:34).

Father arrived, he taught his disciples how to live missionally (13:1, 20, 35). As Jesus himself was sent to the world (6:69; 10:36), they were also sent as holy and distinctly one with the Father and the Son (17:14-26; 20:21). In chapters 18-20, Jesus completed his unique mission, which is the sacrificial death for people. As a consequence, forgiveness was given for the disciples to proclaim (20:23). They were sent to bear witness to Jesus by performing signs greater than he performed and obeying the guidance of the Holy Spirit (13:20; 14:12; 15:26-27; 17:20; 19:35; 20:30-31; 21:24). At the same time, they also had to live Jesus's life in mutual indwelling. The community of the disciples was steered toward bearing the fruit of love, unity, and testifying to God, who is invisible.

I propose the following outline of John's Gospel:

1. 1:1-18 Prologue: God's Sending of the Unique Son and a Witness
2. 1:19—12:50 Jesus's Missional Signs and Teachings in His Public Ministry and His Witnesses
3. 13:1—20:31 The Completion of Jesus's Unique Mission, the Holy Spirit and the Disciples' Continuing Mission as Witness in the Sending Formula
4. 21:1-25 Epilogue: The Inauguration of the Disciples' Mission

In the introduction to 1:1-18, John notes that the Word became flesh (incarnation). Jesus was in the bosom of God, and life is in Jesus (1:1-4). His life is the light of people. He became tabernacled in order to dwell in the midst of his people and believers (1:11-12, 14), and made himself known as God's Son (1:18, 34). In this short prologue, John recapitulates his own christological and missional theology. Jesus is "the unique Son who comes from the Father" (μονογενοῦς παρὰ πατρός, 1:14). In the same verse, two expressions indicate that Jesus is the sent one. *Firstly*, the word is μονογενοῦς (adj. "unique" or "only" [3:18]). Chapter 3, v. 16 describes that "God gave his Son" [to the world] (τὸν υἱὸν τὸν μονογενῆ ἔδωκεν). His giving of this unique Son parallels the phrase "God sent the Son into the world" in 3:17 (ἀπέστειλεν ὁ θεὸς τὸν υἱὸν εἰς τὸν κόσμον). *Secondly*, the words are παρὰ πατρός ("from the Father"). In 6:46; 16:27, 28, Jesus introduces himself as the Father (ὁ ὢν παρὰ τοῦ θεοῦ ["the one *is/came* from God"], ἐγὼ παρὰ [τοῦ] θεοῦ ἐξῆλθον ["I came from God"], ἐξῆλθον παρὰ τοῦ πατρός ["I came from the Father"]). These expressions echo the phrase of 1:14 (παρὰ πατρός). The purpose of Jesus's sentness is to testify to the Father's words and deeds through himself (8:38, ἃ ἐγὼ ἑώρακα παρὰ τῷ πατρὶ λαλῶ·καὶ ὑμεῖς οὖν ἃ ἠκούσατε παρὰ τοῦ πατρὸς ποιεῖτε [8:40; 10:18; 15:15; for "truth," 1:9; 17:8]). He is a witness that reveals the Father (1:18; 14:10–11). Thus, in the introduction (1:1–18), John deals with the central theme that the incarnation of the Word is the event in which the Father sends the Son (20:21). Jesus himself testifies, through the Gospels, that he is from the Father, and the person who believes in him bears eternal life, not judgment (12:44–50; 20:30–31). The purpose of Jesus's witness as mission is for people to believe he is from God (16:27, πεπιστεύκατε ὅτι ἐγὼ παρὰ [τοῦ] θεοῦ ἐξῆλθον).

In 21:1–25, John depicts that Jesus comes to the disciples in order to both complete his earthly ministry and to let them return to following him (21:20, 22). Following means to testify to Jesus and his work (21:24). He commands his disciples to care for the flock that he saved through his death (10:7–18; 21:15–17). As he protected them to the end (6:39; 13:1; 18:9), so, too, must they protect his flock in love, which is the origin of Jesus's sacrificial death (3:16). Therefore, in the epilogue, Jesus sends them by lovingly serving his flocks and giving them the task of following him (20:21).

Second, between the prologue and epilogue, John composes his story in two sections, as described below. Some literary characteristics support the division mentioned above:

John 12:37–50 summarizes the first part. This section includes several critical words, such as *faith, light, darkness, world, judgment, salvation, my words* or *logos*, and *eternal life*. This vocabulary characterizes Jesus's public ministries and his missional purpose for the salvation of the world (12:47c):

1. Jesus emphasizes "faith" in him and his Sender (12:37–44, 45, 46, 49).
2. He does not judge the world, but rather saves it by giving "words" to the people of the world. The Father gave these words to him. Those who believe in him and his Sender are no longer in darkness but are in light. This first section is found toward the end of 12:37 (αὐτοῦ [Jesus's] σημεῖα ["signs"] πεποιηκότος ἔμπροσθεν αὐτῶν).

Chapter 12, v. 37 has public teachings in view, but 20:30 sums up the setting that runs from 13:1 through 20:30. The sayings of 12:37 and 20:30 clarify the identities of those who witnessed Jesus's signs, according to their reactions. While 12:37 means αὐτῶν [them], to be Jews among "the large crowd" (12:9, 11, 12), 20:30 points out τῶν μαθητῶν [disciples]. John portrays that, although people saw Jesus's signs, not all of them believed in Jesus (1:11; 3:14; 12:42; and 20:29). The audience's identity is the marker of the division between these two sections. Here, John draws attention to three characteristic points:

Firstly, as Jesus's audiences differ between 1:19—12:43 (12:44–50) and 13:1—17:26 (18:1—19:42) with 20:1—21:25, John employs the term ὑπάγω (*hypagō* + πρὸς τὸν πατέρα ["depart for the Father or the place"]) for Jesus's return to the Father (7:28, 33; 13:3; 16:27-28; 20:17). Jesus uses the word in the polemical context (7:33; 8:14, 21, 22; 12:35); by contrast, he refers to his coming back to the Father for the disciples (13:3, 33, 36; 14:4, 5, 28; 16:5, 17 [disciples]). The former case appears in the dialogue with unbelievers or disputants, such as religious authorities and Jews. They did not know where Jesus will return to (12:35; cf. 7:35); by contrast, the latter knows where Jesus returns to (14:4; 16:5, 10).

Secondly, John draws technically on the usage of you, we, and they. From chapter 12, John uses "you" (plural). Then, he deliberately accentuates the noun (13:19-20, 21, 34, 35; 14:1, 3, 4, 13, 15-21, 24-30; 15:3-5, 7-12, 14-20, 27; 16:1, 4-7, 10-15, 20-27, 31-33; 20:21, 23; "we," 16:30; 17:11; "they," 17:8-26; 18:5, 6). The pronouns *you*, *we*, and *they* point to the disciples. Chapters 13-21 pay particular attention to both the faith community and its life as a group of disciples. Relatively, while chapter 1 utilizes *we* or *I*, chapters 2-12 indicate that believers and unbelievers, even antagonists (*we*, or *they*), are commingling. The subjects *we* and *I* are separated from *you*.[4] The former are witnesses, except for several times (for [unbelieving or unknowing] Jews, 3:2; 6:30, 52; 8:33, 41, 48; 9:24, 34; 11:47-48; for Samaritan, 4:12), whereas the pronoun *you* consists both of nonbelievers or believers.[5] Here, *we* as the unbelieving religious authorities are hostile toward Jesus (11:47). Through this usage, John highlights that, although *you* or *they* as unbelievers characteristically contrast with *we* as believer or witnesses (3:11; 4:22, 42), the major purpose of Jesus and the witnesses in ministry is that people might follow and believe in both him and the Father (10:27, 38; 11:15, 42; 12:36 [believing authorities, 12:42]). Therefore, chapters 1-12 are involved with the evangelism and people's rejection of Jesus, the Father, or the witnesses (*we*). However, from chapter 13, John states that Jesus separates the believing disciples from unbelieving disciples (*his own*, 13:2, 11, 18, 21-30). In the second section (chs. 13-21), *we*, the disciples, are sent to be witnesses in life following Jesus's ascension, and are to set aside proclamatic witness.

Thirdly, John divides Jesus's mission during the public ministry period of making himself and the Father known to people, through the disciples'

4. For [believing] "we" (1:14, 22, 41, 45; 4:42; 6:5, 42, 66-69; 9:31), "I" (Jesus or John the Baptist, 1:30, 31, 33, 34; 5:19, 30, 31; 6:51; 8:55; 9:5; 10:9, 11, 14; 11:25; 12:44-50), "you" (for believers, 1:51; 3:28; 4:35; 6:61-63, 67, 70; 7:7-8, 33, 47; 11:15; 12:8; for unbelievers or unknowing people 2:19; 3:12; 4:22, 32; 5:19, 20, 25, 40, 42-45; 6:26, 27, 32, 36, 43, 61-64; 7:19, 22-23, 35; 8:15, 17, 19, 21-26, 28, 31-32, 36-39, 42, 44-47, 51, 54, 56, 58; 9:27, 41; 11:49; 12:19, 36); for they (Pharisees or high priests, 9:16; 11:56; unknowing people, 10:6; Jesus's sheep, 10:27).

5. The "we" of Nicodemus, or the "we" of the Samaritan, who does not know the regeneration of the Holy Spirit or the Messiah is different from Jesus's word "we" as the eyewitnesses (3:11).

continuing mission, after his return to the Father. The author parallels Jesus's sentness and people's acceptance through his public ministry with the disciples' sentness and people's acceptance through the disciples' mission.

1. John 1:19—12:50 includes both Jesus's public ministry and people's reaction to him.[6] John frames the structure of *see* or *hear-believe* and *see* or *know-witness* (1:33, 34, 46, 49, 51; 2:9, 18, 22, 23; 3:2, 11, 32). This section focuses on seeing and believing in Jesus's signs; those who met Jesus historically emphasized the reality of believing in him through his signs.[7] As Jesus invites people to himself through signs (1:39; 2:23; 3:2), his followers lead people to faith in him by testifying to what they saw and heard (for *lead* and *faith*, 1:43, 51 [4:52–53] and 4:29, 42; for eye-and-ear-witness, 1:34, 46, 49; 2:23; 3:2, 11, 32; 4:42 [5:19, 30]). Faith is the central theme of leading people to receive eternal life throughout the entire Gospel (3:15). Ultimately, the Johannine themes of "[eternal] life or living water," "faith," "light," and following are the goals of God's mission that are fulfilled through Jesus's sentness (3:16–21). Furthermore, in 5:1—12:50, believers see and experience Jesus's signs, and ultimately believe in him (9:38). As John describes how believers react to Jesus's signs in 1:19—4:53, he narrates the increasing numbers of believers as a main theme. However, he begins to emphasize the increasing numbers of unbelievers in spite of the observation of Jesus's signs (5:47; 6:36). They persecute him, which is why unbelievers do not pay attention to Jesus's identity that is revealed by the divine signs, but rather focus on his pedigree or birth place (*Joseph's son* or *Galilee*; 6:42; 7:16, 19, 27, 52) and violation of the Sabbath law (5:1–8, 47; 6:39; 9:16). They conclude that Jesus is a sinner (9:27) and that they must kill him for the benefit of the nation (7:19; 11:50–52). They do not see the work of Jesus and the Father (5:17–18), nor do they accept that Jesus comes from the Father.

In these chapters, John deals with disputes over Jesus's identity (6:42; 7:15, 27, 52; 8:12–13; 9:5, 16; 10:11, 30, 36) and the conflict between believers and unbelievers (5:47; 6:36, 43, 68; 7:5, 45–52; 12:19).

---

6. John also explains why Jesus came to earth in 1:19–51. He is "the lamb of God who takes away the sins of the world" (1:29, 36), the "son of God" who reveals God (1:34), and the "king of Israel" (1:49; 12:13). In this paragraph, too, John emphasizes that the disciples become witnesses to the people as Jesus did (1:39 and 1:46). At the same time, those who come to Jesus become followers of him (1:43). They will be witnesses of what Jesus is doing (1:51). After Jesus returned to the Father, they are sent to the world, to bear witness to what they had seen with Jesus from the beginning (15:27). That is why they follow Jesus.

7. Thompson, *Incarnate*, 63–86.

Interestingly, this conflict is tied to a controversy over the question of whose disciples they are: are they Moses's disciples? or are they Jesus's disciples? (9:27–30). The Pharisees call themselves Moses's disciples. In the Jewish rabbinic tradition, to be a disciple of Moses implies that their teachings originate in Moses, who conversed with God (9:28–31; cf. Exod 33:11).[8] By contrast, a believer would appeal to Jesus's coming from the Father as a way of defending the Pharisees' accusation (9:29, 30). Jesus's originality is placed in God (10:38), and he teaches his disciples what he sees and hears from God (3:32). They must keep Jesus's words (8:51). John highlights that Jesus comes from the Father to deliver his words to the world, while the Jews place the originality and authority of their teachings in Moses. This points out Jesus's inauguration of his community. At the same time, Jesus demonstrates his sacrificial death for nations (10:11, 17; 12:20–25, 33). The author inserts his understanding in the statement of the high priest (11:50–52). His confession clarifies how Jesus gives eternal life to the world. Although the persecution of unbelieving Jews leads Jesus to death, his sacrifice was already determined by the Father in order to accomplish salvation in his missional economy (3:16–18; 17:1, 18; and 20:21). Finally, John accounts for Jesus's death (12:20–33) and judgment on the last day (12:47–48). His judgment is the completion of his mission.

2. John 13 begins to highlight the mission of the disciples after Jesus's return to the Father (13:1). Jesus teaches that they are sent into the world after his ascension so that they might live in union with God and participate in mission as witness (for life-witness, 13:15, 34–35; for evangelism, 13:20). He foretells his death as his own mission on the cross (chs. 18–19, specifically 19:30). The author unfolds the story of Jesus's death in chapter 1, and also points to its meaning in chapters 10–12. In chapter 13, however, John includes an interpretation of his washing act for the community's lifestyle in mutual indwelling (chs. 13–17). He talks about the community living Jesus's life after his departure, and emphasizes that they are sent (20:21) in order to continue his mission (13:20; 14:12; 15:26–27). At the same time, they are in a holy union with the triune God because they share in God's life and character, and their identity and lives testify to Jesus in the world (17:1–26).

Therefore, on the one hand, the first section (chs. 1–12) emphasizes the eyewitnesses who know that Jesus is the savior of the world (4:42). In this section, John is involved with testimonies of Jesus's sentness through

---

8. Beasley-Murray, *John*, 158.

his teachings and signs in his public ministry.⁹ The central purpose of his sentness is to reveal (or bear witness to) his Sender to the world and to give life to the people by faith. The prologue of the Gospel involves the Son's sentness (John 1:1–18). God uncovers himself to the world through Jesus in the form of a tabernacle, and Jesus reveals the Father's presence in his life and actions as signs (10:37–38). John selects several signs in order to testify to the *missio Dei*. According to Merrill C. Tenney, John's term *sign* (σημεῖον) aims at bearing witness to the truth.¹⁰ When Jesus performs signs, one of the major purposes is to reveal his identity in the union with the Father (5:17–18; 10:38; 12:44) so that people trust in him (4:48; 6:30; 10:25; 11:15). His teachings show the motivation, purpose, and result of the Father's sending of the Son (3:16–17; 7:28; 8:28–29).

On the other hand, the second section (chs. 13–21) highlights the credibility of many eyewitnesses and their lifestyles in the unity-relationship with God, and how this influences the people who do not see him (20:29–31; 21:24–25). This second part focuses on how the disciples live a life of witness to Jesus, the Spirit, and the Father in the world (13:35; 15:26–27; 17:23), particularly after Jesus has returned to the Father. The purpose of a life of witness is to participate in the significance of Jesus's life, teaching, and death. Jesus sent the disciples into the world by being consecrated to God (John 17), and his purpose is to make his and his Father's love known to the world (17:23). The disciples participate in the missional significance of foot washing, which signifies the love and service of Jesus's death (13:14–15, 16, 20, 34–35). The fruits of their lives are to bear witness to God in the world (13:35; 15:8, 27; 17:23). The central theme of the disciples' life-witness appears more concretely in both Jesus's washing action (13:5) and the disciple's understanding of the action (13:7, 12, 14). That is, they should live Jesus's life by *abiding* (μένω) in him, so they must make fruits of his commandments and words (14:20–21; 15:4–17).¹¹ Their fruits reveal their identity as Jesus's disciples, which bear witness to Jesus and the Father for the world (13:35; 17:23). However, in spite of the structures of the two sections, the Gospel is united by its missional frame. That is, while John divides the Gospel into two parts by using sending language at the end of each section (12:44–50 and 20:19–31), these sections eventually focus on the ultimate task of Jesus's sentness for his death and resurrection in the course of John's story.¹² Jesus's resurrection from the dead would be the most dramatic "sign" (20:28

---

9. Dodd, *Historical Tradition*, 276–78.
10. Tenney, *John*, 28–29.
11. Michaels, *Gospel of John*, 802–3.
12. Culpepper, "Plot," 353–57.

and 2:18, τί σημεῖον δεικνύεις ἡμῖν between 2:22-25 and 20:24-31).[13] John purposely points to Jesus's crucifixion and resurrection as the sign from chapter 1. On the one hand, Jesus tells Nathanael that "you will see greater things than these" (μείζω τούτων ὄψῃ, 1:50). As some scholars observe, these "greater things" might indicate that Jesus reveals his glory by way of "greater works" (2:11; 11:40; 14:12 [τὰ ἔργα]).[14] The climax of these greater things is his crucifixion and resurrection that gives faith to the unbelievers (3:12-15; 11:25; cf. 7:39).[15] Those events point out that Jesus both glorifies the Father and is also glorified in the account of his death (12:23, δοξασθῇ ὁ υἱὸς τοῦ ἀνθρώπου; 12:28, πάτερ, δόξασόν σου τὸ ὄνομα. ἦλθεν οὖν φωνὴ ἐκ τοῦ οὐρανοῦ· Καὶ ἐδόξασα καὶ πάλιν δοξάσω; for "hour," 12:23 and 13:31-32).

On the other hand, readers encounter controversy over signs in the continuation of John's story (2:18). Jesus had already shown his first sign in 2:1-11, though the readers would not agree with the Jewish question in this debate. However, Jesus's answer to their inquiries includes a "sign" to the Jews apart from the first sign (2:11), which refers to his physical resurrection (2:20-21). Through this sign, the disciples know who Jesus is and then believe in his sayings (1:50; 2:22; 20:24-29). Although people believe in him by way of other signs (2:23; 3:2; 12:37; 20:30), their full understanding and faith must be dependent on these two events (3:12-15; 14:29). In order to save the world through these events, God sent his Son. Likewise, Jesus sends his disciples into the world (17:18; 20:21). The sent ones also follow Jesus in life and do the "greater things" in order to be witnesses to God and Jesus, except for Jesus's death as the sacrificial lamb (11:49-50, [12:24]; 13:15, 20, 34-36 and 21:19, 22; 14:12; 15:27; 19:31-37).

Therefore, John begins with the Son's coming into the world and ends with his sending of the disciples (1:14 [19] and 20:21 [21:22-25]). The Johannine Christology is the unifying theme of the Gospel, and this perspective focuses on the *missio Dei*, namely God's sending of the Son.[16] The ultimate intention of Jesus's sentness is to reveal the Father and to fulfill his salvation and work (1:18; 4:34, 36; 5:18; 6:37-38, 40; 8:29; 9:3; 11:52; 14:10).[17] Above

---

13. Crowe, "Chiastic Structure," 71, 77-81.
14. Barrett, *Gospel according to St. John*, 186; Thompson, *John*, 54.
15. Bruce, *Gospel of John*, 62.
16. Loader, *Jesus*, 41; John talks about the organic narratives and various themes for his community, from the christological and missional perspectives (Lightfoot, *St. John's Gospel*, 21; Barrett, *Gospel according to St. John*, 14; Schnelle, "Recent Views of John's Gospel," 353-56).
17. Jesus's signs and works demonstrate that he reveals the Father to the disciples and the world through the unity-relationship between the Father and himself (14:7-12; 17:21-22, 24) (Köstenberger, *Missions of Jesus*, 72-74).

all, Jesus's sacrificial death is his unique mission. Additionally, the author is engaged in describing the disciples' mission through the sending formula. As Jesus enables the disciples and the world so that they might know and believe in both him and his work (11:15, 42; 13:19; 14:29, 31; 17:23, 26), they are sent to bear witness to God and Jesus so that people might believe in Jesus (6:28–29; 17:20–21, 23; 19:35; 20:31; 21:24). Accordingly, though John's Gospel consists of two sections (chs. 1–12 and 13–21), these sections make up an entire book that follows a christological and missional thematic structure, which is framed by sending language and its formulae.[18]

SENDING LANGUAGE AND SENDING FORMULAE

John's sending language and its formulae constitute a missional frame of the Gospel. John begins his story with the Son coming into the world through the event of incarnation, which follows the formula "the Father sent the Son" (1:14; 3:17; 17:18; 20:21). This basic formula is extended to another one that describes that the Father sent the Son to save the world.[19] These formulae are accompanied by the complementary phrase that "God loved the world so he gave the unique Son" (ἠγάπησεν ὁ θεὸς τὸν κόσμον, ὥστε τὸν υἱὸν τὸν μονογενῆ ἔδωκεν, 3:16), or the frame of "as . . ., so . . ." in order to make the connection between the Son's mission and the disciple's mission. Moreover, the formulae and the frame focus on Jesus's death and resurrection, which explains both the purpose and nature of the *missio Dei* and the disciples' mission. Here, I will briefly observe John's use of the sending language and its formulae in order to understand the nature of God's sending act. Then, I will explore how the author explains both the concept of mission and the mission of Jesus and his disciples.

---

18. For a more detailed study of the structure of John's Gospel, see Mlakuzhyil, *Christocentric Literary Structure* (1987).

19. John uses the term κόσμος seventy-six times (cf. Mark, four times; Luke, five times; Matthew, eleven times). This makes it clear that John focuses on the world in association with the purpose of his epistle (20:30–31). "The world" appears in John as both a positive and a negative. The former means the good creation of God (1:1–3, 9; 9:5; 14:29; 17:18) as the redemptive object (3:16, 17b; 4:42; 6:14, 33, 51; 8:12; 12:46, 47), and the latter connotes the entity of protestation against the Creator (1:10; 3:17a, 19; 7:7; 14:17, 27; 15:18, 19; 16:8, 11, 20, 33; 17:9, 14, 15, 16) as the judged object (9:39; 12:31). John sees that this world must be recovered by God through Jesus, who is the Savior of the world (4:42; cf. 3:17) and who takes away the sin of the world (1:29). Here, "the world" is negative.

Sending Language

John explains the nature and purpose of Jesus and the disciples' sentness throughout the entire story of the *missio Dei* (20:21). By way of sending language and sending formulae, God's sending act is described as missional: (1) God lets the sent one complete his special task and will, and (2) God makes himself known to the world through the sent one by sharing life and identity with him. These two points appear in the use of sending language (πέμπω and ἀποστέλλω) as follows:

Table 1. John's Usage of ἀποστέλλω and πέμπω

ἀποστέλλω	πέμπω
1:6 ἀπεσταλμένος παρὰ θεοῦ	1:33 ὁ πέμψας με
3:17 ἀπέστειλεν ὁ θεὸς τὸν υἱὸν	4:34 τοῦ πέμψαντός με
4:38 ἐγὼ ἀπέστειλα ὑμᾶς	5:23 τὸν πέμψαντα αὐτόν
5:36 ὁ πατήρ με ἀπέσταλκεν	5:24 τῷ πέμψαντί με
5:38; 6:29 ὃν ἀπέστειλεν ἐκεῖνος	5:30 τὸ θέλημα τοῦ πέμψαντός με
6:57 ἀπέστειλέν με ὁ ζῶν πατήρ	5:37 ὁ πέμψας με πατὴρ
7:29 κἀκεῖνός με ἀπέστειλεν	6:38, 39 τὸ θέλημα τοῦ πέμψαντός με.
8:42 ἐκεῖνός με ἀπέστειλεν	6:44 ὁ πατὴρ ὁ πέμψας με
9:7 ἀπεσταλμένος	7:16 τοῦ πέμψαντός με
11:42; 17:8 σύ με ἀπέστειλας	7:18 τὴν δόξαν τοῦ πέμψαντος αὐτὸν οὗτος
17:3 ὃν ἀπέστειλας Ἰησοῦν Χριστόν	7:28; 8:29 ὁ πέμψας με
17:18 καθὼς ἐμὲ ἀπέστειλας εἰς τὸν κόσμον, κἀγὼ ἀπέστειλα αὐτοὺς εἰς τὸν κόσμον	7:33; 12:44, 45 τὸν πέμψαντά με
	8:16, 18 ὁ πέμψας με πατήρ
17:21, 23 σύ με ἀπέστειλας	9:4 τὰ ἔργα τοῦ πέμψαντός με
20:21a καθὼς ἀπέσταλκέν με ὁ πατήρ	12:49 ὁ πέμψας με πατὴρ
	13:16 τοῦ πέμψαντος αὐτόν
	13:20a τινα πέμψω ἐμὲ
	13:20b τὸν πέμψαντά με
	14:24 τοῦ πέμψαντός με πατρός.
	14:26 ὃ πέμψει ὁ πατὴρ
	15:21 τὸν πέμψαντά με
	15:26 ὃν ἐγὼ πέμψω ὑμῖν παρὰ τοῦ πατρός
	16:5 πρὸς τὸν πέμψαντά με
	20:21b κἀγὼ πέμπω ὑμᾶς

John uses two words for *send* to delineate the same usage for God's sending of Jesus and the Spirit, except for in the people's case (for ἀποστέλλω, 1:19, 24; 7:32; 11:3; 17:18; 18:24; for πέμπω, 1:22; 12:44, 45; 16:7; 20:21). The diagram shows some of the following characteristics:[20]

1. 4:34 and 38 link the sending act to the sent one's achievement of the Sender's will and work ("ποιήσω τὸ θέλημα τοῦ πέμψαντός με καὶ τελειώσω αὐτοῦ τὸ ἔργον" [4:34; 8:29; 9:4] and "ἐγὼ ἀπέστειλα ὑμᾶς θερίζειν" [4:38; 11:42]. Also, the verb πέμπω in 14:26; 15:26; and 16:7 points out that the sent Holy Spirit has special works.[21]

2. 5:30, 36, and 37 convey the intersectional structure of the two words. These verbs are involved in the Sender's works, along with the unity of the Sender and the sent one. The phrase "the Father sent (ἀπέσταλκεν or ἀπέστειλεν) me" (vv. 36, 38) and "the Father who sent (πέμψας) me" (vv. 30, 37) focus on the Father's sending of Jesus.

3. 7:16, 18, and 28 (πέμψας), with 29 (ἀπέστειλεν) (cf. 7:32, 33), 12:49, and 14:24, show that the Father's sending act entails his giving of words to the sent one.

4. 17:18 and 20:21 parallel one another:
   a. καθὼς ἐμὲ ἀπέστειλας . . ., κἀγὼ ἀπέστειλα αὐτοὺς . . . ("As you sent me . . ., so I have sent them . . .")
   b. καθὼς ἀπέσταλκέν με ὁ πατήρ, κἀγὼ πέμπω ὑμᾶς ("As the Father has sent me, so I am sending you")

The above-stated observations point out that John's sending language is used in two cases. The first case takes place when John explicates Jesus's sentness, which draws attention to the sent one's accomplishment of the Sender's work (10:37). Jesus has completed the work that the Father gave him to do "in the name of the Father" (5:43; 10:25; 12:28; 17:3). Thompson

---

20. On the one hand, in the case of verb active aorist participle, John prefers πέμπω to ἀποστέλλω. On the other hand, he customarily uses the verb ἀποστέλλω in the indicative sentence. Secondly, the aorist participle of πέμπω is usually adjusted to the Father, except for 1:22 and 20:21b. However, there is no difference in their meanings in light of John's repetition of 17:18 and 20:21.

21. In the Old and New Testaments, the Spirit is the sign of the eschatological hope for God's coming salvation of humanity and of all nations (Ezek 36 and 37:1–14; John 3). This is why the Spirit signals God's inaugurating of the new creation in the scheme of his reign's fulfillment (Barrett, *Gospel according to St. John*, 24; Beker, *Triumph of God*, 101). There, people are living with Jesus Christ and worshiping the true God (John 4:24).

argues that Jesus is participating in the Father's saving and judging works.[22] By completing the Father's work, Jesus reveals the Sender's will and goal (John 3:13–14; 5:19, 30).[23] Jesus identifies his will with that of the Sender (5:18, 30). His wording follows the Semitic linguistic habit; *Mishnah Ber* 5:5 illustrates this fact well, describing that the sent one is tantamount to the Sender. Namely, an agent is a plenipotentiary who can make a contract with someone other than himself, beside the Sender, for he has already received authorization and empowerment from the Sender (John 3:35; 13:3; 17:2; cf. 5:22, 26, 27). According to Peder Borgen, 17:18 and 20:21 manifest "the unity between the agent and his Sender."[24] Specifically, in 17:18 and 20:21, John uses ἀποστέλλω and πέμπω simultaneously, and both are involved in the accomplishment of the Sender and the sent one's purpose. John's usage differs from K. H. Rengstorf's observation, who argues that "when *pempein* is used in the NT the emphasis is on the sending as such, whereas when *apostellein* is used it rests on the commission linked with it."[25] He continues to argue that John uses *apostellein* to show the connection between Jesus's authority and God's, while *pempein* means God's sending of Jesus as such. However, John interchangeably uses two Greek words, *apostellein* and *pempein*, for a specific commission throughout his Gospel (8:42 with 11:42; 5:24 with 30; 14:26 with 15:26; 13:20 [*apostellein**17 and *pempein**24]).[26] In short, John portrays, in the sending frame, that Jesus's works are equivalent to those of the Father (8:16, 19; 12:44, 45).

The second case describes John's clarification of the unity-relationship between the Sender and the sent one (5:[18]23; 17:21; cf. *glory* and *honor* [1:14–17; 17:24]).[27] Although the Father's role is different from that of the Son, they are in unity. As the Father does, so also does the Son give life to the world (5:18–29). Their oneness does not only refer to the equality of working, but also to the union of identity (5:17, 23; 10:30 [32], 36–38).[28] In particular, when John utilizes the terminology ἁγιάζω (*make holy or sanctify*) in the frame of sending, he refers to the oneness of the Sender and the sent (17:18–19, 23). John highlights that "Jesus and the Father are one" (10:30).[29] This idea presupposes his other understanding that Jesus

---

22. Thompson, *John*, 233–34.
23. Thompson, *John*, 309.
24. Borgen, "God's Agent," 128–32.
25. Rengstorf, "ἀποστέλλω, πέμπω, κτλ," 404.
26. Stibbe, *John's Gospel*, 40.
27. Akala, *Son-Father Relationship*, 128.
28. Thompson, *John*, 128–29.
29. Köstenberger and Swain, *Father, Son, and Spirit*, 43–44, 182, 185.

distinguishes himself from the Father, who is greater than all others (14:28). John repeats the clear distinction of the Father and the Son throughout his Gospel (5:44; 6:27; 17:3; 20:17).[30] If so, what does the oneness of the Father and the Son mean? The very idea is articulated in the phrasing of 10:38 and 17:21 ("the Father is in me, and I in the Father" and "You, Father, are in me, and I in you," respectively). These phrases are involved with the unity-relationship between the Father and the Son.[31] Therefore, the fact that he was consecrated in the frame of sending signifies that Jesus belongs to the Sender in the sharing of life, identity, and work (10:36), so he bears witness to the Father (10:38). Mark L. Appold pays attention to the theme of *erga* (5:17, 18), in which Jesus discloses his identity (7:7; 9:3) in oneness with the Father (10:38).[32] Jesus has an inseparable mutual relationship with the Father, without the distortion of God's identity (5:25-27; 20:28 [*God* and *Lord*]; cf. "I AM . . ." formula).[33]

Sending Formulae

John structures the sending formulae in order to explain the mission of Jesus and the disciples. The simplest structure shows that the Sender sends his agent(s) to any place or to any people:

First, (1) the Sender + sends + the sent one(s) + into the place or to someone (1:6, 33 [Baptist John]; 1:22, 24 [priests and Levites]; 5:23, 36, 38; 6:29, 57; 7:29, 33; 8:42; 9:7 [Siloam]; 11:3 [Martha and Mary], 42; 12:44, 45; 13:20; 15:21 [disciples]; 16:5, 7 [Jesus's sending of the Spirit]; 17:3, 8, 18, 21, 23; 20:21 [Jesus's sending of the disciples and 17:18]; 1:19; 5:33 [Pharisees]; 17:18; 18:24; 20:21); (2) the sent one + be sent + to accomplish (to do) the Sender's will/command (4:34, 38 [disciples]; 5:30; 6:38 [39]; 7:16, 32 [Pharisees]; 9:4 [we]; 12:49), the Sender's glory (7:18), or the Sender's word (14:24, 26 [teaching and reminding and the Spirit]); and (3) the Sender + testifies + to the sent (5:37 [36]; 8:18; 15:26 [the Spirit's testimony]), + be with (8:16), or + leads (6:44). In these formulae, John describes the following characteristics:

Firstly, these phrases clarify the identity of the Sender and the foundation of the sent one's authority. For example, in the discussion of his authority, John the Baptist testifies that he was sent by God to baptize people with water (1:25, 33; 3:23-25). This clarifies both him and his sending by

---

30. Barrett, "Christocentric," 8; Thompson, *God of the Gospel of John*, 72.
31. Thompson, *God of the Gospel of John*, 187-88.
32. Appold, *Oneness Motif*, 19, 21-24.
33. Hurtado, *Lord Jesus Christ*, 380, 394.

determining the order of the Sender on the basis of the action that might be controversial among those who support the cleansing ceremony of the Jews (3:23–25). The same applies to Jesus and his disciples (3:11 and 9:4). Above all, Jesus emphasizes,

    a. ὅτι καταβέβηκα ἀπὸ τοῦ οὐρανοῦ οὐχ ἵνα ποιῶ τὸ θέλημα τὸ ἐμὸν ἀλλὰ τὸ θέλημα τοῦ πέμψαντός με (John 6:38, "For I have come down from heaven, not to do my own will but the will of him who sent me" [ESV]).

    b. ὅτι ἐγὼ ἐξ ἐμαυτοῦ οὐκ ἐλάλησα, ἀλλ᾽ ὁ πέμψας με πατὴρ αὐτός μοι ἐντολὴν δέδωκεν τί εἴπω καὶ τί λαλήσω (12:49, "For I have not spoken on my own authority, but the Father who sent me has himself given me a commandment—what to say and what to speak" [ESV]).

    c. ὁ μὴ ἀγαπῶν με τοὺς λόγους μου οὐ τηρεῖ· καὶ ὁ λόγος ὃν ἀκούετε οὐκ ἔστιν ἐμὸς ἀλλὰ τοῦ πέμψαντός με πατρός (14:24, "Whoever does not love me does not keep my words. And the word that you hear is not mine but the Father's who sent me" [ESV]).

These verses pay attention to the facts that "he came from the Father," or was sent "to testify about the Father's words and do his will" under the Father's authority (cf. 5:36, 38; 7:29; 8:42; 17:8, 29). Therefore, to believe in the sent one is to also believe in the Sender (12:44, 45). In the same way, Jesus sends his disciples (17:18; 20:21). They, too, send Jesus Christ in order to bear witness so that the world will know and believe (17:3, 20). At the same time, the disciples were sent to the harvesters of Jesus (4:34, 38) and those who proclaimed his forgiveness and judgment (20:21, 23 [12:48]).[34] Above

---

34. In 17:18b, ἀπέστειλα is used by the author's present point of view after Jesus's resurrection (20:21) (Brown, *John XIII–XXI*, 762; Barrett, *Gospel according to St. John*, 510). The author of the Gospel bears witness to Jesus (20:30–31; 21:24 [17:3]). He ends the story of his testimony about Jesus and the Father in the sending formula (John 20:21[17:18]. Verse 20:21b states, καθὼς ἀπέσταλκέν με ὁ πατήρ, κἀγὼ πέμπω ὑμᾶς; here, John describes Jesus's identity and role by comparing his sentness with that of the disciples. This phrase refers to the nature of their missional identity and role. Raymond E. Brown notes that this statement demonstrates the Father's sending of the Son as a model for the disciples' sentness (Brown, *John XIII–XXI*, 1036). He views that this formula reflects the continuity of Jesus and the disciples' mission. The nature of their mission already emerges in chapter 17 (specifically, 17:18, καθὼς ἐμὲ ἀπέστειλας εἰς τὸν κόσμον, κἀγὼ ἀπέστειλα αὐτοὺς εἰς τὸν κόσμον). Although John spells out the term "the world" and the past (aorist) tense of Jesus's sending of the disciples in the form of prayer, he employs the same structure of "as . . ., so . . .," clarifying the parallelism of both sentences (17:18 and 20:21) (Köstenberger, *Missions of Jesus*, 186).

all, they receive the Holy Spirit, whose sayings are Jesus's words (14:26). This means that the testimony of the disciples should be Jesus's teachings, known by the Holy Spirit (15:26–27), and they are to bear witness alongside the Holy Spirit. As the Holy Spirit is sent to judge the sin of the world (16:7), so, too, should the disciples forgive the sin of the world or retain its sin (20:23). Under the authority of the Jesus and the Father, their mission is that the world might believe in Jesus in order to have eternal life ([6:57], 17:3; 20:31).

Secondly, in the description of Jesus's sending, the Father testifies to Jesus through his work. God's witness implies a mutual relationship with the Son; Jesus and God are treated equally as one.

- a. καὶ ὁ πέμψας με πατὴρ ἐκεῖνος μεμαρτύρηκεν περὶ ἐμοῦ. οὔτε φωνὴν αὐτοῦ πώποτε ἀκηκόατε οὔτε εἶδος αὐτοῦ ἑωράκατε (John 5:37, "And the Father who sent me has himself borne witness about me. His voice you have never heard, his form you have never seen" [ESV]).

- b. ἐγώ εἰμι ὁ μαρτυρῶν περὶ ἐμαυτοῦ καὶ μαρτυρεῖ περὶ ἐμοῦ ὁ πέμψας με πατήρ (8:18, "I am the one who bears witness about myself, and the Father who sent me bears witness about me" [ESV]).

Jesus says that by working with the Father, he also receives his Father's honor (5:23, "all may honor the Son, just as they honor the Father" [πάντες τιμῶσι τὸν υἱὸν καθὼς τιμῶσι τὸν πατέρα]). This means that Jesus shares the Father's honor by working with him in a mutual relationship (5:18–19). John highlights that the Sender + is + true or greater than the sent one (7:28; 13:16). Although Jesus himself is the incarnate Word and testifies in the *ego eimi* statements that he is the object of faith that gives eternal life (6:35; 8:12; 10:9, 11; 11:25; 14:6; 15:1), he as the sent one always subordinates himself to the Father. Hereby, Jesus is to bear the words and works of the Sender. Likewise, in the unity-relationship, Jesus sends his disciples (13:20; 15:21; 17:18; 20:21), and they share life and life-patterns with one another (13:15, 34–35; 15:3–8). Their walking, speaking, and doing of the "greater works" in Jesus's life-pattern is to be manifested in his character and identity through the mutual indwelling (14:12). Eventually, in this concept of mutual indwelling, they concentrate on witnessing to the Sender.

Second, on the one hand, John is talking about Jesus's unique mission throughout the whole Gospel. John 3:14–21 shows a salient sending formula: the Sender + sends (Past, Present, Future) + the sent + into the place + To Infinitive (purpose) (3:17; 20:21 with 23) or a resultant phrase (5:24 [6:39]). This formula not only serves to present the purpose of God's sending, but to also explain God's mission through Jesus's sentness. God gave Jesus to the world (3:16 [δίδωμι/"give"]), and John describes that giving as equal to sending. When God and Jesus give the Holy Spirit (14:16 [δίδωμι]; cf. 20:22 [λαμβάνω]), their acts are their sending of the Spirit (14:26 [πέμψει], 15:26 [πέμψω]). God's giving of the Son explains the purpose of his mission (cf. 17:18; 20:21). In 13:16–21, his sending of Jesus is rooted in his love for the world; he wants to save it before judging it at the end of days (12:48). The method of his salvation appears in Jesus's unique mission (3:14–15; 10:11, 17; 11:50–52; 12:24). In 3:14–15, the expression "lift up" refers to Jesus's crucifixion to remove the sins of the world (1:29; 8:28; 12:34), which I will discuss again below. His cross is to be seen by all (19:37). The accomplishment of his unique mission is the content of his disciples and the testimony of the Holy Spirit, and is the source of the work of forgiveness and judgment toward sin (16:7–11; 20:23).

In short, John's sending language and its formulae characterize two natures of mission. *Firstly*, the sent one should complete the assigned task according to the Sender's will. The purpose of sentness is this achievement. *Secondly*, the Sender is united with the sent one in order to witness himself both through and in the sent one's life, identity, action, and words. In the sending formulae, John describes Jesus's witness in the unity-relationship between the Sender and the sent one. At the same time, ultimately, John also characterizes the nature of the disciples' witness in the sending formulae (13:20; 17:18; 20:21). As Jesus accomplishes the work of the Father, so, too, are his disciples sent to do Jesus's work (for evangelism, 4:34–38; 14:12; 17:20 with 18:37; 21:15–19 with 13:36; 15:27; 20:23; for life-witness, 13:34–35; 17:23). Eventually, the important themes presented in these formulae can be summarized in two ways. *Firstly*, the sent ones are to bear witness to their union with him. They should do the work of the Sender and deliver his words. *Secondly*, Jesus's sentness has a special purpose; it is meant to accomplish God's salvation. Furthermore, he sends his disciples out in order to continue his witness and mission under the completion of his unique mission.

WITNESS IN JOHN'S GOSPEL

In the sending formulae, the word μαρτυρία, or μαρτυρέω, (*witness* or *testimony* [noun] or *witness* or *testify* [verb]) is used as an important subject (1:6–8, 15, 19, 32; 3:28, 32–33; 15:26–27). John uses the term to preach the gospel and to testify to God and himself through deeds or signs as a way of making someone believe. The essence of the "witness" is that God's presence, along with their identities, are "known" through the inner and outer lives of the disciples. John emphasizes this presence of the Father in Jesus, concentrating on what the Father reveals through his life. This is the same principle that is found as Jesus's indwells in the midst of his disciples, which he reveals throughout their lives (14:10–11; 20:19, 26).

John uses the terms μαρτυρία and μαρτυρέω forty-seven times throughout his Gospel. His use primarily concentrates on evangelism that makes people believe in Jesus Christ, *the Son of God* (20:31).

a. a. 1:7, 8, 15, 19, 32, 34 (3:26); 5:33: John the Baptist testifies to *the light*, or the Son of God, through proclamation. The witness of John the Baptist aims to lead people to faith.

b. b. 3:11, 32, 33 (4:44); 8:13, 14, 18; 19:35: Jesus testifies to what they know and see about himself or about the truth. His purpose is to make people accept his testimony.[35]

c. c. 3:28; 4:39; 15:27; 21:24 (12:17, for the crowd): The disciples bear witness to Jesus so that people will believe in him.

These verses suggest that (1) God sends witnesses, and (2) Jesus and his disciples become witnesses so that people can have the faith needed to receive eternal life. *Firstly*, God sends agents to accomplish his work, and they are to bear testimony while accomplishing their tasks. John the Baptist had to bear witness to Jesus during his mission of baptizing people (1:29–34). In particular, John borrowed the mouth of John the Baptist and preached that Jesus and his testimony were true (3:31–36). *Secondly*, Jesus and his disciples were sent for witness (3:32–33; 15:27; 17:20; 18:37). The purpose of their testimony is to bring the world to salvation, not judgment, by faith (3:36). To this end, their testimony should reveal God (1:18).

The Nature of Witness

The concept of witness in the Fourth Gospel has two characteristics: one is a witness of life, and the other is evangelism. John's focus is that these two are integrated.

First, witness is a life-witness. It is "be revealed" or "be known" (13:35; 17:23). Jesus shows the Father in mutual indwelling (14:9–11). Whoever sees him can see the Father. This is known by Jesus's love for the Father and his obedience in 14:31. Jesus discloses his Father through life by loving him and keeping his word (14:31). The manner of his witness was self-sacrifice,

---

35. In 7:7 (8:13), Jesus testifies that what the world does is evil.

self-giving, and humble service in life (13:14-15). He witnesses to his Father's love toward the world by giving his life for many (11:50-52 and 3:16; 12:23-26; 13:1; 15:10; 17:12; [18:19]; 21:5-23). He testifies to his own love for his people by laying his life down for them (6:39 and 17:12; 10:11, 14, 17; 13:1). Surely, he bears witness to the Father's work in him through the greatest sign, which is his self-sacrificial death for others and for the resurrection (3:13-14; 10:11; 12:24, 32-34; 19:35, 37; 20:24-29). The disciples see Jesus, and they know and believe that the Father sent and loves him (17:25-26).

The mutual indwelling between the Father and Jesus is the essential relationship between Jesus and his disciples. They also dwell in Jesus, and Jesus abides in them (14:20). This unity is a characteristic of the disciples' witness (17:21). Above all, their unity with God must presuppose their complete oneness (17:23). Becoming one results in keeping Jesus's new commandment (13:34; 14:21; 15:17), which is to love one another. As Jesus loves the Father and fulfills his will, so, too, must the disciples keep his words (13:34-35). They should sacrifice themselves as servants who wash each other's feet in love and service. This practice is the disciples' way of living Jesus's life-pattern, which results in unity as both the fruit of mutual indwelling and the life-sign of witness (15:1-5, 10; and 13:35; 15:8).

Second, witness is evangelism. Jesus's evangelistic activity concentrates on teaching and proclamation (4:21, 42, 44, 50, 53; 7:16, 37-39, 45-46; 8:14; 10:25; 12:50; 14:24, 29; for the truth [18:37]). To make people believe in himself, Jesus bears witness to his identity and missional purposes through the following *ego eimi* statements:

a. "The Bread of Life" (6:35, Ἐγώ εἰμι ὁ ἄρτος τῆς ζωῆς): while talking about the Bread of Life, Jesus emphasizes that God's work is to believe in the one whom God sent (6:29). Faith in Jesus enables people to have eternal life on the last day (vv. 37-38).

b. "The Light of the World" (8:12, Ἐγώ εἰμι τὸ φῶς τοῦ κόσμου): those who believe in Jesus are meant to follow him as the light of life. The goal of Jesus's evangelism is to make people into both believers and disciples (v. 31). If they do not believe in him, they belong to sin and this world, and eventually die because of it (vv. 14, 21-24 [9:35-41]). Above all, his witness echoes what the Father taught him and what pleases him (vv. 28-29).

c. "The Door of the Sheep" (10:7 [9], Ἐγώ εἰμι ἡ θύρα τῶν προβάτων): Jesus is the door of salvation for sheep. People can only obtain life through him, which highlights the need to believe in him.

d. "The Good Shepherd" (10:11, Ἐγώ εἰμι ὁ ποιμὴν ὁ καλός): as the Good Shepherd, Jesus gives up his life (vv. 15–17). Soon, his death saves his flock, and following him is the way of eternal life (vv. 26–27).

e. "The Resurrection and Life" (11:25, Ἐγώ εἰμι ἡ ἀνάστασις καὶ ἡ ζωή): Jesus says that believing in him is the way of living without dying forever (v. 26). For people's faith, he carries out signs (10:38), which shows God's work and glory so that all may believe in him (9:3; 11:4, 40, 45, 47; 12:11). This is also Jesus's evangelistic ministry as the light of the world (9:4–5 and 11:9).

f. "The Way, the Truth, and the Life" (14:6, Ἐγώ εἰμι ἡ ὁδὸς καὶ ἡ ἀλήθεια καὶ ἡ ζωή): it is Jesus who will lead the disciples to the Father (14:5–6).

g. "The True Vine" (15:1, Ἐγώ εἰμι ἡ ἄμπελος ἡ ἀληθινή): Jesus is the source of the disciple's life. When they live in union with Jesus, they bear his fruit. This primarily suggests that they live in mutual indwelling with Jesus. At the same time, their lives demand to keep the commandments that Jesus teaches his disciples (15:1–17, [14:15]).

A common theme of these statements is that Jesus is the life-giver (10:28) and ῥήματα ζωῆς αἰωνίου ("the words of eternal life," 6:68). People understand why they must believe in him. Although Jesus is distinguished from the Father, he also has power to give life and the authority to judge the world (5:27; 10:36). As a result, his work is always subject to the Father. He strives to make God and his work known to the world so that they might believe and live in the life of God. For this purpose, God sent him. Likewise, the disciples are sent to do evangelism, or verbal proclamation ("Come and See," 1:26–36, 39, 46; 3:11, 22–30; 4:29, 39; "witness [to the truth]," 5:33; 15:27; 17:20; 19:35). Jesus lets his disciples verbally proclaim both him and his words to other people so that they might believe and obey him (14:31; 17:20; 4:38). As a way of enabling the disciples as they continue his mission, Jesus provides them with the Holy Spirit (15:26–27; 20:22).

Meanwhile, their evangelism will divulge the evils of the world. People would rather hate them, for the world does not know Jesus and the Sender (15:18, 21, 24; 16:3). As the disciples forgive anyone's sin, some will not accept the preaching of the gospel and will remain in wickedness (3:19–20; 8:34–35, 38, 44; 20:23). Thus, the disciples' mission also encounters the concomitance of salvation and condemnation and judgment, just as Jesus's mission did (3:17–18; 9:39, 41; 12:47–48).

Therefore, the purpose of evangelism is to make people into Jesus's disciples (following or disciple of the truth [3:21; 8:31–32] or disciples of Jesus [8:12, 31; 10:27; 12:26; 15:8; 21:22]). The purpose is also God's will, who sent his Son to give eternal life to the world ("eternal life or God's Kingdom" [3:5, 15–18; 6:40, 47, 51–54, 58; 12:50; 17:2; 20:30–31], "life" [4:53; 5:24; 6:44; 10:10], "living water" [4:11; 7:38], "salvation" [3:17; 5:34]; vs. "judgment" [3:16; 12:47–48]). Eternal life is defined as worshiping in spirit and truth, living in the unity of God, and living as a child of light in the light of life (1:12; 12:36). Just as the Father sent Jesus, he also sends his disciples into the world in order to "draw people from darkness into light" (12:46) and away from judgment (12:46–50).[36]

In the Gospel, John is inseparably involved both with what Jesus and his disciples are to hear and proclaim, and also with what they show through their person, character, and actions in their whole life. Therefore, the Johannine witness is *integrated witness*. Jesus not only reveals God through person, identity, and signs in the unity-relationship (9:3; 14:7–10, 20, 31; 17:21), but also communicates the Father's word to the world through teaching and proclaiming. Eventually, John describes Jesus's unique mission and the disciples' entrusted mission in the sense of *integrated witness*: "to be the witness, to do the witness, and to say the witness."[37]

JESUS'S MISSION AS INTEGRATED WITNESS

Although John characterizes Jesus's evangelistic activities during his public ministry period or his ongoing work through the Holy Spirit as well as his life-witness through his doings and sacrificial death, Jesus's witness does not separate seeing from hearing (3:31–36; specifically, 3:32, ὁράω and ἀκούω; 5:36–37, φωνή and ποιέομαι; cf. 9:35–41; 20:8 [βλέπω and πιστεύω]). Jesus not only reveals God and his work through person, identity, and signs (9:3; 14:7–10), but also communicates to the world the Father's word by teaching and proclaiming it in the unity-relationship (1:14, 18; 3:16, 31–32; 5:19; 6:46; 7:16; 8:26, 38; 9:3; 10:32, 36; 12:50; 14:10–12, 20a). This is the mission of Jesus as witness, which manifests the Father in order that people might

---

36. Bauckham, "Did Jesus Wash," 216. The disciples' mission explicitly appears in the healing of a blind man (9:1–41). After being sent, the blind man continues to bear witness to Jesus. In this respect, the mission of Jesus, in which he reveals his Father, is related to the mission of Jesus's disciples in which they reveal him. The testimony of the disciples is "derivative and their light merely reflective. It is the Father's own testimony that establishes the truth of Jesus and his work (5:31–38)" (Miller, "They Saw His Glory," 144).

37. Guder, *Be My Witnesses*, 91–177.

believe in him (7:28–29, [10:30]; 12:44–45; 14:1 [faith in the Father and Jesus himself], 14:31).

Life-Witness in the Unity-Relationship

Jesus's mission begins with God's sending act, which expounds the nature of *missio Dei* (John 3:16; 20:21). The nature is embodied in incarnation and resurrection, and death (1:14; 8:42; 10:11–17; 11:50–52; 12:24–26; 16:28; 17:8; 20:19–23).

Incarnation and Resurrection

John narrates Jesus's sentness in light of mission as witness in the account of incarnation and resurrection (1:14, 18; 20:19–23).[38] Jesus manifests God to the world by sharing God's identity and role (1:18; 14:8–10).

First, Jesus is the incarnate One of the Word (1:1-18; cf. 5:22–39, 46–51, 57). When John uses the term σκηνόω ("to live in a tent") in the narrative of incarnation, Jesus is "the visible manifestation of the presence of God."[39] The Father was made known to the world in the form of the Word's incarnation (1:14a, 18; 14:7–11). According to Barrett, God's self-revelation is also the form of a tabernacle (1:14b).[40] In this form, John employs the verb σκηνόω, which appears in the New Testament five times (John 1:14; Rev 7:15; 12:12; 13:6; 21:3).[41] John's Gospel expresses the phrase "He dwelled 'in the midst of' us" (John 1:14a, ἐσκήνωσεν ἐν ἡμῖν). In general, the root of ἐσκήνωσεν (the verb aorist indicative of σκηνόω) is *skene* ("a place of shelter, of lodging and dwelling, or of a movable cultic tent," "transcendent celestial tent, tent

---

38. Jesus came from the Father in holiness (6:69; 8:42; 16:27, 28). The Father consecrated Jesus when he sent (10:36; cf. 17:19). The Father and the Son are mutually in one another (10:38). In 10:36, Schnackenburg rightly argues that the word *hagiajo* includes the "concept of ratification or sealing," for the term is associated with the Father's giving of the earthly task to Jesus (Schnackenburg, *Gospel according to St John*, 2:311). God imparts the Spirit to Jesus to completely bear witness to "what he has seen and heard in the presence of the Father" (3:32–34; 6:46) (Schnackenburg, *Gospel according to St John*, 2:311).

39. Barrett, *Gospel according to St. John*, 165.

40. Barrett, *Gospel according to St. John*, 165.

41. The author of Revelation defines the phrases to "shelter (literally, 'tent over') them" (Rev 7:15) and "to live" in "them [heavens]" (12:12), "a tent" (13:6), or "with them" (21:3). Revelation describes God's temple in 7:15, heavens in 12:12, and God's tent in 13:6 and 21:3.

or dwelling").⁴² In studying a cognate word (*skenoun*) in the Old Testament and Wisdom literature ("the Creator of all . . . chose the spot for my tent, saying, 'In Jacob make your dwelling [*kataskenoun*], in Israel your inheritance'" [Sir 22:4]), Raymond E. Brown focuses on the use of the very term in association with a tent that God dwells in ("Tabernacle" [Exod 25:8–9]).⁴³ God's tabernacle ("pitching a tent") symbolizes his dwelling amid his people, which is a concept that was later expanded to describe the function of the temple (κατασκηνώσει τὸ ὄνομά μου ἐν μέσῳ οἴκου Ισραηλ τὸν αἰῶνα, Ezek 43:7 [LXX]).⁴⁴ If Brown is right, Jesus's sentness as incarnation, who dwells in the midst of people as God, witnesses, or reveals, the invisible God's dwelling among his people.⁴⁵ This becomes more evident as he stands among his disciples during his resurrection. By confessing him as God, the disciples believe that Jesus reveals God (20:19–23).

Here, attention is given to John's expression ἐσκήνωσεν ἐν ἡμῖν ("he dwelled 'in the midst of' us"). John uses the metaphor of "glory" with this expression (John 1:14). This indicates that he is looking at Jesus's incarnation in terms of the fulfillment of eschatological expectations.⁴⁶ I presume that John echoes Ezekiel's eschatological promise of the restoration of his people. The sign of the promise's fulfillment is that YHWH establishes his tabernacle "in the midst of" them. Ezekiel anticipates that YHWH will "put his sanctuary (מִקְדָּשִׁי) 'in the midst of'" (ἐν μέσῳ αὐτῶν LXX) his people (37:26; cf. 37:28; 48:35) at the time of his restoration of all Israelites to the land ("all the house of Israel," 36:10; 37:21).⁴⁷ In 37:27, Ezekiel links a sanctuary to a tabernacle.⁴⁸ YHWH will place his "tabernacle" (מִשְׁכָּן, Ezek 37:27; LXX κατασκήνωσις "taking up residence" or "a place to live") "among them [Israel]" (ἐν αὐτοῖς LXX; עֲלֵיהֶם "upon them").

---

42. Danker, Bauer, and Arndt, *Greek-English Lexicon*, 928.

43. Brown, *John I–XII*, 32, 33.

44. Brown, *John I–XII*, 33.

45. Cf. Schnackenburg, *Gospel according to St John*, 1:269–70.

46. Blumhofer, "Gospel of John," 120n58.

47. Ezekiel concentrates on the rebuilding of the new temple amid Israel's twelve tribes (chapter 48).

48. David names the very place אֹהֶל ("tent," Pss 15:1; 27:5–6; 61:4) and מִשְׁכָּן ("tabernacle," Pss 43:3; 84:2; 132:5, 7). In particular, מִשְׁכָּן points to "the place where YHWH's glory or his name dwells" (Pss 26:8; 46:5; 74:7; 78:60) instead of the tabernacle, and in 2 Samuel 15:25, David recognizes the place as "dwelling place" or "abode" (נָוֶה). Frequently, the term מִקְדָּשׁ is used for sanctuary, shrine, temple, sacred thing, or holy place (Exod 25:8; Num 10:21; 18:29; Lev 16:33). These designations are usually associated with the fixed temple, regardless of the nomadic or semi-nomadic context (Haran, *Temples*, 17).

From the eschatological perspective of the fulfillment of God's mission, Ezekiel and other postexilic prophets anticipate that YHWH's glory will come back to the temple (Ezek 44:4). God's glory symbolizes the restoration of YHWH's enthronement (43:2, 7; 48:35).[49] However, in comparison to Ezekiel, none of the postexilic prophets refer to the return of YHWH's glory to the temple. J. Daniel Hays argues that other postexilic prophets and biblical texts do not mention the return of YHWH's glory.[50] Although Haggai talks about God's glory, he emphasizes that the temple will be filled with glory by the treasure that God brings from all nations (Hag 2:6–9).[51] According to Robert P. Carroll, Haggai portrays the new temple as "the center of wealth."[52] As Haggai is concerned with YHWH's upcoming restoration of the temple's glory, Zechariah states that the return of YHWH's glory will take place in the future (2:5) and take residence in the temple (8:3–9). Specifically, for LXX translators, Zechariah 8:3 clarifies that YHWH "will return" (qal active [שַׁבְתִּי; ἐπιστρέψω/future active]) to Zion and "will dwell in Jerusalem" (ἐν μέσῳ Ιερουσαλημ). David J. A. Clines claims that, in Zechariah, Zerubbabel would not restore YHWH's glory, for the filling of the temple with glory through wealth is attributed to God himself.[53] Likewise, Malachi claims that YHWH seems to not return to the Jerusalem temple (Mal 3:1, 7). In this respect, the postexilic prophets are concerned with YHWH's future eschatological restoration of both the land and the temple.[54]

If John comprehends Jesus's sentness as the event of the return of God's glory (John 1:14b), the author of the Gospel would take into consideration Jesus's tabernacle in light of Ezekiel's new temple.[55] Ezekiel prophesies that

49. Bedford, *Temple Restoration*, 69.

50. Hays, *Temple*, 12.

51. Cf. YHWH will make the temple and fill it with glory by bringing the wealth of all nations (2:9) (Clines, "Haggai's Temple," 63, 65, 66). He concludes that Haggai's temple is a "treasure-house" of silver and gold from all the nations (Clines, "Haggai's Temple," 65, 71).

52. Carroll, "So What Do We Know," 41, 65, 71.

53. Clines, "Haggai's Temple," 80.

54. Plöger, *Theocracy*, 45, 47, 76, 109–10.

55. John continues to depict the resurrected Jesus as the sanctuary (temple), which is "moving about with all the Israel (cf. John 1:11)," in the midst of Jesus's disciples (ἔστη εἰς τὸ μέσον, 20:19; cf. 1:14). They might abide in Jesus (μείνητε ἐν τῷ λόγῳ, John 8:31 with 15:7). Jesus also declares "peace" (εἰρήνη) to the covenant people who are God's, and God is their Father and God (20:17) in terms of the covenant of peace in Ezekiel 37:26 (Kim, *Ideal King*, 106). The picture of a peace-giver (John 20:19) is associated with the crowd's exclamation (μὴ φοβοῦ, θυγάτηρ Σιών, 12:15a) for the king of Israel (ἰδοὺ ὁ βασιλεύς σου ἔρχεται, 12:13b, 15b), who is the anointed One of God and his Son (20:31) (Carson, *Gospel according to John*, 432). This is the fulfilment of God's indwelling-place on earth. When Jesus spoke to the disciples, the *missio Dei* began with Jesus's incarnation

God's glory, which left the temple (Ezek 11:23), will come back to the new temple (43:2–5; 44:4). In the account of Jesus's incarnation, John employs the expression "glory" for the imagery of the temple (1:14). This means that John's use of these expressions signifies the fulfillment of God's eschatological promise. The scheme of God's promise and fulfillment is the foundation of God's sending of both the Son and the Spirit (John 1:14 and 20:21–22). In the Prologue, John illustrates Jesus's incarnation in the form of "tabernacle." Interestingly, he narrates the risen Jesus, whose body is the temple (2:21).[56] In

---

and was fulfilled through his death and resurrection. Its result is the establishment of God's indwelling place (temple) in the midst of his people. John indicates that the risen Jesus's body is the *new temple*. The temple is the result of God's forgiveness of his people's sins (Ezek 44:4). God's mission actualizes the lives of the world and humanity in the *new temple* by living according to the life-pattern of the new creational and covenantal order (Isa 52:1–10; 60:1–9; 63:18–19; Zech 8:3) (Marinkovich, "What Does Zechariah 1–8," 96). In this regard, John accounts for the following points in terms of the relatedness between forgiveness and mission.

56. Most recently, studies about Temple-Christology in John have related to the fulfillment, or replacement, of the temple, its institutions, and Jewish festivals. (1) G. K. Beale and Köstenberger investigate the temple theme in the Fourth Gospel (John 1:14, 51; 2:14–22; 4:10–14, 21–26; 7:37–39; cf. 20:22) in terms of Jesus as the fulfillment of the symbolism surrounding the Jewish background (Beale, *Temple*, 192–200; Köstenberger, "The Destruction," 215). Specifically, Köstenberger demonstrates that Jesus fulfills Jewish religious institutions (1:14, 51; 2:14–22; 4:19–24) and festivals (7:1—8:59; 10:22–39) in terms of the realization of Jewish religious symbolism (Köstenberger, "Destruction," 228). He goes on to verify that the Fourth Gospel is aimed at defending the faith of the Johannine community against the Judaism or Pharisaism that formed after the destruction of the temple. He focuses on Jesus the Messiah as the embodiment of the Jewish symbolism of the temple and its entire festivals, apart from the typological imageries of the Old Testament (Köstenberger, "Destruction," 220–21). (2) Stephen T. Um deals with the Johannine temple theology and the Spirit's eschatological figure. He links the Spirit to water in the Jewish background, which is the source of the "new creative and eschatological life" in the new temple (Um, *Temple Christology*, 161, 171, 189–90). Um investigates Jesus as the new temple (John 7:38–39) in light of the temple imagery of Ezekiel and Zechariah (Ezek 47:1–9 and Zech 14:8). Their link is the phrase "living water(s)" (Um, *Temple Christology*, 156–63). This living water symbolizes the Holy Spirit, who enables worshippers to participate in the True Temple, the "person of Jesus" (Um, *Temple Christology*, 190). Finally, Um notes, "He (Jesus) is the 'eternal cosmic-human Temple of God' who tabernacle among his people 'by its totally different form of proximity,' a fact which symbolized the ushering in of the eschatological presence of God's Temple in the messianic age" (Um, *Temple Christology*, 154). (3) Alan R. Kerr begins with a study of Jesus's temple-cleansing in terms of the destruction of the temple (AD 70), which symbolizes a shift from the old temple to the new temple (John 2:13–22) (Kerr, *Jesus' Body*, 2, 4, 7, 11–49). According to him, the Fourth Gospel is a reaction to the destruction of the Jerusalem temple (Kerr, *Jesus' Body*, 34–66). Kerr agrees with Mary L. Coloe's argument that Jesus replaces the temple in terms of God's presence in him (John 1:51 with Gen 28:12–22; John 4:1–26) (Kerr, *Jesus' Body*, 6; Coloe, *Dwelling*, 215, 219, 308). Kerr tries to demonstrate that Jesus substitutes the "temple-as-building" for "temple-as-community" (13:1–38; 14:2, 23) (Kerr, *Jesus' Body*, 33, 57, 144,

the narrative of resurrection, John accounts for Jesus's standing "in the midst of" the disciples, as the temple sanctuary will be in the center of Israel's tribes (Ezek 37:28; 48:21). These are God's covenant people (John 20:17–23).[57] John also echoes Ezekiel 37 in John 21. Ezekiel understood YHWH's sanctuary, or tabernacle, within the context of YHWH's restoration. YHWH will place the everlasting sanctuary in the midst of the restored Israel.

Firstly, in Ezekiel 37, YHWH promises to tabernacle among Israel forever in the frame of his eschatological restoration, as follows:

1. YHWH will give *rûaḥ* (רוּחַ) "Spirit," "breath," or "wind" to dry bones so that they might live (Ezek 37:5).
2. YHWH will restore the whole of Israel (37:15–22).
3. YHWH will save and cleanse the people of Israel so that they will be his and he will be their God (37:23).
4. YHWH will establish his servant David as king over them (37:24–25).
5. YHWH will make a covenant of peace with them (37:26).
6. YHWH will dwell (pitch a tent) "in the midst of" them forever (37:26–28; 44:8). Specifically, "My dwelling place" (37:27, מִקְדָּשִׁי) is translated into LXX κατασκήνωσις.[58]

Secondly, in John 20, the author shows the fulfillment of Ezekiel's promise within the context of sending by reminding his readers of Jesus's incarnation in the form of tabernacling.

1. The risen Jesus dwells "in the midst of us" (John 1:14).[59] He is Israel's king (1:49; 12:13; cf. 18:33, 39; 19:21).[60]

206–68). However, Kerr's theory among the above-mentioned theories lacks evidence for the following reason: in John, there is nothing of direct reference to the destruction of the Jerusalem temple in AD 70 (Köstenberger, "Destruction," 215–16). Instead, it should be highlighted that people can mutually live in Jesus by sharing life with the Father by the Spirit.

57. The important factor is the covenant-language "My God and Your God, My Father, and Your Father." This expression is both covenantal and relational (Ezek 11:20b; 36:28; cf. Jer 31:31–34; 32:36–41) (Scheuer, *Return of YHWH*, 115).

58. This word indicates "a central place of worship as the dwelling place of God (cf. Exod 25:9; Lev 15:31)" (see, Swanson, "מִשְׁכָּן").

59. Jesus's coming to Samaria signifies the unity of Israel. In light of Ezekiel, the unity of the whole of Israel indicates God's restoration of his people by entailing his cleansing of their sins and dwelling among them (Ezek 37:15–28) (Blumhofer, "Gospel of John," 159, 161). According to John, the pronoun "us" means believers—whoever believes in Jesus Christ (1:12; 20:19-29).

60. John never directly designates Jesus as the son of David, nor does he specifically use the imagery of the Davidic line, apart from the use of the Synoptic Gospels' "the

2. Jesus consecrates both the world and the disciples (1:29; 13:1-20; 17:19).

son of David" (Mark 10:47; 12:35-37; Matt 1:1; 19:30, 31; 20:9; 21:9; Luke 1:27, 69) (Bornkamm, *Jesus of Nazareth*, 173; Bock, "Son of David," 444). The absence of the christological designation causes scholars' vehement debate over Jesus's identity as "the offspring of David" (John 7:42) or "the king of the Jews" (18:33, 39; 19:21) (Brown, *Community*, 13; Ashton, *Understanding the Fourth Gospel*, 262). On the one hand, Mavis M. Leung emphasizes that the reason John keeps silent about Jesus's Davidic kingship is that he wants to reveal Jesus's divinity (Leung, *Kingship-Cross*, 47). In this sense, he suggests several explanations: *first*, John tries to draw attention to "the Jewish ignorance of Jesus's true origin" by interweaving Jesus's identity and his birthday in John 7:40-44; *secondly*, John evades the connotation of Jesus's Davidic kingship in terms of the national-political-military Davidic Messiah whom had been longed for by the Jews from the late Second Temple era to the first-century church (4Q174, 4Q285; 4 *Ezra* 13:26-27; Luke 1:71; Acts 1:6; Mark 12:35-37) (Leung, *Kingship-Cross*, 47-48; Collins, "Zechariah 9:9," 38). Brown supports Leung's first theory. He claims that "the king of Israel" (John 1:49) refers to a messianic king of believers, like Nathanael, but not of the Jews (Brown, *John I-XII*, 87). In particular, he believes that the concept of the very messianic king is not contingent on a nationalistic sense, but on a divine one. Nathanael's confessional designations ("Son of God" and "King of Israel") are subject to a higher Christology in light of Jesus's divinity than a lower Christology in terms of the background of the Davidic king (2 Sam 7:14; Ps 2:6-7). This is why Jesus's disciples gradually realized the divine status of Jesus, as a disciple confessed Jesus to be "Lord" and "God" (John 20:28), and then the readers of the gospel received their proclamation by faith (Brown, *John I-XII*, 87-88). Concerning Leung's second theory, M. de Jonge makes it explicit that John 18:28—19:16 is central to Jesus's kingship (Jonge, "Jesus as Prophet," 165). According to John, Pilate employs the title "the King of the Jews" from a Jewish national point of view (19:1-3) (Beale, *Temple*, 192; Koester, *Symbolism*, 225-27). He seemingly endeavored to crucify Jesus under the title of a political crime against the Caesar of the Roman Empire (John 18:33). His decision revealed Jesus's identity as the king of the Davidic line (18:37; 19:7). By the same token, while reciting Zechariah 9:9, or 12:10, John uses the term "the King of Israel" (John 12:13; cf. 1:49). The title may possibly be connected with the imagery of the Davidic kingship (cf. 2 Sam 7:14, Ps 2:7; 1 *Enoch* 105:2; 4 *Ezra* 7:28-29; 13:52; 14:9; Mark 1:11; Rom 1:3) (Daly-Denton, *David*, 185; Appold, *Oneness Motif*, 91; Barrett, *Gospel according to St. John*, 186; Blumhofer, "Gospel of John," 344-47). On the other hand, John develops Jesus's Davidic kingship in light of the universal kingship across the world. To be sure, Jesus is the Messiah, but in this Gospel, he is such by virtue of being Son of God. It is easy enough to see that this is so: it becomes more speculative to suggest why this is so. John may represent a universalizing of the traditions of Jesus's Davidic descent: Jesus now exercises his messianic office, not only as "King of Israel" (1:49; 12:13) or "King of Jews" (18:33, 39; 19:3, 19, 21), but as the "King of Israel who has authority over all flesh" (Thompson, *John*, 7). John's understanding of Jesus's kingship would result from his "retrospective post-Easter viewpoint" (Schnelle, "Recent Views of John's Gospel," 356). Undo Schnelle states, "The retrospective post-Easter viewpoint is for John both a theological scheme and a narrative perspective; it allows the Fourth Evangelist to translate theological insights into narrated history" (Schnelle, "Recent Views of John's Gospel," 356). In short, my opinion is that Jesus's universal kingship includes the Davidic king imagery and divine king imagery simultaneously in the Gospel.

3. Jesus gives his covenant words to the disciples ("τὸν πατέρα μου καὶ πατέρα ὑμῶν καὶ θεόν μου καὶ θεὸν ὑμῶν," 20:17c).

4. Jesus comes and stands "in the midst of" (εἰς τὸ μέσον) the disciples (20:19b).

5. Jesus gives "peace" (εἰρήνη) to the disciples (20:19c, 21).

6. Jesus breathes the Spirit upon the disciples (20:22).

In the Gospel, this structural and thematic frame supports that John intends to show God's promise to Ezekiel and Israel. Brian Neil Peterson proposes that Ezekiel 37:1–14 and 15–28 are related to John 20:22.[61] He pays attention to the phrases "receive the Holy Spirit" (Ezek 37:1–14 and John 20:22) and "the covenant of peace" (Ezek 34:25; 37:26; and John 20:19, 26).[62] Peterson does not consider that John corresponds the narrative of Jesus's being "in the midst of the disciples" with that of his tabernacling "in the midst of 'us' [disciples]." However, John describes Jesus's presence "in the midst of the disciples" through the missional structure by recalling Ezekiel 37 in both John 1 and 20. Of particular importance is Ezekiel's emphasis that nations know (Ezek 37:28a, וְיָדְעוּ הַגּוֹיִם) that (כִּי) I, YHWH, consecrate (קַדֵּשׁ) Israel, when "my sanctuary" (cf. "holy places," LXX; cf. Isa 8:14)[63] is (verb qal indicative infinitive, בִּהְיוֹת) "among" ("in the midst of," ἐν μέσῳ) them forever.[64] This phrase clarifies the symbolic role of the sanctuary in expressing YHWH's forgiveness of Israel and his dwelling among Israel in the future (36:23; 43:9).[65]

To put it briefly, the risen Jesus is the fulfiller of YHWH's promise. When Jesus stands in the midst of his disciples, the disciples see and believe in him to be "my Lord and my God" (20:28). This means that the disciples recognize Jesus to be the one who shares the divine identity with God. As Jesus's incarnation is to bear witness to the invisible God (1:14, 18), so must his resurrection be the most important testimony of the Father and himself.

---

61. Peterson, *John's Use of Ezekiel*, 170–71.

62. Peterson, *John's Use of Ezekiel*, 166.

63. YHWH will be a sanctuary among two houses of Israel.

64. This verb pattern appears in Joshua 5:13 (בִּהְיוֹת יְהוֹשֻׁעַ בִּירִיחוֹ, "when Joshua was by Jerico"). Additionally, the verb בִּהְיוֹת (qal active infinitive) is translated into LXX ἐν τῷ εἶναι. This expression means "while (for present infinitives), or as, when (for aorist infinitives)" (Wallace, *Greek Grammar*, 595). In the New Testament, Matt 13:4; Luke 3:21; and Heb 2:8 use the sentence of ἐν τῷ + the infinitive.

65. Ezekiel's idea was handed over by Zechariah. YHWH will cleanse Israel from sin and impurity (Zech 13:1). God's forgiving act is the expression of his restoration of the covenant (13:9) as Zechariah follows Ezekiel's language of God's dwelling among his people (2:11) and living water flowing from Jerusalem (Zech 14:8 and Ezek 47:1–12).

Second, Jesus's incarnation is the starting point of his role in a witness during his public ministry period. Jesus was sent into the world as the Father's witness.

- a. 8:42, ἐγὼ γὰρ ἐκ τοῦ θεοῦ ἐξῆλθον καὶ ἥκω· οὐδὲ γὰρ ἀπ' ἐμαυτοῦ ἐλήλυθα, ἀλλ' ἐκεῖνός με ἀπέστειλεν ("for I came from God and I am here. I came not of my own accord, but he sent me," ESV).
- b. 16:27c-28, ἐγὼ παρὰ [τοῦ] θεοῦ ἐξῆλθον. ἐξῆλθον παρὰ τοῦ πατρὸς καὶ ἐλήλυθα εἰς τὸν κόσμον· πάλιν ἀφίημι τὸν κόσμον καὶ πορεύομαι πρὸς τὸν πατέρα ("I came from God. I came from the Father and have come into the world, and now I am leaving the world and going to the Father," [ESV]).

John repeats the same expression in 17:8. ἔγνωσαν ἀληθῶς ὅτι παρὰ σοῦ ἐξῆλθον, καὶ ἐπίστευσαν ὅτι σύ με ἀπέστειλας ("they have come to know in truth that I came from you; and they have believed that you sent me"). Each of these verses understand that Jesus came from the Father and was sent from the Father.

- a. 8:42, ἐκ τοῦ θεοῦ ἐξῆλθον ... με ἀπέστειλεν ("I came from God ... he sent me").
- b. 16:28, ἐξῆλθον παρὰ τοῦ πατρὸς ... πορεύομαι πρὸς τὸν πατέρα ("I came from the Father ... I am going to the Father")
- c. 17:8, παρὰ σοῦ ἐξῆλθον ... με ἀπέστειλας ("I came from the Father ... he sent me")

The phrase πορεύομαι πρὸς τὸν πατέρα in 16:28 is associated with 14:12, 28 (ἐγὼ πρὸς τὸν πατέρα πορεύομαι, "I am going to the Father"). The latter is interwoven with the Father's sending of the Son and the Spirit (14:24, 26). In chapter 16, Jesus's act of going to the Father presupposes that the Father sent both he and the Spirit for witness (16:5, 7 [15:26]). Accordingly, when these three verses point to the purpose of Jesus's sending, they reveal two characteristics of Jesus's witness. *Firstly*, because the source of Jesus's sending is the Father, his testimony conveys what he sees and hears from the Father (8:38). Above all, he says that his act of doing the Sender's work is his mission (9:4). The emphatic point here is that what he is doing reveals the Father's work (9:3, φανερωθῇ τὰ ἔργα τοῦ θεοῦ). *Secondly*, Jesus unites with the Father (16:32, ὁ πατὴρ μετ' ἐμοῦ ἐστιν). Their unity is connected through the mutual indwelling concept (17:21).[66] Thus, Jesus reveals the Father through everything that

---

66. Thompson, *God of the Gospel of John*, 114, 117.

he lives.[67] He manifests glory through works (2:11, [5:41; 8:50]; 8:54; 9:24; 11:40; 12:41), and such things are the Father's works. In other words, he discloses God and his glory (5:44; 7:18; 12:43; 17:22). Although Jesus had his glory before creation, his glory is revealed with the aim to make the world know the Father and his sending of Jesus (17:24–26). Thus, the purpose of Jesus's witness is to present the invisible God and his glory through his identity, life, words, and actions (1:18; 14:10–11; 12:41; 20:28; cf. 12:16).[68] Jesus is God's witness as the true revealer (14:8–9; 17:8, 25).[69]

Therefore, the reason why Jesus was sent from the Father is to reveal the Father through and in him. Jesus gives testimony of the Father to the world through the mutual indwelling and unity-relationship that he has with him. The nature of his witness, or sentness, is that, regardless of time or place, he must bear witness to the Father through all that he does in life.

Sacrificial Death

In the literary context of 3:11 and 3:31–32, John portrays God's sending act (3:[2], 13, [16], 17, 31) and witness (vv. 11, 28, 32–33). He continues to concentrate on the purpose of God's sending of the unique Son in the frame of his mission, which is the salvation of the world through the Son's "being lifted up" (death, 8:28; 12:32–33) (vv. 14, 15–21; cf. 8:13–14 [witness]–16 [sentness]–20 [death]).

God gave Jesus to the world as a sacrifice (3:13–14); this sacrifice has a twofold missional meaning. *Firstly*, Jesus's death is meant for the eschatological salvation of Israel and other nations, through the act of purification (1:29; 3:16–18; 10:11–17; 20:23; especially Israel first and then other countries [11:51 and 52]).[70] *Secondly*, the Son's sacrificial death is to bear witness to God's love and service for the world (3:14–15, 16, [10:11; 11:50–52]; 12:24–26). John primarily crystallizes the missional purposes and meanings of God's sending of the Son within the literary-theological context of 3:14–17.

---

67. Jesus fully shows the Father God to his disciples in terms of the relationship between the Father and the Son and the continuance of their activities in life and action (4:34; 5:36; 9:3; 10:32, 37–38; 14:10) (Barrett, "Christocentric," 75; Thompson, *God of the Gospel of John*, 141). The relationship may demonstrate the "complete unity" of Jesus and God, which "implies the superiority of 'agency'" (Thompson, *God of the Gospel of John*, 142).

68. Thompson, *God of the Gospel of John*, 114; Blumhofer, "Gospel of John," 127–28.

69. Schnackenburg, *Gospel according to St John*, 2:311; 3:68–69.

70. Culpepper, "Pivot," 30.

Jesus's "Being Lifted Up" (3:14–15)

The author of the Gospel links the imagery of Jesus's "being lifted up" on a cross to the matter of eternal life in 3:14–15 (cf. 12:33b–34c, ποίῳ θανάτῳ ἤμελλεν ἀποθνῄσκειν and ὑψωθῆναι τὸν υἱὸν τοῦ ἀνθρώπου). The term "lift up" (ὑψόω) testifies to Jesus's sacrificial death (8:28; 12:23, 28, 32, 32–34; 13:31–32).[71] Jesus's sacrificial death is meant to bring God's salvation of his people to rescue them from judgment (19:31–37 [12:48]).[72] John identifies this death as the sacrifice of the "Lamb of God" (1:29, 36).[73] The purpose of this victim is to remove sin. We must here briefly consider the Lamb of God in 1:29, along with the death of Jesus as described in 19:31–36 (18:28).[74] The former refers to the atonement of sin, while the latter refers to the paschal lamb found in Exodus 12.[75] Scholars generally agree that the Passover sheep have no concept of atonement.[76] What lamb does Jesus's death on the cross indicate? Instead, they pay attention to the imagery of the suffering servant of Isaiah 53:7 to explain how the servant dies for many people's sins (לָרַבִּ֔ים וַעֲוֺנֹתָ֖ם ה֥וּא יִסְבֹּֽל ["bears the sins of many," Isa 53:11]).[77]

---

71. Brown, *John I-XII*, 476–77; Ridderbos, *Gospel of John*, 410; Brown and Moloney, *Interpreting the Gospel*, 204.

72. Schnackenburg, *Gospel according to St John*, 3:15.

73. The term ὁ ἀμνὸς τοῦ θεοῦ is used twice (1:29, 36) in the Gospels: when referring to the flock of Jesus, πρόβατον (10:1, 2, 7, 11, 13, 15, 26) and ἀρνίον (21:15; cf. for Jesus, Rev 5:6; for a lamb, Rev 13:11).

74. With regard to Jesus's death for the forgiveness of sin, Loader understands that John 4:35; 5:36; 10:18; 12:17; 14:31; 17:4; 18:11; and 19:30 point out Jesus's death as a sacrifice for sinners (Loader, *Jesus in John's Gospel*, 148, 149). These verses can be understood in light of the completion of the Father's will, which means to take away the sin of the world (4:34). Loader attempts to examine the identity of "the lamb of God" whether it is the Passover Lamb (*hyssop*, John 19:29), the Isaianic vulnerable lamb as YHWH's suffering servant (Isa 42:1; 53:7), or a sacrificial lamb for sins (Loader, *Jesus in John's Gospel*, 149–60). Loader suggests the possibility of the Passover Lamb based on two proofs: (1) in 19:29, John uses "a plant" (ὕσσωπος [*hyssōpos*]) for "ritual purification" (Exod 12:22; Lev 14:4–6, 49–52; Num 19:18) (Loader, *Jesus in John's Gospel*, 161); and (2) John would link Jesus's body with the Passover lamb in John 19:36 and Exod 12:46 (Ps 34:19–20). Loader senses that the concept of vicarious sacrificial atonement is unclear in John 6:51; 11:50; 15:13, and in the story of Jesus's passion (Loader, *Jesus in John's Gospel*, 149–60; cf. Bultmann, *Theology*, 2:54; Boer, *Johannine Perspectives*, 233).

75. Koester, *World of Life*, 113.

76. Koester, *World of Life*, 113.

77. Thompson, *John*, 47; R. E. Brown identifies the Lamb of God with "the apocalyptic lamb" and "the suffering servant" (Brown, *John I-XII*, 58–63).

However, Isaiah does also not imply "taking away many people's sin."[78] If this is true, how can we understand this problem? First of all, let us briefly examine the things that John describes concerning the death of Jesus. He uses terms related to purification, such as νίπτω and λούω (*wash* and *bath*, 13:6, 10), καθαρισμός (*purification*, 2:6; 3:25), καθαρός or καθαροί (*clean, pure,* or *purity*, 13:10, 11; 15:3), ἁγνίζω (*purify*, 11:55), and ἁγιάζω (*make holy*, or *sanctify*, 17:17, 19 [for Jesus, 10:36]). Of these words, *purify* is also used in Jewish cleansing ceremonies. Their ceremonies are also symmetrical with baptism (3:22–26),[79] in which an important element is water. While John the Baptist introduces him as the sheep of God that removes sin through the testimony of Jesus, the background of the story is baptism with water. Based on this observation, it is presumed that Jesus's sacrifice as the Lamb of God contains purification (13:4–11). Most of all, while John alludes to Jesus's death as the sacrifice of the paschal lamb, he simultaneously focuses on the Passover. Through the feast, Jesus is offered to God as a sacrifice. This allows us to consider how both the paschal lamb and the feast of the Passover were performed in the Old Testament. My suggestion is that Jesus's death as the sacrificial lamb carries the twofold meaning shown below:

First, Jesus is the Sacrificial Lamb on the Passover for Purification.

Jesus's crucifixion as a sacrificial lamb is meant to take away, or purify, the sin of the world on the Passover. The term *lamb* is interchangeable with a ram for an offering to God. In particular, Genesis 22:13 shows that Abraham offered a ram to God instead of Isaac. Abraham and Isaac both employ the term שֶׂה in their dialogue. This word refers to "a small four-footed mammal like a sheep or a goat."[80] In Exodus 12:3, 4, 5; 13:13, the author indicates שֶׂה as a paschal lamb (πρόβατον [LXX]). The blood of this paschal lamb saves people from the angel who judges Egypt. This lamb and the Passover are characterized by:

a. The placement of the paschal lamb's blood with hyssop on the top and on both sides of the doorframe (Exod 12:22).

b. The passing over by the Lord when he sees the blood of the doorposts, preventing them from destruction (v. 23).

---

78. Köstenberger assumes that in "Isaiah 53:7 and 10, there would be a reference to the forgiveness of sins by way of a substitutionary sacrifice" (Köstenberger, *Missions of Jesus*, 110). He pays attention to the ἀμνὸς appearing in Isaiah 53:7 (LXX) and John 1:29. However, the way in which these texts use the word seems to not support that the Isaianic imagery of the lamb would be for the forgiveness of the sin of the world (cf. Brown, *John XIII–XXI*, 60–63; Koester, *World of Life*, 219–24).

79. Lindars, *Gospel of John*, 109–10.

80. Swanson, "Ὁράω."

c. The feast of the Passover celebrating YHWH's salvation of Israel (v. 27).

d. The bones of the lamb going unbroken (v. 46; Num 9:12; Ps 34:20).

The difference between Exodus and Numbers is that, while a family unit slaughters the paschal lamb (Exod 12:3, 21), the native Israelites and colonists kill the lamb (Num 9:14). Additionally, in Numbers 28:16–25, the sacrifices were diversified by the offering of calves and rams, along with the paschal lamb. The former focuses on the blood of the Passover and God's salvation, while the latter is also concerned with the sanctification of worshipers. Of course, despite the size of the sacrifice and the expansion of participants in the latter situation, they both aim to commemorate YHWH's deliverance of Israel from Egypt (Num 33:3; Deut 16:1–6).

On the other hand, in the preexilic and postexilic history of Israel, there are three cases:

Firstly, in 2 Chronicles 30:17, the Levites killed the paschal lamb for unclean people (MT, "because there were many in the assembly who had not consecrated themselves, therefore the Levites [rush to] slaughtered the Passovers for all the unclean people, to consecrate their lamb to YHWH," (כִּי־רַבַּת בַּקָּהָל אֲשֶׁר לֹא־הִתְקַדָּשׁוּ וְהַלְוִיִּם עַל־שְׁחִיטַת הַפְּסָחִים לְכֹל לֹא טָהוֹר לְהַקְדִּישׁ לַיהוָה). The priests, who cleansed themselves, slew the Passover sheep for the unconsecrated people (2 Chr 30:15–17) in order to eat the Passover (30:18–19; cf. John 18:28). For others who did not sanctify themselves in order to eat the lamb, Hezekiah prayed to God to forgive them according to the sanctuary's rules of cleanliness (2 Chr 30:18–19).

Secondly, in 2 Chr 34:30–31, King Josiah and Israel renewed the covenant with God according to the law, so they kept the Passover (34:33; 35:1–19; cf. 2 Kgs 23:22–23). EsdA 1:1, 6 describes Josiah's celebration of the Passover. According to the law of Moses, both the priests and the Levites offered sheep and calves (1:8; EsdA 7:12). Before the priests slay the paschal lamb, the people should take away all idols (περιαιρέω LXX 2 Chr 34:33 and αἴρω John 1:29), or the priests must primarily consecrate themselves to kill the paschal lambs (2 Chr 30:15; 35:6; cf. Ezra 6:20).

Thirdly, in Ezra 6:19–21 and Ezek 45:21–25, the priests and the Levites kill the Passover lamb "for all the returned exiles" or "for himself [king] and all the people of the land," respectively. In particular, Ezekiel 45:22 recounts that καὶ ποιήσει ὁ ἀφηγούμενος ἐν ἐκείνῃ τῇ ἡμέρᾳ ὑπὲρ αὐτοῦ καὶ τοῦ οἴκου καὶ ὑπὲρ παντὸς τοῦ λαοῦ τῆς γῆς μόσχον ὑπὲρ ἁμαρτίας (LXX, "On that day the prince shall provide for himself and all the people of the land a young bull for a sin offering," ESV). Here, they offer young cattle as a sin offering, along with sheep (v. 23; cf. 45:15, "a sheep to make atonement for them," LXX). This shows that the Israelites who returned from captivity sanctified themselves (cf. 45:15). However, in the case of Ezekiel, they offer the paschal sacrifices after YHWH's glory returns to the temple (43:2).

In particular, after both the monarchy and the Babylonian captivity, the Passover sheep and cattle were also used to sanctify the king, the priests, the people, and the temple. In John's day, if the concept of sanctification was included in the temple offering, the concept of sanctification would have had to deal with the death of Jesus on the Passover.[81] I presume that this sanctification is an important factor for the restored Israel in the fulfillment of Ezekiel's prophecy of receiving the Holy Spirit as it flowed out of the temple.

According to Ezekiel, YHWH will lead Israel to the land and "cleanse" or "purify" (טָהֵר; LXX καθαρίζω or καθαρισμός) the people of the nation with water. In other words, YHWH will place his sanctuary in the midst of them forever (37:28), after all Israelites are restored to the land ("all the house of Israel," 36:10; 37:21). Ezekiel emphasizes the Jews' observation of the laws and the role of the Spirit. YHWH will let them reside there by cleansing them from sins and keeping the laws in the new Spirit (by מַיִם טְהוֹרִים ["pure water," 36:25, 26–27]; by דָּם ["blood," 43:18–27]). The sign of the establishment of the new temple is to flow out of the living water, from there into the sea, so that the water there might refresh wherever its river flows so that creatures may live there (47:1–12; cf. 36:22–28). The land, in which the new temple is centered (48:10, 21), might be allotted to the Gentiles who live with the Israelites (47:21–23). I suppose that John would

---

81. The "common Judaism" revolved around the Jerusalem temple as society's religious-political center, under "the agreement of the parties and the populace as whole" (Wardle, *Jerusalem Temple*, 118, 170; Sanders, *Judaism*, 12). Most "common" Judeans endeavored to hold the purification of the temple (1 Macc 2:12; 14:36) and their Jewish identity and life according to the Mosaic law and the temple ritual worship (2:22, 29, 40, 50; 4:36–40); according to Maccabees, Judeans thought that purification meant cleansing (1 Macc 2:12; 14:36) for holiness (2 Macc 2:18; 14:36; cf. 15:18, "the consecrated sanctuary") (Kampen, "Books of the Maccabees," 19; Wardle, *Jerusalem Temple*, 81). This purification ceremony occupies an important place in the Jewish "purification ceremony" (John 2:6; 3:25; 11:55). The Jews should also be a cultic community (Lev chs. 1–7, 11–15). They had the responsibility of participating in annual temple services at festivals and purification rituals (*Wars* 4:5, 2, 6, 3). Philo highlights that "there is one temple of the one God," to which people must offer their sacrifices. The one temple is the Jerusalem temple, at which the priests should "offer prayers and sacrifices" for the nations (Spec. Leg. I 66; Leg. Ad Gaium 156, "through those who offer the sacrifices" to Jerusalem). *V. Mos.* II 174 and *Ebr.* 66 note that the temple service can be recapitulated to "prayer and sacrifice." Philo's *Moses* 2.71–75 notes that in the wilderness, Moses made "a portable sanctuary" (φορητός ἱερόν) as a "tabernacle" (σκηνήν) to offer sacrifices there (*Moses* II 74) before constructing the "notable Temple" (περίσημος ναός) in the land (2.72, 73).

deliberately set Jesus's purification of the people through his sacrificial death against the purification ceremony of the "common Judaism" in the first century (2:1–11; 13:10).[82] If John deliberately connects the Jewish purification with Jesus's events (2:6; 3:25; 11:55; 18:28), Jesus's death would fulfill the ritual purification for the nation and the scattered children of God who are consecrated to him. Jesus's consecration ("make holy") is associated with purification (John 2:6; 3:25; 10:36; 15:3; 17:17, 19; 18:28; for Jewish festivals, 10:22).[83] Given that John alludes to the eschatological fulfillment, the author may understand Jesus's sacrificial death in light of Ezekiel (5:13; 37:23–28; 43:12–25; 45:18–25; 46:4–13).

According to Ezekiel,

1. God is jealous for the temple (ζήλῳ μου, Ezek 5:13; cf. Ps 68:10 [LXX, ὁ ζῆλος τοῦ οἴκου σου κατέφαγέν με]).

2. On the Passover (τὸ πασχα ἑορτή), the priests purify the sanctuary by putting the blood of an offering on the temple's doorposts (45:18–20).

3. The king offers a young bull and rams (Ezek 43:23, אַיִל; for lamb [כֶּבֶשׂ, 46:5, ἀμνός, 46:6]) for all the people of the land (ὑπὲρ παντὸς τοῦ λαοῦ τῆς γῆς) and for sinners (ὑπὲρ ἁμαρτίας, 45:22, 23; 46:4–13).

According to John, Jesus

1. takes away merchants and sacrificial animals because of his jealousy, which results in the purification of the temple (Ὁ ζῆλος τοῦ οἴκου σου, John 2:13–17);

2. offers his blood for the nation(s) on the Passover (ὑπὲρ τοῦ λαοῦ, 19:34 and 11:51–52; 13:1, [Israel's king, 1:49; 12:13, 24]);

3. is "God's Lamb" (ἀμνὸς) who takes away the sin of the world (1:29, 36; cf. 13:5–10);

4. dies for his own people on Passover (τὸ πασχα ἑορτή, 13:1; 20:17, 22). Jesus is the [good] shepherd who lays his life down for his people (ὁ ποιμὴν [ὁ καλός], John 10:11; 12:13).

John reiterates YHWH's jealousy for the temple in Ezekiel. As the prophet emphasizes that the Israelites defiled the sanctuary and God vented his anger toward them, which is associated with his jealousy (Ezek 5:11, 13a, ἐν ζήλῳ μου and τὴν ὀργήν μου, קִנְאָה ["jealousy," Zech 8:2], John reports that Jesus took away the merchants and animals from the temple in his zeal

---

82. Cf. Jones, *Symbol of Water*, 63–64.

83. Corell, *Consummatum Est*, 72; Chennattu, *Johannine Discipleship*, 93; Bauckham, "Did Jesus Wash," 95, 97–98, 103–5; Beasley-Murray, *John*, 234; Thompson, *John*, 282.

for his Father's house (John 2:16, Ἄρατε ταῦτα ἐντεῦθεν ["take away these from here"]; 2:17, Ὁ ζῆλος τοῦ οἴκου σου ["The jealousy of your house"]). He made a whip to drive out sheep or cattle, to pour out the merchants' money, and to stir up his anger (John 2:15). His wrath is YHWH's jealousy (Ezek 16:42; 23:25; 35:11; 36:6; 38:19).[84] Both authors pay attention to the result that people might know YHWH through God's anger and jealousy (Ezek 5:13b [ἐπιγιγνώσκω], John 2:17 [μιμνήσκομαι]). However, God's wrath and jealousy also entail his redemptive work that he purifies his people with water so that they are able to receive the Spirit (Ezek 36:25, טָהֵר ["clean" or "purify"], 36:26, 28, and John 20:17, 22 [covenant and the Spirit]). As Ezekiel prophesized that God dwells in the midst of his people as the sanctuary by establishing the eschatological temple (Ezek 37:26, 28; 41:1—47:12), John also testifies that God resides in his own people through the *new temple* (John 1:11, 14; 2:21; 20:19). The hallmark of these temples is the fullness of glory (Ezek 43:5 and John 1:14). In this respect, Jesus is the eschatological temple for his people (John 2:21). God must primarily purify the land and take away his people's sins so that they can participate in the festival, receive the Spirit, and know God (Ezek 39:12, 16, 19, 28-29; 43:18-27; 45:18-25; John 1:29; 2:8-11, 22; 7:2, 37-39; 11:40; 12:1; 13:1; 20:22, festival and glory]). In the imagery of Ezekiel's eschatological temple, the focus should be on animal sacrifices during the Passover and the Feast of the Unleavened Bread. When Ezekiel points to the "ram" (אַיִל) as a sacrificial animal, it is equivalent to כֶּבֶשׂ ("lamb," Ezek 46:4-7, 11; John 1:29, 36; cf. Gen 22:7-8, 13; Exod 12:3, 4, 5; Num 15:5, 11; Ps 114:4, 6; Ezek 34:17-19; Ezek 6:9). If John echoes the fulfillment of Ezekiel's eschatological temple and its animal sacrifices in his Gospel (Ezek 36, 37 with 45:7-8, 18-27; John 1:29, 36; 11:51-52; 19:34), the author of the Gospel likely deals with a sacrifice for God's purification on the Passover (John 19:33, 36; cf. Exod 12:10).[85]

If my idea is appropriate, the first meaning of Jesus's sacrificial death is purification in light of Ezekiel's Passover and sacrifices for both purification and God's salvation. When YHWH restores his people again, he is present among them, sanctifying the temple and the people. His presence presupposes the return of his glory to the temple, and with purification and worship, living water comes from the temple to save the dead sea (Ezek 47:1-12). All of the Israelites and the foreigners residing among them are living in the land (vv. 13-23). The picture of God's eschatological promise is fulfilled through Jesus. In the Gospel of John, Jesus comes as God's

---

84. Lappenga, "Whose Zeal," 141-59; Voorwinde, *Jesus' Emotions*, 116-38.

85. Barrett, *Gospel according to St. John*, 176, 558; Belle, "Christology and Soteriology," 448-49.

glory and becomes the temple. He cleanses the physical temple, washes his people, offers himself as a sacrifice, and stands "in the midst of" his disciples (John 1:14 and 12:41; 2:13–18; 3:22–26; 4:1–2; 13:4–11; 19:30; 20:19, [26]). The risen Jesus also gives his eternal life by providing them with the Holy Spirit as promised, as his blood and water flow from the sides of his body on the cross (7:37–39; 19:34; 20:22). Accordingly, God washes away the sins of the world and wants to be with the Son as he shares his life with him. This life-giving is the beginning of a relationship, and God lives in the unity-relationship with Jesus. Jesus's sacrifice is, in this sense, the fulfillment of the Father's heart and will.

Second, Jesus is the Sacrificial Lamb for Salvation.

Jesus's sacrificial death concentrates on God's salvation for his sheep and nation (10:17; 11:51–52; cf. Isa 53:6–7, 11; 55:5). John says the world is in darkness and in sin. In 8:34, people are slaves to sin, and their father is the devil (John 8:41–44). Jesus was sent to set them free (8:32). In John's Gospel, sin is unbelief, and the result is condemnation and judgment (3:18–19; 9:39–41).[86] Through his death, Jesus brings them to faith. He sounds like a brass serpent, demonstrating that he is the "Lamb of God" to the world (3:14–15). Brown's argument makes sense that Jesus's death for the people, specifically the ingathering of the dispersed children of God, alludes to one flock in 10:16 in reference to the Old Testament imagery ([Isa 11:12]; Mic 2:12; Jer 23:3; Ezek 34:16).[87] In particular, for YHWH's gathering of "all Israel," Ezekiel 36:24–25 (cf. 37:21; Isa 56:8) reverberates in John 11:50–52 of the ingathering of "the people" as God's children. John clarifies in 11:50–52 that Jesus died for "the nation," which is the Jews, as well as the scattered children of God throughout the world (John 11:50–52; 18:14). God saves many people through Jesus's crucifixion (12:24; 18:14; 19:34).[88] Jesus's sacrificial death as God's Lamb is the fulfillment of God's eschatological salvation for both Israel and the Gentiles (Isa 2:3; 43:5; 56:7; 60:6; Jer 23:2; Ezek 34:12; 37:21; Zech 14:16).[89] Accordingly, Jesus's death best illustrates God's saving work.

In short, the sacrificial death of the Johannine Jesus on the cross is meant both for God's purification of the people's sins and for saving them. At the same time, the incident is a witness to the sign. He lets everyone, even those who stabbed him and those who followed him, "see" him (John 19:35, 37), and they "see" God raise him up. They become the witnesses to

---

86. Koester, *World of Life*, 115.
87. Brown, *John I–XII*, 442–43; Lightfoot, *St. John's Gospel*, 230.
88. Dodd, *Interpretation*, 349n2.
89. Barrett, *Gospel according to St. John*, 407.

God's glory through Jesus's death and resurrection. Just as Lazarus's death and being raised from the dead reveal God's glory, Jesus's incidents also show his glory so that people are able to see (11:40; 12:23, 28, 33-34). Jesus's crucifixion is the greatest witness to both the beginning and completion of God's salvation for the world (8:28 [τότε γνώσεσθε ὅτι ἐγώ εἰμι]; cf. "lift up" for both events in 3:14-15; 12:34).

Jesus's Sacrifice of Love (3:16-17)

The sending formula of 3:17 clarifies the purpose of Jesus's sending by the Father, which is meant for salvation (ἵνα σωθῇ ὁ κόσμος δι' αὐτοῦ), but not judgment (3:17, 19; 5:24; 12:44-47, 48).[90] Salvation refers to eternal life.[91] In order to give life to the world, the Father sent the Son.

Within the parallel structure of John 3:16-17, the phrase ἀπέστειλεν ὁ θεὸς τὸν υἱὸν εἰς τὸν κόσμον (3:17a, "God sent the son into the world"]) is associated with τὸν υἱὸν τὸν μονογενῆ ἔδωκεν (3:16b, "he gave the unique son"). The phrase ἀποστέλλω ("send") corresponds to δίδωμι ("give"). The verb *give* demonstrates that God loves the world and its people to the point that he gives them eternal life (3:16a). Similar cases of this verb's usage appear in John 6:31-35 and 17:2-4. John states that the Father gives the bread of life (6:32), which is Jesus (6:35).[92] In 17:2, 4, for the life of the world, the Father gives all authority to the Son (17:2) so that he might complete the work that the Father gave him (4:34; 5:36). Therefore, God sent the Son into the world in order to give it life. In other words, the Son's mission is to give life to the world by faith (3:15). In 3:17, his giving of life is associated with "having eternal life" (3:16b), "being saved" (3:17b), and "doing the truth in light" (3:21).

Jesus's death is a self-sacrificial and self-giving event that originated from God's love and service (3:16; 12:24-26; 13:14, 34-35). With regard to Jesus's death for the nation and God's people (11:50-52), M. C. de Boer claims that the preposition ὑπὲρ (11:50) needs to be translated to "for the benefit of, for the sake of, or to the advantage of."[93] He observes that 13:37-38 and 15:13 deal with the disciple's imitation of Jesus; thus, the preposition "for" refers to an act of self-devotion.[94] In the same sense, the shepherd's sacrifice expresses his love for sheep (10:7-18). Thompson points out that ὑπὲρ

---

90. Barrett, *Gospel according to St. John*, 434.
91. Brown, *John I-XII*, 147.
92. The Father gives the *Paracletos* to the disciples (14:16).
93. Boer, *Johannine Perspectives*, 233.
94. Boer, *Johannine Perspectives*, 233.

means "for, on behalf of, or for the unspecified benefits of others," which is why the good shepherd dies not for this particular reason, but for his sheep (10:15b, 17–18).[95] This narrative focuses on the fact that Jesus brings life to the world through his sacrificial and self-giving death in the sense of fulfilling God's eschatological salvation for the world.[96] Ultimately, God's forgiveness of sin through Jesus's sacrificial death is given to the world through the disciples' mission, occurring through their forgiveness of anyone's sins (1:29; 21:23). Jesus's death was a testimony both to the Father and to his love for the world (3:16; 13:1 [10:11–15 and 21:15–17]). He reveals the Father on his cross, which discloses the glory of the Father (11:40; 13:31–32). John speaks of his death as an act of service for many (12:24–26). Love and service are embodied in the triune God's attributes, life, and activity, and were testified to through Jesus's death, that is, his life and sacrifice.

Therefore, Jesus was willing to be lifted up, or die, for others according to God's Old Testament promise (John 3:14–15). His death is the culmination of his sentness that fulfills the Father's will.[97] The disciples, whom Jesus sends with the Spirit, lead people to believe in Jesus and in his sacrificial death. By faith, they can be forgiven or accepted by God and live eternally in his presence. The eternal life of these people is the achievement of Jesus's unique mission.[98] Jesus's sacrificial death is a revelation of God and of his own love through life.

Evangelism

The author of the Gospel uses terms such as λέγω, λαλέω, γινώσκω, ἀκούω (8:14; 10:6, 16, 27) and λόγος, ῥῆμα, φωνή (5:24, 47; 6:68; 8:47; 10:3, 16; 14:10; 15:7; 18:37). These words characterize Jesus's mission as evangelism, which focuses on his testimony of both the Father and himself as the sent one, so that he might evangelize people in order for them to believe, become disciples, and live in the eternal life and light (11:25–27, 39–40, 42, 45; 12:11, 17–19, 36).

Firstly, to hear Jesus's voice is to believe in both him and the one who sent him, and is done in order to gain eternal life (5:24; 14:24). This eternal life avoids death and judgment on the last day (5:25; 6:39, 44; 12:47–50). In order to bring eternal life to the world, Jesus was sent to testify to God and his salvific work (μαρτυρέω 5:39; 8:13, 17; 18:37). Above all, by using the sayings

---

95. Thompson, *John*, 226.
96. Thompson, *John*, 226; cf. Morris, *Gospel according to John*, 374n116, 376n119.
97. Köstenberger, *Missions of Jesus*, 139.
98. Köstenberger, *Missions of Jesus*, 75.

of ἐγώ εἰμι (6:20, 35, 41, 48, 51; 8:12; 10:7, 9; 10:11, 14; 11:25; 14:6; 15:1, 5), Jesus declares that hearing, knowing, and believing in him are the will of the Sender for the salvation of individuals and the world (6:28; 12:36; 14:24; 17:3).

Secondly, to hear Jesus's voice is to know and follow him (the structure of φωνή-ἀκούω-γινώσκω-ἀκολουθέω, 10:3, 4, 27). First of all, to follow means to become his disciple. John demonstrates that Jesus "teaches" people to be his disciples (διδάσκω, 7:14, 16, 17, 35). Jesus's teaching also aims at allowing them to "know" (οἶδα or γινώσκω, 7:28; 8:28) and to be believers (8:28-30, 31). Ultimately, Jesus's evangelistic ministry is meant to make people into his disciples so that they can live in his word and eternally be in the light (8:12, 13, 31, 51).

Thirdly, through the Samaritan woman, Jesus emphasizes his harvesting work as his mission. This harvest refers to letting people believe both in Jesus as the savior and in his Word (4:39-42; cf. Luke 10:2, Ὁ μὲν θερισμὸς πολύς, οἱ δὲ ἐργάται ὀλίγοι δεήθητε οὖν τοῦ κυρίου τοῦ θερισμοῦ ὅπως ἐργάτας ἐκβάλῃ εἰς τὸν θερισμὸν αὐτοῦ). In particular, Luke 10:1-20 resembles the context of Matt 10:1-42, and John also echoed Matt 10:40 and Luke 10:16 (John 13:20) to Jesus and his disciples. His mission is to preach the gospel for soul-salvation. Thus, the goal of his harvest reveals that it is an evangelistic task that intends for people to obtain eternal life (4:36).

In his Gospel, John presents that the two points of Jesus's evangelism attend to bringing people both to the light and to God's rulership. Jesus leads people to "life," which he gives through his death. These points refer to this "life" in the light, along with the worship of God in "Spirit and Truth" (4:24; 17:3).

Life in the Light (3:17-21)

Jesus's evangelism highlights that God's sending of the Son aims to deliver the world from darkness into light. He, who was sent as the light, saves people so that they might live in the light (1:9; 3:17-21; 8:12; 12:46). John 3:17-21 clarifies what salvation means in comparison with judgment or condemnation (κρίσις, 3:19); this latter word explains the current status of the world and of people.

  a. ἠγάπησαν οἱ ἄνθρωποι μᾶλλον τὸ σκότος ἢ τὸ φῶς (19b, "[people] loved the darkness rather than the light").

  b. αὐτῶν πονηρὰ τὰ ἔργα (19c, "their works were evil").

People love "darkness" (σκότος) more than "light" (φῶς) because of their evil deeds (3:20a). Σκοτία ("darkness") appears eight times in the Gospel of John (1:5*2; 3:19; 6:17; 8:12; 12:35*2, 46; 20:1). Two cases among these verses state "walk in darkness" (8:12; 12:35). In these instances, the word *walk* (περιπατέω) means to live. John links "to walk in darkness" with "sin" (ἁμαρτία, 8:12, 21). Throughout the Gospel, the author splits "sin" into two groups (1:29; 8:21, 24, 34, 46; 9:34, 41; 15:22, 24; 16:8, 9; 19:11; 20:23):

a. The first group (8:21, 24, 34; 9:34; 19:11; 20:23) underlines that people sin in their lives.

b. The second group (9:31, 41; 15:22, 24; 16:8, 9) describes that peoples' ignorance of the Sender and the sent one is sin, and that hating Jesus and the Father is also sin, even though they know who the Sender is.

The first group claims that people are living as the "servant of sin" (8:34), namely Satan's slaves (8:44). The second one emphasizes that sin is that people do not know Jesus and the Father (15:21–23, to hate Jesus and the Father; cf. 8:12–20). These groups are eventually subordinate to the fact that people are walking in darkness. Blumhofer observes that "throughout the Gospel, John has noted that human behaviors occur alongside this divine hardening: the love of human glory and the love of darkness."[99] Their lives result in death (8:21–25; cf. 5:29); therefore, John defines sin as evil deeds or evil life, and the ignorance of the true God (cf. 17:3). Death and judgment are given to the world in darkness or sin. Jesus testifies that the world is evil because it lives in this light (7:7), and asks the world to be free from the slave of sin by becoming his disciple (8:31–34). The people of the world are to live the life of Jesus's disciple (8:31; 13:34–35; 14:15), and this is the first goal of Jesus's evangelism. His disciples believe in both God and him, and keep his words (8:31; 13:35; 17:6–8). For those who have unbelief and disobey these words, God's judgment and wrath will rest upon them (3:18, 36; 8:24; 9:39; 12:48). Jesus proclaims faith (9:35–37), but at the same time, he also teaches that unbelief is sin itself. The result is death (8:24, [15:6]). On the other hand, if he teaches that anyone lives in the light, he or she will not die in sins (8:12–51). Therefore, he preaches that people will move from the darkness to the light by way of faith and his words.

The other characteristic point is that John connects judgment with "the ruler of this world" (12:31; 14:30; 16:11). The ruler has nothing in Jesus (ἐν ἐμοὶ οὐκ ἔχει οὐδέν, 14:30c). Along the same vein, those who do not receive Jesus's washing "have no part with him" (οὐκ ἔχεις μέρος μετ' ἐμοῦ, 13:8c).

---

99. Blumhofer, "Gospel of John," 312.

Jesus washes his disciples in order to be consecrated and holy (13:10; 15:3), and so that they might belong to the Father and to him, but not to the world (17:14, 16, 21). The servants of sin and evil cannot abide in God's household "forever" (8:35, 34–44, 47). These contrasting points signify that the ruler reigns over the world in darkness and in sin (evil lives and deficiency of God's knowledge) in order to bring death and destruction to people (17:12). In contrast to the ruler of the world, when Jesus was sent into the world as *the light*, the ultimate goal of his mission shone a light on the world that was in darkness (1:4; 8:12; 12:47).[100] In other words, God's sending of the Son intends to make the world live in Jesus, the light, by faith (12:44–47).[101]

Therefore, as the light of the world, Jesus's mission is meant to bear witness to God so that the world can believe in him (1:1–4; 9:5; 10:37–38).[102] At the same time, Jesus as *the light* testifies to the truth (8:32; 18:37).[103] To

---

100. Dodd, *Interpretation*, 348n2; Lenski, *St. John's Revelation*, 894–96; Herbert, *Mishnah*, 179–80.

101. The motif of light is used by John within the context of the Feast of Tabernacles (*m. Sukkah* 5:1–4; cf. "the Feast of Dedication," 1 Macc 4:52–59; 2 Macc 2:18–36; 10:5–8). According to Gale A. Yee, these texts present similarities between the Feast of Tabernacles and the Feast of Dedication. The Feast of Dedication is the commemoration of the temple purification event through Judas Maccabeus (1 Macc 4:36–51; 2 Macc 10:1–4). In particular, 2 Macc 2:18–36 describes the light ceremony (Yee, *Jewish Feasts*, 86). During the ceremony of the Feast of Tabernacles, priests implemented symbolic and religious ceremonies, such as the outpouring of water on the west side of the altar and the lighting of several candles on golden candlesticks in the temple precinct (Dodd, *Interpretation*, 348; Danby, *Mishnah*, 179–80). Specifically, John highlights that Jesus utilizes these symbolisms to unfold his identity (Dodd, *Interpretation*, 351). The expression ἐγώ εἰμι τὸ φῶς τοῦ κόσμου (John 8:12) presents that Jesus understands himself to be united with God, who is "the bearer of life and light" (1:1–4; 10:37–38). According to C. H. Dodd, the phrase "the light of the world" (8:12; 9:5) indicates God himself in the Rabbinic tradition. Dodd objects to the influence of Zoroastrianism with respect to the antithesis between light and darkness, whereas he suggests the understanding of light in the context of the glory of the Old Testament (Dodd, *Interpretation*, 206). By using ἐγώ εἰμι, Jesus explicitly indicates that he recognizes self-divinity (Isa 60:1–2, 19–20; cf. Ps 27:1; 36:9) in opposition to "the Jews" who do not believe Jesus (John 8:25) and eagerly kill him (8:58–59; cf. "children of the devil," 8:43–44) (Koester, *Symbolism*, 140). His understanding of identity is pertinent to his mission. He reveals God by sharing the Sender's identity.

102. Culpepper, *Anatomy*, 89; Köstenberger, *Studies*, 164–67; For the discussion on the divine name, *Ani-w'hu*, and "the bearer of light" (see Dodd, *Interpretation*, 349–50, 351).

103. Köstenberger, *Studies*, 164–67; cf. Keener proposes that the eschatological light from Zech 14:7 and the pillar of fire in the wilderness (Exod 13:21; cf. Ps 78:14; 105:39; Neh 9:12, 19) limit the meaning of the statement of Jesus's light (Keener, *Gospel of John*, 739). That is, he observes that the imagery of light should be extended to the scope of life (8:12; 9:4; 11:9; 12:35) (Keener, *Gospel of John*, 739). Virtually, the light metaphor is accompanied by "walking in darkness" in contrast to "lamp of the world," which

know the light of the truth means to live according to God's words and command for eternal life (1:9; 8:28, 32; 12:50).[104] For this reason, Jesus made people follow him (1:43). Their following presupposes that they believe in him, know him, hear his voice and ultimately follow him (9:35–36; 10:16, 27). Jesus continues to teach them his words, making them disciples (8:12, 31–32; 10:1–6).[105] This means that Jesus saves people so that they know God and walk in *the light*, namely himself (8:12; cf. 1:37–38, 40, 43; 10:4, 5, 27; 12:26; 13:36–37; 21:19, 22). When John calls the disciples "sons of light" (12:36), this emphasizes the unity of the holy Father and the holy Son (17:11). Those, who are walking in light and knowing God, are believers. They belong to God by being consecrated in truth (17:19). John 3:21 identifies people who follow the truth (cf. 8:12, 32), revealing their deeds in light. Jesus gives his new commandments to believers so that they might produce fruits, and the world might recognize God and Jesus through the fruits of these believers (13:35; 15:1–17; 17:23). For this reason, Jesus makes them holy and sends them into the world (17:17–19 [cf. 10:36]). Therefore, the fact that Jesus, as *the light*, consecrates the disciples shows that they are not only living in the mutual relationship with God, but are also revealing God to the world according to the sending formulae.

Worship in "Spirit and Truth" (4:23–24)

The purpose of Jesus's sentness for evangelism is to find true worshipers of God in "Spirit and Truth" (John 4:23–24). This theme is well-represented in 4:20–22. These verses utter that "Jerusalem is the place of worship" or "salvation is from the Jews." John tells us that Jesus is from God in 1:41, 49; 3:2, 15–21, and 31–36; and in 2:16 he refers to the temple in Jerusalem as "my Father's house."[106] In these verses, Jesus emphasizes the act of worshiping

---

is called God's Wisdom or Torah (Ps 119:105, 130; Prov 6:23) as the agent of God's creation, revelation, and salvation (Prov 8:1–36 with John 1:1–18).

104. With regard to the fulfillment of the Isaianic servant, James Hamilton argues that the expression "walking in the light" (John 8:12; 9:5; 11:9–10; 12:35–36) should be understood in terms of the fulfillment of "the Isaianic motif of the Servant as the 'light to the nations'" (Isa 9:1; 42:6; 49:6; cf. also 60:1, 3; 1 *Enoch* 48:4) (Hamilton, "Influence of Isaiah," 154; cf. Koester, *World of Life*, 137). Hamilton connects "He" of ἐγώ εἰμι (8:24; cf. Isa 48:5 with John 13:19) with "My servant and I am He" of Isaiah 43:10. Hamilton's opinion makes a strong point in that John identifies Jesus as the chosen One (cf. Isa 42:1 with John 1:34) (Hamilton, "Influence of Isaiah," 155–56).

105. Köstenberger, *Missions of Jesus*, 131, 177–80.

106. Thompson, *John*, 104.

the Father (4:21), saying that now is the time to worship God everywhere, and that the Father is looking for true worshipers such as these (4:23).

For this purpose, the sent Jesus focuses on evangelism. He invites a Samaritan woman to the worship of God. After she knows Jesus's identity, the Samaritan woman immediately discards her water bucket and enters her neighborhood, and she then brings the people there to Jesus. She participates in Jesus's evangelism, and Jesus speaks of this as fulfilling the will of the Sender, which means to gather fruit at harvest. His activity is to make people believe (4:42). Many Samaritans believe in him as the Savior of the world, and in Galilee, both an official and the whole family believe in Jesus (4:53). In describing these stories, John demonstrates in chapters 4 and 7 that the role of Jesus's verbal proclamation is to bring together those who worship God in Spirit and Truth. In other words, true worshippers in Spirit and Truth are those who receive Jesus's proclamatic invitation to his "living water" (7:37–38). This theme of "living water" is central to the conversation with the Samaritan woman. In comparison between 4:14–15 and 7:37–38,

> *A* Jesus says to the Samaritan woman: ὃς δ' ἂν πίῃ ἐκ τοῦ ὕδατος οὗ ἐγὼ δώσω αὐτῷ, οὐ μὴ διψήσει εἰς τὸν αἰῶνα, ἀλλὰ τὸ ὕδωρ ὃ δώσω αὐτῷ γενήσεται ἐν αὐτῷ πηγὴ ὕδατος ἁλλομένου εἰς ζωὴν αἰώνιον (4:14, "but whoever drinks of the water that I will give him will never be thirsty again. The water that I will give him will become in him a spring of water welling up to eternal life" [ESV]).

> *B* The woman asks: Κύριε, δός μοι τοῦτο τὸ ὕδωρ, ἵνα μὴ διψῶ μηδὲ διέρχωμαι ἐνθάδε ἀντλεῖν (4:15, "Sir, give me this water, so that I will not be thirsty or have to come here to draw water" [ESV]).

> *B'* Jesus invites: Ἐν δὲ τῇ ἐσχάτῃ ἡμέρᾳ τῇ μεγάλῃ τῆς ἑορτῆς εἱστήκει ὁ Ἰησοῦς καὶ ἔκραξεν λέγων · Ἐάν τις διψᾷ ἐρχέσθω πρός με καὶ πινέτω (7:37, "On the last day of the feast, the great day, Jesus stood up and cried out, 'If anyone thirsts, let him come to me and drink'" [ESV]).

> *A'* Jesus proclaims to people: ὁ πιστεύων εἰς ἐμέ, καθὼς εἶπεν ἡ γραφή, ποταμοὶ ἐκ τῆς κοιλίας αὐτοῦ ῥεύσουσιν ὕδατος ζῶντος (7:38, "Whoever believes in me, as the Scripture has said, 'Out of his heart will flow rivers of living water'" [ESV]).

Here, the woman's plea links with Jesus's invitation. In 4:14, Jesus promises "a spring of water welling up to eternal life" to the thirsty person. Then,

7:37–38 shows that he invites thirsty people to drink the living water (cf. Isa 43:20; 44:3; Joel 3:18; Zech 14:8; Prov 18:4). In particular, in 7:37–38, Jesus's invitation and proclamation contain two important themes of evangelism.

First, in 7:38, Jesus declares that only believers can drink the living water. The believers believe in God and Jesus (3:18). That faith is living in his word (8:31). To follow Jesus (8:31) and to keep his commands (13:34–35; 14:15; 15:15; and 17:6, 7–9) is to live a fruitful life (15:8). What the Holy Spirit does is to continue the mission of Jesus. He comes to earth, teaches, reminds, and keeps producing fruit by doing (14:26). Jesus brings the truth and the new commandment to people (3:21, 23–24; 8:32; 13:34–35; 17:16–19; 18:37).[107] His mission is to make people know the true God and worship only him in Truth (4:23–24; 17:3).[108] Jesus's significant role, as the sent one, is to deliver the Father's words to people (17:2, 6–8). These words are to make people his disciples (8:31–32) so that they might be the "children of light" living in eternal life (12:36, 49–50).[109] Additionally, as Jesus and the Father are reciprocally abiding in the bond of holy union, Jesus's word sanctifies the disciples to unite with God (10:36; 17:17, 19, 21, 23). In this respect, to worship God is to keep his commandments in the unity-relationship with God. In short, Jesus's sentness aims to make God known to people, and to enable them to live in the light and the truth. Their lives concentrate on worshipping the true God and obeying his words (17:3).[110]

---

107. God's salvation brings all people into worship of the one true God because they know him and his salvific work (Martens, *Plot*, 87–91; Marshall, *Beyond the Bible*, 77; Wright, *Mission of God*, 75–80; Gorman, *Abide and Go*, 113). Christopher J. H. Wright states that God allows people to know him as the true God by way of redemptive events and revelation (Deut 4:32–34; 5:6; Ps 68:8; Amos 3:1–2) (Wright, *Mission of God*, 42–44). This entails God's self-manifestation of identity and character (Deut 5:6; Exod 6:6–8; 34:6–7; Isa 45:18–19). Just as God revealed himself to his chosen people and all nations through salvation from Egypt and covenant at Sinai, God reveals his trinitarian identity and character to the world through his saving activity of the Son's incarnation and death-resurrection and the giving the Spirit (Deut 4:34; Luke 9:31; Col 2:15) (Wright, *Mission of God*, 49, 51). Salvation from sin enables people to know the glory of the true God and his work in Jesus Christ (2 Cor 4:6; cf. Exod 20:2–3; Ps 96:1–3). It relates to "knowing who God is and what he has done" (Hos 2:15; 12:9) (Wright, *Mission of God*, 59).

108. Thompson, "Gospel according to John," 190.

109. Cf. Green, *Why Salvation*, 11.

110. Living Jesus's words in this spirit of truth means mutual indwelling. Jesus aims to deliver the knowledge of God to the world and embodies God's love for the world by giving eternal life to believers (John 3:16–17; 20:30–31) (Thompson, "John," 191). Thompson matches knowing God to "participating in the relationship of life-giving dependence" (5:25–26) (Thompson, "John," 192). She focuses on the mutual relationship of the Father and Son on their sharing of "an intimate and reciprocal knowledge, mutual love, and unity of will and work" (Thompson, "The Gospel according to John," 189). It

Second, Jesus maintains his evangelistic work through the Holy Spirit. Living water refers to the Spirit (7:39).[111] After Jesus was glorified, he gave the Spirit to his disciples (20:22). God sent the Son to die on a cross by flowing out blood for the worshippers.[112] John links Jesus's blood to life-giving water, namely the Holy Spirit (4:10, 11, 14; 7:37-39; and 19:34).[113] Those who receive this living water become the true worshippers of the true God (17:3).[114] In this regard, the Spirit's primary mission is to provide eternal life for people. The Holy Spirit is "the source of eternal life" and living water as such (7:38-39); this water flows out of Jesus (4:14 with 7:39; cf. 14:17).[115]

---

belongs to God and becomes one with him (14:20; 15:4, 7, 10; 17:9-10). This is defined as living as united with God (17:23). For this work, the Father sent Jesus (17:18), and he sanctified those who believed in him, sending them into the world. Although they are in the world, they are not of the world, but of God (17:16). They too, like Jesus, have the purpose of sending the world to worship God in truth and spirit (17:20).

111. On the cross, water and blood flowing from the side of Jesus's body symbolizes living water as the Holy Spirit (John 19:34 and 7:37-39) The outflowing of living water is the fulfillment of the eschatological temple in the Old Testament (Isa 43:20; 44:3; 55:1; Ezek 47:1-12; Joel 3:18; Zech 14:8). The ceremony of living water is directly associated with the Holy Spirit (Isa 43:3; 29:8; Ps 42:1-2; cf. John 3:5) (Koester, *Symbolism*, 173). Dodd rightly argues that "water" in Jewish literature is Torah, Wisdom, or Holy Spirit (Dodd, *Interpretation*, 138). Isaiah 44:3 and Ezekiel 36:25-27 equate "clean water" to "My Spirit." The Holy Spirit is "the source of eternal life" and living water as such (Michaels, *Gospel of John*, 467; Jones, *Symbol of Water*, 160). Jesus's giving of living water is the sign of the fulfillment of God's "harvesting" mission (John 4:10, 14, 35-38) (Barrett, *Gospel according to St. John*, 233-35). He welcomes believers to himself regardless of their ethnic identity (Jews [12:11], Samaritans [4:39-42], Galileans [4:45], Greeks [12:20-23]). When some Greeks come to him (12:20-23), Jesus declares that his death is for many fruits (12:25). He connects his sacrifice with death for nations (7:39; 11:50-52). Again, Jesus gives the Spirit as living water to believers, which flows out of his body as the temple (2:21). This is the accomplishment of God's eschatological promise for life (Ezek 47:8-12).

112. Belle, "Christology and Soteriology," 448-49; As living waters flow from the temple (Ezek 47:1-12; Zech 14:8), the water springs out of the body of Jesus (John 7:38) (Blumhofer, "Gospel of John," 148). R. Alan Culpepper impressively succeeds in his comparison between Jesus's invitation to living water and his blood as a Paschal lamb on the cross by pointing out the irony of the thirst of the one who gives "living water" (John 19:30; cf. Exod 12:22) (Culpepper, *Anatomy*, 195); The flowing rivers of living water (John 7:38) are not only derived from Zechariah 14:8, but are also tightly bound up with the flowing blood of Jesus from his body as the eschatological temple (John 19:34) (Kerr, *Jesus' Body*, 239-41; Barus, "John 2:12-25," 135).

113. Morris, *Gospel according to John*, 724; Michaels, *Gospel of John*, 967-70.

114. The temple is Jesus, to which all nations are gathered to worship the true living God (Wright, *The Mission of God*, 488, 489, 527). Eventually, the purpose of salvation is the restoration of both worship and the relationship between God and humanity (Gombis, "Participation," 108).

115. Michaels, *Gospel of John*, 467; Jones, *Symbol of Water*, 160.

Koester rightly argues that "living water" not only flows from Jesus, but also from those who drink the water as they can be "a channel of the activity of the Holy Spirit."[116] He points out the Spirit's important missional role, noting that the Spirit is the pivotal object of the Son's mission. He died on the cross and rose from the dead in order to rescue people from judgment and condemnation. He gives believers the Spirit, who is living water and the source of eternal life (6:35). This is the ultimate goal of the Father's mission. He sent the Son and the Spirit so that people might be saved from the judgment of sin and unrighteousness, or injustice, meaning that those who believe in the Son and the Father can participate in eternal life through the Spirit.

Above all, attention is given to the phrase that "the water that I will give him will become in him a spring of water welling up to eternal life" (4:14 and 7:38). This saying means that Jesus will enable his true worshippers to live by the Holy Spirit's work, and they will live in worshipping God in Spirit and Truth. It is the Holy Spirit's missional work that reminds us of Jesus's teachings, makes us understand them, and makes us live. Of course, the identity of the Johannine Spirit is a "miraculous divine power" as an "eschatological gift" that makes believers new creatures.[117] At the same time, however, it should be emphasized that the Holy Spirit is "another paraclete," who is the "Spirit of the truth" (14:16, 17, 25, 26; 15:26; 16:7–11, 13–15; cf. 1 John 2:1) beyond an impersonal power ("a life-giving power figure," John 3:3, 5, 6; 6:63; 7:37, 38). Then, "another" paraclete speaks, hears (16:13), glorifies (16:14), and bears witness to Jesus (15:26). Additionally, the Spirit convicts concerning sin, righteousness, and judgment (16:8). These accounts support the fact that the Spirit takes over mission from Jesus (16:7). As soon as the risen Jesus breathes the Spirit into the disciples, the Spirit becomes the subject of Jesus's mission (20:19–23) by advancing it in the world (15:26, 27). Jesus's breathing of the Spirit is associated with the Father and his sending of the Spirit (15:26a). The Holy Spirit leads the new creatures toward the true worship of God through new birth and eternal life (John 3:3; Ezek 37:5, 14; Joel 2:28). The Spirit-Paraclete completes Jesus's mission in unity with both the Father and the Son, and is sent by the resurrected Son and the Father.[118] The Holy Spirit continues to restore humanity and these creatures to God's new life so they might practice the truth and reveal their deeds in God (John 3:21, ὁ δὲ ποιῶν τὴν ἀλήθειαν ἔρχεται πρὸς τὸ φῶς, ἵνα φανερωθῇ αὐτοῦ τὰ ἔργα ὅτι ἐν θεῷ ἐστιν εἰργασμένα).

---

116. Koester, *Symbolism*, 180.
117. Bultmann, *Theology*, 1:153, 155, 159.
118. Brown, *Spirit in the Writings*, 77.

Therefore, God's eschatological salvation aims at the restoration of worshipping the true God. For this reason, after Jesus completed his mission through his sacrificial death, the Holy Spirit actualizes salvation on earth (19:30). With the Spirit, Jesus's disciples, who are living in truth and holiness as they keep God's commandments, are sent into the world in order to fulfill God's mission over the entire world (14:15, 17, 26; 17:17–19; 20:21).[119] Ultimately, Jesus maintains his evangelistic mission by giving the Holy Spirit to the believers so that they might live in the unity-relationship with him.[120] They receive the Holy Spirit, who is the living water that never thirsts. This Holy Spirit is "the spirit of truth" (14:17) that keeps the words of Jesus that must be done (14:26). Believers worship God in this Spirit of Truth.

THE DISCIPLES' MISSION AS INTEGRATED WITNESS

Jesus sent his disciples into the world just as the Father sent him (17:18; 20:21). John uses the frame of "as . . ., so . . .," along with sending language (10:36, 38; 13:20; 17:17–18; 20:21), to teach that the disciples' mission has continuity with Jesus's mission (13:16, 20, 36; 14:12). As Jesus was sent to bear witness to the Father in life, both in action and proclamation, so also do the disciples preach the gospel (14:25–26; 15:27; 17:20) and testify to God by living as consecrated to him in the world. Such a life-pattern involves keeping the word of God (17:6).[121] In other words, those who belong to God manifest him both through true worship and through keeping Jesus's words (4:24; 17:6). Just as Jesus revealed the name of the Father, they, too, should live a life of testimony that makes the Father and Jesus known to the world (13:35; 17:6, 21).[122] Life-witness and evangelism, or verbal-proclamation, are distinguished in terms of conceptual understanding; in essence, though, both of them are inseparable from the mission of Jesus and the disciples.

Life-Witness

Jesus emphasizes that to see him is to see the Father (John 14:9). This is Jesus's life-witness. As Jesus shows the Father and his work to the world, the Father reveals himself in and through him (4:36–38, 42; 5:32, 34, 36, 37;

---

119. Jenny, "Holiness, Holy," 598.

120. Dunn, *Jesus and the Spirit*, 66, 352, 354.

121. In the phrase "τὸν λόγον σου τετήρηκαν," the word τηρέω means "obey" or "observe" in the Gospel (Ridderbos, *Gospel of John*, 551).

122. Schnackenburg, *Gospel according to St John*, 3:174–77.

10:25). They witness to one another through the unity-relationship (14:10). When Jesus sends his disciples (17:18; 20:21), he commands them to bear witness to him for the salvation of the world (4:38; 17:3, 20). However, this witness does not simply mean evangelism. Rather, during Jesus's absence on earth, John articulates the disciples' life-witness to the world (13:15, 20; 17:21). As the Father works in the life of Jesus in order to reveal himself, Jesus also works in the lives of the disciples in order to testify to himself (5:36, 37; 8:18; 10:25). This is made possible through holy association.

Life-Witness in the Unity-Relationship

John uses the frame of "as . . ., so . . ." to explain the unity-relationship. The unity is life-sharing (17:18; 20:21), meaning that they are sent into this world in order to bear witness to his identity, life, and deeds in the way they share life with Jesus (3:21).[123] John parallels Jesus's sentness to that of the disciples through the frame of holiness:

a. John 10:36, 38: ὃν ὁ πατὴρ ἡγίασεν καὶ ἀπέστειλεν εἰς τὸν κόσμον ("whom the Father consecrated and sent into the world" [ESV]).

b. John 17:17–18: ἁγίασον αὐτοὺς ἐν τῇ ἀληθείᾳ . . . καθὼς ἐμὲ ἀπέστειλας εἰς τὸν κόσμον, κἀγὼ ἀπέστειλα αὐτοὺς εἰς τὸν κόσμον ("Sanctify them in the truth . . . as you sent me into the world, so I have sent them into the world").

In 10:36, Jesus argues that he was consecrated (ἁγιάζω, to make holy or sanctify) and sent into the world. John implies the use of "holiness" in the Old Testament.[124] The word etymologically refers to "separation" or "set

---

123. Love and unity are foundations for the disciples' mission. Those things are sources of witness in their lives in that the disciples are "to witness to Jesus and to represent him accurately" (Köstenberger, *Missions of Jesus*, 189). This is because "Jesus is both the perfect revelation and the ultimate sacrifice—the disciples are to witness to Jesus's person and work through their words, works, and lives (cf. 14:12; 15:26–27; 16:8–11; 17:18)" (Köstenberger, *Missions of Jesus*, 196).

124. Cf. for Christopher J. H. Wright, the core concept of his understanding of mission is holiness (Lev 19:2, "You shall be holy, for I am Holy") in view of God's people's ethical life (justice and righteousness) on the basis of covenant and election (11:44–45; cf. 1 Pet 1:15–16) (Wright, *Mission of God's People*, 124). God summons people to his holiness by making the holy covenant relationship (Exod 6:6; 19:5–6; Lev 26:12; Deut 26:17; Isa 11:5; Jer 7:23; Ezek 11:20). The term "holiness" does not just signify that God separates his covenant people from the world, although the meaning of the words *consecrate* (קָדַשׁ) and *be holy* (קָדוֹשׁ; cf. ἁγιασμός) are dedication to God or moral purity (Rom 6:19, 22; 1 Cor 1:30; 1 Thess 4:3, 4, 7; 2 Thess 2:13; Titus 2:15; Heb 12:14; 1 Pet 1:2) (Swanson, "מְשָׁרֵן"). Rather, they are continually living in society by sharing God's

apart" (וַיְקַדֵּשׁ אֹתוֹ [Gen 2:3]).[125] The Hebrew terms *qadas*, *qodes*, and *qados* are translated into English as sanctify, holiness, and holy. These words characterize that something, or human beings, is not merely separated from impurity, but also belongs to the Holy One (Lev 19:2 and 20:26; Exod 28:40-43; cf. Exod 12:43-49; 19:10; 29:42-44; 31:13; Lev 16:1-24; 23:27; Deut 5:12).[126] Therefore, the fact that God sanctifies people to him means that they are mutually sharing life and nature in holiness (Lev 19:2). John describes this unity-relationship form as a mutual indwelling ("He is in me and I am in him," John 10:38; 14:10, 11; 17:17-18).

In 10:38, Jesus insists on his unity-relationship with the Father (ἐν ἐμοὶ ὁ πατὴρ κἀγὼ ἐν τῷ πατρί). John describes this relationship in holiness and his sentness from above (John 5:18, 23, 37; 6:46, 50-51). Jesus shares the Father's identity, life, and deeds (10:30, 36-38). Although the Father sent him into the world, they are united together in this holy relationship (10:28-30; 14:10). In particular, his deeds bear witness to the Father's work in order to give eternal life (10:25, 32, 37). In 14:7-10, his life and deeds reveal the Father through their oneness. Likewise, Jesus says that his disciples will do his works after his return to the Father (14:12).

In 15:2-17, the disciples are already cleansed so that they may make much fruit. They are united with Jesus in the mutual indwelling relationship. After Jesus purifies their whole bodies and their feet, they are prepared to bear his fruits (13:5). On the one hand, their practice of love is not simply placed within the frame of command-obedience (cf. 13:16 and 15:20; 15:15a), but within the concept of friendship (15:15b).[127] However, on the other hand, their reciprocal love is the fruit of their mutual abiding in Jesus (15:4-5). This relational picture is expressed through the mutual indwelling of the "words," or "commandments" of love (15:7, 9-10, 12, 17). The lives of the cleansed disciples reveal their own identity as Jesus's disciples (13:35; 15:8).

In 17:17-18, John adjusts the Father's sanctification of the Son in his sending act to Jesus's sending of the disciples. As the Father is united with the Son in holiness, Jesus and the disciples are also one (17:20). In particular, the sent disciples' dwelling in God, which is equivalent to their oneness, bears witness to Jesus's sentness (17:18, 21, 23). Above all, Jesus demands

---

life and character in the mutual relationship of the covenant, for he sends them into the world of his creation, which must be restored.

125. Gammie, *Holiness*, 9, 23.

126. In particular, Leviticus 20:26 clarifies the concept of holiness. The reason Israel is holy is because God is holy (Lev 19:2). According to Exodus 25:8-9 and 29:43, after building the tabernacle, YHWH ratifies its holiness. As the holiness of the tabernacle roots in God himself, so, too, is Israel's holiness bound with God (Lev 20:3, 26; Exod 19:6).

127. Cf. Ridderbos, *Gospel of John*, 520.

that his disciples keep his commandments (14:15). This is because their holy lives are related to keeping Jesus's new commandments in the mutual indwelling between them and Jesus (14:20). In 13:34–35, their observation of the commandments also bears witness to their own identity as Jesus's disciples in the world. They were washed by Jesus and purified. This cleansing is the beginning of the union between Jesus and his disciples. Jesus repeatedly spoke of unity with them in chapters 13–17, and this unity presupposes that they first become fully one (17:23). The essential way of living as one is to love one another; this love comes from humbly serving one another, and Jesus demonstrates their life-witness to the world.

Therefore, in their lives, the disciples are to bear witness to the world, of both Jesus and the Father through their holy relationship. This is not a communication model in which disciples become humble in cross-cultural countries through an incarnational way.[128] Incarnation means that Jesus came to earth as a dwelling place for God's presence (1:18; 14:10a). God not only reveals himself in Jesus's life and works, but he also saves sinners through the Son so that he may dwell among them. In this sense, as Jesus reveals his Sender in life, identity, and deeds, so do the disciples also represent God in this intimate relationship. Köstenberger designates this idea as a "representational model."[129] The disciples' lives are not meant to just represent Jesus, but rather to "re-present" him in the relationship.[130] In other words, their lifestyles do not simply represent Jesus as an ambassador, but "re-present" him in and through them.[131]

The disciples' lives do not simply "re-present" Jesus in the sense of imitation, however. Through a new interpretation of Jesus's teachings within a context, they must live Jesus's lifestyle according to the unity-relationship.[132] For this purpose, Jesus sends the Holy Spirit along with the disciples

---

128. Stott, *Christian Mission*, 27.
129. Köstenberger, *Missions of Jesus*, 217.
130. Köstenberger, *Missions of Jesus*, 216–17.
131. Köstenberger, *Missions of Jesus*, 119.
132. With regard to the life-pattern in the era of new creation, James D. G. Dunn proposes that John 20:21 is related to God's new creation in terms of "Jesus as the author of a new creation as he was of the old (1:3)" (Dunn, *Baptism*, 177). Burge supports Dunn in that Jesus's work embarks on a new era (Burge, *Anointed Community*, 122). The Father brought the life of the new creation through Jesus in order to inaugurate the new era. Then, he sent the Spirit and believers to live and to let the world live the new life of the forgiveness of sins (20:23). This is the participation of believers in the *missio Dei*. John develops their life language by reshaping mission language. At the same time, he emphasizes that such a life means "walking" in truth (8:12; cf. 1:37–38, 40, 43; 6:2; 10:4, 5, 27; 12:26, 36, 44; 13:36–37; 21:19, 22).

(20:22).¹³³ This Spirit is meant to lead the Johannine community in bearing witness to Jesus through the daily lives of its people in missional environments. In other words, the Spirit allows John and his community to remember and interpret Jesus's teachings in order to bear fruits in a life-setting (15:1–10, 16).¹³⁴ In 14:15–26, Jesus teaches that the disciples observe the commandment of love, and their practice verifies their love for Jesus and the Father's love for them. In this context, the Holy Spirit's sentness is meant to let the disciples remember Jesus's teachings and actions in a contextual aspect (14:26; cf. 7:39).¹³⁵ Bilger Olsson understands that "the understanding is described as a 'remembering' of Jesus's words and Scriptures" (14:26; 16:13–14).¹³⁶ In other words, the Spirit helps these people understand Jesus by interpreting, translating, and teaching his tenets within a specific context (14:17, 26; 16:13).¹³⁷ Olsson aptly draws attention to the phrase Ταῦτα λελάληκα (the perfect tense of λαλέω ["to speak"]) in 14:25. He notes that "the Paraclete will realize all Jesus's sayings to the disciples, he will interpret them in their situation and thus give rise to new insights and experiences."¹³⁸ John 16:13 verifies that the Spirit's work in a context leads the community "into all the truth."¹³⁹ Their lives make the fruit of love. This fruit is love and unity, which begins from the Father and the Son Jesus (3:16 and 15:12; 13:34; 14:21; 15:10; 17:11, 21–23; cf. 1 John 2:3–5): "You love one another, even as I have loved you, that you also love one another."

Eventually, the disciples must live Jesus's life and reveal their identity as Jesus's disciples and God's children (13:35; 1:12; 15:1–15; 17:1–26).¹⁴⁰ Their lifestyle is service in humility and a practice of love through purification and consecration. Jesus utters that such a life reveals both their identity as his disciples and God's love to the world (13:35; 17:23).

---

133. Brown, *Spirit*, 92; Mathew, *Johannine Footwashing*, 367; Jesus is the light of the world for life (John 1:4; 8:12) (Danby, *Mishnah*, 179–80; Dodd, *Interpretation*, 348n2, 351). John interweaves Jesus's bearing light with knowing God (1:1–4; 10:37–38). John 7:29 and 8:28, 32, 38 depict that Jesus is the one who reveals the Father and is the light of the truth (Culpepper, *Anatomy*, 89; Köstenberger, *Studies*, 164–67). Jesus teaches all people to know the Father (1:9).

134. Barus, "John 2:12–25," 136–37.

135. Barus, "John 2:12–25," 131.

136. Olsson, *Structure and Meaning*, 263–64.

137. Olsson, *Structure and Meaning*, 266, 268, 271–72.

138. Olsson, *Structure and Meaning*, 269, 270–71.

139. Nissen, *New Testament*, 93; Parsenios, *Departure*, 81.

140. Thompson, "His Own Received Him Not," 270; Hock, "Jesus, the Beloved Disciple," 207; John clarifies Jesus's life and his disciples' lives in the love-relationship (3:16; 13:1–20; 15:1–17).

Evangelism

Jesus tells his disciples about what he had received from the Father (17:8). The Holy Spirit will come in Jesus's name and allow them to remember his teachings (14:24, 26).[141] Just as Jesus himself came to earth in order to proclaim the Father's word and to testify to his name, the disciples are also sent to bear witness (14:31; 17:6, 18, 20). Above all, they should be harvesters in the end times. Their role is found in the way that Jesus himself invites people to life, or how the Samaritan woman invites her villagers to Jesus. To elucidate the disciples' witness, John uses two missional themes: harvesting and "come and see" (1:39, 46; 4:29).

Harvesting (4:35-38)

The θερίζω ("harvest") is the purpose of Jesus's sending of the disciples (John 4:35-38). In the Synoptics, the theme of harvesting depicts the proclamation of God's kingdom through Jesus and his disciples (Matt 9:37-38; Mark 4:29; Luke 10:2), and Jesus asks his disciples to pray that God sends reapers to them.[142] Similarly, John also emphasizes the inception of the harvest time (John 4:35).[143] Within the context of sending, John continues to resonate with the evangelistic statement of both Matthew and Luke, and when Jesus sends his disciples into the village, he gives these statements to them (Matt 9:35; 10:1; Luke 10:1-3; John 4:38). Jesus sends them to reap believers through their witness (ἐγὼ ἀπέστειλα ὑμᾶς θερίζειν) in John 4:38, 39, 41; and 13:20 (receiver [λαμβάνων]; cf. "welcome you," Matt 10:40 [Ὁ δεχόμενος ὑμᾶς ἐμὲ δέχεται, καὶ ὁ ἐμὲ δεχόμενος δέχεται τὸν ἀποστείλαντά με] and also in Luke 10:16 [ὁ ἀθετῶν ὑμᾶς ἐμὲ ἀθετεῖ· ὁ δὲ ἐμὲ ἀθετῶν ἀθετεῖ τὸν ἀποστείλαντά με; Luke 10:10, δέχωνται ὑμᾶς]). The harvesting statement becomes a biblical foundation for the Samaritan woman's

---

141. In an epistemological aspect, the Spirit allows the Johannine community to know Jesus's words and deeds (John 16:14-15). The community's knowledge of Jesus is dependent on the Spirit's generating people "from above" (3:3) (cf. Mathew, *Johannine Footwashing*, 366), so that they might participate in light by following the truth (3:21). Tricia Gates Brown observes that the Spirit lets people born from above transfer night into day so that they might experience the transformation of their epistemology in knowing Jesus's identity and believing in him (Brown, *Spirit*, 113). Brown insists on John's deliberate parallelism between Nicodemus's ignorance of something spiritual (3:1-22) and his new recognition (19:38-42) (Brown, *Spirit*, 119). She continues to propose that Nicodemus is a representative of believers who are born by the Holy Spirit from above (4:10-14; 7:39; 19:34) (Brown, *Spirit*, 122).

142. Bruce, *Gospel of John*, 115.

143. Carson, *Gospel according to John*, 230.

evangelism (John 4:42). She led other Samaritans to faith in Jesus by way of her verbal witness and proclamation (4:39, 42; cf. 15:27; 17:20).

When some Greeks come to him, Jesus professes that his death is meant to make many fruits (12:20–25). In the sense of mission, his sacrifice gathers God's scattered people (11:52).[144] Jesus teaches his disciples how to follow him (12:26), and the way to do so is to serve him by participating in his death so that much fruit is produced (13:20, 36; 20:19), which reaps the harvest (4:35–38). Through this verbal proclamation, as Jesus allows people to have faith and eternal life, so, too, do the disciples (4:34; 10:42; 20:29, 30–31).[145] For this reason, Jesus sends his disciples into the world (20:21).[146] Even though they are excommunicated or killed by owing to their testimony, their evangelism is to ultimately serve God (16:2, 8–12).

"Come and See" (1:39, 46; 4:29)

Jesus's invitation has two meanings: *firstly*, he gives eternal life to those who respond to the calling by faith; *secondly*, he asks them to follow him by inviting unbelievers to himself for the purpose of eternal life. The phrase "come and see" (ἔρχεσθε καὶ ὄψεσθε, 1:39; ἔρχου καὶ ἴδε, 1:46; δεῦτε ἴδετε, 4:29) indicates the disciples' evangelism of leading people to faith (1:50; 4:42; 10:27–28; 11:26).

---

144. Thompson, *John*, 109.

145. Köstenberger, *Missions of Jesus*, 185.

146. With respect to the Holy Spirit's role in mission, Köstenberger states that "to fulfill their God-given role as sent ones of Jesus, Jesus's followers needed the Spirit (20:22). Using Jesus's followers as his instruments, the Spirit will convict people in the world of their sin, (un)righteousness, and judgment (cf. 16:8–11). The mission of the Messianic community is that of extending to unbelievers the forgiveness of sins made possible through Jesus's completed work (see 17:4; 20:23)" (Köstenberger, *Studies*, 157). John 14–16 presents that the Holy Spirit plays a role in allowing the community of Jesus to gain a much deeper comprehension of Jesus's words recorded from his public ministry (16:13; cf. 14:12), promoting missions to the world (Nissen, *New Testament*, 231). Jesus's followers reap the fruits of his public ministry and gather the eschatological harvest in the age of the Holy Spirit (Köstenberger, *Studies*, 124). In this respect, Beasley-Murray rightly states that "the emphasis is the continuing ministry of the Lord with and through his disciples, by whom the glorification of the Father in the Son will be continued" (Beasley-Murray, *John*, 255). By the same token, Aelred Lacomara states that "his (Jesus) mission will be an unending one, assuring the preservation and communication of the words of Jesus to the end of time (John 14:16). 'The Spirit is the living bond which guarantees unity between the eternal witness of the church and the eye-witness testimony of the first disciples'" (Lacomara, "Deuteronomy," 82).

a. Jesus tells two of John's disciples to "come and see" his dwelling (1:39). One of them, Andrew, finds Simon Peter in order to introduce Jesus as the Messiah. Peter, too, became a follower.

b. When Jesus meets Philip, he says, "Follow me" (1:46). This expression is understood in the same context as "come and see." Philip follows Jesus, immediately visiting Nathanael and preaching, "Come and see."

c. When a Samaritan woman realizes that Jesus is the Messiah, she immediately goes to his neighborhood and asks people to "come and see." Her acts take on the role of Jesus's harvesting worker in light of 4:34–38.

First, Jesus's "come" message is repeated in many forms. In 6:35, he does not go hungry, and the believer shall not thirst forever (ὁ ἐρχόμενος πρὸς ἐμὲ, ["the one who comes to me"]). He was sent to do the will of God. *Firstly*, those who are thirsty must believe in Jesus (6:29). In addition to this case, Jesus also invites people to come to himself in 7:37–39. His invitation will cause people to believe in him, and to also have eternal life on the last day. This is Jesus's evangelism, in which the disciples must also participate (15:27). They are to be Jesus's evangelistic witnesses that preach him to the people and bring them to faith. *Secondly*, Jesus died in order to fulfill God's will. He completes his own task by declaring on the cross, "It is finished" (19:30). God's will is that people trust in Jesus's death (6:29–30 and 8:28–29; 12:32–34). His death is for the removal of sins (1:29), and his crucifixion must be testified (19:35; 20:31; 21:24). Furthermore, they must execute the forgiveness or retainment of sins (20:23). This proclaims the salvation and judgment of Jesus so that hearers will believe and have eternal life (cf. 6:40, 54; 17:2–3).

> 5:24 Ἀμὴν ἀμὴν λέγω ὑμῖν ὅτι ὁ τὸν λόγον μου ἀκούων καὶ πιστεύων τῷ πέμψαντί με ἔχει ζωὴν αἰώνιον καὶ εἰς κρίσιν οὐκ ἔρχεται, ἀλλὰ μεταβέβηκεν ἐκ τοῦ θανάτου εἰς τὴν ζωήν ("Truly, truly, I say to you, whoever hears my word and believes him who sent me has eternal life. He does not come into judgment, but has passed from death to life" [ESV]).

Here, Jesus emphasizes believers' salvation and freedom from judgment. This is his evangelistic ministry, and he sends disciples for his work. Until Jesus judges unbelievers at the end of days, his disciples should continue his evangelism. Jesus says that it is "indicative of the work of God" that each man and woman should be a believer out of his or her sins (9:3). Here, we must distinguish between Jesus's present judgment and the futuristic judgment of the last day. While the latter will be the final condemnation, the former takes place now in that their reaction belongs to a future judgment. Some are freed from present judgment by faith, but some remain in their sins and unbelief (9:35-41). When Jesus witnesses himself and proclaims salvation and judgment, the salvation and judgment of people are now divided according to their belief and unbelief (3:17-18; 7:39; 12:47-48). On the basis of Jesus's evangelistic work, the disciples' mission must also proclaim Jesus, his salvation, and his judgment, causing believers to be free from the slavery of evil while unbelievers will have sin as it is to them (9:41; 15:21-24). Although some will persecute the disciples as they persecuted Jesus, some will listen to them and keep their words (15:20). Just as Jesus testifies to the truth before those who kill him, so should they also be witnesses (18:37; 21:18-22). Therefore, in order to gain believers, they must testify to Jesus (15:27; 17:20; 20:31 [20:29]). This is how they take part in God's mission.

Second, meanwhile, "come and see" connects with "follow me." Jesus asks people to "follow me" (ἀκολούθει μοι, 1:43) in order to give them life (10:27-28). His followers will have the light of life through his witness and faith (8:12, 13; 11:26). In 8:12, the term ἀκολουθέω ("follow") notes that following Jesus is the only way of walking in the light of life. John explains "following" in relation to 10:27, which describes a flock of lambs following their shepherd.[147] Jesus as the light illuminates all people residing in the world, in order that they will walk in the light.[148] John continues to use the word περιπατέω ("walk," 8:12) for the disciples, who walk in the light (8:12; cf. 1:37-38, 40, 43; 6:2; 10:4, 5, 27; 12:26; 13:36-37; 21:19, 22).

The disciples must participate in the work of the light of the world (9:4, "our work"), just as Jesus achieved the Father's work (9:3). In the Fourth Gospel, the disciples are not only identified as the "children of light" receiving Jesus, the son of God, but also as those who oppose the Jews that appear as representatives of the unbelieving world of darkness (1:10-11).[149] They, as the "children of light" (12:35, 36; 11:9-10), illuminate the world by witnessing to the invitation and promise of Jesus (6:35, 51; 8:12; 11:25; 15:5) to life in the light.[150] In this sense, Jesus's calling ties with the disciples' inviting work ("come and see," 1:39, 46; 4:29), which leads people to faith and eternal life (1:50; 4:42; 10:27-28; 11:26). As Jesus undertook the Father's will (4:34), his disciples' inviting activity is to

---

147. Thompson, *God of the Gospel of John*, 200.
148. Davies, *Rhetoric*, 199-200.
149. Booth, *Selected Peak Marking Features*, 56-59; Köstenberger, *Studies*, 161.
150. Bultmann, *Gospel of John*, 342; Ball, *"I Am" in John's Gospel*, 163.

harvest the crop for eternal life (4:36). For this work, as the Father sent Jesus to make the world trust in himself, so, too, does Jesus send his disciples to make people believe in himself (4:34, 38 [5:40]; 12:44-46).

Therefore, the above-mentioned two missional themes (harvesting and "come and see") teach that the purpose of the disciples' sending is to preach the gospel of Jesus Christ. They bear witness to Jesus Christ on earth, as Jesus testified to God and carried out his work. In this sense, John clarifies the concept of mission as evangelism, or verbal-proclamation.[151] Köstenberger defines mission as "the specific task or purpose which a person or group seeks to accomplish, involving various modes of movement, be it sending or being sent, coming and going, ascending and descending, gathering by calling others to follow, or following."[152] He focuses the Johannine concept of mission on the accomplishment of tasks given by either a sender or sent ones.[153] Köstenberger's study also provides linguistic evidence of John's emphasis on his recipients' evangelistic activities for unbelievers. To be sure, John highlights Jesus's fulfillment of God's eschatological salvation for all nations, including the Jews and the Gentiles. Specifically, John's evangelistic tasks, such as *bring*, *lead*, and *gather* appear in John 10:16 and 11:52 (cf. 1:46; 3:28-36, evangelism and faith). The verb *lead* in 10:16 can be understood through the shepherd figure. Just as a shepherd leads his sheep, Jesus's redemptive mission is to lead his people.[154] These linguistic studies support John's missional concept in association with God's eschatological redemption in the Gospel. According to Thompson, Jesus's account that this shepherd "must lead them out" (*kakeinan dei agagein*) means that Jesus as the good shepherd finds and gathers God's people in one flock by "bringing all people to himself" (12:32) "through his own death" (11:52).[155] These words show that, first and foremost, the task of Jesus's mission is to die for all nations, and, at the same time, for the scattered sheep of God's flock constituting Israel (1:11), the

---

151. Mission language constitutes the following terms in John: "send" (ἀποστέλλω / πέμπω, for Jesus [*43 times]; for disciples [*3 times]; for general [*2 times]); "come" (ἔρχομαι), "go" (πορεύομαι / ὑπάγω), for Jesus [*44 times]; for disciples [*13 times]); "descend" (καταβαίνω), "ascend" (ἀναβαίνω), for Jesus [*11 times]; for disciples [not used]); "follow" (for Jesus [not used]; for disciples [*17 times]); "bring," "lead" (ἄγω), and "gather" (συνάγω) for Jesus [*2 times]; for disciples [*2 times]). Köstenberger sets these words aside in another group: "work" or "do" (for Jesus [*70 times], "sign" (for Jesus [*16 times]; for disciples [not used]], "harvest" or "bear fruit" (for Jesus [*3 times]; for disciples [*5 times]) (Köstenberger, *Missions of Jesus*, 27-31). These terms characterize the mission of Jesus and the disciples.

152. Köstenberger, *Missions of Jesus*, 31.

153. Köstenberger, *Missions of Jesus*, 181-85.

154. Lenski, *Interpretation of St. John's Gospel*, 739.

155. Thompson, *God of the Gospel of John*, 227.

Samaritans (4:39–42), and the Gentiles (7:35; 10:16).[156] Thompson claims that Jesus's redemptive work goes beyond the eschatological restoration of Israel, expanding to God's salvation for the nations.[157] It is the union of both Israel and the Gentiles in the scheme of God's eschatological redemption.[158] John's descriptions and eschatological symbols are engaged in expounding Jesus's identity and mission. In other words, the Father, as the Sender, bears witness to the sent Son by working in and through him. They are signs and proofs, and they describe the mission of the Sender and the sent. Therefore, John employs the mission paradigm of sending and ingathering.[159] Just as Jesus bears witness to the invisible God and his kingdom in order to invite unbelievers to himself, so also is the Johannine community sent to invite people to eternal life by faith in Jesus (1:39–41; 4:29; 12:20–22). To be sure, Jesus stresses the responsibility of his disciples with respect to their witness of him (4:35–38; 15:27), just as the Holy Spirit testifies to Jesus (14:16–17; 15:26; 16:7–15).[160] In Jesus's farewell prayer, he makes it clear that the reason he sends his disciples into the world is "for those also who believe in Me through their word" (17:18, 20).[161]

However, in John's Gospel, the evangelism of Jesus and the disciples, in the frame of *command-obedience* for the completion of a task, must be accompanied with life-witness in the frame of *mutual indwelling* (15:14; cf. Matt 28:19–20).[162] When Jesus is sent into the world, he and the Father are one of mutual indwelling (John 10:30; 17:22). Jesus abides in the intimate-relationship and in fellowship with the Father. Therefore, Jesus is thoroughly devoted to bearing witness to the Father and his will (17:6), and his love for the Father and obedience of the Father's command makes him devoted to verbal proclamation (14:31; 17:8). Jesus's mission is essentially possible when he shares the will, life, and identity with the Father in this unbroken relationship. Love and trust in the relationship leads him to an evangelistic witness of the Father and his name (17:7). Jesus never leaves the unity-relationship with the Father (14:10) so that people might see Jesus and the Father in oneness and come to faith in Jesus's words (17:7, 8, 11). John does not separate the evangelism of Jesus and the disciples from their lives of

---

156. Thompson, *God of the Gospel of John*, 254–55.

157. Thompson, *God of the Gospel of John*, 254–55.

158. Brown, *John I–XII*, 443.

159. Robinson, *Priority*, 61–63.

160. The Spirit bears witness to Jesus Christ with the regenerated faith communities (Barrett, *Gospel according to St. John*, 90). He leads the community's proclaiming activity in the world (Burge, *Anointed Community*, 36).

161. Koester, *World of Life*, 133.

162. Ridderbos, *Gospel of John*, 520.

being consecrated to God (14:6, 7, 8, 10, 11 [ὁράω and λέγω; γινώσκω and πιστεύω; ἀλήθεια and ζωή]).

SUMMARY

John speaks of Jesus's witness to the Father, his work, and his death, centering on God's sending of the Son. Jesus fulfills the purpose of the Father's sending and sends his disciples into the world with the Holy Spirit so that they continue his mission as witness (15:26–27). John discusses the process and meanings of fulfilling the purpose of Jesus's sentness in the whole structure, while also talking about his public ministry and teachings in two sections. In this structure, John demonstrates that the disciples' mission must be a testimony of life and proclamation: (1) the first section (chs. 1–12) teaches that Jesus's work and witnesses lead people to faith and eternal life; and (2) the second book (chs. 13–21) deals with Jesus's accomplishment of God's mission through death and resurrection, where John describes how the disciples can continue Jesus's mission during his physical absence on earth.

First, John explains the meaning of mission through sending language in his missional structure. *Firstly*, the sent one should accomplish the work of the one who sent him. *Secondly*, the sent one must bear witness to the Sender by sharing his life and identity within the unity-relationship. (1) Jesus completes the giving of eternal life to people through his ministries, sacrificial death, and testimony of the truth. (2) as being sent, Jesus was incarnated in the form of tabernacling, the so-called dwelling place, for God's presence in the midst of his people (1:14). God manifests himself through his tabernacle. In other words, God is present in Jesus, and Jesus simultaneously reveals himself in his presence while in the midst of his disciples (1:18; 20:19–29). This self-revelation of God and Jesus allows people to receive eternal life by making them know, believe, worship, and live in God's reign. Finally, the language and formula of sending emphasizes that the sent one's evangelism is never separated from its life-witness in the unity-relationship of mutual indwelling between the Sender and the sent.

Second, in the missional structure based on the sending formulae, John explicates Jesus's and the disciples' mission as integrated witness. *Firstly*, Jesus's *integrated* witness as mission is accomplished by teaching the words of God's truth and laying his life down to save the world (3:16–17). His teachings and sacrificial death enable the world to move from darkness to light or judgment to salvation, and to worship God. His crucifixion, in particular, is the demonstration of God's love and forgiveness, which testifies to self-giving and self-sacrificial commitment, as well as the essence of God's mission. As a result, people might live in truth and in unity-relationship with God; this is the ultimate goal of Jesus's sentness. *Secondly*, the disciples' mission does not inherently become a sacrifice for the forgiveness of sins, nor does it inherently give eternal life. Instead, their mission is an *integrated witness* of both life-witness and evangelism of Jesus and God's salvific work. They must evangelize people in the eschatological scheme of harvesting and invitation toward the salvation that Jesus accomplished. As Jesus invited the Galilean, Samaritan, Greek, and Jew into faith for eternal life, so also do the disciples proclaim the words so that the world might believe in Jesus and follow him (17:20). More importantly, their evangelization is inseparable from life-witness, which bears witness to God while sharing their lives and identities with the triune God in the holy relationship. John portrays that, when Jesus sends them in the frame of "as . . ., so . . .," he is commanding them to perform the forgiveness that he has fulfilled (20:21, 23).[163] Their mission must entail love and service in humility (13:16, 20). This is the nature of their *integrated witness* as mission, which remarkably appears in the foot-washing narrative (13:1–38).

---

163. Cf. Estrada, *Pneumatology*, 285–87.

3

Understanding the Foot-Washing Narrative in Light of Mission as Integrated Witness

THIS CHAPTER AIMS TO explore the missional meanings of the foot-washing narrative (John 13:1-38). John alludes to *integrated witness* as both life-witness and evangelism in the narrative, which consists of Jesus's symbolic deed and his interpretation for the purified community. The disciples are consecrated so that they can participate in Jesus's life and evangelistic (or verbal-proclamatic) ministry (13:15-17, 20, 35). They are sent into the world in order to bear witness to God through their witness of life and verbal proclamation.[1] In this study, I will deal with (1) the scholarly debate over the foot washing in regard to mission, (2) the literary context and structure of the foot-washing narrative, (3) the meaning of Jesus's foot-washing act

---

1. The sending language and sending formulae provide clarification as to how God reveals himself through Jesus, along with what he fulfills. His self-manifestation and works show his nature and doing. To explain the divine life and activity, John uses terms such as: "forgive" (*1, ἀφίημι, 20:23), "love" (*37, ἀγαπάω [3:16] and *7, ἀγάπη [5:42]; *13, φιλέω [5:20] and *6, φίλος [15:13]), and "service" (διακονέω, 12:2, 26*2). This vocabulary is the key to understanding the missional themes found in the Gospel's sending frame: (1) forgiveness illustrates the purpose of God's sending act, (2) love expresses the origin and nature of sending, and (3) service is a mode used by the sent ones in order to fulfill the Sender's will. John shapes these themes in the sending formulae to tell how God fulfills his mission.

(vv. 1–11), and the interpretation of Jesus regarding the foot washing within the Johannine community (vv. 12–38).

SCHOLARLY DISCUSSIONS OF THE FOOT-WASHING NARRATIVE FOR MISSION

Within the context of John, some scholars present the missional meanings of chapter 13 in diverse ways. I will briefly look into their arguments and evaluate them.

First, Herold Weiss interprets the mission of John's community as its martyrdom, through which it participates in Jesus's death within the historical context. The disciples' death serves as a witness (21:19).[2] At first, Weiss argues that the foot-washing narrative includes the interpretation section for the community's preparation for persecution and martyrdom in light of 16:2, 4a.[3] Additionally, Weiss focuses on "having a part" between Jesus and the disciples. This "part" ties into Jesus's washing act that makes the disciples clean for their religious rites. In his day, the Jewish people would have needed their "cleanliness," gained through a sacrificial offering, in order to go into the presence of God. Of course, Weiss does not regard the cleansing concept as "the ritualistic metaphor of cleansing from sin."[4] Although he suggests that the disciples are purified by Jesus's blood,[5] this cleanliness makes no reference to the purification from sins. Instead, his cleansing concept focuses on their preparation for death and standing in the presence of God. Just as Jesus himself is washed by Mary for standing in front of God through his death, so, too, have the disciples washed their feet for martyrdom and sanctification, through which they complete the process of standing in the presence of God.[6] Besides, Weiss believes that the cleansing concept should be connected to Jesus's words for the disciples' abiding in him on the basis of 15:3.[7] Their indwelling means that they bear the fruit of true discipleship in him, which is joy in both persecution and martyrdom, while also being the disciples' participation in Jesus's death as they follow him.[8]

---

2. Weiss, "Footwashing," 321.
3. Weiss, "Footwashing," 301, 306–7, 315.
4. Weiss, "Footwashing," 319.
5. Weiss, "Footwashing," 317–18.
6. Weiss, "Footwashing," 300, 307–10, 312–14.
7. Weiss, "Footwashing," 320.
8. Weiss, "Footwashing," 312; Thompson, "His Own Received Him Not," 268, 272.

Weiss aptly points out that Jesus's washing act challenges his disciples to participate in his death. Above all, it is a stunning insight that martyrdom is a type of witness within the context of their lives. In addition, his observations surrounding the meanings of indwelling in Jesus and bearing fruit seem to have grasped the literary flow of chapters 13–15. However, it is questionable as to whether the purification concept of sin will be completely excluded from the symbolic meaning of Jesus's washing act.[9] At first, in this discussion, there needs to be agreement that the narrative is rare in its mention of the early churches' sacramental praxes, like baptism and Eucharist.[10] But if John primarily refers to Jesus's sacrificial death on the cross itself, the symbolic act might include the removal of the sin of the world, as testified by John the Baptist. After Jesus completes his mission, he sends his disciples to carry out forgiveness of anyone's sins (1:29; 20:23).[11]

Hence, the foot-washing narrative premises that John describes people under Satan and sin, owing to their unbelief and evil deeds (8:34–44; 9:40–41). If the phrase Οὐχὶ πάντες καθαροί ἐστε ("not all of you are clean," 13:11b) is associated with Jesus's statement ἤδη ὑμεῖς καθαροί ἐστε διὰ τὸν λόγον ὃν λελάληκα ὑμῖν ("you are already clean because of the word that I have said to you," 15:3), Jesus points to Judas Iscariot, who remains in Satan and sin because of his unbelief. Meanwhile, those who belong to Jesus by faith in his words are "already clean." In the previous chapters, John has already connected sin with unbelief and a life that is in darkness or under Satan (cf. 3:18–20; 8:34, 38, 44; 9:35–41). In chapter 9, Jesus's washing act results in opening a sinner's eyes so that the person can believe in him (9:7, 11, 35–38). Therefore, when Jesus cleanses people from their sin, namely that of unbelief, his washing act indicates his restoration of sinners to holiness, so that they might belong to the holy God and Jesus in mutual indwelling (10:36; 15:3–4, 7; 17:11; 17:17, 23; cf. Lev 10:3, 10; 11:44). In the foot-washing narrative, Jesus's purification of his disciples might wash them so that they can belong to him (13:8). Consequently, the cleansing concept is bound to the disciples' mutual indwelling with the holy God and Jesus (10:36; 14:20; 17:11).

Second, in observing 13:1—20:31, H. A. Lombard and W. H. Oliver suggest that 13:1–30 introduces Jesus's mission and 13:31—17:26 utters

---

9. Brown, *John XIII–XXI*, 567.

10. Schnackenburg, *Gospel according to St John*, 3:21–22; Carson, *Gospel according to John*, 466; Mathew, *Johannine Footwashing*, 37–38.

11. Loader, *Christology*, 325; Carson, *Gospel according to John*, 465; Thompson, "His Own Received Him Not," 261; Gibson, "Johannine Footwashing," 58.

the disciples' mission.¹² In particular, they observe that the Passover-motif (Jesus's hour), Mission-motif (His coming back to the Father), and Love-motif appear in chapters 13–17. Along with such an understanding, they focus on the expression μέρος μετ' ἐμοῦ from a missionary point of view. They translate the phrase as "taking part/partaking with Jesus," which symbolically implies Jesus's death and the disciples' ethical lives in union with him.¹³ Lombard and Oliver go on to call the phrase a "μέρος-concept," which ultimately connects their sentness to that of Jesus. In other words, the disciples should show the nature of Jesus's "doing" as his service of love through "their missionary task and doing."¹⁴

To be sure, Lombard and Oliver rightly divide the narrative into two sections of both Jesus's death and the interpretation for the disciples.¹⁵ *Firstly*, Jesus's recognition of his hour indicates the crucifixion. *Secondly*, the "μέρος-concept" suggests a missionary life in that the disciples unite with Jesus after his departure to the Father (cf. 15:3; 17:23).¹⁶ However, within the structural analysis of chapter 13, it is not appropriate to distinguish between 13:1–30 for Jesus's mission and 13:31—17:26 for the Johannine community's discipleship. Instead, in my opinion, it is convincing that John makes a distinction between vv. 1–11 and vv. 12–38. John explicitly presents the transition of the verb tense from "will know" (future) to "know" (present) (vv. 7, 12).¹⁷ First of all, if Jesus's death and washing action are linked, his exemplary interpretation is engaged in the disciples' missional lives as the sent community in vv. 14–15 (cf. 17:18 and 20:21). As 13:1–11 is involved with Jesus's symbolic death, 13:12–38 deals with the community's missional life-pattern.

Third, in studying John 13–17, Teresa Okure senses that the foot-washing narrative provides the disciples with a model that allows them to follow Jesus in their mission (13:15); this model is humility (13:1–17). She divides 13:1–11 and 13:12–17, noting that the former talks about "visual symbol," while the latter refers to "conceptual symbol."¹⁸ Verses 1–8 describe the master's symbolic act, along with what the disciples should do. Their

---

12. Lombard and Oliver, "Working Supper," 361.
13. Schnackenburg, *Gospel according to St John*, 3:25.
14. Lombard and Oliver, "Working Supper," 363.
15. Coloe, *Dwelling*, 136.
16. Loader, *Christology*, 330–35.
17. Brown, *John XIII–XXI*, 561–62; Thompson, *John*, 281, 282; Morris, *Gospel according to John*, 611, 620; Lindars, *Gospel of John*, 452; Mathew, *Johannine Footwashing*, 140–46.
18. Okure, *Mission*, 196–97.

deeds are acts of humble service. In addition, as Jesus conducted the "life-giving service," his disciples should also imitate his love for the world.[19] Above all, Okure emphasizes that the scope of the disciple's mission is the entire world. She concentrates on John's expressions "all flesh" or "the world" (1:9, 10a; 3:16–17; 16:28; 17:2). Although Jesus focuses on his "self-revealing mission" in Palestine, the scope of his mission is the world.[20] On the other hand, his disciples should "witness to the reality of God's salvation (15:27; 1 John 1:1–3; 4:9, 14)."[21] Okure connects the "fruiting" of discipleship with the disciples' harvest (4:31–38; 13:16; 15:16).[22] This is because the disciples' mission focuses on "missionary fruitfulness" (15:1–8, 16), leading them to believe in Jesus (17:20).[23] It is within this context that she argues that the practice of love and service as discipleship brings authenticity as Jesus's disciples are sent into the world during their missionary activity period.[24] Therefore, they should "do both by their life of mutual love and service in the community (13:35) and by proclaiming to others the knowledge of Jesus's life and work as they had personally witnessed it (17:20; 20:30–31; 21:24)."[25]

In my opinion, Okure aptly views that the mission of Jesus and his disciples is to preach the gospel in both Judea and the world. In particular, the disciples' missionary activities aim to testify to the salvation that God has accomplished through Jesus so that the world will believe. Their mission has a "harvesting nature."[26] Unlike Wiess, they are not deported, rejected, or treated with hostility by the world, but rather are committed to the eschatological representatives of God for the sake of the world's salvation.[27] Their

19. Cf. Köstenberger, *Missions of Jesus*, 139.
20. Okure, *Mission*, 198.
21. Okure, *Mission*, 200.
22. Okure, *Mission*, 212; Köstenberger, *Missions of Jesus*, 141, 133; Köstenberger pays attention to πολὺν καρπὸν φέρει ("bear much fruit," 12:24). This phrase might refer to "diaspora Jews and Gentile proselytes into the orbit of God's salvation and community" (Köstenberger, *Missions of Jesus*, 133). He continues to link the phrase with the expression φέρει καρπὸν πολύν in 15:5 [16]. Jesus's death is the tunnel of gathering, or bringing, of his scattered people into salvation. His disciples also bring people to the community, which metaphorically means "bearing much fruit." But, in the context of chapter 15, the phrase indicates the disciples' union with Jesus in mutual indwelling and their bearing much fruit of love or discipleship (15:5, 8, 9–17) (Schnackenburg, *Gospel according to St John*, 3:100).
23. Okure, *Mission*, 201.
24. Okure, *Mission*, 204.
25. Okure, *Mission*, 200.
26. Okure, *Mission*, 212.
27. Okure, *Mission*, 33.

mission is to build a new world for those who live more actively "here and now."[28] Accordingly, the disciples' practices of love and service within the faith community are "visible proof" (13:35; 15:19).[29] She argues that the disciples' keeping of the commandments visibly joins the Father and Son's love and service for the sake of the world.[30] However, in her argument, the practice of love and service tends to be seen only as occurring in John's community, although the scope of mission is appropriately expanded to the world.[31] Moreover, their action is limited to the proof of missionary activities. In my estimation, the Johannine community is sent into the world in order to live in the midst of it. They must live Jesus's life pattern in both the faith community and the world. The scope of their lives is not separated from the world. Even though the world may expel them, hate them, or persecute them, in such a situation, their way of life should be a witness to Jesus and God's salvation, as such a life pattern must be realized in the faith community. In this sense, "bearing many fruits" refers to the fruits of life that come from the mutual indwelling relationship with Jesus, rather than gaining converts through evangelism.[32] Instead, the missionary concept might be understood through 13:20. Those who receive the Sent one believe in the Sender and his words, which is echoed in 12:44–50.

Fourth, Michael Gorman regards the foot-washing narrative as a mission discourse (13:1—19:42). The narrative deals with Jesus's "saving, loving death and the preparation of his disciples to continue his salvific, loving mission in the Spirit's power and with Father's blessings."[33] He particularly draws attention to chapters 13–17, noting that they contain Jesus's final meal and Farewell discourse, which are the "extended commentary on the foot washing" of Jesus. Jesus's act implies "Jesus's impending death" and "the manifestation of love."[34] Gorman observes that Jesus's washing of the disciples' feet shows that God and his love are revealed through Jesus's death. Moreover, it is a correct understanding of the structural aspects of chapter 13 that the disciples understand the nature of Jesus's death so as to missionally participate in the very death. Gorman identifies Jesus's actions as a

---

28. Okure, *Mission*, 206.
29. Okure, *Mission*, 207, 209.
30. Okure, *Mission*, 207–8.
31. Okure, *Mission*, 212–13.
32. Loader, *Christology*, 331.
33. Gorman, *Abide and Go*, 76.
34. Gorman, *Abide and Go*, 85.

"living parable, or an icon, of both the saving and the ethical and missional significance of his death."[35] His significant observations are as follows:

Firstly, Gorman understands the disciples' mission as "doing" or "participation." His concern is with the term "share" (μέρος, 13:8), which is understood as "transformative participation in his death."[36] For Gorman, the core of "share" or Jesus's model is "doing" (13:8, 15). Comparing 14:12 with 15:3–5, 7–8, he concludes that the disciples participate in Jesus's sacrificial love, which is "doing" within their mutual indwelling relationship with him. This is why the "doing" is actually "participating" beyond imitating.[37] *Secondly*, Gorman pays attention to the scope of mission. His understanding of John's centrifugal mission concept for the world is distinguished from the centripetal concept for the faith community. His interpretive foundation is rooted in the analysis of the "*doulos*-proverb" and "*apostolos*-proverb" (13:16).[38]

a. Gorman understands that this community resembles Jesus's example of washing one another's feet and practicing love and service in the relationship between the Sender and the Sent one(s).[39]

b. In connection with the missionary implications covered by Matthew's Gospel (10:24), he attempts to comprehend the Johannine community from the outward-oriented perspective.[40] Thus, he rejects the sectarian approach. Instead, he argues that the missional nature of the Johannine community is centrifugally directed toward the world, as presented in the foot-washing narrative.

---

35. Gorman, *Abide and Go*, 87.
36. Gorman, *Abide and Go*, 88.
37. Gorman, *Abide and Go*, 90.
38. Gorman, *Abide and Go*, 92; For me, it is unclear whether Gorman's views regarding the similarity between John 13:16 and Matt 10:24 support his idea of the "*doulos*-proverb" and "*apostolos*-proverb." The contexts of these texts are different, as the Matthean text is associated with John 15:20 in that the world persecutes the disciples, just as it did Jesus. My concern regards the statements in which Jesus is called Lord and Teacher, and that his deed is an example. The disciples should do as servants and deliver the Sender's words, as Jesus does. As emphasized throughout John's Gospel, the sent Jesus always obeys his sending Father (4:34; 12:49–50; 14:31). Likewise, the sent disciples must absolutely be subordinate to the will and deeds of the Sender (Burge, *Anointed Community*, 202). In spite of this controversial textual issue, Gorman's observation of the disciples' scope of doing in the community and in the world is appropriate.

39. Gorman, *Abide and Go*, 93.
40. Gorman, *Abide and Go*, 94.

Consequently, it is appropriate to first address that Gorman understands the disciples' participation in Jesus's model as doing in the unity-relationship. As Barrett argues, Jesus's humble act of service is not just humiliating himself.[41] Likewise, the disciples' love and service should originate from the depth of love and be embodied in doing (3:16; 13:1, 15).[42] This is their participation in Jesus's sacrificial and self-giving death. Gorman rightly points out the missional scope of Jesus's disciples, as Okure suggests. As Jesus was sent into the world, so, too, is the Johannine community sent into the world, without a distinction between the world and the faith community. They must live to the life-pattern of Jesus's love and humble service in both the community and the world (13:20; 15:20; 17:23).[43] However, in dealing with the concepts of centrifugal and centripetal participation, Gorman does not discuss the evangelism of the Johannine community in the interpretation of 13:20.[44] As Okure observes, the Johannine community is essentially the witnesses for evangelism (13:20; 17:18 and 20:21).[45] Within the context of the foot-washing narrative, this will be explained when Jesus should return to his Father. He demands during his physical absence on earth that they live as evangelistic (proclamatic) witnesses and as witnesses of life after his death and resurrection (13:19).[46] This presupposes that the disciples' live lives of both evangelism and life-witness as sent people, through the integrated perspective.[47]

Overall, with regard to the missional meaning of the foot washing, Weiss highlights the martyrdom of the disciples as witness, while Lombard, Oliver, and Gorman emphasize the disciples' unity with Jesus. The former perspective focuses on maintaining John's community as disciples within the context of historical persecution or ex-communication from synagogues. The latter, however, focuses on discipleship in which they bear Jesus's fruit in mutual indwelling with him. The difference between Okure and Gorman is that the Johannine community should enact a missionary task, practicing love and service within them, or should participate in Jesus's love and service in terms of "doing." These suggestions raise three questions: (1)

---

41. Barrett, *Gospel according to St. John*, 441.

42. Coloe, *Dwelling*, 143.

43. Brown, *John XIII–XXI*, 2570; Bruce, *Gospel of John*, 286; Schnackenburg, *Gospel according to St John*, 3:24–25; Köstenberger, *Missions of Jesus*, 109.

44. Gorman, *Abide and Go*, 83–84.

45. Bruce, *Gospel of John*, 288.

46. Culpepper, "Johannine Hypodeigma," 143–44.

47. Schnackenburg, *Gospel according to St John*, 3:25; Köstenberger, *Missions of Jesus*, 109.

the above-mentioned scholars provide various structural analyses (13:6–11 and vv. 12–20 in 2:1—21:25 [Weiss]; 13:1–11 and vv. 12–17 in chs. 13–17 [Okure]; 13:1–30 and 13:31—17:26 [Lombard and Oliver]; 13:1–11 and vv. 12–20 in 13:1—19:42 [Gorman]). A question arises as to how the structure of the foot-washing narrative can be understood; (2) Weiss highlights that Jesus's washing act prepares the disciples' martyrdom, while Gorman emphasizes that John's cleansing concept implies participation, more than purification from sins. However, some scholars claim that Jesus's death signifies the washing of sins.[48] If Jesus's washing act parabolically, or symbolically, means his death on the cross itself, what does his death mean within the entire structure of John's Gospel, or within chapters 13–21? And (3) Okure and Gorman deal with the disciples' mission scope both in the community and in the world. However, Okure is involved with the community's missionary task as evangelism (verbal-proclamation), while Gorman highlights the "transformative participation" in Jesus's action in terms of discipleship as missional life within two contexts. Of course, Okure and Gorman agree that there are two different concepts throughout the entire gospel. If so, how can the foot-washing narrative be read? Does it include the meaning of a missionary task or of missional life, or does it imply something else?

To begin, I will investigate the foot washing within John's literary context and structure. And then, I will exegete the passages of 13:1–38 to find out how the text references the missional meanings for Jesus and the disciples' mission.

LITERARY CONTEXT AND STRUCTURE OF THE FOOT-WASHING NARRATIVE

John relatively concentrates on Jesus's mission during his public ministry period in chapters 1–12. This is the Gospel's witness to Jesus. From chapter 13, John externalizes the significance of Jesus's mission for his community in the frame of sending and "as . . ., so . . ." (17:18; 20:21). Jesus completes his mission through the crucifixion-resurrection ("it is completed," 19:30 [cf. εἰδὼς ὁ Ἰησοῦς ὅτι ἤδη πάντα τετέλεσται, John 19:28]), and then, he launches the new mission of sending out the Holy Spirit and the disciples. In this literary context, the foot-washing narrative is located at the beginning of the second section (chs. 13–21). The author characterizes the meaning of Jesus's unique mission and the disciples' missional identity and role in the structure of the foot-washing narrative.

---

48. Loader, *Christology*, 325; Carson, *Gospel according to John*, 465.

The Foot Washing in Chapters 13-21

The author describes the mission story of Jesus and his disciples in the literary context of the final meal, farewell discourse, passion, resurrection, and Jesus's re-sending of the disciples. Jesus prepares for his death in the foot-washing narrative in order to make its meaning known to his disciples after the events take place (13:7). At the same time, he teaches them what their life pattern should be (13:1).

First, in chapters 13-21, John focuses on the theme of Jesus's death (and resurrection), which is central in the first section (chs. 1-12). His death is for his flock, namely the nation and scattered children of God (10:11; 11:50-52). It also implies Jesus's sharing his part with them through the washing of them or releasing them from the slavery of sin (cf. 1:29; 8:34-36). In the foot-washing scene (13:1-11), the author symbolically depicts Jesus's death in order to sanctify it as an act of washing the disciples. By linking this scene with the event of the cross and the scene of forgiving and restoring the disciples in chapter 21, it is explicit that chapter 13 provides a preview of his death.

Firstly, in the opening narrative of the second section (13:1-38), John deals with Jesus's symbolic deed.[49] In 13:2, 11, 18, 21, and 26, the theme of betrayal plays a pivotal role in explaining the meaning of his act, from the narrative of the foot washing to those of the passion and resurrection. From chapters 13 through 19, John highlights that although Judas Iscariot, Pilate, and the unbelieving Jews handed Jesus over to death, they did not drive the event; rather it was done by the Father and Jesus himself (13:3, 26; 19:11, 30 [παραδίδωμι]). Through his sacrificial death, Jesus washes people and makes them his own ones. His crucifixion is the culminating event in God's sending story (3:16; 10:15; 11:51-52; 12:23, 24, 32-43; 19:30). Jesus teaches them to participate in his death and glory (13:8, 31-32, 36), and sends them to live as he lived by consecrating both the faith community and the world, forgiving anyone's sins and taking care of others ([13:15]; 20:23; 21:15-17).

Secondly, in chapters 13-21, one of the crucial events of the story-plot is the theme of betrayal and restoration (13:2, 10, 21, 36-38; 21:15-23). The author repeats the theme of betrayal in Jesus's passion narrative (18:3-5, 15-18, 25-27), and also at the moment of Peter's denial of Jesus, which is contrary to his confession (13:37 and 18:15-18, 25-27; cf. 16:32 for the disciples' dispersion). John deliberately confronts Peter's betrayal with Jesus's

---

49. John divides the story of the supper into two parts by way of "when": 13:1 (πρό) and 13:31 (Ὅτε). The former deals with the commemoration of Jesus's death and the interpretation of the Johannine community, while the latter engages in the lifestyle and role of the true faith community.

protection (18:8–9, 19–24) by placing the high priest's interrogation of Jesus between the various pieces of his account of Peter's refusal. He dissolves this conflicted situation (21:15–18) when he writes: "Simon, son of John, do you love me more than these? He said to him, Yes, Lord; you know that I love you" (21:15, ESV). John finishes his story by showing that Jesus allows Peter to follow and die for him (13:36–38 and 21:18, 19). This scene, in which Jesus encounters Peter and the other disciples, except for Judas Iscariot, refers to his restoration (21:1–23).[50] Thus Jesus models his own words: "having loved his own who were in the world, he loved them to the end" (13:2; cf. 1:11).[51]

Second, John pays attention to the faith community's new lifestyle. He has two structures for Jesus's foot-washing event that account for the symbolic acts and their interpretation (13:1–11 and 13:12–38). Jesus interprets his actions as the practice of love and service. The expression "love one another" (15:12, 17) in verses 13:34–35 is parallel to the phrase "wash one another's feet" (13:14). Loving one another is Jesus's new commandment and is the model of life he practices (13:15). This model is linked to three concepts:

Firstly, in 15:1–17, Jesus sanctifies the disciples so that he might be one with them as they bear the fruit of love (15:2–4). Unity is an important theme in chapters 13–17, and tells readers that Jesus and his disciples are united in the sharing of life through the phrase "abide in" (μένω ἐν) (14:20; 15:4–7). In chapter 17, this expression is connected with "be in us" (ἐν ἡμῖν ὦσιν), which means that they are in oneness with God (17:21, με ἐν αὐτοῖς ἦ κἀγὼ ἐν αὐτοῖς, 17:26b). Jesus makes them perfect and unites them with God (17:23), providing the missional principle for the disciples' witness in that they saw the Father in and through Jesus in order to believe his testimony (14:7–11; 17:8). Namely, in being united with Jesus, they can bear witness to his abiding in them (14:17, 20). When Jesus is shown in and through them, they are able to make the world believe in him, in the Holy Spirit, and in the name of the Father (10:38; 15:8; 17:6, 11). Therefore, they must also live just as Jesus lived through a life of sacrificial love and humble service during his physical absence (13:1, 15).[52] Although they are in the world, they no longer belong to it (15:19; 17:16), which is why the disciples must live the unity-life of the Father and the Son in holiness. This holy unity is actualized in making the fruits of love (15:4; 17:21), which is the essence of God's sending of the Son and the Spirit (3:16; 13:16, 20; 14:15–17, 26; 15:26;

---

50. Judas Iscariot is not Jesus's own (13:1); he is "the son of destruction" (17:12).
51. Bruce, *Gospel of John*, 278.
52. Boer, "Jesus' Departure," 2–4.

17:18; 20:21). For these reasons, Jesus protects the disciples to the end, and gives them the Spirit so as to unite them with himself and the Father.

Secondly, the model of Jesus's life-pattern is the essence of discipleship. Peter's following of Jesus is to live Jesus's life and to care for his flock through love and service (10:7–18; 21:15–18). Eventually, Peter dies both for Jesus and for them (21:19, 22). In 18:32 and 21:19, John deals with ποίῳ θανάτῳ ἤμελλεν ἀποθνῄσκειν ("by what kind of death he was going to die") and ποίῳ θανάτῳ δοξάσει τὸν θεόν ("by what kind of death he was to glorify God"), describing their link to death. The author reminds readers that Jesus's death is a self-sacrificing event for the people by repeating the passage of 11:50–52 in 18:14. In the light of his sacrificial death, Peter's discipleship involves self-denial, sacrifice, and the protection of his flock without abandoning his following of Jesus (13:1; 17:12; 18:9, 19; [20:27; 21:15–22]).

Thirdly, the foundation for the model-interpretation of Jesus's symbolic action lies in the work of the Spirit-Paraclete. The Spirit comes to remind and teach Jesus's work (14:26; 16:14 [13:19 with 14:29]); thus, the disciples can bear witness with the Holy Spirit (13:20; 15:26–27). Above all, the coming of the Holy Spirit and his work make it possible for the disciples to live as a missional community, or as missional disciples, and not as part of the world that is being sent out of the earth during his return to the Father (13:34–35; 16:28, 33; 17:9, 14–16, 18, 21, 23). Even though the world hates them, the disciples must believe that they are sent from the Father and must live as witnesses until Jesus comes again (15:18–27; 16:27, 30; 17:3, 6, 8, 18, 21; 19:35; 20:21–23, 29; 20:31; 21:24).

Thus, the second section of chapters 13–21 tells how the purified and consecrated disciples should unite with him as Jesus's missional community and live as holy people during his period of absence. Within this context, the foot washing is not just the beginning narrative of Jesus's discourses (chs. 13–17) and salvific events (chs. 18–21), but also includes Jesus's teaching and model for the missional life of the faith community that remains in the world after his resurrection and ascension (13:1, 7 with 13, 15, 33, 36; 14:23–24; 17:8; 20:21 and 23; 21:15–19).

The Thematic Layered Structure of Chapter 13

John mirrors the scene of Jesus's foot washing in 13:1 when Jesus "returned to the Father," and at 14:2 in "I am going to prepare a place for you." Specifically, in 13:19, he emphasizes πιστεύω ("believe") only after another work has taken place, while chapter 14 highlights both the disciples' present faith in Jesus (14:1, 10–12) and the work of the Holy Spirit (14:16–18, 26). Of course, these themes, which are covered in chapter 13, are found through chapters 14 to 21, so Jesus's death and his mission are not cut off. Nevertheless, it should be seen that the primary scope of Jesus's foot-washing narrative is 13:1–38, in that the events thematically constitute the layered structure.

Jesus knew the hour of his return to the Father (13:1). The phrase ἦλθεν αὐτοῦ ἡ ὥρα ἵνα μεταβῇ ("his hour had come to return") presupposes that the time at which he would finish the purpose behind his sentness had come (19:30). John inserts the statement of Judas's betrayal between Jesus's actions, exhibiting the layered structure (A–B–C–A'–B'–C'). Moreover, after Judas Iscariot leaves the space, Jesus continues the dialogue about glorification, the practice of love (the new commandment) during his absence, and Peter's betrayal and later turn toward following him (13:31–38 [21:19]).[53]

A 13:1a Jesus's return to the Father (hour)
B 13:1b He loved his own people (life)
C 13:2 Judas Iscariot's betrayal (παραδίδωμι ["hand over" or "betray"])

A' 13:3–5 Jesus's return to the Father (hour)
B' 13:6–10 Peter's miscomprehension and Jesus's *part* (life)
C' 13:11 Judas Iscariot

A' 13:12a After Jesus washed the disciple's feet (hour)
B' 13:12b–17 The disciples' comprehension and action (life)
C' 13:18 Judas Iscariot

A' 13:19–20 Before it happens and whoever accepts me (hour)[54]
C' 13:21–30 Judas Iscariot (παραδίδωμι) in the dialogue between Jesus and other disciples
B' 13:31–38 The disciples' doing and following (life)

This structure presents Jesus's washing act and the disciples' responses in the dialogue between them. The account (13:1–38) consists of two parts:

---

53. Jesus utters that his washing of the disciples' feet is proper for those who have already bathed. Martinus C. de Boer claims that Jesus did not wash Judas's feet, and so rectified the discrepancy between John 13:2, 10b–11 and 18:21–30 (Boer, "Jesus' Departure," 285). But 13:5, 12 makes clear that Judas was included in the twelve disciples (Mathew, *Johannine Footwashing*, 324). According to Thompson, Jesus's washing, which includes Judas the betrayer, reflects his love toward enemies (Thompson, "His Own Received Him Not," 264). More importantly, as Jesus says, "all have been clean," he excludes Judas Iscariot from the other disciples (15:3 and 17:19).

54. Cf. 20:19–31.

(1) Jesus's action (vv. 1–11) and (2) its interpretation (vv. 12–38).⁵⁵ John divides the narrative into these two parts by using prepositions of time: πρό and ὅτε (*before*, 13:1 and *when*, 13:12). Before the Passover, Jesus washes his disciples' feet. In that moment, they did not know what Jesus was doing (ἄρτι [*just now*]), but will understand its meaning "after these things" (μετὰ ταῦτα, 13:7). In contrast, after finishing the act and returning to the table, Jesus questions, "Do you know what I have done for you?" (13:12). For this different time situation, John contrasts ποιῶ . . . γνώσῃ (the present tense of *do* and the future tense of "know," v. 7) and γινώσκετε . . . πεποίηκα (the present tense of *know* and the perfect tense of *do*, v. 12).

In the first part (13:1–11), Jesus demonstrates his love and sacrificial life (his *part*, 13:1, 8) for his own people, the so-called purified and consecrated people, in that he died for them. Regarding the theme of death, John compares Jesus's "taking off of the garment" (τίθησιν τὰ ἱμάτια, 13:4) with "his receiving of the garment" (ἔλαβεν τὰ ἱμάτια αὐτοῦ, 13:12; 10:15 [the shepherd's death]). This latter expression is echoed in 19:23, 40. Technically, John places the "receiving of his garment" (ἔλαβον τὰ ἱμάτια αὐτοῦ) before Jesus's cross (19:23) with the "receiving of Jesus's body" (ἔλαβον τὸ σῶμα τοῦ Ἰησοῦ, 19:40). If this observation is correct, Jesus's expression of μετὰ ταῦτα ("after these things," v. 7) stresses that Ὅτε οὖν ("after therefore," v. 12) points out his death afterward. Additionally, the disciples' incomprehension of Jesus's act is "paralleled earlier in the gospel by two statements of the evangelist to the effect that the disciples did not understand at the time, but did so after Jesus's resurrection (2:22) or after his glorification (12:16)."⁵⁶ John deliberately draws attention to the disciples' understanding after Jesus's crucifixion and glorification (13:7, 19; 14:29 [later]).

In the second part (13:12–38), John articulates the language of life through the words *model, do, love,* or *follow* (13:15, 17, 34, 36 [37–38; cf. 21:18–19]). Especially, these words are bound with "washing one another's feet" (13:14). John parallels two phrases:

a. καὶ ὑμεῖς ὀφείλετε ἀλλήλων νίπτειν τοὺς πόδας (13:14b, "You also ought to wash one another's feet")

b. καὶ ὑμεῖς ἀγαπᾶτε ἀλλήλους (13:34b, "You must also love one another")

John draws a parallel between "washing one another's feet" and "loving one another." This comparison highlights that both purified individuals and consecrated communities of the disciples participate in Jesus's life by

---

55. Schnelle, "Recent Views of John's Gospel," 355–56.
56. Bauckham, "Did Jesus Wash," 420.

loving one another. Jesus's act represents his sacrificial death as the expression of love and service (3:16; 12:24-26), and the disciples follow his life-pattern (13:15, 34, 36). Culpepper's understanding is remarkable in that John interweaves the foot washing with the new commandment (love) in terms of the teaching the same meaning that is embodied through Jesus's crucifixion. Culpepper's idea is powerful because Jesus taught that his disciples should practice love and serve by externalizing Jesus's model (foot washing / love / die) so that others might realize that they are becoming his true disciples (13:35).[57] Accordingly, Jesus symbolizes his washing act in the form of a prediction in 13:1-11, while he accounts for the interpretation of the disciples' foot washing in 13:12-38. Although Judas's departure could be criterion for separating the scene of 13:1-30 from that of 13:31-38 (Ὅτε οὖν ἐξῆλθεν, v. 31), John's distinction between Judas and the other disciples begins with verses 1-2. Therefore, chapter 13 pays attention to Jesus's sacrificial death and its significance for the life of the disciples in the world (13:15, 34-35). His death accomplishes God's salvation of the world and reveals his love and truth. The disciples are saved not only to live eternal life by belonging to his "part" in the holy-relationship with God, but are also sent into the world in sanctification in order to participate in Jesus's mission. Within the frame of "as . . ., so . . ." and sending (13:16, 20), Jesus consecrates them into both life-witness and evangelism, which, in other words, embodies the discipleship of "model" and "follow" (13:15, 36).

THE SYMBOLIC MEANING OF JESUS'S FOOT-WASHING ACT (VV. 1-11)

Jesus washes (or purifies) the feet of "his own people" (13:1) and teaches them how to live his lifestyle in the community (τεκνία, "little children" [13:33; cf. 1:12]) according to his new commandment (13:15, 34-35; 14:15; 15:12). They are consecrated to Jesus (15:3), meaning that their union with the Father and the Son is in mutual indwelling (17:21). They form a new community by faith and truth (17:17-19; "the Spirit of the truth" [15:26]). This faith community is the significant goal of God's mission (3:16; 17:18; 20:21).[58] It is for this community that Jesus dies on the cross (12:24). I argue

---

57. Culpepper, "Johannine Hypodeigma," 146.

58. The mission of God has the purpose of establishing his own people through Jesus's death and faith. When Jesus incarnated in flesh, "his own people" did not accept him (John 1:11; 5:44-47), but those who do believe in him might become his new people (1:12). These new people are Jewish, Galilean, Samaritan, and Greek believers (2:23; 4:42, 45, 53; 12:20) (cf. for 10:16 ["other sheep"], see Estrada, *Pneumatology*, 43). They are born of water and the Spirit from above (3:3 [γεννηθῇ ἄνωθεν . . . οὐ δύναται

that Jesus's washing act symbolizes his sacrificial and self-giving death for the accomplishment of his exclusive mission for the purification and unity-relationship of the disciples with the holy God (12:50; 15:3; 17:17, 19; cf. 1:29; 3:16).

Jesus's Sacrificial and Self-Giving Death

When interpreting Jesus's foot washing, several scholars suggest that his action reflects the early church's ritual practice (Eucharist and baptism).[59] In the New Testament books, washing the body (bathing) is remarkably adjusted to washing of sins within the context of baptism, which refers to purification from sins, holiness, or righteousness, figuratively (1 Cor 6:11; Eph 5:26; Titus 3:5; Heb 10:22; 2 Pet 2:22). In particular, while the word λούω ("bath") means the washing of the body in Acts 9:37, 16:33, and 22:16 states that the washing of the body is associated with baptism. Luke's use of the word seems to have been prominent in his day.[60] However, the Johannine

---

ἰδεῖν τὴν βασιλείαν τοῦ θεοῦ] and 3:5 [γεννηθῇ ἐξ ὕδατος καὶ πνεύματος... οὐ δύναται εἰσελθεῖν εἰς τὴν βασιλείαν τοῦ θεοῦ]). Born from above parallels with born with water and Spirit. John states that living water is the Spirit (7:38–39). Jesus is the giver of living water and the Spirit to believers (3:15; 4:14; 20:22). He must be lifted up in order to give them eternal life (3:14–15; 10:10–11), who are Jesus's own people (10:26–28).

59. Whallon, "Pascha," 127; Erwin, *Encyclopedia*, 60; Jeremias, *Eucharistic Words*, 49, 82; Brown, *John XIII–XXI*, 561–62.

60. There are two different opinions of the foot washing. *Firstly*, Oscar Cullmann argues that this verse is evidence of the ongoing cleansing of the Eucharist (Cullmann, *Worship*, 109). For Cullmann, John 13:10 demonstrates that it is no longer necessary for a second baptism, but rather insists that the sacrament of the fellowship of love is repeated in the Eucharist; eventually, the foot washing incorporates the significance of baptism and the Eucharist (Cullmann, *Worship*, 108–9). In this respect, the foot washing suggests fellowship between he and the disciples, as realized in the early church. Similarly, Beasley-Murray conceivably focuses on the following significant question: "Why did the author omit all reference to the words of Jesus concerning the bread and wine in the Supper?" (Beasley-Murray, *John*, 225). This scholar claims that John intends not only to situate the bread and wine of the Lord's Supper in John 6, but to also "reproduce teaching that gave their meaning" in order to deliver the doctrine of the Eucharist to the Johannine community (Beasley-Murray, *John*, 225–26; cf. Lacomara, "Deuteronomy," 84). In a linguistic aspect, M. J. J. Menken clarifies the relationship between 6:31, 51c–58 and 13:18, observing John's intentional use of the verbs ἔδωκεν and φαγεῖν. As a result, according to Menken, it is inappropriate that John was not interested in sacraments (Menken, "Translation of Psalm," 65). Likewise, A. J. B. Higgins suggests the apologetic purpose of John against the miscomprehension of the Jews with respect to blood and flesh (the elements of sacrament) (Higgins, *Lord's Supper*, 76). Higgins's idea is conceivable because 6:52 presents the ignorance of the Jews. He goes on to argue that, even though baptism is carried out once to cleanse believers from their sin without a need for repeating, it is maintained by way of the Eucharist in terms of the purification of

Jesus's washing act does not clarify the baptismal meaning.⁶¹ Instead, the narrative is primarily engaged with Jesus's death for purification in 13:1.⁶²

First, Jesus's hour indicates his death (ἦλθεν αὐτοῦ ἡ ὥρα, "His hour had come," 13:1).⁶³ The term *his hour* (ὥρα) is a technical word used in

---

"post-baptismal sins" (Higgins, *Lord's Supper*, 84). *Secondly*, Rudolf Bultmann argues that the foot washing does not imply baptism, but rather that Jesus's practice of service through his disciples can be united with him in terms of fellowship (Bultmann, *Gospel of John*, 468, 470, 472). In a word, Bultmann emphasizes the lasting service of believers who were already purified by way of Jesus's words (15:3) (Bultmann, *Gospel of John*, 472, 473). Ernst Käsemann also insists that worship and sacraments do not occupy the crucial position of the Gospel of John; therefore, it is doubtful that some try to understand the event of the foot washing in terms of the Eucharist or baptism (Käsemann, *Testament of Jesus*, 32–33). In my opinion, Jesus's washing act primarily symbolizes his purification of the disciples and the world through his sacrifice regardless of the early churches' sacramental or ritual practices. At the same time, the narrative involves the ethical interpretation of Jesus's act for the faith community's life as Jesus's disciples.

61. Moloney, "Sacramental Reading," 238–39; Thomas, *Footwashing*, 177–84; John highlights the phrase Οὐχὶ πάντες καθαροί ἐστε (13:11) so that the members of the Johannine community might be baptized and be allowed to join the Eucharist ceremony, although none of them could participate in the eternal life-giving meal (Culpepper, *Anatomy*, 95; Koester; *World of Life*, 180). The First Epistle of John 2:19 supports this with a pivotal clue: "They went out from us, but none of them belonged to us." Brown explains this phrase by reciting Exodus 12:16 ("no servile work will you do") and 12:43 ("no foreigner will eat of the Passover") (Brown, *John I–XII*, 342). John makes it clear in 2:19 that the Johannine community had secessionists who rejected Jesus and the Father (16:3; 1 John 2:22–23). It is striking that these secessionists, like Judas, did not originally belong to Jesus's community, but rather to the ruler of the world (14:30–31; 17:9, 12, 15). This means that if Jesus's disciples listen to his word and follow his new commandments, they need not need be afraid of situations in which they cannot physically see Jesus, as they can overcome the world because they have already participated in Jesus's water and blood (1 John 5:4–6; cf. 1 Cor 11:23).

62. Additionally, Tertullian mentions the foot washing in *de Corona* chapter 8 ("admitting indeed that we use along with others these articles") (Tertullian, "Chaplet," 85). This record means that some early churches continued to undertake the practice, interpreting the act as the service of the servant or of the serving life.

63. Schnackenburg, *Gospel according to St John*, 3:12, 23. Jesus's "hour" indicates the incident ("before it takes place," [13:19, πρὸ τοῦ γενέσθαι]). John writes two more verses, explaining that before that time comes, Jesus will give his disciples faith. In 14:29, Jesus repeats a similar phrase of καὶ νῦν εἴρηκα ὑμῖν πρὶν γενέσθαι, ἵνα ὅταν γένηται πιστεύσητε ("and now I have told you before it happens, so that when it takes place you might believe"). The same is also done in 16:4, ἀλλὰ ταῦτα λελάληκα ὑμῖν ἵνα ὅταν ἔλθῃ ἡ αρα αὐτῶν μνημονεύητε αὐτῶν ὅτι ιγὼ εἶπον ὑμῖν. What these expressions have in common is that Jesus prepares his disciples for their future in both. However, these verses have contextual differences: (1) 13:19 in Jesus's foot-washing act and Judas's betrayal, (2) 14:29 in the context of God's giving of the Holy Spirit, and (3) 16:4 in the context of the future persecution (Bernard, *Exegetical Commentary*, 468–69). Hence, the event in 13:19 is different than those in 14:29 and 16:4, as Jesus implies in his washing the disciples' feet. This event is primarily about death, and the disciples who have

John's Gospel. Although the hour in 13:1 refers to Jesus's *return* to the Father (13:3b),[64] it is certainly involved with his crucifixion (for death, 2:4; 12:23 [καιρὸς 7:6, 8]; for ascension, 13:1 [cf. for the eschatological future and present, 5:25, 28; cf. 12:32–33]).[65]

In 8:28, Jesus says, "when you have lifted up the son of the man" (Ὅταν ὑψώσητε τὸν υἱὸν τοῦ ἀνθρώπου). Here, the expression ὑψόω ("lift up") means that his death will make him known to the people. John develops the use of the hour for Jesus's death and resurrection in 13:7, 19 (μετὰ ταῦτα ["after these things"] and ὅταν γένηται ["when it takes place"]), linking the foot-washing narrative to Jesus's *being lifted up* by paying attention to the time in which the disciples will know Jesus or will believe in him. Above all, John clarifies the meaning of the phrase "his hour" in 7:30 (ἡ ὥρα αὐτοῦ). His hour is directly linked with the phrase ζητέω + ἀποκτεῖναι, which is used seven times (5:18; 7:1, 11, 19, 20, 25 with 30 [8:37, 40]). This hour is indicative of Jesus's death in the situation in which the unbelieving Jews' attempt to kill him. Jesus declares that his *being lifted up* is the hour of his *glory* and crucifixion (12:23–24, 32–34). At the same, the time of Jesus's return is associated with his death and resurrection.[66] John juxtaposes *hour* and *end* (τέλος) (13:1), which occurs in 19:30 (τετέλεσται); consequently, John stresses that Jesus's event points to his death. Robert H. Gundry makes it explicit that John 19:28 and 30 are directly connected to 13:1 in terms of Jesus's fulfillment of works, signs, and words.[67] Through both the foot washing and his teachings, Jesus anticipates his death, resurrection, and ascension. Accordingly, Jesus's departure to the Father presupposes his death

---

a "part" with him follow him in the way of death (13:8, 36–37 and 21:18–21). Jesus's crucifixion is for his flock, and gives it eternal life (10:11, 18, 28–29; 11:51–52; 12:24, 32–34; 21:15–17). In other words, his sacrificial death is the fulfillment of God's mission, and at the same time is a witness that reveals God.

64. Jesus's "hour to return" in 13:1 implies that he will depart to the Father after he completes the goal of his sentness. His mission is clarified through Jesus's saying on the cross ("it is completed," 19:30 [cf. εἰδὼς ὁ Ἰησοῦς ὅτι ἤδη πάντα τετέλεσται, John 19:28]). In John 13:3, Jesus's return (πρὸς τὸν θεὸν ὑπάγει) is associated with his coming from the Father (ἀπὸ θεοῦ ἐξῆλθεν). This pair of sending language reflects that Jesus's foot-washing narrative exists throughout the entire flow of John's Gospel. John also repeats this paired language in 16:27b–28 (ἐγὼ παρὰ [τοῦ] θεοῦ ἐξῆλθον. ἐξῆλθον παρὰ τοῦ πατρὸς καὶ ἐλήλυθα εἰς τὸν κόσμον· πάλιν ἀφίημι τὸν κόσμον καὶ πορεύομαι πρὸς τὸν πατέρα. Here, the phrase παρὰ [τοῦ] θεοῦ ἐξῆλθον is expressed in 8:42 (ἐγὼ γὰρ ἐκ τοῦ θεοῦ ἐξῆλθον), in which John identifies coming with being sent (ἔγνωσαν ἀληθῶς ὅτι παρὰ σοῦ ἐξῆλθον, καὶ ἐπίστευσαν ὅτι σύ με ἀπέστειλας [17:8b]).

65. Paschal, "Sacramental Symbolism," 157n18, 170; Köstenberger, *John*, 471.

66. Hays, *Gospels*, 334.

67. Gundry, "New Wine," 292–96.

on the cross for many people's lives (12:24–25, 32–34).⁶⁸ This salvific event must be completed before his return to the Father (13:1 and 19:30).

Second, the main character of the story proves the connection of Jesus's act and his death event (Ἰούδας Ἰσκαριώτου and παραδίδωμι, "Judas of Iscariot" and "hand over," 13:2). John repeats his description of Judas Iscariot as the betrayer who hands Jesus over to death (6:71 with 7:1; 12:4 with 12:7; 13:2; cf. 18:2–5⁶⁹). In the foot washing, John forms an *inclusio* as to Jesus's death as the result of Judas's betrayal, which clarifies the relationship between Judas as a betrayer and Jesus as a sacrifice.⁷⁰ In this structure, Judas's action (παραδίδωμι) is antithetical to that of Jesus. This use manifests the author's intention (cf. 10:17, 18, "Jesus gives up his life" [ἐγὼ τίθημι τὴν ψυχήν μου and ἐξουσίαν ἔχω θεῖναι αὐτήν]), and the author tries to demonstrate that Jesus's death is not passive. That is, Judas Iscariot was not the one who handed Jesus over to death (παραδίδωμι, 6:71; 7:1; 12:4; 18:2–5; or by Pilate, 19:16).⁷¹ Rather, he gave himself over (παραδίδωμι) to death (19:30; cf. 10:18) through the hands of Judas and Pilate under the authority of the Father (δίδωμι, 13:3 with 26–27 and 19:9). In particular, Jesus gave "a dipped piece of a bread" to Judas Iscariot in the foot-washing narrative (13:26, 30). If this piece symbolizes Jesus's flesh (6:39 with 13:1; 6:51–54), his gift symbolizes his handing over of himself to Judas Iscariot (13:27, 30; and 6:70–71; 7:1).⁷² Accordingly, John's technical words hand over and give indicate Jesus's sacrificial death between chapters 13 and 19.

Third, Jesus's authority is performed for his death (πάντα ἔδωκεν αὐτῷ ὁ πατὴρ εἰς τὰς χεῖρας, "The Father had given all things into his hands," 13:3). This phrase appears in 3:35 (ὁ πατὴρ . . . πάντα δέδωκεν ἐν τῇ χειρὶ αὐτοῦ). The Son can give eternal life to believers and judge unbelievers (cf. 5:27). In 17:2, Jesus has authority over all flesh and can give it eternal life (ἔδωκας αὐτῷ ἐξουσίαν πάσης σαρκός). More importantly, this authority includes Jesus's right to lay his own life down, as well as to take it back again

---

68. Käsemann, *Testament of Jesus*, 19; Cory, "Wisdom's Rescue," 114; Hamilton, *God's Indwelling Presence*, 88.

69. This passage does not include the term Ἰσκαριώτου, but does belong to the story of Jesus's trial and death.

70. Orchard, *Courting Betrayal*, 170.

71. Παραδίδωμι is John's technical term for Judah of Iscariot (6:64, 71; 12:4; 13:2, 11, 21; 18:2, 5; 21:20), the unbelieving Jews and religious authorities (18:30, 35, 36; 19:11), and Pilate (19:16). However, the most significant usage is that the subject of Παραδίδωμι is Jesus in 19:30. Namely, Jesus's death is his choice. He fulfills the work of the Sender (19:30).

72. Brown and Moloney, *Interpreting the Gospel*, 264.

(10:18).⁷³ Eventually, Jesus uses this right to willingly die for the nation (18:14 with 11:50-52; 19:10 [cf. 18:6]). Therefore, 13:3 points to the exercise of his authority at the moment of death that the Father gives to him.

Fourth, Jesus's actions in the process of washing his disciples' feet implies his crucifixion (τίθησιν τὰ ἱμάτια καὶ λαβὼν λέντιον διέζωσεν ἑαυτόν, "[Jesus] laid down his outer garments, and taking a towel, tied it around himself" [13:4]). The expression of τίθησιν τὰ ἱμάτια ("lays down the outer garments") is connected to the scene of soldiers' ἔλαβον τὰ ἱμάτια αὐτοῦ ("took his garments," 19:23). They took his garment, but ultimately Jesus handed it over to them as a way of surrendering himself to the crucifixion (19:10, 11, 23, 30). Brown concentrates on the verbs τίθησιν ("lay down," 13:4) and λαβὼν ("take up or receive," John 13:12; 10:17, 18), as these terms indicate the death of Jesus by portraying the motion of taking up the robe and life.⁷⁴ Surely, John utilizes terms like "laid down" (13:4) and "took up" (13:12) in order to connect his symbolic behavior with his self-giving death on the cross. John uses the identical term of lay down for both the Good Shepherd (10:11, 15, 17, 18) and Lazarus (11:34) when referring to their deaths.⁷⁵ In the foot-washing narrative, Jesus's act of washing the feet subordinates his motions (τίθημι and λαμβάνω ["lay down" and "take up," 10:11, 15, 17, 18; 13:4]). Additionally, Jesus's washing of the disciples' feet would be understood as an act of servanthood, to which people were accustomed in the first century (13:8).⁷⁶ Schnackenburg observes that Jesus's taking off and putting on of his outer garment implies humble service, and at the same time is relevant to the message of his laying down and taking up his life (10:17).⁷⁷ In 12:24-26, Jesus ties the matter of death to that of service (διακονέω, "serve"). In regards to this idea, John already informed readers of a washing act in preparation for Jesus's death by paralleling ἐκμάσσω ("wipe dry") in 12:3 (cf. 11:2) and 13:5. Chapter 12:1-8 is involved with the commemorational deed of Jesus's burial (12:7), placing aside the concept of helping the poor (12:8). The disciples could not understand the meaning of the act until they saw Jesus's resurrection from the dead (12:16). As Mary commemorates Jesus's death (12:7), Jesus himself indicates that his death cleanses the disciples (13:10).

73. Ridderbos, *Gospel of John*, 458.
74. Brown, *John I–XII*, 551.
75. Ridderbos, *Gospel of John*, 137.
76. Malina, *Windows*, 40; Keener, *Gospel of John*, 908; Mathew, *Johannine Footwashing*, 374; Herodotus mentions in his book *Erato* (*The History of Herodotus*) that the captive women had to wash the feet of the long-haired (the Persians) (σαὶ δ' ἄλοχοι πολλοῖσι πόδας νίψουσι κομήταις, 6.19.2).
77. Schnackenburg, *Gospel according to St John*, 2:384; 3:17–18.

Fifth, as John testifies to Jesus's dialogue with Peter in 13:6–9, 24 (as opposed to the description of Judas Iscariot in 13:2, 18, 21, 26–30), he contains the anticipation of Peter's denial within the parallel structure of 13:21–30 and 13:36–38.[78] In sharp contrast to Judas's treachery, Peter will later follow him (ἀκολουθήσεις δὲ ὕστερον, 13:36).[79] Here, the term "follow" refers to death, to which glory is subsequent.[80] While Jesus forbade him (13:36, 38), he mentions in 21:19–20 that Peter will follow him by dying. Peter's death is equivalent to Jesus's death in that both glorify God (13:31–32). John already describes Peter's following of Jesus's sacrifice as bound with Jesus's action of tying a towel around his own waist (13:4); διαζώννυμι ("tie around") is cognately associated with Peter's death (ζώννυμι ["tie a belt around"], 21:18*2).[81] After Jesus's crucifixion and resurrection, Peter will be able to follow him (ὕστερον, "afterward").

In short, these five points show that the foot-washing narrative primarily deals with Jesus's sacrificial and self-giving death on a cross. The Father sent the Son in order to give the world eternal life (3:16–18). The Son fulfills his mission as service (12:24–26, διάκονος), namely through his sacrificial death (13:1, 3).[82]

Purification and Relationship of Unity with the Disciples

The purpose of Jesus's foot-washing narrative is to explain the meaning of his sacrificial death (13:19; 20:31). Through death, Jesus allows believers to

---

78. Interestingly, Judas does not participate in this dialogue with Jesus.

79. Peter asks a question, "Where are you going?" He will go to the Father (7:34–36 and 13:33, 36). However, Jesus protests that nobody questions about where he goes in 16:5, which points to the distinction between 13:36 and 16:5. While the former concentrates on the time of Jesus's death, the latter associates with the time of his ascension. Therefore, although these chapters both deal with Jesus's farewell, the focus of each is different (Thompson, *John*, 295–98).

80. Barrett, *Gospel according to St. John*, 453.

81. Louw and Nida, *Greek-English Lexicon*, 525.

82. Brown, *John XIII–XXI*, 564. In John's Gospel, the verb *serve* (διακονέω) emerges from 12:2, 26 (*2). These cases are engaged in the people's service for Jesus. In contrast, the verb δουλεύω (8:33) indicates the Jews' status as the servants of sin (8:34). In the case of the nouns διάκονος (2:5, 9; 12:26) and δοῦλος (4:51; 8:33, 34, 35; 13:16; 15:15*2, 20; 18:10*2; 18, 26), John uses the former for servants or people, who serve Jesus and know him, and the latter for the ordinary servants, who are subject to the master (4:51; 8:34–35; 13:16; 18:10, 18, 26) and do not know his will (15:15). Jesus's disciples must be his friends who know the master's will (15:15), although they are never greater than the master in the relationship between the Sender and the Sent (13:16).

"share *part* in him" by purifying them, which means their unity-relationship with God (13:8).

Purification

Jesus's washing of the disciples' feet with water signifies the twofold dimension of purification (cf. 1 John 1:9, "ἀφῇ ἡμῖν τὰς ἁμαρτίας καὶ καθαρίσῃ ἡμᾶς ἀπὸ πάσης ἀδικίας").[83] In the first dimension, his washing act is meant to cleanse people from their sins by way of death (13:10; cf. Ezek 36:25, 33; 37:23).[84] The author uses three cases of the water-motif in the whole Gospel.[85] One of them is the purification ceremony. In the beginning of the story, John pays attention to water in contrast to the Jewish purification ceremony. God sent John the Baptist to baptize people with water (1:26, 29, 33). John's baptism causes a debate between Jews and his disciples about the purification ceremony (3:25). The Jews would have two traditions.

   a. It is required that priests or the Israelites perform a purification rite to advance to God (Lev 16:24 [17:16]; Exod 30:18-20). In particular, the priests must wash their hands and feet before

---

83. In 1 John, the author matches forgiving with cleansing.

84. The foot washing means that the disciples are cleansed from their sins through his blood. R. E. Brown observes that "in the Book of Glory the Last Supper and the Discourse that precede the action of glorification serve to interpret that action. The foot washing in 13 dramatically acts out the significance of Jesus's death—it is a death that cleanses the disciples and gives them a heritage with him" (Brown, *John XIII-XXI*, 542).

85. Other two cases are: *First*, John uses the water-motif as a symbolic meaning for eternal water or to the Holy Spirit. In the conversation with the Samaritan woman, water for eternal life is linked to worship, and in the scene of Jesus's invitation to living water, living water refers to the Holy Spirit (John 4:14; 7:37-39). Those who receive living water are residing in the Spirit, whom God gives through Jesus (14:16, 26; 20:22). In Jer 17:12-13; Ezek 47:1-12; and Zech 14:8, God himself becomes a spring of water or the fulfillment of the promise of water flowing from the temple or from Jerusalem (cf. Isa 49:10; 55:1). John says in 4:14 that the water he gives becomes a spring of water. The water points to the Holy Spirit at 7:38-39. Obviously, this concept is different from the meaning of water for washing in chapter 13. Nonetheless, John is to emphasize that the blood and water of Jesus first purify anyone's sins so that they can live with the holy God. The author of the Gospel places the water-motif for purification or consecration along with the water imagery as the Holy Spirit in the literary context of the Gospel (4:14; 7:38-39). *Second*, John highlights the pool of Siloam (9:1-12). A blind man is sent to wash his eyes. This scene draws attention to the Sender. With the emphasis that he opens the blind man's eyes, John insists that Jesus or the blind are not sinners, but ironically, the Jews' sins remain (9:7, 11, 16, 25, 31-34, 41). The washing story of the blind man is related to Jesus's judgment of unbelievers' sins in the context of debating over who is a sinner(s). The subsequent chapter shows that Jesus is the light setting his disciples free from the bondage of sin (8:12, 31-36).

entering the Tent of Meeting (Exod 30:17–21; cf. Yoma 3:3 [for the high priests' regular cleanness for Yom Kippur]; Ps 26:6 [for a person's vindication of innocence]).

b. The Jews should wash their hands before a meal like bread (Berakhot 53b), or they had to wash their hands before the service (Berakhot 15a; cf. Matt 15:1–2; Luke 11:38).

Among them, the first one is similar to John's use. The author highlights the purification ceremony for entering into the presence of God rather than their eating of food. The Jews prepare for their participation in the temple festivals (11:55; cf. 2:6; 3:25). In addition, John's cases are different from a regular meal ceremony in that Jesus and his followers are already in the middle of a meal (2:3; 12:2; 13:4). Therefore, if John makes use of the water-motif for purification or consecration, his washing of the disciples' feet seems to prepare them for standing in front of God. However, John goes on to develop the idea of abiding in or mutual indwelling in chapter 15. This notion also ties to holiness or sanctification (15:3; 17:23). That is, John describes that Jesus washes or consecrates his disciples to be united with himself and the holy God in life (14:20; 15:3–6; 17:11, 19). Eventually, Jesus's washing the feet of the disciples with water implies purification or consecration for their union with God in Jesus.

While illustrating the water-motif, the author repeatedly talks about the subject of death or resurrection.[86] Jesus's death bears the meaning of the sacrifice of God's lamb to remove the sins of the world (1:29). However, a question arises: does John's purification idea include the cleanness of sin? Strictly speaking, it is not clear in the Gospel whether the water-motif has a direct connection with the cleansing of sin. The baptism accounts or narratives of water do not mention the purification of sin (1:29; 3:22–26; 4:1–2 and 2:1–11; 4:6–14; 5:2–9; 7:37–39; 9:7–11; 13:1–14; 19:34). Nevertheless, it cannot be denied that John implies Jesus's washing of the world's sins through his death because of two reasons.

Firstly, John parallels the phrase ὑμεῖς καθαροί ἐστε ("you are clean," 13:10) with the phrase ἤδη ὑμεῖς καθαροί ἐστε ("you are already clean," 15:3).[87] Within the context of the narrative, Jesus's washing signifies his

---

86. E.g., "water (baptism)," 1:29; 2:7; 3:23, 26; 4:6, 14, 46; 5:3; 7:38; 9:7, 11; 13:5; 19:34; 21:11–12; "blood," 6:54; "death or resurrection," 2:21–22; 3:14; 4:47, 50, 53; 5:21–30, 54, 56; 7:19, 25; 8:20, 21–24, 28, 34; 10:11, 15, 17, 18; 11:24–25, 13, 44, 50–52; 12:7, 24, 32–34; 13:36–37; 18:32; 19:30–37; 21:18–22.

87. John uses the term "wash" in the narrative of the born blind man (9:6–7, 11). The narrative is irrelevant to the matter of the individuals' private sin (9:2–3). Rather, the washing of the man's eyes is associated with the matter of "seeing" or "knowing" (9:12; 10:36, 38). People, who are in sin and darkness, cannot see Jesus and God (9:40–41;

people's purification (cf. Exod 30:17-21; 40:31-32; Zech 13:1).[88] When his act symbolizes his death on the cross (John 19:34), the sacrifice is given for the people (10:11; 11:51-52; 12:24; 17:17).[89] Even from the beginning of the story, John premises that Jesus is God's Lamb designed to take away the world's sin and to be slain for the sake of the people (1:29, 36; 10:11; 11:51-52; 12:24). John describes Jesus's death as a paschal sacrifice within the context of the Passover (12:1 [11:53, 57]; 18:28, 39; 19:14, 32, 36).[90] Although John modifies συντρίβω ("break into pieces or crush") from an active verb into a passive verb, he recites Exodus 12:46 (ὀστοῦν οὐ συντρίψετε ἀπ' αὐτοῦ [LXX]; cf. Num 9:12) in John 19:36 (Ὀστοῦν οὐ συντριβήσεται αὐτοῦ).[91] The author portrays Jesus's death as the sacrifice whose death saves his own people (13:1; 11:49-53; 18:8-9, 19) and initiates the birth of the new people (20:17).[92] Above all, as observed in the chapter 2 of this study, one of the purposes of the Passover sacrifices is for the washing of the people's sins. Jesus cleanses his people from sins to restore them to the holy-relationship with God.

Secondly, John accounts for Jesus's death in the scheme of God's eschatological promise and fulfillment (2:21; 7:38; 19:34; [10:11, 15, 17; 12:24] 20:22). John cites Zechariah 12:10 at the scene of Jesus's death (John 19:37). If John is mindful of Zechariah's prophecy in account for Jesus's "being pierced his side," it can be assumed that water flowing from Jesus's body is

---

12:35; cf. *Tob* 5:10; 14:10) (Hahn, *Mission*, 138; Beale, *Temple*, 177, 199). By contrast, as Jesus washes the blind man's eyes so that he can see both himself and the Father, he purifies people so that they can live in light (8:12; 9:37-38; 12:36). The author recalls John the Baptist's saying of Jesus in the end of the blind man's story. The phrase "everything John said about this man was true" (10:41) recalls John the Baptist's declaration, "the Lamb of God to take away the sin of the world" (1:29).

88. Barrett, *Gospel according to St. John*, 556-57; cf. Barrett proposes that John amended the story of the foot washing from the synoptic account of Jesus as ὁ διακονῶν (Luke 22:27). Chapter 13 verses 1-30 is a special section which connotes that Jesus's sacrificial blood cleanses his disciples from their sins (1:29; 19:34), just as he washed the disciples' feet (Barrett, *Gospel according to St. John*, 436).

89. Mlakuzhyil, *Christocentric Literary Structure*, 325.

90. Barrett, *Gospel according to St. John*, 410-11; Jones, *Symbol of Water*, 151.

91. Higgins, *Lord's Supper*, 85.

92. With regard to the birth of God's eschatological community, D. A. Carson understands the fulfillment of Jesus for "the paschal role of head of the family" by highlighting the unique term of John τεκνία, except for seven times found in 1 John (cf. Gal 4:19). This idea supports that Jesus sets up his family-community through his death, resurrection, and the Holy Spirit ("regeneration," 3:3, 6), and becomes the head of the community (cf. Eph 4:15-16) (Carson, *Gospel according to John*, 483). This community contains "God's children" who are dispersed (τὰ τέκνα τοῦ θεοῦ, 11:52). Jesus lays down his life for his own people (10:3, 4), as God's children who believe in him and the Father (1:10-12 and 13:1, 19-20), by loving them to the end.

resonant with Zechariah's "fountain" (John 19:34; Zech 13:1). Zechariah's water-motif illustrates that God will cleanse the sin and defilement of both the house of David and inhabitants of Jerusalem. Here, washing or purifying "sin" (חַטָּאת) and "uncleanness" (נִדָּה) with water primarily has a similarity of consecrating the priests and Israelites with water (Num 19:9, 13, 20, 21). Their cleansing and consecrating act symbolizes that they make themselves holy for YHWH's possession (Ezek 36:22-28; Zech 13:1-2, 9 [cf. Lev 20:24; Ezra 9:11b]. If "blood" and "water" in the place of Jesus's crucifixion imply the imagery of washing away Israel's sin and impurity, then Jesus's washing act, which connotes his death, might refer to washing or consecrating people's sin to make them holy for God's possession. This reflects their reciprocal holy union (John 13:1; 17:6, 11; Zech 2:10–13; and John 1:14; 20:19).

In the second dimension of purification, Jesus's death is bound with the concept of "forgiveness" (ἀφίημι), which appears in 20:23. John uses the term to mean "depart from" and "release" from sins within the frame of Jesus's eschatological salvation, rather than in the scheme of repentance and forgiveness of sins (cf. Luke 24:47).[93] Jesus allows sinners to depart from and be released from the servanthood of sin in darkness so that they might become children of the light (8:34; 9:41; 12:36; 20:23).[94] In the water-motif narrative of Siloam in 9:1–41, John links the washing narrative of the blind man with the theme of forgiveness and retainment of sins. First of all, the author clarifies the nature of forgiveness by describing Jesus's declaration that the sin of unbelievers "remains" (μένει, 9:41 with 20:23b [κρατέω, "retain"], 8:31; 9:36–37 [9:27], 13:35). That is, freedom from sin means that the children of the light have God's words, or the truth (8:31–32; 12:36, 50). In this sense, John's term ἐλευθερόω ("set free") matches with the concept of "forgiveness" (ἀφίημι) (8:32, 33, 36).[95] When anyone becomes Jesus's disciple, they are set free from sin by the truth (8:31). This truth allows sinners to be consecrated in order to live in unity with God (17:14–19; cf. Isa 55:7). As a result, Jesus's purification of his disciples brings them into the holy relationship with the Father and himself, in which they might have this part of life in Jesus (13:8; 17:19–26). They no longer belong to the world, but rather belong to God through Jesus, who has all authority and protects them from evil until the end (13:3a with 17:2; 13:1, 12; 17:15).

In short, in the foot-washing narrative, Jesus's washing act symbolizes his cleansing of people's sin and releasing them from sins (forgiveness) to erect his consecrated community (15:3; 17:23). Those who are washed will

---

93. Brown, *John XIII–XXI*, 1040.
94. Ridderbos, *Gospel of John*, 645.
95. Emerton, "Binding," 329–30.

be clean and share Jesus's life in mutual indwelling. This concept should be understood in the same context as that believers are free or released (forgiven) from sin to live in him (8:31–34; 20:23).

Relationship of Unity

Jesus's purification makes the unity-relationship between him and the disciples. This relationship means that through his death as a sacrifice, Jesus allows the disciples to share his "part," or "side" (μέρος, 13:8).[96] The term μέρος points not only to the disciples' participation in Jesus's death, but also resides in his life.[97] They must dwell in his nature and way of life in the unity-relationship. Their lives are ones of witness that follow Jesus, and they should share his portion as his sacrificial death, or life-pattern, in love and humble service (21:18–21 and 22–23). For this reason, Jesus gives the Spirit to the disciples so that they might live in both he and the Father after the resurrection (John 14:12–21; 20:22).[98]

John interweaves the disciples' participation in Jesus's *part* or *share* with the inevitability of Jesus's washing of the disciples' feet. This indicates that the disciples' cleanness and purification are connected with their unity with Jesus, or their dwelling in him (14:20).[99] They might share Jesus with the Holy Spirit to make fruits (14:16–17, 21). Contrary to this, Judas Iscariot shares Satan's thinking and activity, although he still receives a piece of bread from Jesus (13:2, 26–27).[100] This distinction matches with that of one

---

96. Coloe, *Dwelling*, 124–25.

97. Thompson, "His Own Received Him Not," 272.

98. Cf. Chennattu suggests that μερὶς should interrelate with חֵלֶק (Num 18:20 MT; μερὶς LXX) in allusion to the "God-given portion of the land, but in the second part, God becomes the נַחֲלָה for Aaron and his family members. To have a נַחֲלָה with God implies accepting God as their possession or inheritance. This status can prevail with Yahweh, 'You shall be my people and I shall be your God (Ezek 36:28)'" (Chennattu, *Johannine Discipleship*, 95).

99. Bauckham, "Did Jesus Wash," 415.

100. John describes that Judas received a morsel of bread, concluding that he finished his death as a paschal lamb (John 19:36; Exod 12:46; Num 9:12) (Higgins, *Lord's Supper*, 77; Koester, *World of Life*, 113–17). Interestingly, John does not mention a lamb at the supper before the Passover (Luke 22:1–7; cf. Matt 26:17–18; Mark 14:12) (Whallon, "Pascha," 128). This is why Jesus replaced the morsel of bread that was given to Judas with his flesh within the context of his vicarious physical death. Orchard highlights the quotation of Psalm 41:9 in John 13:18 (Ὁ τρώγων μου τὸν ἄρτον ἐπῆρεν ἐπ' ἐμὲ τὴν πτέρναν αὐτοῦ) in terms of the prediction's fulfillment (18:2–5) (Orchard, *Courting Betrayal*, 171–72). His impressive observation is that John parallels Ὁ τρώγων μου τὸν ἄρτον (13:18) with ὁ τρώγων μου τὴν σάρκα (6:54, 56), so as to make it evident that the morsel of bread given to Judas is connected with the destruction of Jesus's flesh because of Judas's betrayal.

part belonging to Jesus's kingdom and the other part belonging to this world (19:36, 37). The former who shares Jesus's *side* or *part* might belong to God and his death, life, and glory (17:14; 13:31–38 with 21:18–23), while the latter kills Jesus by not being part of his circle of disciples. John clarifies Judas's separation from Jesus's side by comparing the phrase μετὰ τῶν μαθητῶν αὐτοῦ (Jesus and "with his disciples") with the phrase μετ' αὐτῶν (Judas and "with them [soldiers and some officials]") in 17:12; 18:2 and 18:5.[101] Judas betrays Jesus by loving money, and he belongs to Satan, even though he received a piece of bread from Jesus (13:26–30). While the disciples are cleansed by Jesus, Judas remains in the sin of the world (8:44). By this, he was excluded from Jesus's purification.

Jesus enables believers to live the pattern of a new life according to his model (13:15) and new commandment (13:14, 34–35). Jesus might abide in them in a mutual relationship (chs. 13–17, 20) so as to make fruits of the vine (13:34–35 with 15:1–27; cf. Ps 80).[102] Their mutual indwelling imagery is bound with the concept of a shared life with Jesus in the Holy Spirit (14:26). Rekha M. Chennattu aptly observes that the wine and the branches in John 15 figuratively indicate the relationship between Jesus and his disciples in life.[103] That is, Jesus allows the disciples to reside in him (15:4–7) in order to keep the new commandment of love (vv. 9–17). Therefore, Jesus's purpose of purification is not only to enable people to dwell in him, but to also form the unity-relationship between them and God (ἁγιάζω 17:17, 19; αὐτοὶ ἐν ἡμῖν ὦσιν, 17:21).

Furthermore, Jesus's washing the feet of the disciples entails the meaning of the disciples' ongoing purification, through which he allows them to live in mutual indwelling, or in the unity-relationship by purifying them (13:34–35; 15:2, 3–8; 17:23; cf. Lev 20:26). In the foot-washing narrative, the focus is on the statement: Ὁ λελουμένος οὐκ ἔχει χρείαν [εἰ μὴ τοὺς πόδας] νίψασθαι (NA28) (John 13:10, "the one who has been bathed does

---

101. "The Jews" who reject Jesus (8:21–22; cf. 7:1, 19–20, 30; 8:37, 40) are of the devil (8:44, 47) and must die in their sins (9:41; 8:24, 26). Catherine Cory observes that "the phrase 'You will die in your sins' is used in the LXX to refer to the fool who refuses wisdom (Prov 24:7–10) or to the unrepentant wicked person (Ezek 3:18–19). In the Fourth Gospel, sin is the circumstance of one's refusal to believe, after having heard the words and having seen the work that Jesus does (John 9:34; 15:24; 16:9)" (Cory, "Wisdom's Rescue," 110n28).

102. Brown, *John XIII–XXI*, 557; Paschal, "Sacramental Symbolism," 171–72; Jesus makes the new covenant with his disciples as presented in the Synoptic Gospels (Mark 14:24; Luke 22:20; Matt 26:28), which allude to "my blood of the covenant" and "the fruit of the vine" (τό γένημα τῆς ἀμπέλου, Mark 14:24–25; Luke 22:18, 20; Matt 26:28–29).

103. Chennattu, *Johannine Discipleship*, 85.

not need to allow himself to be washed" [except for his feet] [translated by Wallace).[104] John utilizes two words for washing: λούω and νίπτω. However, with regard to a reading of the phrase (εἰ μὴ τοὺς πόδας νίψασθαι), a critical question is whether the author equates λούω and νίπτω. The former word is used for washing (bathing) the entire body nine times (in the New Testament, John 13:10; Acts 9:37; 16:33; 22:16; 1 Cor 6:11; Eph 5:26; Titus 3:5; Heb 10:22; 2 Pet 2:22), while the latter is engaged in washing a part of the body, such as the hands or face (Matt 6:17; 15:2, 20; 27:24; Mark 7:2, 3; John 9:7, 11, 15; 13:5, 6, 8, 10, 12, 14; 1 Tim 5:10).[105] This distinction between two terms is clear throughout the Old Testament (LXX). In particular, in Leviticus 15:10-12, 16, the translator makes use of these words distinctively: λούω for the body, and either νίπτω or πλύνω for hands, feet, or clothes. He associates λούω with the concept of "fully being purified" (Lev 15:8-13, 16; λούσεται τὸ σῶμα αὐτοῦ ὕδατι, 16:24 [LXX]), but not with "partially being washed" (cf. *De somniis* 1.148). If the use of these two words is different in Greek, then washing (bathing) of the entire body is separate from the washing of the disciples' feet. However, although it is necessary to acknowledge that these two terms are each typically used for a particular case (the whole body or hands and feet), those words have no difference in meaning (for holiness, Ex 29:4; 40:12-13; Lev 16:4, 24; 2 Chron 4:6; for washing of sin(s), Lev 15:11, 13 and Deut 21:6-8; Isa 1:16; Ezek 16:4, 9; Pss [LXX] 25:6; 57:11; 72:13), and indicate the foot washing in John 13.[106] In other words, even though John employs the use of λούω for the entire body as a parallel for the washing of feet (13:10, 14), he intends to signify the same meaning of λούω and νίπτω in 13:10 (purification or consecration).[107] If so, Jesus's washing of the disciples' feet, who are already bathed, means their continuous consecration of the faith community in the world. They must live Jesus's life in the unity-relationship with the holy God (17:11, 19; cf. 1 John 1:9; 2:1, 2)[108]

104. Wallace, *Greek Grammar*, 427n54; The representative reading, albeit peculiar, is the text of Tertullian Origen: οὐκ ἔχει χρείαν νίψασθαι (Metzger, *Textual Commentary*, 240). Origen Augustine, syr[h,pal], byz Let Cyril, Chrysostom, and D it[d] have an analogous reading, even though they have different forms (Thomas, *Footwashing*, 19-25). These readings do not contain the phrase εἰ μὴ τοὺς πόδας; by contrast, P[66] and P[75] include this expression. Despite a discussion about the date of the papyrus, these sources were likely written between the second and third centuries. In this study, I accept the reading of P[66] and P[75], except for the adverb μονον, depending on the reading of NA[28].

105. See Metzger and Mathew's study (Metzger, *Textual Commentary*, 204; Mathew, *Johannine Footwashing*, 41-45).

106. Schnackenburg, *Gospel according to St John*, 3:21.

107. Barrett, *Gospel according to St. John*, 442; Beasley-Murray, *John*, 234.

108. Carson, *Gospel according to John*, 465-66; Morris, *Gospel according to John*, 550.

The author highlights that the disciples are continually clean by Jesus (13:10; 15:2). This way makes them live in Jesus and fruits (15:4–5).

In short, chapter 13 is the beginning of John's second section (chs. 13–21), which constitutes Jesus's redemptive events and farewell for his disciples during his absence. The foot-washing narrative is engaged in the symbolic meaning of Jesus's death on a cross (13:1–11). His crucifixion is a sacrifice that purifies people so that they can be united with God and Jesus through mutual indwelling.

JESUS'S INTERPRETATION OF THE FOOT WASHING FOR THE JOHANNINE COMMUNITY: MISSION AS INTEGRATED WITNESS (VV. 12–38)

In the second part (13:12–38), John provides the missional interpretation and explanation of Jesus's act for the community's witness. The disciples are sent to bear witness to Jesus in the world (13:16, 20, 35, 36), and this witness is both life-witness and evangelism. The former is a witness toward the community and to the world that occurs by living Jesus's life-pattern in terms of relational unity and mutual indwelling, while the latter is a witness of proclamation and preaching of Jesus's words, as Jesus teaches the truth so that the disciples and the world can live as children of light and his followers. These two witness concepts must be treated as one.

Life-Witness: Love and Humble Service

Life-witness as mission means to testify to God in both life and identity. As Jesus reveals the Father through his life and character (10:38; 12:45; 14:9–11), so, too, must his disciples reveal God in their lives according to his words and deeds (13:35; 17:21, 23). John describes that the second meaning of the foot-washing narrative (13:12–38) relates to its interpretation for the faith community, while the first meaning accounts for Jesus's washing action (13:1–11).[109] In beginning this part of interpretation with the word *understand* (vv. 7, 12), the author notes that Jesus asks the disciples to live out his life pattern, or model (13:14–15). They should wash one another's feet, which means following him and loving one another (13:34–35). This way of following is the nature of the washing's interpretation (13:36).

First, Γινώσκετε τί πεποίηκα ὑμῖν; ("Do you understand what I have done for you?" John 13:12).

---

109. Hultgren, "Johannine Footwashing," 540; Bauckham, "Did Jesus Wash," 415.

Jesus emphasizes that the disciples will know what he is doing "after these things" (13:7). The phrase "after these things" shows a difference other than usage (5:1; 6:1; 7:1; and 21:1). Apart from 13:7, John employs the expression as the transition within the story. That is, these cases manifest the geographical and temporal changes of events. However, in 13:7, the author does not pay attention to the geographical movement, nor the temporal change, of some events. Rather, these things point to specific events. R. E. Brown connects 13:7 ("What I am doing you do not understand now, but afterward you will understand" [Ὃ ἐγὼ ποιῶ σὺ οὐκ οἶδας ἄρτι, γνώσῃ δὲ μετὰ ταῦτα]) with 12:16: ("His disciples did not understand these things at first [ταῦτα οὐκ ἔγνωσαν αὐτοῦ οἱ μαθηταὶ τὸ πρῶτον], but when Jesus was glorified, then they remembered [τότε ἐμνήσθησαν] that these things had been written about him and had been done to him").[110] Jesus's disciples did not understand "these things," but then remembered that "these things" were written about him and "these things" they had done to him. Brown's focus is on the fact that 12:16 includes John's theological intention of Jesus's resurrection.[111]

After completing his washing of the disciples' feet, Jesus took off his outer garment (13:12, ἔλαβεν τὰ ἱμάτια αὐτοῦ) and asked, "Do you understand what I have done for you?" This question focuses on the disciples' present comprehension, and Jesus begins to explain how the disciples live his lifestyle (13:15, 17). Schnackenburg aptly observes that John develops this interpretive aspect of Jesus's washing act for his recipient community as a way of participating in his sacrificial death.[112] The disciples are allowed to participate in the life that results from Jesus's unique mission in the mutual relationship (13:34–35; 14:20; 14:7–10 [10:38] with 13:35; 17:23), as well as in his ongoing mission as witness (13:20; 15:27; 18:37 with 17:20; 20:31; 21:24).

Second, καὶ ὑμεῖς ὀφείλετε ἀλλήλων νίπτειν τοὺς πόδας ("You also ought to wash one another's feet," John 13:14).

Some scholars are concerned with the verb νίπτω ("wash"). They assert that the foot washing was involved with the believers' practices of love, such as hospitality, or service in humility, in light of the early Christian church's use of the term (1 Tim 5:10).[113] John Christopher Thomas connects

---

110. Brown, *John XIII–XXI*, 552.

111. Brown, *John I–XII*, 463.

112. Schnackenburg, *Gospel according to St John*, 2:23; Bruce, *Gospel of John*, 283.

113. E.g., Rudolf Schnackenburg argues that the event, as such, does not reveal the explicit meaning by highlighting the phrase "what I am doing you do not know now, but afterwards you will understand" (John 13:7) (Schnackenburg, *Gospel according to St John*, 3:2). It is associated with the misunderstanding of Peter and the readers of the

the episode of a sinful woman (Luke 7:36–50) with the foot washing (John 13:1–20), so as to highlight her service and subordination through the anointing and her action so with love.[114] He suggests an interesting opinion that the story of John 12:1–8 includes a meal (hospitality) and anointing (washing). In reality, John 13:1–20 implies the remaining element, the so-called service of love through Jesus as a servant.[115] Such a practice of service is repeated in 1 Tim 5:10, which supports that the act of John 13:15 was implemented by the early church community (Rom 12:13; 1 Tim 3:2; Titus 1:8; Heb 13:2; 1 Pet 4:9) according to the comprehension of the disciples.[116] Accordingly, the foot washing would constitute their preparation for both his departure and their service.[117]

Yet the phrase ἀλλήλων νίπτειν τοὺς πόδας ("to wash one another's feet") in 13:14 means that the disciples wash one another's feet within their own community, which does not literally point out the hospitality of strangers (cf. 1 Tim 3:2).[118] Of course, their practice of love could undeniably include hospitality toward guests or strangers (Abraham [Gen 18:1–18]; Joseph [43:24]; Abigail [1 Sam 25:41]; Aseneth [Jos. Asen. 13:15; 20:15]). Nevertheless, the foot washing enacted by Jesus and the disciples is more inclusive in light of Jesus's sacrificial death (cf. John 12:7). When Jesus uses ὑπόδειγμα (13:15, "example," "model," or "pattern"), he reminds the disciples of his death's significance,[119] repeating that they understand his act and practice (13:17). Jesus's death is the practice of love and service that gives eternal life to people and brings them into an intimate relationship with God (3:14–21; 10:10; 12:24–26; 14:20; 15:4–5, 8; 17:21). His event and

---

Gospel up to Jesus's death on the cross. Schnackenburg suggests not only the indirect relationship between John 13 and Luke 22:27, but also the difference between them in that the foot washing in John is based upon the performance of a slave (3:16), rather than just the service of a man like Luke (3:40–41). Nevertheless, he mentions that the core message of the story (John 13) is the service of Jesus's love through his death (John 15:13; 1 John 3:16) (Schnackenburg, *Gospel according to St John*, 3:41, 54).

114. Thomas, *Footwashing*, 57.

115. Thomas, *Footwashing*, 87.

116. Thomas, *Footwashing*, 57–58; Seland, "Resident Aliens," 573.

117. Thomas, *Footwashing*, 59–60.

118. In particular, Arland J. Hultgren suggests the eschatological hospitality as divine hospitality. He argues that the disciples' cleanliness is not dependent on a ritual praxis, but rather on their sharing of Jesus's part as his destiny by believing the word (13:8; 15:3) (Hultgren, "Johannine Footwashing," 543). If this divine hospitality is associated with God's forgiveness, Jesus's death would probably reflect God's acceptance of sinners (Ezek 43:26–27): "they will make atonement for the altar and cleanse it, so they will consecrate it . . . I will accept you."

119. Mathew, *Johannine Footwashing*, 214–18, 406.

symbolic act should be entailed by the removal or purification of sins across the world that God loves (1:29; 3:16). Accordingly, washing one another's feet is a means of practicing love and humble service, which are embodied both in Jesus's sacrificial and self-giving death, and in his consecration of the disciples (13:36–38 with 21:18–23; 15:3; 17:23).

More importantly, "one another's foot washing" implies sacrificial love and humble service within the community and in the world. John intersects the phrases "to wash one another's feet" (13:14) and "to love one another" (13:34). The disciples are to love one another according to Jesus's new commandment. As Jesus humbly practiced his love by serving his disciples as he washed their feet, his disciples should do the same. Above all, in light of Jesus's death, the essence of their love and service is self-sacrifice for both the community of the disciples and the world.[120] Jesus gave himself up to love and served his nation and the scattered people of God (10:11; 11:50–52; 12:26; 18:14). He made it their way of life as a "model" (13:15). This love and service is not merely the act of imitation, but also the fruit of the mutual love between Jesus and the disciples within the relationship of their mutual indwelling (15:4). John describes that Jesus's model was exemplified through his life in the unity relationship between the reciprocal love of Jesus and the Father (14:31; 17:23).

Firstly, Jesus loves the disciples who betray him, and he restores them so that they might follow him. Although Peter and other disciples betrayed and left him, Jesus sought them out again and entrusted them with his mission (21:15–17). He restores their love for him through similar situations of their betrayal (18:15–18, 25–27), in which John repeats the word ἀνθρακιά ("charcoal fire") between 18:18 and 21:9. The author highlights that Jesus washes away Peter's reproach before calling Peter and the other disciples back to him. R. E. Brown argues that 21:9–13 alludes to forgiveness, as Jesus invites the disciples who have betrayed him to the meal (13:12; 16:32).[121] By the same token, the disciples should practice Jesus's act as a life-pattern in the community by washing one another's feet.[122] Their act must be mutual, sacrificial, self-giving, and selfless (13:14, 34–35).[123]

Secondly, Jesus serves the disciples, and even an enemy, through the form of servanthood.[124] In particular, he washes the feet of his enemy, Judas

120. Koester, *Symbolism*, 133.
121. Brown, *John XIII–XXI*, 1098.
122. Mlakuzhyil, *Christocentric Literary Structure*, 325.
123. Mlakuzhyil, *Christocentric Literary Structure*, 286.

124. John depends on Luke's servanthood: "The Lukan service is presented as opposite of the customary understanding of social hierarchy. To be great means not to sit at the table, but rather to serve (cf. 12:37). The same could be said of the Johannine

Iscariot. He already recognized Judas as a treacherous person who participated in his ministry (6:70–71; 13:2, 18, 27, 29 [12:6]), and Judas was indeed an enemy of his teacher. In John 13:18, Jesus quotes Psalm 41:9 ("has lifted up his heel against me") in order to emphasize that a friend betrays him so as to become an enemy.[125] Judas was unfaithful and dishonest, owing to his greed for money (13:29 and 12:6). Eventually, Judas hands Jesus over to the religious authorities (18:2). Although Jesus knew who Judas was and what he did (13:29), he allowed Judas Iscariot to attend his Last Supper (13:2, 18, 27) and washes his feet, even though he understood that Judas was not clean (13:10). From the beginning, Jesus came into his own people, who did not accept him (1:11), and serves both them and Judas in humility and faithfulness (13:1, 16, 34). The focus of the foot-washing narrative is that the faith community has a missional context. Accordingly, the community consists of believers and unbelievers, both of whom can see Jesus through their lives that mirror Jesus's life within the inner community.[126]

---

foot washing. The 'Teacher and Lord's washing the feet is precisely opposite to the customs of the time'" (Mathew, *Johannine Footwashing*, 216). Mathew points to a unique instance in the foot washing where Jesus washed the disciples' feet while eating the meal. Here, he did not follow the contemporary custom (Mathew, *Johannine Footwashing*, 217). By the same token, Christoph Niemand argues that slaves' act did not show intimacy or love in Jesus's day, although John interprets Jesus's act as the expression of perfect love (Niemand, "Was Bedeutet Die Fusswaschung," 115–27).

125. Bishop, "He That Eateth Bread," 331–33.

126. The First Epistle of John does not mention the words *go*, *send*, or *evangelize*. However, I presume that the epistle deals with the nature of a missional life in the inner situation of the faith community (1 John 2:3, 6; 3:18; 4:12). In my opinion, the author of the epistle regards his readers as the objects of his mission (1 John 1:2; 4:14). He attempts to teach his readers how to practice Jesus's commandment in the sense of mission (3:23–24). In other words, although the first readers of John's Gospel were not publicly motivated by missional languages like sending language, they were challenged to live a missional life within their particular situation. If some argue that the missional life must mean discipleship, they are right. However, the phrase "we know him if we obey his commands" conceptualizes the missional nature in that believers can know Jesus through one another's lives according to his words (2:3; cf. John 13:35). That is, they love each other through the light. In John's Gospel, their lives are missional. Although the first John did not mention sending language, the author repeats missional language of John's Gospel, such as the mutual dwelling of God and believers (John 17:[18], 21, 26; 1 John 2:24). In this sense, as John's Gospel describes in the foot-washing narrative where Jesus commands them to emulate his life-pattern (John 13:15), the first readers of the Gospel might live in him (cf. 1 John 2:5–6; 3:14–16) (Thompson, *John*, 300). In light of the semantic aspect, Jesus's command in the Fourth Gospel is associated with that found in 1 John:

 a. John 13:15: καθὼς ἐγὼ ἐποίησα ὑμῖν καὶ ὑμεῖς ποιῆτε.

 b. 1 John 2:6: ὁ λέγων ἐν αὐτῷ μένειν ὀφείλει καθὼς ἐκεῖνος περιεπάτησεν καὶ αὐτὸς [οὕτως] περιπατεῖν.

By contrast, Jesus's act is not congruent with the world's way of life. The world is dominated by hate and evil, and therefore hates and denies Jesus and his disciples (μισέω "hate," 3:20; 7:7; 15:18, 19, 23, 24, 25; 17:14). But Jesus and his disciples love and serve within the faith community and in the world, and their lifestyle reveals Jesus and bears witness to their identity of oneness with God (13:35).[127] John highlights the sinful nature of the world under Satan's rulership:

Firstly, the world hated him, rather than accepting him (1:11; 3:20; 5:42; 7:7; 15:24).[128] Thompson defines the word *hate* as "not an internal

---

These two texts emphasize the life pattern of the faith community in accordance with Jesus's life. At first, the recipients of the texts should love one another (John 13:14; 1 John 2:9–10). Their mutual love premises the washing of one another's feet. In the language of 1 John, the act of washing parallels the purification of believers from all sins (1 John 1:7, 9). The terms καθαρίζω ("make clean" or "purify") and ἀφίημι ("forgive") are interchangeably understood in the same line. In particular, forgiveness is both the beginning and end of believers' reciprocal love. First John uses the aorist subjunctive active in 1:9 (ἵνα ἀφῇ); this phrase might mean "a present general condition" (Wallace, *Greek Grammar*, 698). That is, the subject "we" might include the speaker and his congregations "who do sin" (1 John 2:1–6) (Marshall, *Epistles of John*, 111). Forgiveness originates from Jesus's atoning death for the world and believers (2:2). Depending on Jesus's forgiveness of anyone's sins, the believers might confess their sins so that they should love one another by no longer hating one another (1 John 1:9—2:2). This hate belongs to the world that is in the darkness (John 3:20; 7:4; 15:18–19, 23; 1 John 3:13). The author of 1 John recites the language of John's Gospel (John 13:14–15; 15:3–4; 20:23), demonstrating that the foundation of the believers' love is Jesus's atoning sacrifice (ἱλασμός) (John 6:51; 1 John 4:10–11) (Brown, *Epistles of John*, 240; Marshall, *Epistles of John*, 117).

127. Within the aspect of the Johannine community's historical context, the Johannine community would have consisted of diverse believers (Brown, *John XIII–XXI*, 1047). John probably connotes that different ethnic groups and social classes joined Jesus's movement (for Jews, 1:36–50; 3:1; 7:50; 19:38–42 [religious authorities]; for Samaritans, 4:4, 35–38, 39–42; for Gentiles, 12:20–23; for the marginalized and ostracized people like women, 4:6, 9; 11:1; 12:7; 20:11 [8:1–11]) (Thompson, *John*, 108). R. E. Brown argues that the variety found in the community's members gradually increased as Samaritan and gentile Christians entered the Johannine community (Brown, "Other Sheep Not of This Fold," 5–22; *Community of the Beloved Disciple*, 59–88; McGrath, *John's Apologetic Christology*, 9). If it is true that John considers the Samaritan believers of his community, his account for discussion about the place of worship would reflect the debate between Jews and the Samaritans (4:20–25). When this complex community can show the unity of their faith and action in forgiveness, sacrificial love, and service, their witness can turn out to be true throughout the world. In other words, the community's individuals must become an atoning sacrifice for all members, even though this community involves unbelieving disciples, such as Judas Iscariot.

128. John uses the term μισέω ("hate") twelve times (3:20; 7:7*2; 12:25; 15:18*2, 19, 23*2, 24, 25; 17:14); not all people (πάντες, 13:35) accept Jesus (2:24). Some reject or suspect him (1:11; 3:20; 5:23; 10:24; 16:2), while others believe him (1:12; 3:15, 16; 4:39, 45; 6:37, 39, 40, 45; 10:4, 41–42; 11:42; 12:46; 17:7, 10, 21; 18:37). John talks about

attitude or emotion of hostility so much as an external expression of distancing oneself from something or being indifferent to it."[129] This hatred is the nature of the world's ruler, who dislikes God through deceit (8:38, 44). By contrast, Jesus is willing to lay his life down for the world (12:24–25). He practices the Father's love, which motivates his giving of the Son to the world (3:16); his death is a self-giving and sacrificial act for many people (10:11, 15; 11:50–52).

Secondly, Judas Iscariot betrays his master (13:27, 29; 12:6), and his treachery comes from Satan (13:2, 27). John specifies Satan as the father of lies or deception (ψεῦδος), in opposition to truth (8:31, 44, 45). Those who belong to Satan live a lie, while God's true people have no deceit (ἀληθῶς Ἰσραηλίτης ἐν ᾧ δόλος οὐκ ἔστιν, 1:47). The true ones practice the truth in the light, so their deeds have evidently been done to honor God (3:21). By contrast, Satan rules the world with deceit and treachery, in which people live as the servants of sin (8:34, 43). This deceit and betrayal are rooted in avarice (12:4, 6). In wanting to hand Jesus over, Judas Iscariot belongs to Satan (6:70–71).

On the contrary, John highlights Jesus's love despite the hatred of the world (15:18–25).[130] Although the world hates him, who is the light and speaks the truth (15:25; cf. 3:20; 7:7; 12:46), he shows love toward it. Jesus teaches his disciples how to participate in his sacrificial and self-giving love as his friends (15:14); their practice of sacrificial love and humble service through Jesus is a witness of his life in the world (13:35; 14:31; 17:23).[131]

Therefore, the disciples' love and service are rooted in both the Father and Jesus's love and "doing" (3:14–18;[132] 13:1, 34).[133] Their practice is sac-

---

Jesus's sentness and his own people's response within the context of the Jews (1:11): "His own people" in 1:11 (11:48) did not receive him; by contrast, "his own people" in 13:1 believe in Jesus and the Father (13:19). John articulates this antithetical reaction to Jesus within both the Jewish context and the foot washing. John underscores that many disciples did not believe Jesus's explanation in 6:60–71. Their distrust is bound with Judas Iscariot's response to Jesus (6:64, 70; 13:2, 11, 27). In two situations, although they ate the pieces of Jesus's bread and listened to him (ch. 6) or he in Jesus's washing event and received a morsel of bread (13:30), none of them trusted in Jesus.

129. Thompson, *John*, 86.
130. Lappenga, "Whose Zeal," 108–15.
131. This world usually points out "all people" who are the object of the *missio Dei*.
132. Jesus applies his death on a cross to God's salvific work through *Moses's brazen serpent in the wilderness* (Num 21:4–9). God saved Israel from judgment, which resulted in their repentance of sin (21:7). The picture of Numbers 21 alludes to God's forgiveness toward Israel. Accordingly, it can be presumed that when Jesus reminds readers of the event of God's salvation, he focuses on his salvation through forgiveness, which will be fulfilled by way of his crucifixion.
133. John primarily characterizes the reciprocity of love in the mutual relationship:

rificial and altruistic.[134] At the same time, their love and service are aimed toward the community and the world's sanctification to God. The world is accustomed to hatred, betrayal, murder, and greed for money under the servanthood of sin and Satan. It is to this world that Jesus and his disciples practice love, forgiveness, and service in order to reveal God and his salvific works that bring people to God.

Third, the frame of καθὼς and πέμπω ("as . . ., so . . ." and send, 13:15, 20).

This literary frame highlights that Jesus's life is bound with that of the disciples in the missional structure of the Gospel, and is founded on the basis of the frames of "as . . ., so . . ." and the sending language. Jesus undertook

---

(1) love between the Father and Jesus or the disciples (3:35; 5:20; 10:17; 14:23, 31; 15:9; 16:27; 17:23, 24, 26); (2) love between Jesus and the disciples (14:15, 28; 21:15, 16, 17; 16:27); and (3) love between one another in the community of the disciples (13:34; 14:21). That is, when God loves the world, he demands that the people also love him. Therefore, this mutual love demands the trust, dependency, and action of both the subject and the object of love. John 10:17 clarifies that what Jesus abandons his life for is the reason why the Father loves him. The author makes use of the maker of reason or cause (ὅτι). However, Jesus's death is not the prerequisite of the Father's love toward him. Instead, the Son's sacrifice is dependent on the Father's love raising him from the dead. Likewise, the Father loves whoever loves him. In 16:27, John emphasizes that the Father loves those who love Jesus. They should keep Jesus's commandment by loving one another as Jesus loved them (ἀγαπᾶτε ἀλλήλους, 15:12, 17). The phrases of 14:21 and 24 clarify that the people, who both keep Jesus's words and do them, love him and receive the Father's love. In this sense, the loving relationship between the Father and the Son is the same as what the disciples should do (14:31; 17:23).

134. The value of the disciples' sacrificial love and service is not confined to friendship (15:13). Ronald F. Hock argues that John employs love in light of friendship in the Greco-Roman society (Hock, "Jesus, the Beloved Disciple," 195-212). Jesus's saying, "whom he loves" in 13:23, indicates friends' love in 13:1-35 (Hock, "Jesus, the Beloved Disciple," 206). Hock notes that "Jesus demonstrates his love or friendship for the disciples by washing their feet (vv. 4-12). This action, while certainly demeaning for a teacher and supposedly reserved only for Gentile slaves, is not simply 'servant love' or 'a loving act of abasement,' but also an act of friendship, is evident from several of Lucian's stories where friends do things for their friends that are far below their status" (Hock, "Jesus, the Beloved Disciple," 207). However, John does not stop to explain Jesus's love as friendship, but rather develops it into unconditional love. It is this covenantal love between God and the world, or among humanity. This love language and concept characterize their identity and lives. As John employs the term "love" (37 times, ἀγαπάω or ἀγάπη [Matt*8, Mark*5, Luke*13, Rom*8, 1 Cor*2, 2 Cor*4, Gal*2, Eph*10, Col*2, 2 Tim*4, Heb*2, Jas*3, 1 Pet*4, 2 Pet*1, 1 John 28, 2 John*2, 3 John*1, Judah*1, Rev*4] + 13 times φιλέω or φίλη), Greek terms are interchangeable and focus on the relational love (John 15:9, 12, 17; 16:27). This *love* language molds the Johannine community as God's household in Jesus, the *new temple*, and allows them to live God's life and identity as his children (1:12; 15:1-15; 17:1-26) (Thompson, "His Own Received Him Not," 270; Hock, "Jesus, the Beloved Disciple," 207). The Holy Spirit helps believers live such a life in peace and joy (14:26-27; 15:11).

his unique salvific work and revelation in his life in order to save sinners and establish them as a new community. On the one hand, they ought to live Jesus's life under his truth and authority (8:12; 13:3; 17:2).[135] The practice of their lives verifies their identity as Jesus's disciples (13:35), as well as bears witness to the triune God in the holy relationship (17:23).

Firstly, the frame of "as . . ., so . . ." characterizes the sharing of identity and a new life pattern between Jesus and the disciples. John connects the foot-washing narrative with Jesus's command (20:23) in the frame of "sending" language, "as . . ., so . . .," or "belief" (13:16, 20; 20:21, 23; 13:19–20; 17:3 with 18; 20:31). John 13:14–15, 16, 20 is bound with 20:21 by the verb *send*. Mathew highlights the relatedness of Jesus and his disciples in the form of John's structure (13:14–15, εἰ . . . ἐγὼ [if . . . I] . . . καὶ . . . ὑμεῖς [you also] . . . καθὼςἐγὼ [just as I] . . . καὶ ὑμεῖς [you also] . . .), which occurs within the sending frame of 17:18 and 20:19–23.[136] In particular, Jesus states that his disciples remain in the world, as he was consecrated for sentness (17:18–19). They are sanctified in truth (ἐν ἀληθείᾳ). John uses this term, "truth," in the two ways: (1) sayings (1:14; 8:40, 44, 45, 46; 16:7; 17:17, 19; 18:37, 38) and (2) Jesus and the Holy Spirit (3:21, 34; 5:33; 8:32; 14:6, 17; 15:26; 16:13).

Jesus is the bearer of truth, and, at the same time, is the truth itself.[137] John emphasizes that those who receive the truth or Jesus's words become disciples, free from the slavery of sin and of Satan (8:31, 32, 34, 37). These disciples follow the truth, so they come to the light (3:21). Jesus is the light of the world (1:4; 8:12).[138] At the same time, John interweaves Jesus's bearing light with knowing God (1:1–4; 10:37–38).[139] He depicts that Jesus is the one who reveals the Father and is the light of the truth (8:[12]28, 32, 38, 45 12:46[50], and 14:6).[140] He teaches all people to know the Father (1:9). Subsequently, John demonstrates that the disciples' life pattern means "walking" in the truth (8:12; cf. 1:37–38, 40, 43; 10:4, 5, 27; 12:26, 36, 44–46; 13:36–37; 21:19, 22), by which they are consecrated (17:19).[141] Their holiness aims to

---

135. Jesus's kingdom does not belong to the earthly kingdom (17:14; 18:36; 19:20). Therefore, his disciples must live under his rule and command.

136. Mathew, *Johannine Footwashing*, 4, 267–75.

137. As part of the role of Jesus as "light" and "truth," the Spirit was sent by the Father in Jesus's name (14:26) (Mathew, *Johannine Footwashing*, 367). He bears witness to Jesus Christ with the regenerated faith communities and leads the community's proclaiming activity in the world (Barrett, *Gospel according to St. John*, 90; Burge, *Anointed Community*, 36).

138. Danby, *Mishnah*, 179–80; Dodd, *Interpretation*, 348n2, 351.

139. Dodd, *Interpretation*, 349–51.

140. Culpepper, *Anatomy*, 89; Köstenberger, *Studies*, 164–67.

141. Cf. Koester proposes that περιπατέω ("walk," 8:12) is likened to "the ethical

make fruits in the unity-relationship with Jesus (15:2; 17:19–22).[142] Therefore, the disciples, who are in Jesus, must live his life within the frame of the Father and Son's mutual indwelling (15:9). As Jesus lived completely as the light of the truth according to the Father's will and work, so, too, should they live as a light of the truth in the world (12:36 and 13:17).

Secondly, Jesus's washing of the disciples' feet is accompanied by his sending of them (13:20, τινα πέμψω . . ., τὸν πέμψαντά . . .). As Jesus was consecrated for sentness (6:69; 10:36), his disciples' sentness also premises their sanctification to God.[143] This holiness confirms that the disciples belong to God in spite of their staying in the world (15:1–14; 17:14, 18–19; 20:21).

Through Jesus's washing of the disciples' feet, John demonstrates that just as Jesus was sent to purify and consecrate people, the disciples' sentness aims to release or forgive anyone from their sins in order to be united with the holy God and to make Jesus's fruit (15:2, 3; 20:23). As Jesus sets people free from their sins (8:31–34), the disciples also (ἀφίημι ["forgive"] and κρατέω ["retain"], 20:23).[144] John shows that Jesus retains the sins of unbelievers in 8:21, 24. Here, Jesus declares, "You will die *in your sins* (ἀποθανεῖσθε ἐν ταῖς ἁμαρτίαις ὑμῶν)," because of their unbelief in the Sender and in the Sent (8:19, 27–28; 15:22). Likewise, 9:41 states that Jesus *retains* some unbelieving Pharisee's sins (ἡ ἁμαρτία ὑμῶν μένει). The term *sin* (ἁμαρτία) is associated with the fact that, although people saw Jesus and his signs, they hated him and the Father because of their unbelief and ignorance regarding God (15:24; 16:9; for ignorance, 15:12 and 9:30). Therefore, through "forgiveness [releasing]" and "setting free," Jesus's mission aims to restore the people to the role of God's children as the "children of light" (1:12; 11:52; 12:36 and 1:14; 17:18; 20:21; "from death to life," 5:24), who mutually abide in God (14:20; 17:21).[145]

On the other hand, in the frame of "as . . ., so . . ." and sending, Jesus dispatches his disciples into the world (17:18; 20:21). Just as he revealed the invisible Father in his life and fulfilled his salvation by his crucifixion,

---

dimension of discipleship" associated with Jewish literature (Prov 4:17–18, 1QS iii): "the path of the righteous is like the light of dawn," but "the way of the wicked is like deep darkness" (Koester, *Symbolism*, 143).

142. Mathew, *Johannine Footwashing*, 144.

143. Mathew, *Johannine Footwashing*, 326.

144. Köstenberger, *John*, 282–83.

145. For discussion about God's children in John and Jewish literature, see Culpepper, "Pivot of John's Prologue," 2–22, 26–31. In particular, "the nation" in 11:51 is neither the nations nor the Gentiles, but rather Israel (Culpepper, "Pivot," 30). Next, John adds others (including the Gentiles) to the "ingathered people" in 11:52.

the disciples must also practice a sacrificial love, humble service toward the world and, at the same time, forgive anyone's sins (20:23). In other words, they should bring the fulfillment of Jesus's purification and self-sacrificial love to the world.[146]

Thirdly, καθὼς ἠγάπησα ὑμᾶς ἵνα καὶ ὑμεῖς ἀγαπᾶτε ἀλλήλους ("Just as I have loved you, you must also love one another," 13:34b). The frame of "just as ..., also ..." pertains to the mutual abiding of Jesus and his disciples. Their mutual indwelling relationship is equivalent to that of the Father and the Son (14:10). In this relationship, Jesus is willing to die for his sheep by keeping the commandment of the Father's love (10:15a, 17–18; 15:10, 12). Jesus gives the new commandment to the disciples in the same way in which it was given to him (13:34; 14:15). The fact that they observe the commandment means that they abide in Jesus's love (14:20, 23; 15:5, 10). Their mutual indwelling relationship bears fruit (15:4, 5, 16), which manifest their identity as Jesus's disciples in the world (13:35; 15:8). Their relationship with Jesus must be expanded beyond the faith community to the world.[147] It was for this expansion that Jesus sends them into the world (17:18–20).

Fourthly, Ὅπου ὑπάγω οὐ δύνασαί μοι νῦν ἀκολουθῆσαι, ἀκολουθήσεις δὲ ὕστερον ("Where I am going, you cannot follow me now, but you will follow later" (13:36b). John divides the term *follow* (ἀκολουθέω) into three possible cases. The first is defined as belonging to someone, or becoming a disciple (1:37, 38, 40, 43; 8:12; 10:4, 5, 27; 21:20), the second case refers to a simple deed of following someone (6:2; 11:31; 18:15; 20:6), and the third regards the following of Jesus's service or sacrificial death (12:26; 13:36 [37]; 21:19 [20], 22).[148] In a dialogue between Jesus and Peter, the term *follow* indicates the event of death, as found in 13:37. Peter would be willing to lay his life down for Jesus (13:38 and 10:15; 11:50–52).[149] The disciple's act of following Jesus is to walk in Jesus's way. He was sent to serve the world through his words, activities, and death so that the world might receive eternal life by faith (12:24–26, 44–50). His commitment originates in love (3:16; 13:1) and is handed over to his disciples (20:21, 23 [4:34–38]). Accordingly, the fact that Jesus's disciples follow him means that they serve the world through their sacrifice and love. Simultaneously, as Jesus leads people to the light, he also invites them into his forgiveness and eternal life by showing their lives according to the light

---

146. Newbigin, *Open Secret*, 48.

147. Hays, *Gospels*, 338.

148. In 21:20, the beloved disciple's following of Jesus conveys a different meaning than Peter. Jesus specifies the mood of Peter's following, "You follow me!" (Thompson, *John*, 444).

149. Brown, *John XIII–XXI*, 616; Carson, *Gospel according to John*, 486; Morris, *Gospel according to John*, 563.

of the truth. The structure of *thirdly* and *fourthly* is echoed in chapter 21. After restoring Peter through love, service, and forgiveness, Jesus entrusts him with the care of his lambs, for whose lives he died (21:15–17; cf. 10:11–18). Peter's loving service must be accompanied by his self-sacrificial death and self-giving love in life, which fulfills his following of Jesus (21:18–19).

In short, the foot-washing narrative states that, just as Jesus washes their feet, so, too, should his disciples forgive, love mutually, and serve others by way of selflessness, self-giving, and self-sacrifice. Such a life-pattern serves as missional evidence for their sharing of eternal life with Jesus (5:26). The disciples' missional lives transcend the exclusive life-pattern of the world and accept others in love and service, while the world excludes those who have different faiths and values. Through self-giving and self-sacrificial death meant for forgiveness, Jesus washes away the sin of the world and restores it; he washes away the sins of the world's people and restores them (1:29) to the new life-pattern in eternal life (12:36, 46; 20:30–31). His death embodies the model of humble service for his new community (13:1–15). When Jesus sends his disciples into the world, he commands that they forgive anyone's sins (20:23). Their actions must be rooted in God's love and service (3:16; 10:11–15), and the way of their mission is to let those of the world know about Jesus's death, resurrection, and teachings through their evangelism and life-witness.

Evangelism: Verbal-Proclamation

Under his authority over all things, Jesus consecrates his disciples so that they might participate in evangelism about him and the truth (13:3; 17:18). This is placed within the frame of command-obedience. Just as Jesus was sent to bear witness to the Father's name and the truth (17:6; 18:37), his disciples' sentness is also aimed at evangelism, as well as the truth for the world so that it might have eternal life through faith in the scheme of "as . . ., so . . ." (13:20; 15:27; 17:20). Their evangelism must be interwoven with life-witness to God and his redemptive works through Jesus. For these reasons, Jesus washes, or consecrates, his disciples to his side in the unity-relationship with him and the Father (13:8; 15:3; 17:20–21).

Jesus's Authority and Evangelistic Task

The Father handed all things over to Jesus, who God entrusts with authority (13:3, πάντα ἔδωκεν αὐτῷ ὁ πατὴρ εἰς τὰς χεῖρας). In 3:35 (πάντα δέδωκεν ἐν τῇ χειρὶ αὐτοῦ) and 17:2 (ἔδωκας αὐτῷ ἐξουσίαν πάσης σαρκός), his authority is used for giving eternal life to people. Jesus bears witness to the truth with authority so that everyone can listen to him (8:26, 32, 45, 46; 18:37). Knowing the truth is the result of freedom from the slavery of sin and darkness (8:12, 21, 32, 36). Under his authority, Jesus will bring judgment to those who do evil (5:27, 29). Therefore, the preaching of the truth is the proclamation of the saving truth, which is an evangelistic task (8:32; 12:50; 14:6; 17:20; 18:37).[150]

Jesus imperatively sends his disciples into the world to accomplish his work (13:16, 20; 17:18; 20:21) through the frame of "as . . ., so . . .," namely evangelizing unbelievers through their words (17:20) and proclaiming the forgiveness of sin (20:23). The pivotal purpose of the disciples' sentness is to reveal Jesus and the truth to the world (17:3; 13:16, 17; 12:26 with 13:36–38). As Jesus knows the will of the Sender and completes his work (5:17–18, 30; 6:38–39; 8:28–29; 12:50; 14:10; 17:4; 18:37; 19:30), so, too, should they follow him by denying their own will (ἀκολουθέω, 12:26 [1:37, 38, 40, 43; 6:2; 8:12; 10:4, 5, 27; 11:31; 13:36, 37; 18:15; 20:6; 21:20]).

The Disciples' Evangelism

The disciples' preaching is never separated from their life-witness. Jesus is the one who reveals the Father and testifies to the truth, as they ought to testify to Jesus and make the world believe in him (1:1–4; 10:37–38; 18:37).[151] In the union between them and Jesus (17:18, 23), the disciples must proclaim what to hear, see, receive, and know (or understand) by the Holy Spirit (16:13; 17:8; 19:35; 21:24).

In the foot-washing narrative, Jesus allows his disciples to believe in him through his salvific events (13:18). He sends them into the world in order to live (13:16–17) and to bear witness to him and his work, just as he did (3:20). Above all, with regard to the evangelistic task of the disciples, John shows similarities with the Synoptics (ESV):

    a. John 13:20 ὁ λαμβάνων ἄν τινα πέμψω ἐμὲ λαμβάνει, ὁ δὲ ἐμὲ λαμβάνων λαμβάνει τὸν πέμψαντά με ("Whoever receives the one I send receives me, and whoever receives me receives the one who sent me").

    b. Mark 9:37 Ὃς ἂν ἓν τῶν τοιούτων παιδίων δέξηται ἐπὶ τῷ ὀνόματί μου, ἐμὲ δέχεται· καὶ ὃς ἂν ἐμὲ δέχηται, οὐκ ἐμὲ δέχεται ἀλλὰ τὸν ἀποστείλαντά με ("Whoever receives one such child in

---

150. Schnackenburg, *Gospel according to St John*, 2:206–9.
151. Culpepper, *Anatomy*, 89; Köstenberger, *Studies*, 164–67.

my name receives me, and whoever receives me, receives not me but him who sent me").

c. Luke 9:48 Ὅς ἐὰν δέξηται τοῦτο τὸ παιδίον ἐπὶ τῷ ὀνόματί μου, ἐμὲ δέχεται· καὶ ὃς ἂν ἐμὲ δέξηται, δέχεται τὸν ἀποστείλαντά με· ὁ γὰρ μικρότερος ἐν πᾶσιν ὑμῖν ὑπάρχων οὗτός ἐστιν μέγας ("Whoever receives this child in my name receives me, and whoever receives me receives him who sent me").

d. Matt 10:40 ὁ δεχόμενος ὑμᾶς ἐμὲ δέχεται, καὶ ὁ ἐμὲ δεχόμενος δέχεται τὸν ἀποστείλαντά με ("Whoever receives you receives me, and whoever receives me receives him who sent me").

While Mark 9:37 and Luke 9:48 emerge from the debate over who is the greatest among the disciples, Matt 10:40 is situated within Jesus's sending of the disciples on their evangelistic journey. Although within the same context as Mark and Luke, Matthew does not use the phrase (ὃς ἐὰν δέξηται ἓν παιδίον τοιοῦτο ἐπὶ τῷ ὀνόματί μου, ἐμὲ δέχεται). Accordingly, two interpretations of John 13:20 seem to coexist. *Firstly*, if John contains an evangelism concept that appears in both Mark and Luke, he takes into consideration the concept of service in humility. *Secondly*, if John uses this phrase in order to emphasize sending, he intends to place the phrase within the evangelistic context, just as Matthew does. In my estimation, this phrase includes both meanings. If 13:20 is associated with 13:16 (οὐκ ἔστιν δοῦλος μείζων τοῦ κυρίου αὐτοῦ οὐδὲ ἀπόστολος μείζων τοῦ πέμψαντος αὐτόν), it should be observed that 13:16 is echoed in 15:20 (Οὐκ ἔστιν δοῦλος μείζων τοῦ κυρίου αὐτοῦ). John 15:20 deals with the disciples' practice of love and the hatred of the world against them, so it might indicate the disciples' endurance in the world as they practice their mutual love.[152] Their lives are witnesses toward the world.[153] At the same time, John demonstrates in 15:27 that the disciples should bear witness to, or proclaim, Jesus with the Holy Spirit (15:26).[154] The matter of people's acceptance of their evangelism resonates with Luke 10:16 (ὁ ἀκούων ὑμῶν ἐμοῦ ἀκούει, καὶ ὁ ἀθετῶν ὑμᾶς ἐμὲ ἀθετεῖ· ὁ δὲ ἐμὲ ἀθετῶν ἀθετεῖ τὸν ἀποστείλαντά με). Luke elucidates that the one who rejects the evangelists rejects Jesus and the Father. If Thompson is right in saying that John 15:22–24 treats the world's rejection of Jesus's revelation, John alludes to the disciples' apostolic proclamation in the world. Furthermore, John does not neglect another evangelistic activity of Jesus and the disciples in the account of harvesting in 4:35–38, in comparison with Luke 10:2 (Ὁ μὲν θερισμὸς

---

152. Carson, *Gospel according to John*, 525.
153. Thompson, *John*, 332–33.
154. Köstenberger, *John*, 465.

πολύς, οἱ δὲ ἐργάται ὀλίγοι· δεήθητε οὖν τοῦ κυρίου τοῦ θερισμοῦ ὅπως ἐργάτας ἐκβάλῃ εἰς τὸν θερισμὸν αὐτοῦ).

In the frame of "as . . ., so . . .," Jesus sends his disciples as "special messengers" into the world (13:16 [ἀπόστολος], 20). He shows them a model of life so that they can know and live the lifestyle (13:15, 17). At the same time, they are also sent into the world to bear witness to him and his redemptive work of forgiveness (13:20; 20:23). For these reasons, Jesus taught his disciples about the betrayal of another disciple so they could believe in him (13:18–19). In 14:29, Jesus's emphasis is on the disciples' faith, for he has two purposes for them in the frame of 13:20: (1) "whoever receives the one I send receives me," and (2) "whoever receives me receives the one who sent me" (ESV). *Firstly*, Jesus sends the disciple to testify to him and his death in order to make the world know and believe both in him and in his signs for eternal life (17:3; 20:31). John 13:20 echoes 12:44–45 according to the same framework (ESV):

> 13:20 ὁ λαμβάνων ἄν τινα πέμψω ἐμὲ λαμβάνει, ὁ δὲ ἐμὲ λαμβάνων λαμβάνει τὸν πέμψαντά με ("Whoever receives the one I send receives me, and whoever receives me receives the one who sent me").

> 12:44b–45 Ὁ πιστεύων εἰς ἐμὲ οὐ πιστεύει εἰς ἐμὲ ἀλλὰ εἰς τὸν πέμψαντά με, καὶ ὁ θεωρῶν ἐμὲ θεωρεῖ τὸν πέμψαντά με ("Whoever believes in me, believes not in me but in him who sent me. And whoever sees me sees him who sent me").

Here, John parallels "the one who receives me" with "the one who believes in me," and "the one receives the one who sent me" with "the one who sees the one who sent me." In particular, he draws attention to the verb κράζω (cry out, 12:44a). This term is used for Jesus's public proclamation or invitation, along with the witness of people (1:15; 7:28, 37; 1:49 and 12:13).[155] John states that, when Jesus cries out, he intends to make people believe in why the Father sent him (12:46; cf. 11:43). Such a goal of Jesus's public proclamation occurs in John's statement (20:30–31):[156]

---

155. Schnackenburg, *Gospel according to St John*, 2:421.

156. In contrast to the evangelistic purpose of the Gospel, Wayne A. Meeks argues that John does not directly state the Johannine community's mission in the ecclesiological perspective, even though he agrees with J. Louis Martyn's theory regarding the Johannine excommunication from the synagogue (Meeks, "Man from Heaven," 69). Meeks indicates that John does not address the mission activities of the church meant for the evangelism of unbelievers (Meeks, "Man from Heaven," 70–71). He objects to the purpose of the Johannine community's missional activities (evangelism) outside the church because John concentrates on the social identity of the "insiders" of the community within the dualistic

20:30–31 Πολλὰ μὲν οὖν καὶ ἄλλα σημεῖα ἐποίησεν ὁ Ἰησοῦς ἐνώπιον τῶν μαθητῶν [αὐτοῦ], ἃ οὐκ ἔστιν γεγραμμένα ἐν τῷ βιβλίῳ τούτῳ· ταῦτα δὲ γέγραπται ἵνα πιστεύ[σ]ητε ὅτι Ἰησοῦς ἐστιν ὁ Χριστὸς ὁ υἱὸς τοῦ θεοῦ, καὶ ἵνα πιστεύοντες ζωὴν ἔχητε ἐν τῷ ὀνόματι αὐτοῦ ("Now Jesus did many other signs in the presence of the disciples, which are not written in this book; but these are written so that you may believe that Jesus is the Christ, the Son of God, and that by believing you may have life in his name" [ESV]).

Of course, 12:45 and 20:31 never exclude Jesus's life-witness nor John's expectation for the Johannine community's growth in faith, through which they together reveal the Father to the world (14:7, 10–11; 17:23). However, John's use of the word θεωρέω ("see") does not weaken Jesus's proclamation in relation to the term *receive*.[157] This is because Jesus clarifies that the matter of belief and unbelief in him is interwoven with either "receiving" (λαμβάνω) or "rejecting" his words (ἀθετέω). As Jesus was sent to make people listen to and keep the Father's word, so, too, should they proclaim Jesus and his work to the world (12:49–50; 17:17; 20:30–31; 21:24–25).

John 15:27 states that Jesus asks his disciples to bear witness to what they saw through Jesus and his public ministry (ὑμεῖς δὲ μαρτυρεῖτε, ὅτι ἀπ᾽ ἀρχῆς μετ᾽ ἐμοῦ ἐστε). It is for this purpose that he sends the Spirit to them. The Spirit also testifies about Jesus, as Jesus revealed the Father and fulfilled salvation (14:10; 15:26). The disciples should also perform this work; when he sends them (17:18; 20:21), they must testify to Jesus and his redemptive

---

framework of two worlds. He draws attention to John's expressions like "from above" and "the world," which indicate these two different worlds. According to Meeks, the Johannine community would have been a social group isolated from the larger world (Meeks, "Man from Heaven," 70). Like Meeks, Raymond E. Brown insists that John was not written as "a missionary handbook to convert Diaspora Jews," but instead as an "apologetic and polemic" book (Brown, *John I–XII*, lxxiii). Although Brown acknowledges the mission activity for Samaritans and Greeks, he contends that John's written goal (John 20:31) was for the community members, not the unbelievers (Brown, *John I–XII*, lxxviii). Meeks and Brown are concerned with the written purpose of the Gospel, in spite of the fact that they admit to the mission concept within John's Gospel. Essentially, they contend that John does not describe mission(s) as evangelism for unbelievers outside the community, but rather focuses on the ecclesial situation. That is, John's priority was strengthening the faith of the Johannine community. However, in my opinion, Robert Kysar and Sukmin Cho rightly point out that John reflects multidimensional goals (Kysar, *Fourth Evangelist*, 147; Cho, *Jesus*, 31). John engages in education meant for the growth of their faith and evangelism within its missional context. This means that John's written purpose is not directly bound with the matter of "for whom," but rather the matter of everyone's faith in Jesus Christ and the Son of God for eternal life (Carson, "Purpose of the Fourth Gospel," 639–51).

157. Schnackenburg, *Gospel according to St John*, 2:423.

work according to the Holy Spirit (15:26–27). Their verbal-proclamation ties together with their life-witness, with no separation between them.

Secondly, Jesus was sent to the world. He invites all believers to eternal life beyond their ethnic identity (for Jews [1:11], for Samaritans [4:39–42], for Galileans [4:45], for Gentiles [7:35; 12:20]). Furthermore, Jesus turns the Samaritan woman into a disciple for his mission (4:34–42). Jesus leads her restoration toward the true worship of God through the truth and the Spirit (4:24, 28). After dialoguing with him, she publicly confesses her concealed life, saying, "he (Jesus) told me all that I ever did" (4:29). Her testimony plays a role in making her neighbors believe her words (4:29–30, 39), and she bears witness to Jesus's revealing of her actions, which confirms his identity as the Messiah. She becomes a harvester so as to participate in the model of the disciples' mission within the frame of "come and see" (4:29, 35–38). Therefore, the Samaritan woman's story is an example of the mission of Jesus's disciples. In the same vein, the disciples guide the Greeks to Jesus, when they asked Philip to see Jesus (12:21). Their evangelistic task is to invite people to faith and eternal life by sharing a testimony of the salvation that Jesus gave by dying for both the nations and the scattered children of God.

In short, Jesus sends the disciples to carry out the verbal-proclamation of his salvific events and activities. Through their words and deeds, they let the world believe in God so that it might share eternal life with him in Jesus, as Jesus enables them to have the faith required for unity with himself and the Father (13:35).

SUMMARY

The purpose of this study is to examine the missional meanings found within the foot-washing narrative of John 13:1–38. In the preceding study, which has been conducted from the missional perspective of the foot-washing narrative, the main issues were the structural analysis and understanding of the narrative's missional meaning. Scholars have argued for (1) testifying to God through their martyrdom in the world in which Jesus and his disciples are persecuted, (2) sharing the "part" between Jesus and his disciples in doing and missionary tasks, or missionary work as harvesting in the world, and (3) emphasizing the disciples' "participation" as a "doing" of his love and service through mutual indwelling with Jesus, which illustrates the centripetal and centrifugal mission concepts that must be achieved in both the community and the world.

In this study, I briefly analyze what the foot-washing narrative means missonally in the second book (chs. 13–20), and simultaneously, within the structure of the narrative. Then, I exegete the narrative within the literary context (13:1–38) to discover the mission concepts of Jesus and the disciples.

First, the foot-washing narrative reflects John's central theme to be the purification concept of Jesus's death for his disciples' consecration in mutual indwelling. The phrase "hour to return" (13:1, [3]) and the connection between 13:3 and 3:35 show Jesus's return to the Father after his completion of the mission on the cross. Additionally, the phrases "before it takes place" (13:19) and "having a part or share" (13:8) indicate the disciples' participation in Jesus and his mission as an integrated witness of both evangelism and life-witness.

Second, the narrative (13:1–38) marks the beginning of the Gospel's second part (chs. 13–20 [21]). Chapters 13–21 cover two central themes, as follows. The first theme is one of Jesus's death and resurrection. In particular, this death implies purification. Jesus shows his symbolic act in chapter 13, and continues to restore the disciples who betrayed him, apart from Judas Iscariot, in chapter 21. The second theme is one of the purified and consecrated faith community's new lifestyle in the community and the world. They must bear the fruit of love and unity (13:34–36; 17:23). These two themes occupy a major role in the narrative, showing a new way of life by way of Jesus's washing the disciples' feet. His act symbolizes the witness of life that the disciples must follow. Furthermore, the narrative deals with evangelism, which is entrusted by both the Holy Spirit and the disciples (13:20; 15:26–27).

Third, the narrative structure is a layered one (A–B–C–A'–B'–C'). John divides chapter 13 into two parts (13:1–11 and 13:12–38): (1) Jesus's symbolic action and (2) its interpretation for the Johannine community during his physical absence. The narrative presents some implications:

Firstly, Jesus's washing act symbolizes his sacrificial death that was done in humble service and as a demonstration of the Father's love. He died for the world and saves believers. His sacrifice is the event that brings the salvation of the world as Jesus hands himself over to death, and is the result of his service. Through his sacrificial death, he washes people and consecrates them so that they might share a part in him. That is, they might share Jesus's life and identity in mutual indwelling, or in unity-relationship. Above all, his self-giving and self-sacrificial death is meant to bear witness to God's love and service for the world.

Secondly, the interpretation of Jesus's act for the community simultaneously demands their integrated witness of life-witness and evangelism. Jesus's command ("wash one another's feet") requires that the already-consecrated disciples practice sacrificial love and humble service. Their doing is united with God's nature and way of life and is a new ontological and practical life-pattern. Furthermore, they are to love and serve the world equally in the unity-relationship with God. In both their nature and practice, the disciples bear witness to their own identity as Jesus's disciples in the world.

Thirdly, as shown in the structure of "as . . ., so . . ." (13:16), the disciples were sent into the world. They abide in a faith community with Jesus. As Jesus testified to God toward the world as the light of truth, so, too, should they be a light to the world. They escape from darkness and sin by Jesus's setting people free from their sin, so as to live in the light of the truth in unity-relationship with God. They must practice releasing anyone's sins (forgiveness of sins) so that the world might live in the light. Most importantly, the disciples' forgiving work should be accompanied by their fruit of life according to Jesus's new commandment. Their lives are the witness of true life to the world.

Fourthly, the disciple's life-witness is inseparable from evangelism, which Jesus commands the disciples to do. As Jesus testifies to the truth, they are to let the world know the truth through their words, or through verbal-proclamation. They have an evangelistic task of letting people believe in Jesus and become his disciples, who live in the light of the truth.

Therefore, John deals with the mission of Jesus and the disciples as *integrated witness* through the foot-washing narrative. They are bound together in the frames of "as . . ., so . . ." and of sending. Above all, Jesus consecrates the disciples so that they might live in the unity-relationship by sharing life and identity with him. This is their life-witness. At the same time, as Jesus was sent into the world in order to testify to the truth, so that the world might have eternal life by faith, the disciples are also sent to make the world believe in Jesus and receive his eternal life through the verbal-proclamation of the gospel. In other words, they lead the world so that it might live in the light and become Jesus's disciples. Their *integrated witness* must be connected with the intimate relationship they have with the triune God.

4

Missional Implications of John's Gospel for the Future of the Evangelical Mission

THIS CHAPTER AIMS TO examine what the missional implications of John's Gospel are for today's evangelicals and their future. For this study, I will explore how evangelicals understood mission at the Lausanne International Conferences (Lausanne [1974], Manila [1989], Cape Town [2010]) and the characteristics of these conferences. This investigation brings up their contributions and limitations. In particular, with regard to these issues, my emphasis will be on some select evangelicals' understanding of the concept of mission concept in the 2010s, along with the Lausanne International Conferences' interpretation of John's Gospel. Finally, I will pay attention to the missional implications of John's Gospel for the transformation of evangelicals in their missional perspectives and practices.

EVANGELICALS' UNDERSTANDING OF MISSION IN THE LAUSANNE MOVEMENT

Evangelicals, who held three Lausanne International Conferences (1974, 1989, 2010), have presented their agreements about the nature of the church's mission: (1) evangelism as mission, (2) holistic mission, (3) God's mission. Lausanne I employed Jesus's Great Commission for a biblical foundation of mission, which focuses on evangelism and social responsibility (Matt 28:19-20; Mark 16:15; Luke 24:46-48).[1] Then, at Lausanne II and III (Manila and Cape Town), evangelicals had expanded their mission concept. In particular, in understanding mission from a holistic perspective, they transcend the mission concept of evangelism and social responsibility, and then include witness in a holistic aspect of life in God's mission. This change is due to evangelicals' desire to form a more comprehensive concept of missionary work, discussing the definition of mission in various situations in the world.

The Lausanne Covenant (1974, LC)

The 1974 Lausanne International Congress discussed Christian mission in the dichotomous frame of evangelism and social responsibility. The congress defines mission as follows: (1) evangelism as mission is "the proclamation of the historical, biblical Christ as Saviour and Lord, with a view to persuading people to come to him personally and so be reconciled to God" and its result is "obedience to Christ, incorporation into his Church and responsible service in the world" (LC art. 4). The Lausanne Covenant insists that God's people are called for "the extension of his kingdom, the building up of Christ's body, and glory of his name" through witnesses. They argue that the one gospel of Jesus Christ is the only ransom for sinners, and is a mediator in repudiating syncretism and interreligious-dialogue (art. 3) within a corrupt cultural context (art. 10). This concentrates on salvation through believing in Jesus Christ; as a result, mission is purportedly engaged in delivering God's love to sinners and summoning them to believing in Jesus as the only Savior and Lord. For this reason, mission seeks to evangelize unbelievers by "spreading the good news that Jesus Christ died for our sins and was raised from the dead according to the Scriptures, and that as the reigning Lord he now offers the forgiveness of sins and the liberating gifts of the Spirit to all who repent and believe" (art. 4). Evangelism is the major task of the church's mission (arts. 6, 9); (2) the covenant is concerned with "justice and reconciliation throughout human society, and the liberation of men and women from every kind of oppression, alienation, and discrimination" (art. 5). Justice is the matter of the Christian's political engagement as duty and love for neighbor.

However, in spite of the necessity of Christian's social responsibility, the covenant insists on the priority of evangelism under the motto "the whole Church takes the whole gospel to the whole world" (art. 6). The covenant is

---

1. Stott, *Christian Mission*, 25–26.

focused on new resources for world evangelization, which are non-Western churches and para-church agencies (arts. 8, 9). The center of mission is the church (art. 12), which the covenant separates as God's community marked by the cross from a cultural, social, and political institute. They recognized the appropriateness of social responsibilities, those actions were regarded as the bridge of evangelism (LC 1974, arts. 1, 2, 3).[2]

The Manila Manifesto (1989, MM)

At Manila (1989), evangelicals essentially adhered to Lausanne I agreement: "Evangelism is primary because our chief concern is with the gospel, that all people may have the opportunity to accept Jesus Christ as Lord and Saviour" and that "God is calling the whole church to take the whole gospel to the whole world" (MM art. 4, 21). The Manila Congress took over the dichotomous frame that the covenant took toward evangelism and social responsibility. However, they reflected new changes for evangelism and social services in light of a holistic mission or mission as witness in life:

(1) *The Manifesto* mentions the various forms of evangelicals' repentance, such as: the defense of the gospel against the false gospel (cf. arts. 3, 16, 19) and the proclamation of the gospel based on the Bible and truth; the poverty of the poor; dialogue with other faiths without abandoning Jesus Christ's uniqueness as the only means of salvation (cf. art. 7); the expansion of the gospel's scope; the role of the Holy Spirit in transforming power and creating the new community, which consists of diverse ethnicities; laity's witnesses in their settings in life; the wrong lives of churches and Christians within the context; the unity of churches; and their inevitable suffering from the proclamation of the gospel. (2) *The Manifesto* begins to highlight the

---

2. Graham, "Why Lausanne," 30–31; Steuernagel, "Social Concern," 53; Ott and Strauss, *Encountering Theology*, 109; As the chief architect of the covenant, Stott wrote in his book *Christian Mission in the Modern World* that both evangelism and social responsibility constitute Christian mission (Stott, *Christian Mission*, 35). Evangelism essentially testifies to the good news concerning the events of Jesus's life, death, and resurrection for sins, putting aside its results like conversion or methods (Stott, *Christian Mission*, 40, 54); For Stott, evangelism entails conversation (dialogue) around the attitude of preachers' humility, integrity, and sensitivity, which are non-negotiable (Stott, *Christian Mission*, 56, 80, 81). This is because "true Christian dialogue with a non-Christian is not a sign of syncretism but is fully consistent with our belief in the finality (and the supremacy) of Jesus Christ" (Stott, *Christian Mission*, 71). Salvation is accompanied by conversion through repentance and faith in the gospel message (Stott, *Christian Mission*, 114). In particular, conversion includes the holistic sphere of life, so that mission is involved with the social implications of conversion in light of shalom (Stott, "Biblical Basis," 119–21).

unity of life and doing. In particular, it deals with life-witness and evangelism in a life of holiness, love, and compassionate service (arts. 15, 16). (3) *The Manifesto* highlights the subject matter of forgiveness of sins, justice and peace, loving service, and prophetic witness to social responsibility in terms of the kingdom of God (arts. 6, 9). (4) *The Manifesto* states that "God is the chief evangelist" and Christians are his "fellow workers" (art. 2). All Christians and local churches become witnesses in the context of the workplace, and worship without separating worship and witness. (5) *The Manifesto* consents that both Christians and churches should be incorporated with one another for the gospel's proclamation.

At the Manila Conference, evangelicals also emphasized evangelism and the proclamation of truth for the salvation of souls according to Scriptures. But they addressed concepts such as dialogue with other religions, salvation within the political and economic structure, unity of churches and witness of life as important topics in the discussion of the meeting. This expansion of the scope of dialogue is due to the fact that evangelicals had debated over various topics in the diverse circumstances of life around the world until the 1980s. Some of them did not limit salvation to soul salvation. By crossing salvation into the concept of liberation, political and economic activities were regarded as mission. In other words, many evangelicals admit that their mission brings freedom to the world under Jesus's lordship.

Thus, Lausanne II advanced two major discussions. *First*, mission is an integrated mission or holistic mission of evangelical evangelism and social responsibility which is for comprehensive salvation. After the Manila meeting, some evangelical theologians, like Orlando E. Costas, continued to develop a theological foundation for social actions within the dimension of the gospel's proclamation.[3] In *Christ Outside the Gate*, Costas seeks to create an integrative theology of personal and social salvation: "The demands of the kingdom do not encompass only personal and ecclesial affairs, but also social and institutional issues."[4] He argues that Christians carry a twofold eschatological responsibility for (1) the universal liberation of all creation that is (2) under the rulership of Jesus Christ. In particular, while respecting the just institutions, he emphasizes the role of Christians in resisting those that are unjust, which "become possessed of the devil and turn into enemies of justice."[5] More recently, Costas has argued that "the

---

3. Escobar, "Evangelical Missiology," 107; cf. Gutierrez, "Good News," 149–52; Houston, "Good News for the Poor," 153–61.

4. Costas, *Christ Outside the Gate*, 26, 93.

5. Costas, *Christ Outside the Gate*, 93.

evangel is the announcement of the good news of salvation."[6] Salvation is "liberation from the power of sin and death, being born into the family of God, and participation in the reign of Christ."[7] *Firstly*, the proclamation of salvation "witness[es] to the truthfulness of the gospel messages" in light of humanity's struggles for economic justice, human dignity, peace, solidarity, and hope.[8] *Secondly*, the proclamation of the gospel "call[s] for a decision about God's liberating action in Jesus Christ, to invite people to confess him as the Lord and Savior of their lives, to recruit them for God's kingdom, to persuade them to be reconciled to God through his Son, to make them his disciples."[9] In discussions of mission or salvation, these scholars went beyond the concept of spiritual salvation to continue defining the integral mission, including social salvation. Salvation meant being under Jesus's rule by repenting both personal sins and social sins.

Second, some evangelicals emphasize at Lausanne II that mission must be witness in life, and published the Lausanne Report *Proclaim Christ Until He Comes* (ed. J. D. Douglas [1990]). Among the contributors of the book, Camelo B. Terranova insists that Christian life is holiness associated with Jesus's life.[10] This holy life is one lived in the presence of God in order to open new mission fields and evangelize unbelievers. Meanwhile, Roberta Hestenes explores the biblical texts of Matt 28:18–20; Acts 1:1–4; 2:1–4; 1 Cor 12; and Gal 6:10. She emphasizes that Christians' unity and life in the community are to bear witness to Jesus and the Father's salvation.[11] These two theologians focus on the holy life and unity of both Christian individuals and congregations. Their witness in life is not merely a social action, but is also the result of believers' practice of love and service in the church, house, and workplace.[12] In particular, Hestenes aptly points out that Christians' lives are rooted in their "costly, sacrificial, compassionate, caring, and self-denying service to the Christian community" and produce reconciliation in the world (John 15:9–17; 2 Cor 4:5; 5:16–21; 6:3–10).[13] More importantly, Hestenes insightfully observes that the community's unity is relevant to one another's forgiveness, as God has forgiven sinners. She states, "A lack of forgiveness in the life of a fellowship can leave an organization vulnerable

6. Costas, "Evangelism," 33.
7. Costas, "Evangelism," 39.
8. Costas, "Evangelism," 37–41.
9. Costas, "Evangelism," 42.
10. Terranova, "Living Holy," 116–17.
11. Hestenes, "Christian Community," 120.
12. Hestenes, "Christian Community," 121–22.
13. Hestenes, "Christian Community," 120.

to deceit and pretense because the truth will not be handled sensitively and will be forced into hiding. Forgiveness opens the door to restoration and renewed service."[14] Forgiveness enables congregations to share in God's love. However, the Lausanne Committees, Terranova, and Hestenes still cling to the paradigm of mission that the holy lives of Christian individuals and congregations, in unity, aim at evangelism. In other words, the prior purpose of the church is to evangelize the world, despite the fact that it was thought that Christians' re-evangelization is necessary in the church (LC arts. 7, 13). Finally, *the Manifesto* shows the theological development of the integral mission concept, which includes witness in life and evangelistic, or proclamatic, witness.[15]

These discussions provided evangelicals with a variety of spectra on the understanding of mission.[16] However, many evangelicals maintained that the church's priority of mission is evangelization of the world through the verbal proclamation of the gospel.[17] They considered social responsibilities as (1) a means, (2) a result, (3) a partner of evangelism, and (4) conversion according to Jesus's Great Commission.[18]

Cape Town Commitment (2010, CTC)

In 2010, the Cape Town Congress echoed the Lausanne Covenant in their statement that God loves all humanity, and that mission is to "proclaim God's love for a world of sinners" (LC art. 3).[19] But evangelicals who prepared for the conference show theological changes. In the commitment,

14. Hestenes, "Christian Community," 125.

15. Bush, "Challenge Before Us," 60–61; Ford, "Proclaim Christ," 50; Hestenes, "Christian Community," 120.

16. Deborst, "Integral Transformation," 44–49, 52.

17. Adeyemo, "Critical Evaluation," 46–47; The early Christian churches pursued spiritual conversion and the transformation of pagan life into a new lifestyle in Jesus, both through evangelism and the practice of love (social concern) (Ro, "Perspectives of Church History," 16, 18–19). Ro's understanding is different from the Lausanne Covenant, as he notes that: "Although reconciliation with man is not reconciliation with God, nor is social action evangelism, nor is political liberation salvation, nevertheless we affirm that evangelism and socio-political involvement are both part of our Christian duty" (LC art. 5).

18. Adeyemo, "Critical Evaluation," 51.

19. The Cape Town Congress sustains both the biblical pillar of God's mission and the practical pillar of truth and peace (or reconciliation). Of course, in Part II, their truth-focused understanding of mission is meant to "bear witness to Jesus and all his teaching in all nations, in all spheres of society, and in the realm of ideas," from the holistic perspective (Dahle, "Mission in 3 D," 268, 272–75).

they present "unchanging truth" and "changeable truth" in order to both keep the truth of the gospel and realize God's universal plan for the world through changeable situations.

The design of unchangeable truth and changing truth acknowledges the diversity of churches' biblical interpretations and ecclesial traditions according to contexts beyond the frame of the absolute truth. It soon serves as the theological basis for evangelical churches' unity and cooperation. Furthermore, they sought to consider God's mission from his nature, understanding it in a more theological way (CTC art. 1):[20]

(1) The commitment defines mission as the *missio Dei*. God's sending act originates from his whole being and actions (art. 1.c). Just as God loves the world to begin with mission, the church also loves God and the world so as to commit to mission. (2) The commitment demonstrates that "evangelism comes from the overflow of a heart in love with Christ" (art. 7.b; cf. MM art. 5).[21] Evangelism is distinguished from proselytizing in that Christians must share the good news with others beyond forcing conversion onto unbelievers (CTC art. 3.c.1).[22] These evangelistic activities are based on the love that Christians have toward God, along with their response to his calling for compassionate forgiveness of sins, constant love and obedience. Those who might join the family of God by repentance and faith live according to God's command and the Spirit's sanctification in unity, honesty, and solidarity (art. 8.a, b, c). The commitment emphasizes that those lives enable the world to know Jesus and his teachings (art. 4). (3) The commitment specifies the world as the object of God's love. This idea helps evangelicals overcome the dualistic perspective that exists between God's kingdom and the sinful world ("toxic idolatry of consumerism," art. 7). Moreover, the commitment recognizes the world to be the place in which God is present (art. 7.a). Therefore, under Jesus's lordship, Christians should not only

---

20. For some evangelicals, mission as participation in the *missio Dei* focuses on the unity of life and action in terms of the triune God's character (Sunquist, *Understanding Christian Mission*, xiii). Similarly, John R. Franke agrees with David Bosch's idea that "mission is derived from the very nature of God and must be situated in the context of the doctrine of the Trinity rather than ecclesiology or soteriology" (Franke, *Missional Theology*, 62).

21. Thus, Cape Town pays attention to how churches should be motivated in order to evangelize the world. In this document, humanity is the subject of love language. In the first part of the confession of faith, the committees emphasize the subject "we," apart from a case of "We love because God first loved us": "a. We love the living God, b. We love God the Father, c. We love God the Son, d. We love God the Holy Spirit, e. We love God's word, f. We love God's world, g. We love the gospel of God, h. We love the people of God, and i. We love the mission of God" ("Cape Town Commitment," 61–67).

22. "Proselytizing is the attempt to compel others to become 'one of us,' to 'accept our religion,' or indeed to 'join our denomination'" (CTC C.1).

proclaim the gospel, but should also commit themselves to a missional calling in order to fulfill the mandate and stewardship. They make themselves responsible for the distorted world that is filled with poverty, oppression, injustice, and so forth.[23] (4) With regard to "unity in the church," the commitment emphasizes the solidarity of Christians, which works to evangelize the world: "A divided Church has no message for a divided world. Our failure to live in reconciled unity is a major obstacle to authenticity and effectiveness in mission. We urge Christian sisters and brothers worldwide" (art. F 1.b). The congress talks about the unity of the entire church community, but does not address the fact that there is diversity of the community, rather than unity in the church.

At Cape Town, evangelicals raised theological issues of mission. *Firstly*, they developed the concept of command-obedience to mission by their engagement in God's nature from the perspective of his mission. As has already been discussed at the Manila Conference, their understanding of mission concentrates on holistic, or integral, mission of evangelism and social actions in light of God's mission (CTC art. 10). In particular, the Cape Town Commitment emphasizes love and reconciliation in light of God's mission, in both nature and action.[24] Love is a motivational factor for the church as it participates in the *missio Dei* beyond "a command-obedience rationale."[25] Through "the proclamation and demonstration of the gospel," the church restores the world to "love and repentance in all areas of life" (art. 10.b).[26] Therefore, Cape Town inherits the theological frame of the previous Conferences: evangelism and social responsibility in light of command-obedience. At the same time, within the pluralistic context, they also develop the motivation and direction of mission in terms of God's mission, or love, as his nature. The church loves God so as to participate in his mission. Just as the Manila Conference was concerned with the holistic mission, Cape Town also deals with their life in love, reconciliation, and unity, along with the proclamation of the truth and the forgiveness of sins by repentance

---

23. "We do justice through exposing and opposing all that oppresses and exploits the poor. We must not be afraid to denounce evil and injustice wherever they exist. We confess with shame that, on this matter, we fail to share God's passion, fail to embody God's love, fail to reflect God's character and fail to do God's will" (CTC article, 7c). Here the congress speaks of poverty by sending away things that are oppressed, unjust, and poor. The biblical foundation for our commitment to seeking justice and shalom for the oppressed and the poor.

24. Schreiter, "From the Lausanne Covenant," 414–15.

25. Hunsberger, "Is There Biblical Warrant," 60.

26. Wright, "Third Lausanne Congress," 189.

and faith.[27] Therefore, the Manila Conference showed that, as evangelicals maintained the dichotomous frame of evangelism and social responsibility, they also integrated them in terms of God's reign and mission. They began to use mission as witness in order to reveal what they do and how they live. That is, social transformation might take place as believers practice love and service in their routine lives. This means that they live under Jesus's reign. Meanwhile, as part of God's mission, believers must imitate Jesus Christ, which refers both to evangelism and witness in a life of holiness, love, compassionate service, and unity.

Secondly, evangelicals' idea of changeable truth allows for the diversity of churches' interpretation of the truth in various situations ("Jesus Christ is the truth of the universe. Because Jesus is truth, truth in Christ is (i) personal as well as propositional; (ii) universal as well as contextual; (iii) ultimate as well as present" [CTC II, 1]). The fact that Jesus is the truth or that the truth is personal and professional in Christ means that people's perception of the truth can dissimilarly be shaped according to context. In the global and pluralistic world, their acknowledgement of the changeable truth enables them to communicate with Christians who have different theology and traditions within at least the evangelical circle.[28] The result suggests dialogue and cooperation among evangelical churches for mission. Evangelicals, of course, do not abandon the concept of the universal truth. Their biblical interpretation is yet restricted to the scheme of interpretation-application more than a contextual hermeneutic ("the well-adjusted teaching of the Bible" by excluding "a false gospel."[29] Therefore, evangelicals' unity and fellowship are ambiguous.[30]

Thirdly, the focus should be that evangelicals at Cape Town began to emphasize Christians' daily life within diverse cultural and religious contexts (art. 3). They clearly recognize that the modern context is pluralistic, and it is a time when truth is relatively recognized. Christopher J. H. Wright has already raised the following question within this context, concerning the church's mission: "What is needed if we are to bear such confident witness to Jesus in our contemporary world?"[31] He argues that Jesus should be proclaimed as the Truth, for just as YHWH's uniqueness was proclaimed in the Babylonian polytheistic situation, Jesus's unique nature was made

---

27. Concerning the concept of "Christlike living," see Packer, "Work of the Holy Spirit," 102–3.
28. Schreiter, "From the Lausanne Covenant," 90.
29. "Cape Town Commitment," 77.
30. Jørgensen, "Inspiration," 302.
31. Wright, "Difference," 245.

known within the Greco-Roman environment.[32] Wright continues to talk about the declaration of the Truth, while his other focus is on Christian's renewal of the life of Truth.[33] In this sense, he follows Newbigin's assertion that Christian communities can rebuild a "plausibility structure" in unity with the act of faith and by knowing facts, or the Truth, within a pluralized context.[34] Newbigin and Wright's concept of the unity between knowing and action is associated with Myers's "faithful witness" as a type of a missional life.[35] This missional life and knowledge of Jesus characterizes the uniqueness of Christian communities as found within the pluralistic world.[36]

In short, Lausanne I (1974) focused on evangelism and social responsibilities through the frame of command-obedience. However, the following Lausanne II and III expanded these theological frameworks into a holistic perspective, the so-called witness in life. As long as they emphasize mission as both evangelism and social responsibility through Jesus's commission-obedience, many evangelicals have recognized the church's love, service, unity, and holiness as bearing witness to their proclamation of the Truth and the gospel in a pluralistic society.[37]

Characteristics of Evangelical Mission

The concepts of mission that evangelicals have presented through international meetings reveal two distinctive characteristics, which both explain the nature of the evangelical holistic, or integral mission.

First, this mission is characterized by evangelism, which is the proclamation of the gospel according to Jesus's uniqueness and salvation.[38]

---

32. Wright, "Difference," 243.

33. Wright, "Difference," 250.

34. Wright, "Difference," 251; Newbigin, *Gospel*, 7; many Christian communities throughout the world have experienced the forfeiture of the "plausibility structure," which dominates the accepted thoughts and beliefs of a specific culture (Newbigin, *Gospel*, 6–8). Newbigin pointed out, long ago, the fact that such a pluralistic society does not universally accept any belief or value (Newbigin, *Gospel*, 7, 19).

35. Myers, *Engaging Globalization*, 238.

36. Wright, "Third Lausanne Congress," 190–95.

37. The witness of life is "a biblical lifestyle" concerned with "justice, compassion, humility, integrity, truthfulness, sexual chastity, generosity, kindness, self-denial, hospitality, peacemaking, non-retaliation, doing good, forgiveness." It is the life of worship that includes "joy, contentment, and love." Such a lifestyle is practiced by believing in and obeying the Word of God (CTC 6.d). Ultimately, as a model of Matthew's Sermon on the Mount, the acts of the heavenly Father is seen as the life of the church community that reflects his character (3.c).

38. Brown, "Closing Address," 296.

Individuals and society should repent and share the gospel by faith in Jesus, so that they may all dwell in his eternal life.[39] Evangelicals acknowledge the authority of the Bible and its teachings as the truth that evangelism is Jesus's Great Commission for the mission of both Christians and churches.[40] Therefore, their primary question is why. Their "calling to mission" based on biblical grounds asks them for absolute obedience to God's mission, which is meant for his kingdom.[41] The theological frame of evangelicals is described through the eschatological paradigm of "already" and "not yet."[42] In this way, evangelicals focus on the realization of God's reign in people and society. His reign entails his new creation and restoration of the world from sin.[43] Wright notes that, under the Gospel's light, evangelism will change from individual to whole society through Jesus Christ.[44] For this reason, evangelicals' mission concentrates on world evangelization.[45]

Second, evangelicals emphasize doing mission.[46] In view of both the nature of the *missio Dei* and the fulfillment of God's reign, they seek to practice his love and realize justice and truth within the diverse contexts of the world. The second questions are "how" and "what."[47] This can be explained in two ways: (1) evangelicals are concerned with doing through the practice of love and service. Wright follows Stott's idea that "mission concerns his redeemed people, and what he sends them into the world to do."[48] Without neglecting the Great Commission, Stott tries to draw attention to the great commandment: "love your neighbors" who live in a sick society.[49] These theologians emphasize that the church must practically participate in the *missio Dei* by obeying the Lord's command, loving both him and the world. (2) evangelicals are engaged in doing for the goals of personal and social transformation. Deborst states, "Mission is integral: it has to do with the transformation of human life in all its dimensions, not only the individual

---

39. Stott, *Christian Mission*, 42, 115–35.

40. Graham, "Why Lausanne," 3; Bebbington, *Evangelicalism*, 3; Wright, "Third Lausanne Congress," 169–70, 178–80; Netland, "Cape Town Commitment," 428.

41. Stetzer, "Evangelical Kingdom," 99–114.

42. Deborst, "Integral Transformation," 44.

43. Deborst, "Integral Transformation," 58–59; Escobar, *Changing Tides*, 43.

44. Stott and Wright, *Christian Mission*, 36.

45. Stott, *Christian Mission*, 58, 60.

46. Escobar, *Changing Tides*, 112–15; Padilla, "My Theological Pilgrimage," 132; Tizon, *Transformation after Lausanne*, 4–13; Deborst, "Integral Transformation," 52; Jørgensen, "Inspiration," 294.

47. Tizon, *Transformation after Lausanne*, 94.

48. Stott and Wright, *Christian Mission*, 36–38; cf. Stott, *Christian Mission*, 21.

49. Stott, *Christian Mission*, 31–32.

or sacred, but also the social and secular."⁵⁰ As she defines it, the "integral mission" or "holistic mission" carries the purpose of solving social justice, oppressed systems, poverty, and environmental problems within the context of life, realizing the justice and peace of radical discipleship.⁵¹ This aims to change both people and the environment as a whole.⁵²

Thus, for evangelicals, by 2010, mission is integral. They should participate in evangelism through the proclamation of the truth, and also in action for both the practice of love and the transformation of individuals and society.

CONTRIBUTIONS AND LIMITATIONS OF THE EVANGELICAL MISSION

In three international conferences, evangelicals contribute to the paradigm shift of the mission concept. They have expanded the mission as evangelism through the integral mission to the mission of God. Their renewal of the mission definition not only leads to a missiological and practical transformation of mission but also a challenge to reconsider the nature and identity of the church. Of course, it is true that there is still a discrepancy in the debate on the definition of mission in the 2010s and that their interpretations of John's Gospel are still limited to Jesus's Great Commission and the disciples' obedience in terms of the priority of evangelism.

Contributions

Through three international conferences (1974, 1989, 2010), evangelicals have contributed to (1) the paradigm shift of mission and (2) the understanding of the identity of the church.

First, evangelicals' conferences contribute to their paradigm shift of mission. They, including radical evangelicals and Two Thirds World evangelicals, discussed mission in light of both a variety of contexts and issues, and of the *missio Dei*.⁵³ At Lausanne I, they tried to define evangelism and social responsibilities from the dichotomous perspective, through which they distinguish the priority of mission from Christians' social service as

---

50. Deborst, "Integral Transformation," 52.

51. Padilla, "Integral Mission," 42–58.

52. Bebbington, *Evangelicalism*, 3; Tizon, *Transformation after Lausanne*, 3; Marsden, "Evangelical Denomination," 22–23.

53. Tizon, *Transformation after Lausanne*, 40–52.

a complementary role in evangelization. In the 1989 Manila conference, evangelicals drew attention to the entire gospel's proclamation in international missionary activities under the motto "the whole Church [to] take[s] the whole gospel to the whole world."[54] There was a change in the definition of the gospel and salvation here, in that salvation must take place in all areas of life. In particular, they emphasized that "the whole Gospel for the whole person in their sociopolitical, economic, cultural and religious contexts," for which mission is called "holistic mission."[55] And evangelicals more recently tried to define mission, its nature, and the motif of Christians' engagement through the theological lens of the *missio Dei*.

Firstly, after evangelicals presented "mission as transformation" at the 1983 Wheaton Conference, the "transformation" concept found its roots in the Lausanne Covenant, paragraph 5, which states that "the salvation we claim should be transforming us in the totality of our personal and social responsibilities."[56] At the same time, the concept points to "holistic mission" or "integral mission."[57] Under God's reign, mission transforms both the heart of a person and society.[58] Those at the conference discussed how evangelicals would respond to various issues that arise in today's context, such as Economics, Health, Hunger/Agriculture and Water, Relief, and HIV/AIDS (LOP 33, C. Rene Padilla, Bryant L. Myers "Humanitarian Response: Christians in Response to Uprooted Peoples," LOP 5 Christian Witness to Refugees).[59] The preface to the Cape Town Commitment is a serious discussion of environmental issues ("For the World We Serve: The Cape Town Call to Action"). The Cape Town Commitment 1, 7A, emphasizes that the whole earth is the object of mission and is God's mission field, which suffers from both poverty and violence. Preaching the whole gospel to the world is the integral mission, and is done for the sake of restoring the world (CTC pt. 2, IIB, 2A, 2B). This change is not aimed at the evangelicals' hostile understanding of the rapidly changing world and society in light of the dualism of the sacred kingdom and the secular world, but rather to the evangelical churches' participation in mission to the world as the sphere of God's reign. Their concern is with realization of God's rule in the field of

---

54. Douglas, "Manila Manifesto," 12.
55. Tizon, *Transformation after Lausanne*, 65.
56. Tizon, *Transformation after Lausanne*, 7–9, 21–22, 231.
57. Padilla, "Integral Mission," 42–58.
58. Tizon, *Transformation after Lausanne*, 68–69, 243–55.
59. "Holistic Mission (LOP 33)."

human life, resolving various sociopolitical-economic issues.[60] As a result, they seek to transform society.[61]

Secondly, the second paradigm of holistic mission is one of a witness of life. Those in the Manila Congress, on the one hand, developed the concept of mission as life-witness in order to emphasize the need for "being and witnessing," rather than "doing and strategy" for evangelism and outreach by.[62] Several evangelicals try to understand mission in light of the *missio Dei* (CTC 1, 7A).[63] They view that their activities in every field of life are missional. This is because when they participate in God's nature and activities in their situations, they can be witnesses in life.

Second, evangelicals gain an important understanding as to the nature and identity of the church in two ways. *Firstly*, in the Manila Manifesto, they begin to recognize the church as the sent congregations (MM II, 6, 8). They develop a gathering and scattering church, which bears witness to God through worship. The consciousness of this sent church brings forth the fact that all congregations should participate in mission, without discriminating between church leaders and laypeople in missionary activities (CTC II, 6; II, D, 1, 3). *Secondly*, they also recognize that, as a sent church, the missionary activities of the church are not mission, but rather that the church should participate in the *missio Dei*.[64] The concept of the sent church reminds Christians that visible churches are Jesus's one body, which must pursue unity within the big picture of the *missio Dei*. Jørgensen notes:

> The Lausanne Covenant states that 'the church's visible unity in truth is God's purpose.' Evangelism is a call to unity because our oneness strengthens our witness. The 1989 Manila Manifesto takes this a step further and affirms the 'urgent need for churches to co-operate in evangelism and social action, repudiating competition and avoiding duplication.' In the 2010 Cape Town Commitment the strong focus is on 'love'—love of the triune God and love of God's people. This love is the first evidence of obedience to the Gospel and 'a potent engine of world mission.'[65]

Jørgensen observes the Lausanne conferences according to their pursuit of the unity of the church. Since the unity of churches originates in the union of the triune God, their becoming one in truth and love is a witness,

60. Padilla, "Integral Mission," 2–3, 202.
61. Hutchinson and Wolffe, *Short History*, 248, 250–54.
62. Jørgensen, "Inspiration," 294.
63. Tizon, *Transformation after Lausanne*, 67.
64. Jørgensen, "Inspiration," 300.
65. Jørgensen, "Biblical and Theological Foundations," 35.

in and of itself, in the diversity of the world.[66] As Christ's one body, these sent churches should manifest that they are one in love, acting beyond the division of "barriers of race, colour, gender, social class, economic privilege or political alignment."[67] As a result, evangelicals work toward the actual coalition as "global partners" with other evangelical churches.

Therefore, evangelicals' three international meetings have provided transforming mission concepts for the missional roles of contemporary Christians and churches within their contexts. Evangelicals work to overcome the dualistic frame of mission, and also participate in God's mission in light of the ongoing and futuristic realization of his reign.

Limitations

Although many evangelicals attempt to agree to a missional understanding at Cape Town, two issues are presented by those who reacted to the Lausanne movements in the 2010s. *Firstly*, evangelicals have critically discussed the definition of mission. While some evangelicals still argue that mission is primarily evangelism meant for soul-salvation, some are involved with a holistic mission of both evangelism and social service within a sociopolitical and economic situation, or a pluralistic context. *Secondly*, three Lausanne Congresses have interpreted John 20:21, and other passages, from the perspective of Jesus's command and the disciples' obedience. Although they consent that mission is God's and comes from his person and activity, they confine the church's engagement in the *missio Dei* to their own activities. In my estimation, these issues need to be dealt with in the sense of the unity-relationship between God and his people. In particular, John's Gospel describes the mission of Jesus and the disciples through the concept of mutual indwelling, which provides a missiological frame for the unity of life-witness and verbal-proclamation. According to John's perspective, evangelization is not separated from life-witness, which includes services and works in all areas of life.

An Understanding of Mission

The first controversial issue is that of the understanding of mission. On the one hand, some evangelicals agree with the Manila and Cape Town Conferences, which combine evangelism and social engagement in order to

---

66. Jørgensen, "Biblical and Theological Foundations," 39–40, 44.
67. Dowsett, *Cape Town Commitment*, 25–26.

describe an holistic mission for "the transformation of human life in all its dimensions, not only the individual or sacred, but also the social and secular" under Jesus's lordship.[68] Tizon, speaking of this holistic mission, argues that it is in Christians' spiritual DNA to pursue their social responsibilities, for the purposes of social transformation, on the basis of prioritizing evangelism.[69] He defines evangelism as verbal proclamation at the expense of social justice.[70] This social justice is the inherent task of world evangelization, owing to "denouncing injustices and calling governments to repentance" and "promoting the righteousness of the Kingdom of God for and among the oppressed."[71] In particular, at Cape Town, evangelicals agreed

68. Steuernagel, "Latin-American," 316; Deborst, "Integral Transformation," 52.

69. Tizon, "Evangelism," 170; Evangelism and social action are the responsibility of evangelicals (Tizon, "Evangelism," 173). For this reason, Tizon proposes radical discipleship to Christians so that they might participate in the holistic mission without separating evangelism from social justice (Tizon, "Evangelism," 174). He suggests "mission as transformation" or "transformational movement" (Tizon, "Evangelism," 171), through which Christians embody the kingdom of God and change "from a condition of human existence contrary to God's purposes to one in which people are able to enjoy fullness of life in harmony with God" (Tizon, "Evangelism," 177). Accordingly, mission should pursue the transformation of structures, liberation, reconciliation between people, and community building, along with a change of heart, evangelization, reconciliation between God and people, and church planting (Tizon, "Evangelism," 178).

70. Tizon, "Evangelism," 171.

71. Tizon, "Evangelism," 172; Jonathan Leeman divides mission into two concepts: (1) "the broad mission is to be disciples or citizens, and (2) the narrow mission is to make disciples or citizens" (Leeman, "Soteriological," 20). The former concept focuses on being or doing, while the latter is involved in making disciples of Jesus Christ. He combines these concepts together in the scheme of sending and authorizing. Leeman tries to explain mission through the frame of Creation-Fall-Israel-Christ-Church-Glory of the Bible. *First*, he argues that the Bible advocates for holistic mission, or holistic salvation (Leeman, "Soteriological," 22–26). Mission is meant to represent God's character and his kingship over creation (Gen 1:28). In regard to his original purpose for creation, God selected Israel, and sent the Son and the church to "display his wise, holy and loving image for all the world to see" and "embody the justice of God" in their own community (Leeman, "Soteriological," 26). This is "nonverbal witness as life in word and deed" (Leeman, "Soteriological," 34, 41). *Second*, he emphasizes a priestly storyline throughout Scripture. The priestly mission concept is concerned with the vertical and horizontal separation that exists both between God and humanity and among people, and their reconciliation by way of solving the problem of sin through sacrifice and forgiveness (Exod 19:6; Jer 31:31–34; 1 Cor 3:16; 6:17; 1 Pet 2:5, 9) (Leeman, "Soteriological Mission," 27–28, 31). God authorizes the church to "preach a message of reconciliation, to separate holy from unholy [sinners] by identifying repenting sinners with God [reconciling], and to teach them" (Leeman, "Soteriological," 39, 40). This is evangelism through "speaking judge-like words of formal separation, identification, and instruction" (Leeman, "Soteriological," 41). Therefore, Leeman understands that Jesus was sent in order to bring God's glory and love to the world (John 20:21) (Leeman, *Don't Fire*, 50). The world must walk in obedience to the Father's commandment and

that mission was initiated by God, and is God's so-called mission.[72] They concentrate on God's sending act for what he ultimately wants to accomplish. The goal of the church's mission is to proclaim the gospel to all people, to make them disciples, and to establish churches (Matt 28:18–20; Rom 15:7–13; Eph 3:8–11; 1 Thess 5:11; 1 Tim 1:15; Rev 7:9–10).[73] Andy Johnson understands mission as God's mission that is meant for the salvation of the world.[74] For this purpose, God sends his Son to both forgive and save sinners.[75] The church is motivated by love for the glory and the truth of Jesus (3 John 7–8).[76]

However, David J. Hesselgrave criticizes the Cape Town Commitment's concept of a few points: (1) "substitution of the 'we love' formula for either the traditional 'we believe' or 'we affirm' formulas at the beginning of Commitment paragraphs seems to represent a turn away from confessional objectivity and in the direction of existential subjectivity";[77] (2) "this sort of expansionism overshadows the avowed 'centrality' of evangelism and world evangelization."[78] He goes on to argue that evangelism is the proclamation of the truth and the gospel, but is not Christians' practice of love for God and the world;[79] and (3) "to be and remain 'evangelical,' mission

---

live under Jesus's lordship (John 5:19, 30; 8:28; 12:49; 14:10). It is for this mission that Jesus sends his disciples into the world.

72. The theological frame around holistic mission is rooted in the mission of God. Wright understands the Old Testament mission as follows: (1) God's good creation, spoiled by sin and (2) the mission of Old Testament Israel. "Israel was not go to other nations but to be the nation God called them to be, to live as Yahweh's people and in the combination of their worship and the ethical quality of their social life (Deut 4:6–8), to bear witness to the identity and character of Yahweh their God in the midst of nations that knew him not as yet" (Wright, "Response to John R. Franke," 70). In the New Testament, he pays attention to the church's mission mandate in the aspect of how God's mission was accomplished and consummated. This mandatory mission includes five dimensions: (1) Evangelism, (2) Teaching, (3) Compassion, (4) Justice, and (5) Using and Caring for Creation. Wright argues that mission is meant to obey the Great Commission, which is dependent upon Jesus's lordship (Wright, "Response to John R. Franke," 77, 80). This obedience means that believers proclaim the good news of the kingdom and teach people to grow up in faith and discipleship. At the same time, believers should *respond* in faith and in repentance, *experience* in practical and ethical change of life, *do* justice, and *care* about creation under Jesus as the judge and Lord of creation (Stott and Wright, *Christian Mission*, 93; Wright, "Response to John R. Franke," 80–90).

73. Johnson, *Missions*, 28–29.

74. Johnson, *Missions*, 22, 47.

75. Johnson, *Missions*, 32–33.

76. Johnson, *Missions*, 40.

77. Hesselgrave, "Did Cape Town 2010," 84.

78. Hesselgrave, "Did Cape Town 2010," 85.

79. Hesselgrave, "Did Cape Town 2010," 85.

entities must understand and describe Christian mission as witnessing to the truth of the 'evangel' or good news of the gospel of Christ and discipling the peoples of the world in his Name with special attention being given to those who have yet to hear the gospel."[80] Hesselgrave has the mission concept of the narrowed evangelism, noting that "evangelicals must reclaim the apostle Paul as the model missionary, his message as entirely normative, and his methods as most instructive."[81] Similarly, Kevin DeYoung and Greg Gilbert argue that, if mission is the *missio Dei*, the church should participate in God's command until he completes the restoration of shalom and renews the world.[82] However, the church's mission is not equal to God's activity in the world, but rather is merely sent to accomplish specific tasks, such as verbal declaration and making disciples for repentance and faith in Jesus (Matt 15:24; Mark 13:10; 14:9; Luke 24:44–49; Acts 1:8).[83]

By contrast, Wright criticizes DeYoung and Gilbert's mission concepts as being too narrow to include social action as part of the church's mission.[84] Wright espouses Stott's integral mission, which focuses on "to do what" in terms of God's sending act (John 17:18; 20:21).[85] Stott's attention is focused on the matter of "do," "vocation," or "ministry as service" in Jesus's universal lordship. Stott and Wright both emphasize that the church inevitably expresses this mission through a doing-centered frame.[86] Meanwhile, Wright emphasizes that the engagement of Christians in God's mission is his work for the whole creation.[87] Strictly, Wright's opinion of God's mission is different from John R. Franke's. Franke notes that the inner Trinitarian love

---

80. Hesselgrave, "Did Cape Town 2010," 86.

81. Hesselgrave, "Did Cape Town 2010," 88; cf. Hesselgrave, *Paradigms in Conflict*, 141–65.

82. DeYoung and Gilbert, *What Is the Mission*, 28–29.

83. DeYoung and Gilbert, *What Is the Mission*, 29, 31–33.

84. Stott and Wright, *Christian Mission*, 43.

85. Wright, *Mission of God's People*, 23.

86. E.g., Timothy C. Tennent wrote "Lausanne and Global Evangelicalism: Theological Distinctives and Missiological Impact." In it, he argues that "mission refers to God's redemptive, historical initiative on behalf of His creation. In contrast, mission refers to all the specific and varied ways in which the church crosses cultural boundaries to reflect the life of the triune God in the world and, through that identity, participate in His mission, celebrating through word and deed the inbreaking of the new Creation" (Tennent, *Invitation*, 59). Therefore, Christian missions must not merely result from obedience to the Great Commission, but from their joyful response to an invitation to participate in the inner life of the triune God as "a missionary God" and his salvific work for the world (Tennent, *Invitation*, 61).

87. Stott and Wright, *Christian Mission*, 31, 140–41; Wright, *Mission of God's People*, 24–25.

will continue after judgment and completion of redemption, as the concept indicates the action of the Father's sending of the Son and the Spirit. Wright also raises a critical question: "How might we picture the dual nature of the *missio Dei* as, on the one hand, God's eternal purpose for creation and humanity that reflects God's own being as Trinity-in-love and, on the other hand, God's historical mission of bringing redemption and restoration to a world gone awry in sin and rebellion?"[88] He argues that the broad meaning of the *missio Dei* should be distinct from our mission that "we participate in God's creational mission as well as God's redemptive mission, as redeemed humans who are being restored in Christ to the unspoiled image of God."[89] Thus, Wright argues that Christian mission should include evangelism and social activities based on God's redemption and his creation, respectively.

In my judgment, the narrowed evangelism does not fully include God's mission toward the world and Christians' engagement in the mission. Obviously, mission includes evangelism, which asks people's objective confession through Christians' verbal proclamation and making disciples. However, mission must entail their practice of love for God and the world. God sends Christians and church communities to *be* witness, *say* witness, and *do* witness. Here, doing witness includes their social services and activities. They are sent to continually build up the world in all areas under God's reign. Deborst aptly suggests an integral transformational approach ("being," "doing," and "saying").[90] Although she uses the term "integrated whole," she is concerned with an integral transformation of both Christians and society in all areas of life, in light of radical discipleship and God's rulership. This integral transformation focuses on what and why, or who and how.[91]

Meanwhile, mission should reflect God's nature and activity in the inner relationship. To understand the nature of God's sending act, we need to consider the motivation and purpose of his act. Although God's mission is embodied in the frame of creation and redemption, the mission cannot exclude the theme of God's inner relationship. *Firstly,* God calls the world to his unity-relationship. Franke rightly argues that God calls all of creation to participate in the "eternal, relational intra-Trinitarian fellowship."[92] *Secondly,* God sends his people to bear witness to the gospel of his love through

---

88. Wright, "Participatory Mission," 141–42.

89. Wright, "Response to John R. Franke," 143; Stott and Wright's *missio Dei* concept and the church's mission are closer to that of J. Andrew Kirk, who argues that the church responds to the *missio Dei* by testifying to God's activity (Kirk, *What Is Mission*, 31).

90. Deborst, "Integral Transformation," 41–68, 143–44.

91. Deborst, "Integral Transformation," 141.

92. Franke, "Intercultural Hermeneutics," 93.

their lives of his love.[93] He understands mission as Christians' involvement in the attributes of God in light of God's mission. This leads to seeing that mission proclaims and testifies to God's love (John 3:16–17).[94] Accordingly, the nature of the church's mission bears witness to God's love for the world through the emulation of Jesus's self-sacrificing and self-giving love, through the perspective of the *missio Dei* (20:21–23).[95] The end of the *missio Dei* is salvation for believers, which includes the restoration of the created order of humanity and the world and fellowship with the Father.[96] Therefore, mission presents the comprehensive and integrated aspect of God's mission.

The Interpretation of John's Gospel for Mission

The second issue of debate is that of the evangelical limitation on the interpretation of John's Gospel in the frame of command-obedience. Their biblical hermeneutics aims at a proof-texting method, or the biblical foundation for mission approach to reading John through the lens of mission, which is the overarching theme of Scripture. The missional understanding of many evangelicals regarding the Johannine mission do not deeply reflect this unique missional notion of the Fourth Gospel.

At the Lausanne Conferences, most evangelicals tended to interpret John's Gospel in a way that justifies their own mission definition, based on the dichotomous framework of evangelism, social responsibility, and the transformation of both society and people, but not on the *integrated* framework of evangelism and life-witness. They are still concerned with how and why, and their focus is on evangelization and the realization of God's reign according to the socio-political-economic situation. As a result, in dealing with the Gospel, the Lausanne Conferences and the below-mentioned evangelical scholars have not fully explored John's missional meanings and significance in the framework of *integrated witness* from the perspective of mutual relationship. Instead, they interpret John's Gospel by involving themselves with the mission strategy and motivation of the church's sending act for evangelism and social service, each in light of Jesus's Great Commission and the church's obedience.

First, Lausanne I (1974) created a treaty based on several passages from John.[97] It describes the mission of the church as proclamatic witness

93. Franke, "Missional Theology," 57.
94. Franke, "Contextual Mission," 109.
95. Franke, "Contextual Mission," 113, 117.
96. Franke, "Intercultural Hermeneutics," 86.
97. The Lausanne Covenant presents its agreement by using the Gospel of John as

on the basis of God calling and sending his people (John 17:6, 18).[98] Their witness proclaims God's love for the world of the sinners, and calls people to repentance and faith in Jesus Christ (John 3:16-19 [art. 3]). Essentially, the church's mission is to evangelize the world, or to propagate the gospel, within the frame of command and obedience under God's reign (arts. 4, 6, 13).[99] Evangelism is the sacrificial service given to non-Christians, to whom Jesus sends his redeemed people (John 17:18; art. 6). At the same time, the church's unity also enforces Christian witness, which includes both words and deeds (John 17:11-23; art. 6).[100] However, article 7 of the covenant reveals the division between mission and other themes (e.g., truth, holiness, and worship). Evangelicals agree that the church's mission should preach the cross in order to evangelize the world through the sending of missionaries to other parts of the world (John 9:4; art. 8). This means that the priority of the 1974 Lausanne Covenant regarding Christian mission is placed on the proclamation of the gospel and disciple-making, according to the Great Commission.

The Lausanne Covenant includes Stott's understanding of John's Gospel. In 1966, he understood the sending formula as Jesus's Great Commission (John 20:19-23). Jesus imperatively sends his disciples so that they might evangelize the world. They should imitate "the first missionary Jesus's pattern of evangelism": (a) he was born into the world, (b) he lived (dwelt) in the world (1:14), and (c) he took up his cross and died for our sins (12:24-26).[101] Evangelical Christians must be committed to Jesus's command.[102] Their mission does imply proclamation or announcement of Jesus's gospel.[103] In the 1974 Lausanne meeting, Stott defined mission as God's activity that emerges from his nature.[104] The church follows God's sending of the Son, as follows (17:18; 20:21): (a) Christians are sent into the

---

follows: 17:6, 18 (for the purpose of God); 10:35 (for the authority and power of the Bible); 3:16-19; 4:42 (for the uniqueness and universality of Christ); 20:21 (for the nature of evangelism); 3:3, 5 (for Christian social responsibility); 17:18; 20:21 (the church and evangelism); 17:11-23 (for cooperation in evangelism); 9:4 (for the urgency of the evangelistic task); 17:15 (for spiritual conflict); 15:18-21 (for freedom and persecution); 3:6-8; 7:37-38; 15:26, 27 (for the power of the Holy Spirit); and 2:18; 4:1-3 (for the return of Christ) (Graham, "Why Lausanne," 3-9).

98. Graham, "Why Lausanne," 3.
99. Cf. Hunsberger, "Is There Biblical Warrant," 60.
100. Graham, "Why Lausanne," 26-27.
101. Stott, "Great Commission," 39-40.
102. Stott, "Great Commission," 40.
103. Stott, "Great Commission," 41.
104. Stott, *Christian Mission*, 66.

world, as Jesus became incarnate and (b) they are sent into the world not only to save and proclaim the gospel, but to also serve.[105] Samuel Escobar interprets Stott's idea both through the aspects of Jesus's first missionary model for Christians and the incarnate message of God.[106] Meanwhile, Rene Padilla interprets John 18:36 from the political perspective, noting that "to proclaim the Gospel is to proclaim the message of a Kingdom that is not of this world."[107] The world is under the power of darkness and sin (12:31; 14:30; 16:11), which drives humanity to commit evil deeds or sins (3:19; 8:34).[108] God sends his Son as the Savior of the world in order to save them and make them a community *in* the world (3:17; 4:42; 12:47).[109] Padilla pays attention both to Jesus's universal salvation of the sociopolitical aspect, and to individual people's lives through repentance and faith.[110] The purpose of Jesus's salvation is to establish a new humanity under his reign (17:11–18). In my estimation, Padilla's understanding fits well with the topic of John.

---

105. According to Stott, Christian churches might understand both their mission and that of God through the question, "Why and how did the Father send the Son?" (John 20:21) (Stott, *Christian Mission*, 26). Although the Son's mission is never entirely comparable to Christians in that he vicariously died for people in order to give them eternal life (1 John 4:9, 10, 14), Christians could exemplify Jesus's service as an incarnational model (Dan 7:14; Mark 10:45; Luke 22:27; Phil 2:5–8). He shows consistency between words and deeds in his mission, which becomes the basis of the church's integral mission of evangelism and social action through service and love in the world (Stott, *Christian Mission*, 27–33). However, Stott's incarnational model, based on the reading of John 20:21, has two critiques: (1) he regards "Jesus's mission as one of service." Of course, Jesus's mission involves the service of the poor and the marginalized. However, Jesus focused on saving all people, regardless of whether they are poor or rich (John 3:17; 6:57–58; Luke 19:5) (DeYoung and Gilber, *What Is the Mission*, 43–35); (2) he leads Christians toward the idea that they identify their mission with Jesus's mission (Stott, *Christian Mission*, 36–37). John distinguishes Jesus's unique mission from the disciples' continuing mission. While Jesus became flesh in order to save the world through his sacrificial death and resurrection, the disciples must never engage in his redemptive events, nor can they imitate a divine incarnation within a specific context, apart from their proclamation and witness in life. Ott and Strauss argue that the disciples' imitation of the work of Jesus results in the restoration of the culture and sociopolitical system of the society, beyond personal salvation. In explaining incarnation as the nature of mission, they claim that Jesus's incarnation is not a model for ministry approach, a cultural synchronization approach, or a contextual approach, but is rather bound with the relationship between the Sender and the Sent one, or between Jesus and the church in John 17:18 and 20:21 (Ott and Strauss, *Encountering Theology of Mission*, 103).

106. Escobar, "Evangelism," 309.
107. Padilla, "Evangelism and the World," 116–17.
108. Cf. Beyerhaus, "World Evangelization," 289.
109. Padilla, "Evangelism and the World," 120–22.
110. Padilla, "Evangelism and the World," 128–33.

Since Jesus's kingdom is not part of the world, the sent community of Jesus is in the world, but must also realize the value and purpose of radical discipleship within the holistic (political, social, and economic) spheres of life (13:35; 17:23).

In short, the Lausanne Congress made use of John 20:21 in order to understand God's mission. Through this verse, those at the congress emphasized the incarnation and service of Jesus's coming. Furthermore, based on the theme of unity found within John's Gospel, the congress regarded the unity of the church as the essence of her witness. However, the congress did not dig deeper into how the use of, and witness in, the literary structure of John's Gospel is used or explained (1:7, 8).[111] Often times, John 20:21 was interpreted in light of the category of the Great Commission through the frame of command and obedience (Matt 28:19-20; Mark 16:15; Luke 24:47).[112] Arthur P. Johnston pays attention to Jesus's bearing of witness (John 18:37) and the embodiment of the truth in his ministry (14:16).[113] His witness does not mean life-witness, but rather both ministerial deeds and evangelistic proclamation of God's kingdom (5:39; 16:12-15).[114] He continues to argue the priority of verbal proclamation. That is why seeing does not lead people to faith (6:36; 7:3-5; 11:45, 46), although "Jesus's signs are revelation" for their faith.[115] Therefore, Lausanne I comprehended John's mission in order to highlight Christians' evangelistic, or proclamatic, witness for world evangelization (10:27).

Second, the Manila Congress (1989), in succession with the Lausanne Covenant, asserts Christ's uniqueness for salvation, which is given to the world only through Jesus and through faith (14:6).[116] It recognized God as "the chief evangelist," stating that he sends the Holy Spirit of truth for the purposes of repentance and belief through evangelism (MM art. 5; John 15:26-27; 16:8-11). Meanwhile, the conference interpreted John 13:34, 35; 17:21, 23 as a way of showing that God reveals himself by way of Christians' practice of love for one another and their fellowship in unity (arts. 8, 9) (John 15:12).[117] To me, this interpretation is judged as consistent with how John understands his disciples' identity as a sent community of witnesses who must live according to a new way of life that bears the fruit of love

---

111. Adeyemo, "Critical Evaluation," 57–58.
112. Parks, "Great Commission," 483–91.
113. Johnston, "Kingdom," 114.
114. Johnston, "Kingdom," 121.
115. Johnston, "Kingdom," 127.
116. Douglas, "Manila Manifesto," 29.
117. Hestenes, "Christian Community," 120.

(13:35; 17:23). In 1989, however, the priority of mission was still placed on world evangelization.[118] It was believed that Christians must become witnesses who undertake evangelistic (witness) and social (service) ministries according to the integral aspect of Christian mission.[119] Eduardo M. Maling argues that "Christ, the Good Shepherd, died for church growth and world evangelization. He commissioned and commanded his church to do the same. 'As the Father has sent me, I am sending you' (20:21)."[120] The church should proclaim Jesus as the truth of God (8:32, 36; 14:6; 18:37–38).[121] Peter Kuzmic contends that "evangelism is a life before it is a task," for evangelism includes both "how shall they hear?" and "what shall they see?"[122] Interestingly, Manila did not deal with life-witness, but rather with evangelism in light of John's Gospel.

Third, in 2010, on the basis of the Johannine theological concept of love (3:16), the Cape Town Congress developed the language of love in order to define both God's mission and the church's engagement in this mission.[123] God's mission emerges out of his love for the world; meanwhile, Christians love and obey him through evangelization.[124] The conference bases its biblical foundation on the Gospel of John more strongly than previous conferences did, arguing that God's love is the motivation behind the sending of his Son and the giving of a sacrificial and self-giving death for our sins (1:18; 3:16; 14:21).[125] Believers also love him and obey his command so that they

---

118. Ford, "Proclaim Christ," 50, 52–53; Maling, "Importance of the Local Church," 73.

119. Ford, "Proclaim Christ," 50; Hammond, "Laity," 83; The church's mission is not to develop a new work, but rather to maintain Jesus's ministry for the Father's redemptive work. Its task is to proclaim the forgiveness of sins for people's repentance and God's judgment for unbelievers (John 13:20; 20:23) (Tennent, Invitation, 156–58).

120. Maling, "Importance of the Local Church," 74.

121. Kuzmic, "How to Teach the Truth," 198.

122. Kuzmic, "How to Teach the Truth," 199–200.

123. Schreiter, "From the Lausanne Covenant," 416.

124. Dowsett, Cape Town, 170.

125. The Cape Town Commitment contains the structure of repentance-forgiveness-reconciliation (Dowsett, Cape Town, 65). In this structure, forgiveness is a one-time event, and is not continuous (Dowsett, Cape Town, 65). The evangelicals confine the notion of forgiveness to the idea that someone no longer condemns the sin of others. However, John characterizes sin in two dimensions: firstly, God forgives believers once and for all through the purifying event of Jesus's sacrificial death (art. 3, a); secondly, both God and the believers continue in purification and forgiveness (John 13:1, 10). Moreover, John's Gospel does not use the term "repentance," but rather pays attention to the fact that Jesus transfers sinners from the darkness to the light by faith so that they might live the lives of children. John illustrates the transition of their lives as the comprehensive and ongoing work of God. R. J. Schreiter's definition of forgiveness is likely suitable for John's concept, as he views that a victim's forgiveness antecedes a

can devote themselves to saving the world according to this holistic aspect (15:12).[126] In essence, their missional commitment is rooted in both their zeal for Jesus's glory and in the intimate relationship between the Father and his children (14:6). Therefore, theological changes in Cape Town are prominent in comparison to those made in previous conferences (1974, 1989). The most remarkable aspect is the bringing of God's mission to the surface, based on the Gospel of John.[127] Here, God's mission is indicative of his sending of both the Son and the disciples. Together, they focus on proclaiming the gospel and embodying love, which motivates God's sending act. This does not deny the definition of evangelism as mission as determined in the previous two conferences; based on John 4:42, "to proclaim Jesus as 'the savior of the world' is not to affirm that all people are either automatically or ultimately saved, still less to affirm that all religions offer salvation in Christ."[128] Moreover, the congress confirms that Christians preach Jesus Christ according to the Holy Spirit's mission (20:20-21, 28; 14:16-17, 25-26; 16:12-15; 4:23-24; "the gospel of his incarnation, life and ministry in proclamation of the kingdom of God, death on a cross, resurrection, ascension, and descending for judgment").[129] At the same time, their mission includes all dimensions of "evangelism, bearing witness to the truth, discipling, peace-making, social engagement, ethical transformation, caring for creation, overcoming evil powers, casting out demonic spirits, healing the sick, suffering and enduring under persecution."[130]

However, while the Lausanne Conferences see John's Gospel through the lens of a command-obedience under Jesus's Great Commission, it is important to note that God's mission first began with his nature, life, and work. Flemming aptly argues that evangelism, or verbal proclamation, is never

---

wrongdoer's repentance so that the wrongdoer might repent of sins and be restored as a new creation (Schreiter, *Ministry of Reconciliation*, 57–58). God, at first, forgives the world and gives his son over to death in order to purify and restore it. His forgiveness results in the unity and reconciliation of both the world and the church, which must both practice forgiveness in their own situations. Thus, John's Gospel emphasizes the life-witness based on Jesus's life-pattern, while not using the words *proclaim* or *make disciples* (Dowsett, *Cape Town*, 62–63).

126. Dowsett, *Cape Town*, 171–72.

127. Schreiter understands that Cape Town Conference bases its theological foundation on John's Gospel and Paul's Epistles: "The Johannine writings, so central to Cape Town's theological concept of love, also have an ambivalence about the 'world'. The world is seen at once as utterly alienated from God but also the object of God's great love (cf. John 3:16)" (Schreiter, "From the Lausanne," 414–15, 416).

128. Netland, "Cape Town Commitment," 436.

129. Dowsett, *Cape Town*, 184.

130. Dowsett, *Cape Town*, 176, 178.

separated from "being," "saying," and "doing" in life.[131] His idea is based on the perspective that the *missio Dei* is "a witness to the gracious mission of the triune God."[132] Mission sprouts from God's loving character, and as such, he sends his Son to give life to the world (3:16–17; 5:23, 30, 36; 12:44, 49).[133] Flemming observes that (1) "Jesus's mission is more about 'being' than 'doing'"; (2) the mission is not ours, but is God's; (3) John's Gospel underlines "the missional impact of the common life of the Christian community"; (4) "love is both the motivation and character of mission"; (5) the mission is testifying to the truth in words and life; and (6) the mission is "a magnificent synergy between being, doing and speaking the good news."[134] For me, these mission concepts converge upon life-witness and speaking the truth (8:32; 18:37). In Jesus's incarnational sentness as the living Word, he testifies to himself and teaches the truth from God. In John's Gospel, mission is to "do witness," "say witness," and "be witness" (14:10–12).[135]

Finally, in John's Gospel, God's mission is involved with verbally proclaiming his salvation. At the same time, his mission is also engaged with revealing his own life and identity through people, who are in the unity-relationship, to the world. Both verbal proclamation and revealing of God in life are witness. In other words, just as the coming of Jesus arrived through incarnation in order to testify to the Father residing in Jesus himself, so, too, must the disciples be witnesses to Jesus, the Father, and the Holy Spirit that abides among them. It is missional to share person, life, identity, and actions anytime and anywhere within a mutual indwelling relationship (13:1–38; 17:17–19).[136] For this purpose, God consecrates Jesus's disciples from the sinful world and sends them out into it.[137]

MISSIONAL IMPLICATIONS OF JOHN'S GOSPEL FOR THE FUTURE OF EVANGELICAL MISSION

Evangelicals have worked to renew the definition of mission for approximately thirty years, across three separate international conventions. They develop the concept of the holistic mission of evangelism and social responsibilities. They continue to propose the theological frames of: (1) God's

131. Flemming, *Recovering*, 273–76.
132. Flemming, *Why Mission*, xix.
133. Flemming, *Recovering*, 114.
134. Flemming, *Recovering*, 128–30.
135. Cf. Deborst, "Integral Transformation," 44.
136. Kirk, *What Is Mission*, 28.
137. Flemming, *Recovering*, 120; *Why Mission*, 62.

reign, and (2) the *missio Dei*. The former proposal suggests that evangelism and social participation center on the realization of God's kingdom through the salvation of individuals and society. This approach engages with their participation in sociopolitical issues for the transformation of the society. The latter proposal is that the holistic mission refers to the church's involvement in the *missio Dei*. This perspective highlights God's nature and activity, along with the church's calling to mission.

But not all contemporary evangelicals agree with these arguments. Some are in the position of critics, while others either try to understand God's mission as the realization of his reign or through the relationship of God. While participating in this discussion in this section, I will consider the missional implications of the Fourth Gospel for the Johannine community. John implies the community's mission in three ways: (1) the identity of the church community, (2) the relationship between both God and the community and within the community itself, and (3) the understanding of the Johannine mission.

Church as the Sent Community for Mission

The Johannine community is a sent community (John 17:18; 20:21). It dwells in the world but belongs to God (17:23). John likens Jesus's identity to his community as a sent community by highlighting the technical frame of "as . . ., so . . ." (17:18; 20:21). This group is the incarnational and hermeneutical community found in the world.

An Incarnational Community

The fundamental purpose behind Jesus's being sent into this world is to accomplish God's mission. He reveals the Father to the world and accomplishes his work of salvation. The beginning of Jesus's sentness is incarnation (John 1:14), and he himself becomes a tabernacle in order to reveal God (1:18). Anyone who sees Jesus can see the Father (14:9–10), his works disclose the Father (6:39; 9:3; 14:11, 31), and people become believers through him in order to worship God in Spirit and Truth (4:24).

Following the same pattern, Jesus sends his disciples (17:18; 20:21). However, their sentness should be distinguished from the incarnational event of the Word, namely Jesus's own sentness. Some evangelicals use Jesus's incarnation as a model for the contextual missionary activities of the church and translatability of the gospel, emphasizing that Jesus became incarnate in the sociopolitical and economical structure "within the limited realties

Missional Implications of John's Gospel for the Future of the Evangelical Mission 175

of a given time and space."[138] Stott argues that Jesus's incarnation event is a model for Christians' mission, who are sent by Jesus (17:18; 20:21).[139] For Costas, today's missionaries might take Jesus's incarnational model from the Christocentric perspective.[140] Jesus's mission centers on a sacrificial lifestyle and humble service, and his followers imitate this mission pattern.[141] A problem arises, however, as to whether the church can take on Jesus's incarnation as a model. In light of this, Darrell L. Guder raises a critical question: "can and should the unique event of the incarnation of Jesus that constitutes and defines the message and mission of the church have concrete significance for the way in which the church communicates that message and carries out that mission?"[142]

Köstenberger objects to the understanding of incarnation as a method of mission, or for the servanthood-principle of service to human need.[143] The event is unique, as Jesus died on a cross for the sin of the world. The church is simply sent to "re-present" this message of salvation and "giving of life" as it forgives sin (1:29, 36; 3:16–17; 6:53–58; 10:10; 17:2; cf. 20:23), which Jesus accomplished through his death and resurrection.[144] Rather, Köstenberger argues that the model of Jesus's relationship with the Father as Sender can be applied to the relationship between God and the disciples. These disciples must imitate Jesus in order to "re-present" him accurately (1:14, 18).[145] Köstenberger also throws two controversial themes into the discussion. *Firstly*, does John really describe incarnation as a missional methodology, or as a model for the disciple's mission? Can Christians understand, for example, how to convey a message in either an incarnational or a contextual way? *Secondly*, should Jesus's incarnation be considered only as a unique form of his sentness? Is his incarnational pattern discontinuous from the mission of the sent faith community?

On the one hand, the first query should be agreed upon. In John's Gospel, Jesus's incarnation is not "an ongoing process" or "a repeated model"

---

138. Costas, *Christ Outside the Gate*, 107.
139. Stott, *Contemporary Christian*, 357.
140. Costas, *Christ Outside the Gate*, 107.
141. Guder, "Incarnation and the Church's," 174.
142. Guder, *Incarnation*, xii–xiii.

143. Köstenberger, *Missions of Jesus*, 15; by contrast, David Hesselgrave understands that "the incarnational model focus is on continuity between Christ's incarnate earthly ministry and the contemporary ministry of the church today," while the representational model is involved with the discontinuity between the ministries of Jesus and the church (Hesselgrave, *Paradigms in Conflict*, 149–51).

144. Köstenberger, *Missions of Jesus*, 212–15.
145. Köstenberger, *Missions of Jesus*, 216–17.

in that the event presupposes his preexistence and giving of life to people, regardless of the message's translation into cross-cultural and linguistic circumstances.[146] Jesus came as flesh and dwelt on earth as a natural human (1:13, 14; 8:15; 17:2).[147] The incarnation, which can never be repeated again, is a divine event that took place in God's redemptive history in order to bring "heavenly revelation and divine life" (3:31–36; 6:51; 8:32, 45; 17:17; 18:37).[148] However, those who espouse an incarnational model are involved with the contextualization of the gospel in local contexts. Stott, Guder, and Flemming offer two words, "identification" and "contextualization."[149] The former means that "Jesus identified with the human situation," while the latter points to his immersion in the Jewish cultural world.[150] In fact, Flemming senses that "we should view Jesus's incarnation more as a theological lens that helps shape our understanding of mission than as a model to strictly imitate."[151] The incarnational event primarily focuses on the theological understanding of Jesus's identity and divine work. According to Jude Tiersma Watson, however, the incarnational concept of identification and contextualization carries two problems.[152] *Firstly*, the disciples cannot become the Messiah like Jesus Christ, who saves people from distorted and corrupt situations. *Secondly*, the disciples face the danger of contextualizing their own horrible ideas and bad lifestyle into a new context, although they

146. Köstenberger, *Missions of Jesus*, 216; Hesselgrave, *Paradigms in Conflict*, 147; Billings, *Union with Christ*, 124.

147. Thompson, *Incarnate*, 49.

148. Schnackenburg, *Gospel according to St John*, 1:266, 267, 273.

149. Specifically, Dean S. Gilliland states that "as members of the body of Christ interpret the Word, using their own thoughts and employing their own cultural gifts, they are better able to understand the gospel as incarnation" (Gilliland, "Contextual Theology," 12–13). He argues that the young church should critically contextualize the message of the gospel so that the indigenous people might understand it within their own cultural context. This is because Jesus's incarnation is a tunnel through which God's truth is delivered to people (Gilliland, "Contextual Theology," 25). The concept of incarnation as contextualization raises a question: can humanity contextualize the gospel in "Jesus's way," as Jesus became flesh? Can his Jewish identity and ministry in his home country be a model of contextualization and indigenization for today's Christian mission (Guder, "Incarnation and the Church's," 178–79, 181)? Jesus was born as a Jew and lived in the Jewish world. From the beginning, he had a Jewish background, including but not limited to worldview, monotheism, faith, Scripture, and social-ritual contexts. In such a circumstance, he delivered God's message to his people. It is doubtful that Jesus's incarnation, or birth as a Jew, could be a model for contextualization or mission in cross-cultural situations or in other contexts.

150. Stott, *Contemporary Christian*, 356–74; Guder, *Incarnation*, 52; Flemming, *Why Mission*, 70.

151. Flemming, *Why Mission*, 70.

152. Watson, "What Does It Mean," 11.

Missional Implications of John's Gospel for the Future of the Evangelical Mission 177

might contextualize the gospel within the same situation. John does not apply either the incarnational language or the metaphor to the disciples' proclamation and translation of the gospel's message in these cross-cultural contexts. Instead, he emphasizes not only Jesus's unique sentness, which represents his divine identity and ministry, but also his testimony of the divine message that comes from the Father (1:1–18; 7:16).[153] Jesus is the perfect channel of God's communication into the world, while people can play a role in delivering the gospel message to the people (17:20; 18:37).[154] Applying John's incarnational language to a Christian mission model is inadequate, as the incarnate God fulfills his salvation (1:14).[155] Christians must be with the Holy Spirit through the dependent relationship in order to bear witness to Jesus (14:16–18; 15:26–27; 16:15; 20:22).[156]

On the other hand, the second question needs to be understood in terms of existential and relational aspects, along with the dimensions of imitation and representation.[157] This question needs to be understood in light of the form of Jesus's incarnation.[158] The incarnation indicates that God sent him into the world so that he might become the tabernacle. Although he becomes a man and accomplishes specific tasks within a limited time and space, he is the dwelling place of the Sender's presence on earth (1:14, 18). In other words, Jesus is in unity with the Father, and as such, he reveals God in character, life, words, and deeds, as well as he fulfills his works; "God's revelation occurs in the human sphere or in the fleshly sphere."[159] He reveals God's glory to the world (1:14).[160] In the same vein, if Jesus's own incarnation was applied to Christians, it would not be understood as a methodical model, but rather as a relational and ministerial union between the incarnate Son and the sent ones (14:7–11; 17:22–26; 20:21).[161] Moreover, when Jesus sends his disciples, he does not ask for incarnation. Rather, Jesus sends those who dwell in him, and as himself, he teaches them to reveal the Triune God, who is indwelling in them, and to complete his mission. If Jesus abides in them, Jesus appears in their lives, character, doings, words, and ministry

---

153. Guder, "Evangelism," xiii.
154. Thompson, *Incarnate*, 35–36.
155. Guder, *Incarnation*, 50–51; Billings, *Union with Christ*, 124; Flemming, *Why Mission*, 69.
156. Keener, "Sent Like Jesus," 30, 39, 41.
157. Billings, *Union with Christ*, 132.
158. Flemming, *Recovering*, 114.
159. Thompson, *Incarnate*, 34.
160. Schnackenburg, *Gospel according to St John*, 1:266.
161. Guder, "Incarnation and the Church's," 173; Flemming, *Why Mission*, 62.

because Jesus promises that they are to do greater things than him (14:12), while at the same time disclosing himself to them (1:18; 12:45).[162]

Therefore, when Jesus sends his disciples, he is present in the midst of them. The risen Jesus stands among his disciples, whose imagery is that of the tabernacle amid God's people (20:19). Under the picture of the fulfillment of Ezekiel's eschatological promise, Jesus himself gives the Holy Spirit as a temple (Ezek 47:1–12 and John 7:37–39; 20:22). John calls Jesus's resurrected body "the temple" (2:21). He is in them, and they are in him (17:18–20). Therefore, when Jesus sends his disciples, they already reside in the world as part of their union with Jesus. Accordingly, the community's incarnational witness reveals Jesus in them.

Their incarnational witness should show God's love and presence, which Jesus discloses through his sacrificial death (19:30). God loves the world so that he gives his unique son for the eternal life of his sheep, or his nation (1:29; 10:10–11, 17, 28; 11:51–52; 12:24, 33–34). Through his incarnation, Jesus reveals the glory of God to the world by revealing his own glory and love in order to save people from judgment (1:14, 18; 3:14–15; and 12:32; 19:35, 37, [3:16–21, 31–36]; 12:37–50). It is through the foot-washing act that Jesus explains his self-giving death in love and humble service (13:1–38 and 12:26). The way the sent disciples are to participate in Jesus's sacrifice is through love and service in humility. This is their way of life-witness (13:15, 16, 20, 34–35, 36–37). To this end, Jesus sent the church into the world. They are not aliens, but rather are part of the social community that lives in the world.

A Consecrating Community

The church as the sent community is a purified community in light of Jesus's foot-washing narrative. Here, the purification concept does not mean the church is liturgical (John 13:10–11, "pure" or "clean" [καθαρός]). Instead, the concept points out Jesus's consecration of his followers and the communities for their being set apart unto the holy God in the world. Before sending them, Jesus washes them from the worldly life-pattern in order to share his life with them (13:8, 15). They should continue to consecrate themselves from the defilement of evil through Jesus's word, so that they might belong to the holy God and bear his fruit (13:10–11; 15:2–3). Thus, they can have "part" with him who cleanses people from their sin, evil, and defilement (13:8, 36–37). Moreover, they are sent to become a consecrating community either to set the world free from sin or forgive anyone's sin in the world to

---

162. Guder, *Be My Witnesses*, 162–67; Keener, "Sent Like Jesus," 24.

let it participate in God. John understands freedom or forgiveness of sin, which is Jesus's mission (8:32–34; 20:23). In other words, the church is sent to make people set free from the evil of the world in order to follow Jesus. Their following indicates bearing fruit and participating in Jesus's purifying ministry in the holy unity with him. Ultimately, the consecrating churches, which produce Jesus's fruits, reveal God's nature and activity of holiness within both their community and the world.

However, unfortunately, for a long time, some evangelicals have criticized the church for indulging in materialism and sticking to the church's quantitative growth through evangelism.[163] The churches are addicted to growth, materialistic, and consumeristic factors by programs. They seem to be accustomed to the worldly life-pattern and way such as corruption and greed generated in pursuit of wealth.[164] This means that the sent church is not able to be Jesus's witness in the holiness of the church.[165] More recently, many young evangelicals have tried to participate in the spiritual movement beyond the preference of mega-church and church growth. By the early 2020s, they have focused more on "authentic inner life and personhood" than on "group identity and social location."[166]

In this situation, evangelical churches should reconsider their identity as a consecrating community. They are sent to the world, by consecrating both the church and the world. They must remove the pollution of sins from the life of communities and small groups: deceit, corruption, and greed. Just as Jesus humbly washes his disciples' feet in order to join his life, so, too, must the church constantly purify itself and abide in his life. Their consecration pursues not only individual moral life but also the purification of the faith community in relationship with the holy God. Furthermore, they are sent to consecrate the corrupt and defiled of the world.

---

163. Noll, *Scandal*, 75.

164. Today, many megachurches are being criticized by people who recite Dick Halverson, "In the beginning the church was a fellowship of men and women centering on the living Christ. Then the church moved to Greece, where it became a philosophy. Then it moved to Rome, where it became an institution. Next it moved to Europe where it became a culture, and, finally, it moved to America where it became an enterprise" (recited from Larson, *Wind & Fire*, 50). To evangelicals, a challenge is how they can erect an influence on reshaping such stereotyped churches which are held captive to materialism and Victorianism of numeral growth under the influence of church growth theory (McGavran, *Church Growth*, 12–45).

165. Guder, "Evangelism," 147; Kyle, *Evangelicalism*, 67–68.

166. Kyle, *Evangelicalism*, 266.

A Hermeneutical Community

The community of faith is one that is hermeneutical. Until several decades ago, evangelicals focused on transforming their society in order to realize God's reign. However, mission as transformation encounters critical questions, such as who and toward what? Ruth Padilla Deborst suggests an "integral transformation."[167] She continues to ask the question how, insisting that the church should enter society. The church is a social community.[168] In this social community, the church must transform everything in the world that has been polluted with sin into Jesus's life-pattern of love and service. The disciples should free people from the slavery of sin by believing in Jesus so that he might live in them (John 8:31–32, 34–35, 41–44). The disciples' "integral transformation" in society is the essence of the sent community.

Before integrally transforming the world though, the sent community must constantly transform itself. Evangelicals believe that the Bible is a standard of faith, and work to build a community in light of its teachings (cf. the Lausanne Conference documents [1974, 1989, 2010]). Their biblical hermeneutical premise believes that the Bible is the word of revelation inspired by the Holy Spirit. They work to find the original meaning of Scripture, and then apply it to the present situation. Here, I suggest that evangelicals should further expand and understand the hermeneutical role of the Holy Spirit.[169] In John's Gospel, the Holy Spirit is the missional Spirit (15:26; 16:4a; 20:22) that was sent into the world in the frame of the *missio Dei* (20:21–22).[170] The Spirit's role is to interpret, translate, and teach Jesus's words and actions for the Johannine community (14:26; 16:13). John describes that the Spirit's new interpretation within a specific context leads the community "into all the truth" (16:13).[171]

---

167. Deborst, "Integral Transformation," 58.

168. Deborst, "Integral Transformation," 58–59.

169. Hall, "Who Tells," 4; Fowl, *Engaging the Scriptures*, 189; Cartledge, "Text-Community-Spirit," 236–39; Keener, *Spirit Hermeneutics*, 160.

170. Cf. Brown, *John XIII–XXI*, 699–701; In the "Missio Dei Revisited" of the Witness of God, John G. Flett proposes the *missio Dei* concept, which is actualized through the unity of God's nature and act of his internal and external movements (Flett, *Witness of God*, 286–92). At the same time, the concept refers to God's self-witness through "his own proper life" in the world and faith community's response in their own proper life. Their life is a witness to God in "the living history of our fellowship with God" (Flett, "Theology of Missio Dei," 73). For another definition of the *missio Dei*, see Oborji, *Concepts of Mission*, 8.

171. Olsson, Structure and Meaning, 269, 270–71; Nissen, *New Testament*, 93; Parsenios, *Departure*, 81.

Ultimately, the Spirit's role is to let the community of disciples know Jesus and live within the truth according to his teachings. The core of Jesus's teachings is that his disciples follow his words and live in him so as to bear much fruit (8:31; 15:3–12). Their lives are the missional life. Just as Jesus himself practiced it, the disciples must also live according to his life-pattern (13:15, 35; 17:23). Their lives are identified as Jesus's disciples, and testify to God's abiding in them. The Holy Spirit helps the disciples keep Jesus's teachings. Then, it may be said that the interpretative goal of the Holy Spirit is to have his disciples bear the fruit of Jesus's words. The sent community is a small society within the larger world, and their missional life of producing Jesus's fruit must be realized within the community. From this point on, the transformation of the world can begin, and they should lead the larger world into the total transformation of life in which they live. Therefore, the sent church must deal with the role of a hermeneutical community, which interprets Jesus's teachings so that individual disciples can participate in Jesus's life and identity by making fruits of love and service (14:17; 15:1–8, 16, 26; 16:13).[172]

Relationship of Unity for Mission

Until the 2010 Cape Town Commitment, evangelicals had several important discussions regarding unity. However, they tend to understand the unity of the church as a means of evangelism and social transformation.[173] In essence, this unity is directed toward the inherent witness of all believers or communities in Jesus from the moment they are sent into the world, not only for evangelism or partnership. The unity of the Johannine community for mission is clarified through the structure of 10:36 and 17:18. Just as God sent Jesus in holiness, so, too, are the disciples sanctified and sent to the world (17:16–17). This holiness means that Jesus and the disciples belong to the Father (17:9, 11), and John describes this holiness as a premise to live in "mutual indwelling" (10:38; 14:10, 11; 17:17–18). This type of relationship is one that brings unity for mission in the world (17:23). Although they are in the world, the disciples are consecrated to God through Jesus's washing event (13:3–11), which itself is a witness toward the world (13:35; 15:8).

First, the unity of Jesus's disciples originates in his sacrificial and self-giving death. As his washing of their feet implies the symbolic meaning of his sacrifice, he purifies them to be the holy community in the only one

---

172. Olsson, *Structure and Meaning*, 263–64, 266, 268, 271–72; Barus, "John 2:12–25," 136–37.

173. Cf. Van Engen, *Mission on the Way*, 222; Tizon, "Evangelism," 170–72.

God. Jesus sends them into the world. Their oneness testifies to their holy life and identity in the midst of the wicked world (8:31). It keeps holiness in the light and prevents the truth from falling into evil (12:36; 17:15). For these reasons, Jesus sends them the Spirit of the truth in order to lead them toward the truth (16:13). The Spirit will reprove the world of sin, righteousness, and judgment, and will lead the community into the unity of truth so that they might keep the Father's words (14:21-24; 17:8, 14-26).

Second, the disciples must continue to bear the fruit of his sacrificial love in union with Jesus, the so-called "mutual indwelling."[174] The disciples are one in the ontological aspect in that John describes the disciples as a unity of life in 15:4-5. As soon as they are born from above by the Holy Spirit and by faith in Jesus, their persons, identities, and all things in work and life form the unity-relationship with God and Jesus. This new birth imagery is associated with Jesus's sanctification, or consecration, of the disciples that unifies them with the holy God. When he sends them into the world, he perceives that they are living in the world, but not belonging to the darkness and sin of the world. Therefore, their existence itself bears witness to their identity as children of the light (12:36). Individual believers should erect this new unified community. For this reason, they must love one another and serve humbly in terms of "being united to Christ the servant."[175] Their love and service are rooted in sharing the nature and meaning of Jesus's sacrificial death through an intimate relationship with God.[176] That is, the community of the disciples is meant to serve one another, just as Jesus sacrifices himself and washes his disciples' feet (6:51; 10:11, 15, 17-18; 13:12-15; 15:13; 17:21-23).[177] Through reciprocal indwelling, love, and service as the essence of the disciples' mission are that every act should be the nature of their missional life.[178] Since each of their deeds is done within the unity-relationship of God's life, their lives, according to Jesus's life-pattern, are witnesses themselves. Therefore, the nature of Jesus's incarnation shares with his disciples' sentness in order to serve and verbally bear witness to him.[179] As Jesus reveals the Father in him as an incarnate reality (1:14; 14:7-10; 20:21), the disciples' witness should also become "incarnational witness," which is "a way of describing Christian vocation" in life.[180] They reside in the unity-relationship with God.

174. Gorman, *Abide and Go*, 8, 23.
175. Billings, *Union with Christ*, 126, 132.
176. Guder, *Be My Witnesses*, 26-27, 31.
177. Keener, "Sent Like Jesus," 28.
178. Tiersma, "What Does It Mean," 16.
179. Guder, *Incarnation*, 1-4, 9.
180. Guder, *Incarnation*, 9, 16, 27-28.

This relational unity must presuppose the communion of the churches that are scattered around the world. The church is initiated by the mission of God. Just as the Father sent Jesus, so does Jesus send his followers (20:21). The Son's sentness is based on the relational union that is realized within the triune God's inner life. Likewise, the sentness of the believers is also sent in relational association with them. Therefore, the relational unity of the disciples in this community does not simply refer to an agenda that effectively fulfills evangelism, efficiently solves world issues, or seeks theological uniformity.[181] The world has already demonstrated that various Christianities are involved within their specific contexts in God's work.[182] At the same time, those Christianities coexist within a globalized context, communicating with one another.[183] In other words, there exists a unity among diversity. William A. Dyrness calls this church type a "glocal church," which refers to "the multifaceted nature of the church in a global setting."[184] He points out that local churches are creating new global settings based on their contextual theologies and religious traditions. As he observes, today's local churches are forming a hybrid community through exchanges with diverse communities, breaking away from strict monocultural and denominational doctrines and praxis. In this type of situation, evangelicals must dynamically participate in fellowship in order to engage with God's mission. Van Engen defines fellowship as "interpersonal relationships."[185] This means that, in the Lord, the disciples get to know, care for, and enjoy together.[186]

The church community that works for mission should first unite toward the world. This unity occurs through the love and humility of self-sacrifice that Jesus has shown them. Even though these churches must do their best to protect themselves from the world's evils and protect the truth for the sake of congregations, they must also not miss that Jesus washed the feet of his disciples and let them wash one another (13:14).[187] Strictly speaking, living

---

181. Wright, "Trinity," 54–55.

182. Dyrness, "Church in Global Context," 118.

183. Dyrness, "Church in Global Context," 120.

184. Dyrness, "Church in Global Context," 121, 123; cf. Thomaskutty, "Glo[b/c]Alization," 56.

185. Van Engen, *Mission on the Way*, 214.

186. Cf. for a prophetic dialogue, see Bevans, "Prophetic Dialogue," 6–7.

187. Myers argues that Christians have to participate in God's salvific work in the globalizing world that provides people with "a competing and seductive 'good news'" of twin globalisms: "modernity and neoliberal capitalism" (Myers, *Engaging Globalization*, 244). To be sure, globalization allows countries to generate more than 80 percent of global GDP through urbanization (Scott, "Risks of Rapid Urbanization," [2015]). However, the unplanned increasing population of urbanization deteriorates social instability and ruins human dignity by seeking for the utopian illusions of the twin globalisms. This

within holiness and truth is to live by the pattern of Jesus's life. The result of their lives is to become one (17:23). This unity serves as a life-witness toward the world (13:35; 17:23).[188] As the Fourth Gospel shows, the Johannine community would have been organized by a variety of ethnic groups.[189] They would have had to practice the missional significance of Jesus's death as sacrificial love and service so that they might follow Jesus's life by sharing a portion with him (13:8, 36). Their love and service must be that of the relationship between friends, rather than that of a master and slave (15:15). Just as Jesus considered his disciples friends and shared God's work with them, the coalition of faith communities should share the work of the Lord within a mutual intimate relationship and join in the mission of God toward the world (13:14-16, 20).[190] As this unity is realized through the relationship of the triune God, the faith community and the world must also become one in the eternal life of his holiness and truth (8:31-32; 12:50; 17:14-20).

---

phenomenon appears throughout the world. Myers aptly observed that the mission field is no longer "over there." If so, what do Christians have to do? Myers insists that Christians can propose global values and God's creational purpose to the world, which cannot be explained by a flawed anthropology. Albert M. Wolters views that the world distorts the direction and structure of Creation (Wolters, *Creation Regained*, 69-87). This world needs the restoration of God, but Christians' missional responsibility is to correct people's spoiled worldview.

188. Brown, *John XIII-XXI*, 570; Schnackenburg, *Gospel according to St John*, 3:24-25; Bruce, *Gospel of John*, 286; Köstenberger, *Missions of Jesus*, 109.

189. Some scholars suggest that the Johannine community's members were gradually various, as Samaritan and gentile Christians entered into the Johannine community. R. E. Brown argues that Jesus's divinity in oneness with God was not the original belief and theology of the primitive Johannine community, which primarily consisted of Jewish believers. Brown postulates that there was a development of four phases within the context of the Johannine community: phase 1 (mid 50s-late 80s-a pre-gospel phase); phase 2 (90 CE—when the gospel was written—addressing Six Groups within the Johannine Community); phase 3 (100 CE—when the Epistles were written); and phase 4 (after the Epistles, second century). Specifically, he highlights "the entrance of a group of Jews of anti-Temple views and their Samaritan converts as a catalyst toward a higher Christology" (4:4-42) after conflicting with the majority of Jews in a pre-gospel phase. These groups did not focus on the "Davidic messiah" and on Jesus in terms of a high Christology alongside the Prophet like Moses (Deut 18:15-22) (Brown, *Community*, 37-38, 43, 44), and eventually initiated the development of "a theology of descent from above and pre-existence" (Logos-Christology) (Brown, *John XIII-XXI*, 1047).

190. Okure, *Johannine Approach to Mission*, 207, 209; Gorman, *Abide and Go*, 93-94.

Integrated Witness of Life and Evangelism in Mission

The Johannine mission emerged as an integrated witness of life and evangelism. Until modern times, evangelicals have expanded their understanding of mission. Nevertheless, while evangelicals understand mission as evangelism and life-witness, many of them hold a dichotomous structural frame, which often leads them to concentrate more on doing mission, rather than on being witness in daily life.[191] This frame leads to a vehement debate over what should be prioritized within those missional definitions. However, John does not distinguish between life in the unity-relationship and the preaching of the gospel. Rather, he teaches the disciples to live Jesus's life through the mutual indwelling relationship so that they might become witnesses.[192] John underlines evangelism. Accordingly, mission must go beyond church ministries and entertainment, which are motivated by love for God, and should instead be an *integrated witness* of believers' evangelism and life-witness within the unity-relationship with Jesus.[193] In this sense, the dichotomous frames of evangelism and social responsibility as held by some evangelicals' need to be revisited.

Jesus's foot-washing narrative shows two sides of the mission concept: (1) evangelism and (2) life-witness. Jesus sends his disciples into the world, just as he was sent by the Father (13:20; 17:18; 20:21). They abide in him by being consecrated (13:8, 10, 15, 35–36; 15:3–5; 17:23). Accordingly, their mission is to achieve the twofold purpose in the frame of sending and "as . . ., so . . ."

With regard to one of these goals, John claims in the foot-washing narrative that the disciples are evangelists. To receive the disciples and their verbal proclamation is to accept Jesus himself (13:20). Conversely, although their evangelism is rejected, their Lord and Teacher, Jesus (13:14), is also rejected and persecuted, so their suffering is not only theirs (13:16 with 15:20, 21–27; 12:46 with 16:1). In the frame of "as . . ., so . . .," the disciples are sent to proclaim, teach, and testify to this world, just as Jesus did. However, their evangelism never excludes them from living in Jesus. This is another side of their witness in which they live Jesus's life, and are sanctified in order to be united with Jesus (13:8, 15). In the foot-washing narrative, John demonstrates that the disciples' verbal proclamation must never be separated from life-witness. Their sentness should reflect their identity as Jesus's disciples who follow his words (7:31; 13:36; 17:23).

---

191. Jørgensen, "Inspiration," 294.
192. Rutayisire, "Church," 248.
193. Guder, "Incarnation and the Church's," 173–84.

The other goal is to be the witness of life, regardless of what or where it is needed. The person, life-pattern, words, and activities of daily life must bear witness to the Sender in its oneness (17:23). While emphasizing that evangelicals should become witnesses in all areas of life, the dichotomous structure of evangelism and social responsibility tend to engage in doing mission. John, however, highlights life-witness as mission from the integrated perspective of witness. This means that, as they live lives united with God, he is naturally revealed in their lives and characters in association with Jesus's nature, actions, and words. It is not a matter of what social responsibilities they have, but rather what aspects of God's nature, identity, and activities are present in their activities, words, and person. John underlines that Jesus was sent in the incarnate form in order to dwell in the midst of his disciples and the world. He reveals the Father dwelling in him (1:18; 2:21). His identity, words and works witness to the Father (14:7–10). Likewise, when Jesus sends the disciples, they are also abiding in Jesus, who is the temple, the truth, the eternal life, and light of the world (2:21; 3:21; 8:12; 12:46; 14:6). They continue to take fellowship with God, worship, drink living water, and live with him (3:21; 4:24; 7:38; 15:4; 20:21–23). This is possible only when they are in a life-sharing relationship with God. Their witness demonstrates their identity as Jesus's disciples because it reveals the place of the indwelling God in their unity-relationship (13:35; 15:8; 17:23).

First, mission as witness is relational in the mutual indwelling between the Sender and the Sent one(s). Timothy C. Tennent senses that John's sending language reveals the intimate relationship between the Sender and the Sent.[194] The frame surrounding the Sent's knowledge of the Sender clarifies Jesus's intimate witness to the Father; Jesus knows the Father and his will. John states that as soon as the disciples are purified by Jesus, they are united with him and the Father in order to bear fruits. This transcends the command-obedience. Beyond the subordinate conception of the Lord's rule, the will and character of the Sender are also revealed in the mutual relationship between the Sender and the Sent.

The Cape Town Commitment is involved with the why and how of the church's mission, although the congress understands mission as God's mission and the expression of his love (2011, section 1. C). To be sure, John's Gospel clarifies the *missio Dei* (John 20:21) and God's motivation of mission, which is love (3:16). However, John alludes to the nature of mission. His *missio Dei* shows the unity of nature and activity in the mutual relationship between the Father and the Son. (1) Jesus and the disciples invite people into the knowledge of the triune God and life in light through their

---

194. Tennent, *Invitation*, 154.

witness. In using John's sending language, it is understood that salvation is the act of all people knowing God and living in the light, truth, and eternal life (8:12). (2) The disciples' lives are to bear witness to the triune God. Jesus teaches them his life-pattern by washing his disciples' feet within the missional contexts (13:15, 16, 20, 35). They must emulate the meanings of Jesus's symbolic action as his sacrificial death in their lives, and these meanings are embodied in the practice of forgiveness, love, and humble service, which results in the unity of the faith community and of the world. In addition, Jesus never neglects social conflicts, human problems, or political issues in his missional life and works (section E 1). In fact, he deals with a religious conflict between the Jews and the Samaritans, human equality in a community, and political issues during a conversation with Pilate. He takes care of the poor and the disenfranchised, while also regarding a woman's pouring of costly perfume on his feet as an admirable deed (12:1–8).

Ross Hastings argues that the missional nature of the church can become a good answer as to why the church experiences a serious decline in Western societies, specifically within pluralistic contexts.[195] The missional church participates in the love and life of the triune missional God. Hastings defines the term "missional" as "the self-revelation of God in Christ by the Spirit."[196] The Johannine risen Jesus gives his greatest commission to his disciples, in light of fulfilling the new creation, by breathing the Spirit into "the last Adam's race, the new humanity in Christ, or the church."[197] This new creation community is sent by Jesus, just as he was sent by the Father. Thus, Jesus's sent community must be missional ("they will be missional like he is, and as he is").[198] Above all, Hastings pays attention to the community's coming into a specific context, the so-called "new creation context."[199] In particular, Hastings seeks the biblical foundation by linking the missional message of John's Gospel to the nature and mission of the church within the context of the current West.[200]

John's Gospel bears witness to the mission of the loving and sending God, who lets his Son complete his will in words and deeds and reveal his heart (14:10–12; 15:22–24).[201] John conceptualizes this essential aspect of mission, reflecting on the way of new life through which the Johannine

---

195. Hastings, *Missional God*, 16.
196. Hastings, *Missional God*, 23.
197. Hastings, *Missional God*, 36.
198. Hastings, *Missional God*, 30.
199. Hastings, *Missional God*, 30.
200. Hastings, *Missional God*, 33–36.
201. Flemming, *Why Mission*, 55, 57.

community can share love with one another, deriving from the triune God's life.[202] Their mutual sacrificial love witnesses to the "loving, seeking, sending God."[203]

Similarly, Hastings claims that John narrates the missional life of his emergent church. Christians participate in the triune God's mission in the world of his creation. While Flemming engages in a missional life and identity of the community, Hastings focuses on the mission activities of sending, bringing, and missional life in relationship with the triune God.[204] Hastings is involved with the concept of peace found in the story of Jesus's dwelling in the midst of his disciples, in terms of incarnation and resurrection (20:20–21). Thus, he defines the identity and activities of a missional community within the world of God's creative restoration.

God's mission was motivated by his love for the world (3:16), which manifests in Jesus's crucifixion.[205] The church might be involved in Jesus's mission by sharing life and character with him in relationship. The purpose of the church's mission must extend peace to the world.[206]

Second, mission as witness refers to the disciples' love and service for one another, and even to enemies and the world. The foot washing implies that Jesus died for many with selflessness, self-giving, and self-sacrifice. He loved his disciples until the end (13:1), and his love is embodied in the forgiveness of their sins and betrayals. Jesus's sacrifice and love are not alienated from his service in humility for the world (vv. 34–35). These are God's identity and lifestyle in his kingdom. The disciples share in his nature and life-pattern in the unity-relationship, and their lifestyle does not conform to a superficial imitation of Jesus. If they try to simply imitate the intrinsic character and life of the triune God by just showing it, their imitation must transform their person and life-pattern. Just as Jesus lived in his own context, so, too, must today's Christians live according to God's nature, character, identity, and works in specific situations. In this sense, Jesus's lifestyle can be a model for the missional life of Christians today.

The disciples should live a witness of life in all areas and in every moment, both in the faith community and the world.[207] Accordingly, the sent community's *integrated witness* carries an identity of holiness (17:17, 19),

---

202. Flemming, *Why Mission*, 71.
203. Flemming, *Why Mission*, 67–71.
204. Hastings, *Missional God*, 15.
205. Flemming, *Why Mission*, 57–58.
206. Flemming, *Why Mission*, 62–63.
207. Harris, *Mission*, 175; Flemming, *Why Mission*, 63; Thompson, *John*, 373.

which is both separate from and residing in the world.²⁰⁸ Their practices of "forgiveness" (13:8, 10; 20:23), "love" (3:16; 13:34; 14:15, 21, 24, 28, 31; 15:12, 17; 21:15, 16, 17) and "service" (12:2, 26; cf. διάκονος, 2:5, 9; 12:26 and δοῦλος, 4:51; 8:34, 35; 13:16; 15:15*2; 18:10*2, 18, 26) in life bears witness to the truth about Jesus's mission and their identity as his disciples in the world (15:26–27; 18:37; ἀκολουθέω, 12:26 [1:37, 38, 40, 43; 6:2; 8:12; 10:4, 5, 27; 11:31; 12:26; 13:36, 37; 18:15; 20:6; 21:20]).²⁰⁹

Their love and service include both enemies and the world who hate both Jesus and them. As Jesus washes Judas Iscariot and the other disciples that betray him before the cross, so, too, should the disciples love and serve their enemies in both the faith community and the world. Their actions are sacrificial and altruistic. For this purpose, they must forgive one another, just as Jesus forgave his disciples and restored them as his followers (13:36; 21:18–19). Their love, service, and forgiveness result in unity, and they continue to live in unity through these things. This becomes their life-witness to the incarnate Jesus toward the world (13:35; 17:23).

Ultimately, Jesus's disciples are sent for the purposes of evangelism. They must proclaim the gospel in order to make people believe in God and his Son Jesus, so that people might receive eternal life and live in the light (20:31). This gospel contains God's sending act, his fulfillment through Jesus, and his love and service. Their proclamation must be in union with their living of Jesus's life through the unity-relationship. Jesus washes his disciples so that they are consecrated and belong to his part (13:8, 34–35, 36), and he abides in them as he becomes incarnate (1:14, 18; 15:3, 7). Thus, their lives reveal Jesus's person and life-pattern through the mutual indwelling.

SUMMARY

In this chapter, I examined the understanding and discussions that evangelicals have had regarding mission, and reconsidered their mission in light of the Gospel of John. To begin with, I limited the evangelical views explored to those of the international Lausanne Conferences, which were held in 1974, 1989, and 2010.

Throughout these Conferences, those present experienced a gradual change in the mission paradigm. The conferences focused on the frame of command-obedience in Lausanne I (LC), while the very frame was combined with the witness concept of life in Lausanne II (MM) and III (CTC); together, they developed mission as witness. The primary characteristics are

208. Flemming, *Why Mission*, 63.
209. Newbigin, *Open Secret*, 54.

the emphasis of evangelism and social participation based on the uniqueness and salvation of Jesus Christ. Through these Conferences, evangelicals have contributed to overcoming the dualistic frame of evangelical propaganda and social participation, and have developed an integral mission, or holistic mission, beyond the narrowed mission as evangelism. The concept of witness in life was considered important in their discussions regarding mission and its practice.

Evangelicals have two limitations, though. *Firstly*, in the 2010s, there was still controversy surrounding the church's theological motivations and witness as mission. *Secondly*, while the Lausanne Congresses speak of mission as the nature of life, they still have many evangelicals who try to interpret the mission of God (John 20:21) through the lens of Jesus's Great Commission found in the dichotomous framework of evangelism and social responsibility. In contrast, some evangelical scholars have examined the mission concept as integrated witness in the sense of the unity between evangelism and life-witness, which reflects the nature and character of God's mission.

Taking part in this discussion, I focused on the mission of the faith community that John talks about. Throughout his discussion, he shows three concepts. *Firstly*, the church is a sent community meant for mission. (1) This sent community is incarnational in terms of revealing Jesus, who dwells among them. As Jesus presents the Father through himself, they also reveal him to the world. At the same time, the sent community is also a hermeneutical community. (2) They are a consecrated and consecrating community. They should purify individual disciples, the faith community, and the world in the holy-relationship with God. (3) They must live by Jesus's words in this world. Furthermore, they must integrally transform the world according to his words. This integral transformation must take place within the faith community. In order for this to happen, Jesus sent the Holy Spirit out to the disciples' community. The Spirit guides them to live in the truth, and reminds his disciples of Jesus's teachings and life, allowing them to realize those things so that they might walk in the truth. The way they live within their community must spread into the entire world. By doing so, the church must transform the evil world toward God. *Secondly*, the church lives in the relationship of unity for mission. The church community must live in Jesus in mutuality. Just as Jesus was consecrated and sent to this world, they are also consecrated and sent. This holiness means being one with the Father and Son. Moreover, they must form a union-relationship within their community. John offers love and humble service as a way of achieving unity, which should be as mutual as the relationship between friends. Modern evangelical churches, too, must unite with Jesus. That, in and of itself, is the witness that they bring toward the world. At the same time, these churches should also form unity with the world's churches, which is the essence of the church as Jesus's body. Through this action, evangelical propaganda and the practice of love and service should be carried out so that the world can unite with the church. *Thirdly*, the mission of the church is an integrated witness of life and evangelism, which are not separated from one another in John's Gospel (13:8, 10, 15, 16, 20, 35, 36). When Jesus sent his disciples, he made them proclaim the gospel, which is known as evangelism. The world is under sin so that, through the disciples' verbal proclamation, people must come to Jesus and live with him. Jesus had already preached and taught the world how to believe and live in him during his public ministry period, but the disciples must also testify to Jesus in order to make people trust him. In addition, the disciples must be in a united relationship with Jesus, which means that they live in mutual indwelling with Jesus by following his life-pattern in sacrificial love and service. John says that their lives are a witness in and of themselves (13:35; 17:23).

Conclusion

THE PURPOSE OF THIS study is to explore the missional meaning and implications of Jesus's foot-washing narrative (John 13:1–38) within the literary structure of the Fourth Gospel, through which I reconsider today's evangelicals' mission. Throughout these chapters, I defined a missional hermeneutic for the reading of John's Gospel. Most of all, the study paid attention to what John said in his language and literary context, along with what he is saying for today's evangelicals. Accordingly, I suggested both a literary-exegetical interpretation and a theological interpretation. That is, a missional hermeneutic for the study is the interpretation that is both author-centered and reader-centered.

First, I investigated the literary structure of the Gospel and the author's sending language and its formulae. Through my literary-exegetical analysis and theological observations, I found that through sending language and its formulae, John refers to an integrated witness of Jesus and his disciples. *Firstly*, just as Jesus reveals God and his identity through incarnation, sacrificial death, resurrection, and himself, so, too, must his disciples testify to Jesus through their way of life. *Secondly*, Jesus teaches the words of God and proclaims the faith, so that people may live in the light and worship God in Spirit and Truth. Likewise, the disciples, as harvest workers, are sent to invite people to Jesus (cf. "come and see"). They have to proclaim the forgiveness of sins and judgment that Jesus achieved. Thus, they spread the gospel messages of Jesus so that those who believe in him might receive eternal life.

Second, I showed that the concept of integrated witness is well manifested in Jesus's foot-washing narrative in 13:1–38. Jesus's washing act symbolizes his sacrificial and self-giving death on the cross. He gives himself in order to consecrate people so that they might unite with him in the mutual indwelling relationship (13:1–11). At the same time, the narrative provides missional implications for the Johannine community. Jesus gives his life-pattern to the disciples. They must live his life in love and humble service. Their washing of one another's feet points out their practice of love, both in the community and the world (13:12–38). His sacrifice provided his disciples with a life pattern of love and humble service. This first witness-concept in the narrative is the life-witness of Jesus and his disciples. In addition, the second concept is that the disciples are sent out to evangelize the world. They preach Jesus and his words to the community and the world, so that others might follow him in the light and the truth. Thus, my argument is that the Johannine mission is an integrated witness that does not separate evangelism from life-witness.

Third, depending on John's missional understanding of integrated witness, I worked to participate in evangelicals' discussion about mission and their practices. The "integral mission," or "holistic mission," of evangelism and social participation often focuses on doing mission or transformation for evangelism. However, after the 1989 Manila and 2010 Cape Town Conferences, many evangelicals continue to propose that mission comes from God's nature and activity. Of course, some of them integrate evangelism and social service, while others argue for the prioritization of evangelism. Relatively, these two groups do not pay attention to the nature of mission in terms of God's attribute, which reveals his identity. My argument is that the contemporary evangelical mission should be the combination of evangelism and life-witness in the mutual relationship with God in nature, identity, and activities. Soon there should always be an integration of life-witness and evangelism, within both the faith community and the world. John's Gospel presents (1) a sent incarnational, consecrating, and hermeneutical community for mission, and (2) in the unity-relationship between God and them and among the faith-communities so that (3) they should bear the role of a total witness within the community(ies) of Jesus's followers and in the world. Therefore, I propose that evangelicals continue to develop the mission concept and their missional role in the community and the world in light of the Johannine integrated witness.

For future research, I suggest three further areas of study. *Firstly*, in order to understand the unique nature of the Johannine mission concept, comparative studies with other biblical texts are needed. *Secondly*, given that it is tenable that John would have considered the missional implications for his first readers and hearers, who should reveal God and bear witness to Jesus and his gospel in the world, the understanding of John's first readers and their mission should be explored much more from an historical studies perspective. Through this work, we can observe the early church's mission concept(s) in order to better understand current

Christian mission. *Thirdly*, for modern evangelists, a deeper study is needed as to how modern evangelicals should play a role in hermeneutical communities within the global-local context of racial, gender, theological, and traditional diversity.

Bibliography

Adeyemo, Tokunboh. "A Critical Evaluation of Contemporary Perspectives." In Nicholls, *In Word and Deed*, 41–61.
Akala, Adesola Joan. *The Son-Father Relationship and Christological Symbolism in the Gospel of John*. New York: Bloomsbury, 2014.
Allen, R. Michael, and Scott R. Swain. "In Defense of Proof-Texting." *Journal of the Evangelical Theological Society* 54 (2011) 589–606.
Allison, Cregg R. "Theological Interpretation of Scripture: An Introduction and Preliminary Evaluation." *Southern Baptist Journal of Theology* 14 (2010) 28–36.
An, Keon-Sang. *An Ethiopian Reading of the Bible*. Eugene, OR: Pickwick, 2015.
Anderson, Bernhard W. *Understanding the Old Testament*. Englewood Cliffs, NJ: Prentice-Hall, 1986.
Appold, Mark L. *The Oneness Motif of the Fourth Gospel: Motif Analysis and Exegetical Probe into the Fourth Gospel*. Eugene, OR: Wipf & Stock, 2011.
Ashton, John. *Understanding the Fourth Gospel*. Oxford: Oxford University Press, 2008.
Baker, David L. *Two Testaments, One Bible: The Theological Relationship between the Old and New Testaments*. Downer Groves: InterVarsity, 2010.
Ball, David Mark. *"I Am" in John's Gospel: Literary Function, Background, and Theological Implications*. Journal for the Study of the New Testament 124. Sheffield: Sheffield Academic, 1996.
Barr, James. *The Semantics of Biblical Language*. Oxford: Oxford University Press, 1961.
Barram, Michael. "The Bible, Mission, and Social Location: Toward a Missional Hermeneutic." *Interpretation* 61 (2007) 42–58.
Barrett, C. K. "Christocentric or Theocentric? Observations on the Theological Method of the Fourth Gospel." In *Essays on John*, 1–18. Philadelphia: Westminster, 1982.
———. *The Gospel according to St. John*. Philadelphia: Westminster, 1978.
Barthes, Roland. *The Pleasure of the Text*. Translated by Richard Miller. New York: Hill and Wang, 2009.
Barton, John. *Biblical Interpretation*. Cambridge: Cambridge University Press, 1998.
Barus, Armand. "John 2:12–25: A Narrative Reading." In *New Currents through John*, edited by Francisco Lozada et al., 123–40. Atlanta: SBL, 2006.
Bauckham, Richard. *Bible and Mission: Christian Witness in a Postmodern World*. Grand Rapids: Baker, 2003.

———. "Did Jesus Wash His Disciples' Feet?" In *The Testimony of the Beloved Disciple: Narrative, History, and Theology in the Gospel of John*, 191–206. Grand Rapids: Baker, 2007.

———. *John: A Commentary*. Louisville: Westminster John Knox, 2015.

Beale, G. K. *The Temple and the Church's Mission: A Biblical Theology of the Dwelling Place of God*. Downers Grove: InterVarsity, 2004.

Beasley-Murray, George R. *John*. Word Biblical Commentary 36. Grand Rapids: Zondervan, 2015.

Bebbington, David William. *Evangelicalism in Modern Britain: A History from the 1730s to the 1980s*. London: Routledge, 1989.

Bedford, Peter Ross. *Temple Restoration in Early Achaemenid Judah*. Supplements to the Journal for the Study of Judaism 65. Boston: Brill, 2001.

Beker, J. Christiaan. *The New Testament: A Thematic Introduction*. Minneapolis: Fortress, 1994.

———. *The Triumph of God: The Essence of Paul's Thought*. Minneapolis: Fortress, 1990.

Belle, Gilbert van. "Christology and Soteriology in the Fourth Gospel: The Conclusion to the Gospel of John Revisited." In *Theology and Christology in the Fourth Gospel: Essays by the Members of the SNTS Johannine Writings Seminar*, edited by Gilbert van Belle et al., 483–502. Leuven: Peeters, 2005.

Bennema, Cornelis. *Encountering Jesus: Character Studies in the Gospel of John*. Carlisle: Paternoster, 2009.

Bernard, J. H. *A Critical and Exegetical Commentary on the Gospel according to St. John*. New York: Scribner, 1929.

Bevans, Stephen B. "A Prophetic Dialogue Approach." In *The Mission of the Church*, edited by Craig Ott, 3–20. Grand Rapids: Baker, 2016.

Beyerhaus, Peter. "World Evangelization and the Kingdom of God." In Douglas, *Let the Earth Hear His Voice*, 283–302.

Billings, J. Todd. *Union with Christ: Reframing Theology and Ministry for the Church*. Grand Rapids: Baker, 2011.

Bishop, E. F. F. "'He That Eateth Bread with Me Hath Lifted up His Heel against Me'—Jn Xiii.18 (Ps Xli.9)." *Expository Times* 70 (59 1958) 331–33.

Black, David Alan. *Linguistics for Students of New Testament Greek: A Survey of Basic Concepts and Applications*. Grand Rapids: Baker, 1995.

Blauw, Johannes. *The Missionary Nature of the Church: A Survey of the Biblical Theology of Mission*. London: McGraw-Hill, 1962.

Blomberg, Craig. *Jesus and the Gospels: An Introduction and Survey*. Nottingham: Apollos, 2009.

Blumhofer, Christopher Mark. "The Gospel of John and the Future of Israel." PhD diss., Duke University, 2017.

Bock, Darrell L. "The Son of David and the Saints' Task: The Hermeneutics of Initial Fulfillment." *Bibliotheca Sacra* 150 (December 1993) 444–57.

Boer, Martinus C. de. "Jesus' Departure to the Father in John Death or Resurrection?" In *Theology and Christology in the Fourth Gospel: Essays by the Members of the SNTS Johannine Writings Seminar*, edited by Gilbert van Belle et al., 1–20. Dudley: Leuven University Press, 2005.

———. *Johannine Perspectives on the Death of Jesus*. Contributions to Biblical Exegesis and Theology 17. Kampen: Pharos, 1996.

Booth, Steve. *Selected Peak Marking Features in the Gospel of John*. American University Studies 178. New York: Lang, 1996.
Borgen, Peder. "God's Agent in the Fourth Gospel." In *Logos Was the True Light and Other Essays on the Gospel of John*, 121–32. Trondheim, Norway: Tapir, 1983.
Bornkamm, Günther. *Jesus of Nazareth*. Minneapolis: Fortress, 1995.
Bosch, David J. "Towards a Hermeneutic for 'Biblical Studies and Mission.'" *Mission Studies* 3 (1986) 65–79.
———. *Transforming Mission: Paradigm Shifts in Theology of Mission*. Maryknoll: Orbis, 1991.
———. *Witness to the World*. Atlanta: John Knox, 1980.
Brown, Lindsay. "Closing Address: We Have a Gospel to Proclaim." In *The Lausanne Movement: A Range of Perspectives*, edited by Lars Nilsen Dahle, 295–303. Regnum Edinburgh Centenary Series 22. Oxford: Regnum, 2014.
Brown, Raymond E. *The Community of the Beloved Disciple*. New York: Paulist, 1979.
———. *The Epistles of John*. Anchor Bible 30. Garden City: Doubleday, 1982.
———. *The Gospel according to John I–XII*. Vol. 1. 2 vols. Anchor Bible 29. Garden City: Doubleday, 1966.
———. *The Gospel according to John XIII–XXI*. Vol. 2. 2 vols. Anchor Yale Bible 29A. New Haven: Yale University Press, 1970.
———. "Other Sheep Not of This Fold." *Journal of Biblical Literature* 97 (1978) 5–22.
Brown, Sherri, and Francis J. Moloney. *Interpreting the Gospel and Letters of John*. Grand Rapids: Eerdmans, 2017.
Brown, Tricia Gates. *Spirit in the Writings of John: Johannine Pneumatology in Social-Scientific Perspective*. Journal for the Study of the New Testament 253. New York: T. & T. Clark, 2003.
Brownson, James V. *Speaking the Truth in Love: New Testament Resources for a Missional Hermeneutic*. Harrisburg, PA: Trinity, 1998.
Bruce, F. F. *The Gospel of John*. Grand Rapids: Eerdmans, 1983.
Bultmann, Rudolf. *The Gospel of John: A Commentary*. Philadelphia: Westminster, 1971.
———. "Is Exegesis without Presuppositions Possible?" In *Existence and Faith: Shorter Writings of Rudolf Bultmann*, edited by Schubert M. Ogden, 289–96. London: Hodder and Stoughton, 1961.
———. *Theology of the New Testament*. Translated by Kendrick Grobel. London: SCM, 1951.
Burge, Gary M. *The Anointed Community: The Holy Spirit in the Johannine Tradition*. Grand Rapids: Eerdmans, 1987.
Bush, Luis. "The Challenge Before Us." In Douglas, *Proclaim Christ until He Comes*, 58–62.
"The Cape Town Commitment: A Confession of Faith and a Call to Action." *International Bulletin of Missionary Research* 35 (April 2011) 59–80.
Carey, W. *An Enquiry into the Obligation of Christians to Use Means for the Conversion of the Heathens*. Whitefish, MT: Kessinger, 2004.
Carriker, Tim. "The Bible as Text for Mission." In *Bible in Mission*, edited by Pauline Hoggarth et al., 29–42. Eugene, OR: Wipf & Stock, 2013.
Carroll, Robert P. "So What Do We Know about the Temple? The Temple in the Prophets." In *Temple and Community in Persian Period*, edited by Tamara Eskenazi et al., 34–103. Sheffield: Sheffield Academic, 1994.
Carson, D. A. *The Gospel according to John*. Grand Rapids: Eerdmans, 1991.

———. "The Purpose of the Fourth Gospel: John 20:31 Reconsidered." *Journal of Biblical Literature* 106 (1987) 639–51.

Cartledge, Mark J. "Text-Community-Spirit: The Challenges Posed by Pentecostal Theological Method to Evangelical Theology." In *Spirit and Scripture: Exploring a Pneumatic Hermeneutic*, edited by Kevin L. Spawn et al. London: T. & T. Clark, 2011.

Chennattu, Rekha M. *Johannine Discipleship as a Covenant Relationship*. Peabody: Hendrickson, 2006.

Cho, Sukmin. *Jesus as Prophet in the Fourth Gospel*. New Testament Monographs 15. Sheffield: Sheffield Phoenix, 2006.

Clegg, Tom, and Warren Bird. *Lost in America: How You and Your Church Can Impact the World Next Door*. Loveland, CO: Group, 2001.

Clines, David J. A. "Haggai's Temple, Constructed, Deconstructed and Reconstructed." In *Second Temple Studies*, vol. 2, *Temple and Community in the Persian Period*, edited by Tamara Eskenazi et al., 60–87. Sheffield: Sheffield Academic, 1994.

Collins, T. "The Literary Contexts of Zechariah 9:9." In *The Book of Zechariah and Its Influence*, edited by Christopher Tuckett, 29–40. Burlington, VT: Ashgate, 2003.

Coloe, Mary L. *Dwelling in the Household of God: Johannine Ecclesiology and Spirituality*. Collegeville: Liturgical, 2007.

———. "Footwashing (II. New Testament)." *Encyclopedia of the Bible and Its Reception* 9 (2014) 392–494.

———. "Sources in the Shadows: John 13 and the Johannine Community." In *New Currents through John: A Global Perspective*, 69–82. Atlanta: SBL, 2006.

———. "Welcome into the Household of God: The Footwashing in John 13." *Catholic Biblical Quarterly* 66 (2004) 400–15.

Corell, A. *Consummatum Est: Eschatology and Church in the Gospel of St John*. London: SPCK, 1958.

Cory, Catherine. "Wisdom's Rescue: A New Reading of the Tabernacles Discourse (John 7:1—8:59)." *Journal of Biblical Literature* 116 (1997) 95–116.

Costas, Orlando E. *Christ Outside the Gate: Mission Beyond Christendom*. New York: Orbis, 1992.

———. "Evangelism and the Gospel of Salvation." In *The Study of Evangelism: Exploring a Missional Practice of the Church*, edited by Paul Wesley Chilcote et al., 33–45. Grand Rapids: Eerdmans, 2008.

Cotterell, Peter, and Max Turner. *Linguistics & Biblical Interpretation*. Downers Grove: InterVarsity, 1989.

Cranfield, C. E. B., and G. N. Stanton. *The Gospel according to Saint Matthew*. Edited by J. A. Emerton. Vol. 2. 2 vols. Edinburgh: T. & T. Clark, 1991.

Crowe, Brandon D. "The Chiastic Structure of Seven Signs in the Gospel of John: Revisiting a Neglected Proposal." *Bulletin for Biblical Research* 28 (2018) 65–81.

Cullmann, Oscar. *Christ and Time*. Philadelphia: Westminster, 1951.

———. *Early Christian Worship*. Translated by A. S. Todd and J. B. Torrance. London: SCM, 1956.

Culpepper, R. Alan. *Anatomy of the Fourth Gospel: A Study in Literary Design*. Philadelphia: Fortress, 1983.

———. "The Johannine Hypodeigma: A Reading of John 13." *Semeia* 53 (1991) 133–52.

———. "The Pivot of John's Prologue." *New Testament Studies* 27 (1979) 1–31.

———. "The Plot of John's Story of Jesus." *Interpretation* 49 (1995) 347–58.

Dahle, Lars. "Mission in 3 D: A Key Lausanne III Theme." In *The Lausanne Movement: A Range of Perspectives*, edited by Lars Nilsen Dahle, 265–79. Oxford: Regnum, 2014.

Daly-Denton, Margaret. *David in the Fourth Gospel: The Johannine Reception of the Psalms*. Boston: Brill, 2000.

Danby, Herbert, ed. *The Mishnah: Translated from the Hebrew with Introduction and Brief Explanatory Notes*. Peabody: Hendrickson, 2011.

Danker, Frederick W., Walter Bauer, and William Arndt. *A Greek-English Lexicon of the New Testament and Other Early Christian Literature*. Chicago: University of Chicago Press, 2000.

Davies, Margaret. *Rhetoric and Reference in the Fourth Gospel*. Journal for the Study of the New Testament Supplement Series 69. Sheffield: JSOT, 1992.

Davies, W. D. *The Sermon on the Mount*. Cambridge: Cambridge University Press, 1966.

Davies, W. D., and Dale C. Allison. *The Gospel according to Saint Matthew*. Edinburgh: T. & T. Clark, 1988.

Deborst, Ruth Padilla. "An Integral Transformation Approach." In *The Mission of the Church: Five Views in Conversation*, edited by Craig Ott, 41–68. Grand Rapids: Baker, 2016.

Derrida, Jacques. *Of Grammatology*. Baltimore: Johns Hopkins University Press, 1976.

DeYoung, Kevin, and Greg Gilbert. *What Is the Mission of the Church? Making Sense of Social Justice, Shalom, and the Great Commission*. Wheaton, IL: Crossway, 2011.

Dodd, C. H. *Historical Tradition in the Fourth Gospel*. Cambridge: Cambridge University Press, 1976.

———. *The Interpretation of the Fourth Gospel*. Cambridge: Cambridge University Press, 1953.

Douglas, J. D., ed. *Let the Earth Hear His Voice: International Congress on World Evangelization Lausanne, Switzerland*. Minneapolis: World Wide, 1975.

———. "The Manila Manifesto." In *Proclaim Christ Until He Comes*, edited by J. D. Douglas, 25–38. Minneapolis: World Wide, 1990.

———, ed. *Proclaim Christ Until He Comes*. Minneapolis: World Wide, 1990.

Dowsett, Rose. *The Cape Town Commitment*. Peabody: Hendrickson, 2012.

Dunn, James D. G. *Baptism in the Holy Spirit*. London: SCM, 1970.

———. *Jesus and the Spirit: A Study of the Religious and Charismatic Experience of Jesus and the First Christians as Reflected in the New Testament*. Grand Rapids: Eerdmans, 1975.

Dyrness, William A. "The Church in Global Context." In *Theology without Borders: An Introduction to Global Conversations*, 117–56. Grand Rapids: Baker, 2015.

Emerton, J. A. "Binding and Loosing-Forgiving and Retaining." *Journal of Theological Studies* 13 (1962) 325–31.

Enns, Peter. *Inspiration and Incarnation: Evangelicals and the Problem of the Old Testament*. Grand Rapids: Baker, 2005.

Erwin, Fahlbusch. *The Encyclopedia of Christianity*. Edited by David B. Barrett. Translated by Geoffrey W. Bromiley. Grand Rapids: Eerdmans, 1999.

Escobar, Samuel. *Changing Tides: Latin America and Mission Today*. Maryknoll: Orbis, 2002.

———. "Evangelical Missiology: Peering into the Future." In *Global Missiology for the 21st Century: The Iguassu Dialogue*, edited by William David Taylor, 101–22. Grand Rapids: Baker, 2000.

———. "Evangelism and Man's Search for Freedom, Justice and Fulfilment." In Douglas, *Let the Earth Hear His Voice*, 303–38.
Estrada, Rodolfo Galvan. *A Pneumatology of Race in the Gospel of John: An Ethnocritical Study*. Eugene, OR: Wipf & Stock, 2019.
Ferdinando, Keith. "Mission: A Problem of Definition." *Themelios* 33 (2008) 46–59.
Ferreira, Johan. *Johannine Ecclesiology*. Journal for the Study of the New Testament 160. Sheffield: Sheffield Academic, 1998.
Flemming, Dean E. "A Missional Reading of Colossians." In *Reading the Bible Missionally*, edited by Michael W. Goheen, 213–40. Grand Rapids: Baker, 2016.
———. *Recovering the Full Mission of God: A Biblical Perspective on Being, Doing, and Telling*. Downers Grove: InterVarsity, 2013.
———. *Why Mission?* Nashville: Abingdon, 2015.
Flett, John G. "A Theology of Missio Dei." *Theology in Scotland* 21 (2014) 69–78.
———. *The Witness of God: The Trinity, Missio Dei, Karl Barth, and the Nature of Christian Community*. Grand Rapids: Eerdmans, 2010.
Ford, Leighton. "Proclaim Christ." In Douglas, *Proclaim Christ until He Comes*, 49–54.
Fowl, S. E. *Engaging the Scriptures: A Model for Theological Interpretation*. Oxford: Blackwell, 1998.
Franke, John R. "Contextual Mission: Bearing Witness to the Ends of the Earth." In *Four Views on the Church's Mission*, edited by Jason S. Sexton, 107–51. Grand Rapids: Zondervan, 2017.
———. "Intercultural Hermeneutics and the Shape of Missional Theology." In *Reading the Bible Missionally*, edited by Michael W. Goheen, 86–103. Grand Rapids: Eerdmans, 2016.
———. "Missional Theology." In *Evangelical Theological Method: Five Views*, edited by Stanley E. Porter, 52–72. Downers Grove: InterVarsity, 2018.
Gammie, John G. *Holiness in Israel*. Eugene, OR: Wipf and Stock, 1989.
Gennari, Silvia P., et al. "Context-Dependent Interpretation of Words: Evidence for Interactive Neural Processes." *Neuroimage* 35 (2007) 1278–86.
Gibson, David. "The Johannine Footwashing and the Death of Jesus: A Dialogue with Scholarship." *Scottish Bulletin of Evangelical Theology* 25 (2007) 50–60.
Gilliland, Dean S. "Contextual Theology as Incarnational Mission." In *The Word among Us: Contextualizing Theology for Mission Today*, edited by Dean S. Gilliland, 9–31. Dallas: Word, 1989.
Glasser, Arthur F. *Announcing the Kingdom: The Story of God's Mission in the Bible*. Grand Rapids: Baker, 2003.
Goheen, Michael W. "A Critical Examination of David Bosch's Missional Reading of Luke." In *Reading Luke: Interpretation, Reflection, Formation*, edited by Craig Bartholomew et al., 229–64. Grand Rapids: Zondervan, 2005.
Gombis, Timothy G. "Participation in the New-Creation People of God in Christ by the Spirit." In *The Apostle Paul and the Christian Life: Ethical and Missional Implications of the New Perspective*, edited by Scot McKnight, 103–24. Grand Rapids: Baker, 2016.
Gorman, Michael J. *Abide and Go: Missional Theosis in the Gospel of John*. Eugene, OR: Cascade, 2018.
———. *Becoming the Gospel: Paul, Participation, and Mission*. Grand Rapids: Eerdmans, 2015.
Graham, Billy. "Why Lausanne?" In Douglas, *Let the Earth Hear His Voice*, 22–36.

Green, Joel B. "The Bible, Theology, and Theological Interpretation." *Society of Biblical Literature Forum* (September 2004). https://www.sbl-site.org/publications/article.aspx?articleId=308.

———. *Practicing Theological Interpretation: Engaging Biblical Texts for Faith and Formation*. Grand Rapids: Baker, 2011.

———. "Reading James Missionally." In *Reading the Bible Missionally*, edited by Michael W. Goheen, 194–212. Grand Rapids: Baker, 2016.

———. "Rethinking 'History' for Theological Interpretation." *Journal of Theological Interpretation* 5 (2011) 159–74.

———. *Why Salvation?* Nashville: Abingdon, 2013.

Guder, Darrell L. *Be My Witnesses: The Church's Mission, Message, and Messengers*. Grand Rapids: Eerdmans, 1985.

———. *Called to Witness: Doing Missional Theology*. Grand Rapids: Eerdmans, 2015.

———. "Evangelism and the Debate over Church Growth." *Interpretation* 48 (1994) 145–55.

———. "Incarnation and the Church's Evangelistic Mission." In *The Study of Evangelism: Exploring a Missional Practice of the Church*, edited by Paul Wesley Chilcote and Laceye C. Warner, 171–84. Grand Rapids: Eerdmans, 2008.

———. *The Incarnation and the Church's Witness*. Harrisburg, PA: Trinity, 1999.

Gundry, Robert H. "New Wine in Old Wineskins: Bursting Traditional Interpretations in John's Gospel (Part Two)." *Bulletin for Biblica Research* 17 (2007) 292–96.

Gutierrez, Edna Lee de. "Good News for the Poor." In Douglas, *Proclaim Christ until He Comes*, 149–52.

Hagner, Donald A. *Matthew 1–13*. Vol. 1. 2 vols. Dallas: Word, 1995.

Hahn, Ferdinand. *Mission in the New Testament*. Translated by Frank Clarke. Nashville: Allenson, 1965.

Hall, Douglas. "Who Tells the World's Story? Theology's Quest for a Partner in Dialogue." *Interpretation* (January 1982) 47–53.

Hamilton, James. *God's Indwelling Presence*. Edited by E. Ray Clendenen. Nashville: Broadman & Holman, 2006.

———. "The Influence of Isaiah on the Gospel of John." *Perichoresis* 5 (2007) 139–62.

Hammond, Pete. "The Laity." In Douglas, *Proclaim Christ until He Comes*, 81–84.

Haran, Menahem. *Temples and Temple-Service in Ancient Israel: An Inquiry into Biblical Cult Phenomena and the Historical Setting of the Priestly School*. Winona Lake, IN: Eisenbrauns, 1985.

Harris, R. Geoffrey. *Mission in the Gospels*. Eugene, OR: Wipf & Stock, 2004.

Harris, W. Hall. "John." In *The Bible Knowledge Key Word Study: The Gospels*, edited by Darrell L. Bock, 261–388. Colorado Springs: Cook, 2002.

Hastings, Ross. *Missional God, Missional Church: Hope for Re-evangelizing the West*. Downers Grove: IVP Academic, 2012.

Hays, J. Daniel. *The Temple and the Tabernacle: A Study of God's Dwelling Places from Genesis to Revelation*. Grand Rapids: Baker, 2016.

Hays, Richard B. *Echoes of Scripture in the Gospels*. Waco, TX: Baylor University Press, 2016.

———. *Echoes of Scripture in the Letters of Paul*. New Haven: Yale University Press, 1989.

Hengel, Martin. *Judaism and Hellenism: Studies in Their Encounter in Palestine during the Early Hellenistic Period*. Philadelphia: Fortress, 1981.

Hesselgrave, David J. "Did Cape Town 2010 Correct the 'Edinburgh Error'? A Preliminary Analysis." *Southwestern Journal of Theology* 55 (Fall 2012) 77–89.

———. *Paradigms in Conflict: 10 Key Questions in Christian Missions Today*. Grand Rapids: Kregel, 2005.

Hestenes, Roberta. "Christian Community and World Evangelization." In Douglas, *Proclaim Christ until He Comes*, 119–25.

Higgins, A. J. B. *The Lord's Supper in the New Testament*. London: SCM, 1952.

Hirsch, Eric D. *Validity in Interpretation*. New Haven: Yale University Press, 1979.

Hock, Ronald F. "Jesus, the Beloved Disciple, and Greco-Roman Friendship Conventions." In *Christian Origins and Greco-Roman Culture: Social and Literary Contexts for the New Testament*, edited by Stanley E. Porter and Andrew W. Pitts, 195–213. Leiden: Brill, 2013.

Hoskins, Paul M. *Jesus as the Fulfillment of the Temple in the Gospel of John*. Eugene, OR: Wipf & Stock, 2006.

Houston, Tom. "Good News for the Poor." In Douglas, *Proclaim Christ until He Comes*, 153–61.

Howell, David B. *Matthew's Inclusive Story: A Study in the Narrative Rhetoric of the First Gospel*. Sheffield: Sheffield Academic, 1990.

Hultgren, Arland J. "The Johannine Footwashing as a Symbol of Eschatological Hospitality." *New Testament Studies* (1982) 539–46.

Hunsberger, George R. "Is There Biblical Warrant for Evangelism?" In *The Study of Evangelism: Exploring a Missional Practice of the Church*, edited by Paul Wesley Chilcote and Laceye C. Warner, 59–72. Grand Rapids: Eerdmans, 2008.

———. "Proposals for a Missional Hermeneutic: Mapping a Conversation." *Missiology: An International Review* 39 (2011) 309–21.

Hurtado, Larry W. "The Binitarian Pattern of Earliest Christian Devotion and Early Doctrinal Development." In *The Place of Christ in Liturgical Prayer: Trinity, Christology and Liturgical Theology*, edited by Brian Spinks, 23–50. Collegeville: Liturgical, 2008.

———. *Lord Jesus Christ: Devotion to Jesus in Earliest Christianity*. Grand Rapids: Eerdmans, 2003.

———. *One God, One Lord: Early Christian Devotion and Ancient Jewish Monotheism*. London: T. & T. Clark, 2015.

Hutchinson, Mark, and John Wolffe. *A Short History of Global Evangelicalism*. Cambridge: Cambridge University Press, 2012.

Jenny, T. P. "Holiness, Holy." In *Eerdmans Dictionary of the Bible*, edited by David Noel Freedman et al., 598–99. Grand Rapids: Eerdmans, 2000.

Jeremias, Joachim. *The Eucharistic Words of Jesus*. Translated by Norman Perrin. New York: Scribner, 1966.

———. *Jesus' Promise to the Nations*. Naperville: Allenson, 1958.

Johnson, Andy. *Missions: How the Local Church Goes Global*. 9Marks: Building Healthy Churches. Wheaton, IL: Crossway, 2017.

Johnston, Arthur P. "The Kingdom in Relation to the Church and World." In Nicholls, *In Word and Deed*, 109–34.

Jones, Larry Paul. *The Symbol of Water in the Gospel of John*. Journal for the Study of the New Testament 145. Sheffield: Sheffield Academic, 1997.

Jonge, M. de. "Jesus as Prophet and King in the Fourth Gospel." *Ephemerides Theologicae Lovanienses* 49 (1973) 160–77.

Jørgensen, Knud. "Biblical and Theological Foundations: The Triune God and the Missional Church." In *Called to Unity: For the Sake of Mission*, edited by John St. H. Gibaut and Knud Jørgensen, 33–45. Eugene, OR: Wipf & Stock, 2015.

———. "Inspiration and Challenges from Cape Town and Edinburgh to Church and Mission." *Transformation* 29 (2012) 293–303.

Kaiser, Walter C., Jr. "The Meaning of Meaning." In *An Introduction to Biblical Hermeneutics*, 29–48. Grand Rapids: Zondervan, 1994.

———. *Mission in the Old Testament*. Grand Rapids: Baker, 2012.

Kampen, John. "The Books of the Maccabees and Sectarianism in Second Temple Judaism." In *The Books of the Maccabees: History, Theology, Ideology*, 11–30. Leiden: Brill, 2007.

Käsemann, Ernst. *The Testament of Jesus*. Philadelphia: Fortress, 1968.

Keener, Craig S. *The Gospel of John*. Grand Rapids: Baker, 2003.

———. "Sent Like Jesus: Johannine Missiology (John 20:21–22)." *Asian Journal of Pentecostal Studies* 12 (2009) 21–45.

———. *Spirit Hermeneutics*. Grand Rapids: Eerdmans, 2016.

Kerr, Alan R. *The Temple of Jesus' Body: The Temple Theme in the Gospel of John*. Journal for the Study of the New Testament 220. London: Sheffield Academic, 2002.

Kim, Young-Uk. *The Ideal King according to Deuteronomy 17:14–20: An Investigation into Kingship in the Old Testament*. Kampen, Netherlands: Theologische Universitit, 2000.

Kinzer, Mark. "Temple Christology in the Gospel of John." *Society of Biblical Literature* 37 (1998) 447–64.

Kirk, J. Andrew. *What Is Mission? Theological Explorations*. Minneapolis: Fortress, 2000.

Kitzberger, Ingrid Rosa. "Love and Footwashing: John 13:1–20 and Luke 7:36–50 Read Intertextually." *Biblical Interpretation* 2 (1994) 196–206.

Klein, William W., et al. *Introduction to Biblical Interpretation*. 3rd ed. Grand Rapids: Zondervan, 2017.

Koester, Craig R. *Symbolism in the Fourth Gospel: Meaning, Mystery, Community*. Minneapolis: Fortress, 1995.

———. *The World of Life: A Theology of John's Gospel*. Grand Rapids: Eerdmans, 2008.

Köstenberger, Andreas J. "The Destruction of the Second Temple and the Composition of the Fourth Gospel." *Trinity Journal* 26 (2005) 205–42.

———. *John*. Baker Exegetical Commentary on the New Testament. Grand Rapids: Baker, 2004.

———. "John." In *Commentary on the New Testament Use of the Old Testament*, edited by G. K. Beale and D. A. Carson, 415–512. Grand Rapids: Baker, 2007.

———. *The Missions of Jesus and the Disciples according to the Fourth Gospel: With Implications for the Fourth Gospel's Purpose and the Mission of the Contemporary Church*. Grand Rapids: Eerdmans, 1998.

———. *Studies on John and Gender: A Decade of Scholarship*. Studies in Biblical Literature 38. New York: Lang, 2001.

Köstenberger, Andreas J., and Peter Thomas O'Brien. *Salvation to the Ends of the Earth: A Biblical Theology of Mission*. New Studies in Biblical Theology 11. Downers Grove: InterVarsity, 2001.

Köstenberger, Andreas J., and Scott R. Swain. *Father, Son, and Spirit: The Trinity and John's Gospel*. New Studies in Biblical Theology 24. Downers Grove: InterVarsity, 2008.

Krentz, Edgar. "Missionary Matthew: Matthew 28:16–20 as Summary of the Gospel." *Currents in Theology and Mission* 31 (2004) 24–31.

Kuzmic, Peter. "How to Teach the Truth of the Gospel." In Douglas, *Proclaim Christ until He Comes*, 197–203.

Kyle, Richard G. *Evangelicalism: An Americanized Christianity*. New Brunswick, NJ: Transaction, 2006.

Kysar, R. *The Fourth Evangelist and His Gospel: An Examination of Contemporary Scholarship*. Minneapolis: Augsburg, 1975.

Lacomara, Aelred. "Deuteronomy and the Farewell Discourse (Jn 13:31—16:33)." *Catholic Biblical Quarterly* 36 (1974) 66–84.

Ladd, George Eldon. *A Theology of the New Testament*. Grand Rapids: Eerdmans, 1993.

Lappenga, Benjamin J. "Whose Zeal Is It Anyway? The Citation of Psalm 69:9 in John 2:17 as a Double Entendre." In *Abiding Words: The Use of Scripture in the Gospel of John*, edited by Alicia D. Myers and Bruce G. Schuchard, 141–59. Atlanta: SBL, 2015.

Larson, Bruce. *Wind & Fire: Living Out the Book of Acts*. Waco, TX: Word, 1984.

"The Lausanne Covenant" (1974). https://www.lausanne.org/content/covenant/lausanne-covenant#cov.

Lausanne Movement. "Holistic Mission." Lausanne Occasional Paper 33. October 3, 2004. https://www.lausanne.org/content/lop/holistic-mission-lop-33.

Leeman, Jonathan. *Don't Fire Your Church Members: The Case for Congregationalism*. Nasville: B&H, 2016.

———. "Soteriological Mission: Focusing in on the Mission of Redemption." In *Four Views on the Church's Mission*, edited by Jason S. Sexton, 17–62. Grand Rapids: Zondervan, 2017.

Lenski, R. C. H. *The Interpretation of St. John's Gospel*. Vol. 2. 2 vols. Minneapolis: Fortress, 1961.

———. *The Interpretation of St. John's Revelation*. Minneapolis: Fortress, 1943.

Leung, Mavis M. *The Kingship-Cross Interplay in the Gospel of John*. Eugene, OR: Wipf & Stock, 2011.

Lieu, Judith. "Temple and Synagogue in John." *New Testament Studies* 45 (1999) 66–67.

Lightfoot, R. H. *St. John's Gospel: A Commentary*. Oxford: Clarendon, 1959.

Lindars, Barnabas. *The Gospel of John*. London: Oliphants, 1972.

Loader, William. *The Christology of the Fourth Gospel: Structure and Issues*. New York: Lang, 1989.

———. *Jesus in John's Gospel*. Grand Rapids: Eerdmans, 2017.

Lombard, H. A., and W. H. Oliver. "A Working Supper in Jerusalem: John 13:1–38 Introduces Jesus' Farewell Discourses." *Neotestamentica* 25 (1991) 357–78.

Louw, J. P., and Eugene A. Nida, eds. *Greek-English Lexicon of the New Testament: Based on Semantic Domains*. New York: United Bible Societies, 1988.

Luz, Ulrich. "The Final Judgment (Matt 25:31–46): An Exercise in 'History of Influence' Exegesis." In *Treasures New and Old Recent Contributions to Matthaean Studies*, translated by Dorothy Jean Weaver, 271–310. Atlanta: Scholar, 1996.

Malina, Bruce J. *Windows on the World of Jesus: Time Travel to Ancient Judea*. Louisville: Westminster John Knox, 1993.

Maling, Eduardo M. "The Importance of the Local Church to World Evangelization." In Douglas, *Proclaim Christ until He Comes*, 73–77.

Marinkovich, Peter. "What Does Zechariah 1–8 Tell Us about the Second Temple?" In *Second Temple Studies*, vol. 2, *Temple and Community in the Persian Period*, edited by Tamara Eskenazi et al., 88–105. Sheffield: Sheffield Academic, 1994.

Marsden, George M. "The Evangelical Denomination." In *Evangelicals: Who They Have Been, Are Now, and Could Be*, edited by Mark A. Noll et al., 17–30. Grand Rapids: Eerdmans, 2019.

Marshall, I. Howard. *Beyond the Bible: Moving from Scripture to Theology*. Grand Rapids: Baker, 2004.

———. *The Epistles of John*. New International Commentary on the New Testament. Grand Rapids: Eerdmans, 2009.

Martens, E. A. *Plot and Purpose in the Old Testament*. Leicester: InterVarsity, 1981.

Mathew, Bincy. *The Johannine Footwashing as the Sign of Perfect Love: An Exegetical Study of John 13:1–20*. Tübingen: Mohr Siebrek, 2018.

Maynard, Arthur. "The Role of Peter in the Fourth Gospel." *New Testament Studies* 30 (1984) 534–35.

McGavran, Donald A. *Understanding Church Growth*. Grand Rapids: Eerdmans, 1980.

———. "What Is Mission?" In *Contemporary Theologies of Mission*, 15–29. Grand Rapids: Baker, 1983.

McGrath, James F. *John's Apologetic Christology: Legitimation and Development in Johannine Christology*. Cambridge: Cambridge University Press, 2001.

Meeks, Wayne Atherton. "The Man from Heaven in Johannine Sectarianism." *Journal of Biblical Literature* 91 (1972) 44–72.

Menken, M. J. J. *Studies in John's Gospel and Epistles: Collected Essays*. Contributions to Biblical Exegesis & Theology 77. Leuven: Peeters, 2015.

———. "The Translation of Psalm 41.10 in John 13.18." *Journal for the Study of the New Testament* 40 (1990) 61–79.

Metzger, Bruce Manning. *A Textual Commentary on the Greek New Testament*. London: United Bible Societies, 1971.

Michaels, J. Ramsey. *The Gospel of John*. Grand Rapids: Eerdmans, 2010.

Miller, Paul. "They Saw His Glory and Spoke of Him." In *Hearing the Old Testament in the New Testament*, edited by Stanley E. Porter, 127–51. Grand Rapids: Eerdmans, 2006.

Mlakuzhyil, George. *The Christocentric Literary Structure of the Fourth Gospel*. Analecta Biblica 117. Roma: Biblico, 1987.

Moloney, Francis J. "A Sacramental Reading of John 3:1–38." *Catholic Biblical Quarterly* 53 (1991) 237–56.

Moloney, Francis J., and Daniel J. Harrington. *The Gospel of John*. Collegeville: Liturgical, 2005.

Morris, Leon. *The Gospel according to John*. Reprinted as part of the New International Commentary on the New Testament series. Grand Rapids: Eerdmans, 1995.

Mott, John R. *The Evangelization of the World in this Generation*. New York: Arno, 1972.

Moule, H. C. G. *Charles Simeon*. London: Methuen, 1905.

Myers, Bryant L. *Engaging Globalization: The Poor, Christian Mission, and Our Hyperconnected World*. Grand Rapids: Baker, 2017.

Netland, Harold. "The Cape Town Commitment: Continuity and Change." In *The Lausanne Movement: A Range of Perspectives*, edited by Lars Nilsen Dahle, 426–38. Regnum Edinburgh Centenary Series 22. Oxford: Regnum, 2014.

Newbigin, Lesslie. *The Gospel in a Pluralist Society*. Grand Rapids: Eerdmans, 1989.

———. *The Open Secret: An Introduction to the Theology of Mission.* Grand Rapids: Eerdmans, 1995.

Niemand, Christoph. "Was Bedeutet Die Fusswaschung; Sklavenarbeit Oder Liebesdienst? Kulturkundliches Als Auslegungshilfe Für Joh 13, 6–8." *Protokolle Zur Bibel* 3 (1994) 115–27.

Nissen, Johannes. *New Testament and Mission: Historical and Hermeneutical Perspectives.* New York: Lang, 2007.

Nissen, Johannes, et al., eds. "The Gospel of John as Literature: Literary Readings of the Fourth Gospel." In *New Readings in John*, 31–46. New York: T. & T. Clark, 2004.

Noll, Mark A. *The Scandal of the Evangelical Mind.* Grand Rapids: Eerdmans, 1994.

Okure, Teresa. *The Johannine Approach to Mission: A Contextual Study of John 4:1–42.* Tübingen: Mohr, 1988.

Olsson, Birger. *Structure and Meaning in the Fourth Gospel: A Text-Linguistic Analysis of John 2:1–11 and 4:1–42.* Lund: Gleerup, 1974.

Orchard, Helen C. *Courting Betrayal: Jesus as Victim in the Gospel of John.* Edited by Stanley E. Porter. Journal for the Study of the New Testament 161. Sheffield: Sheffield Academic, 1988.

Osborne, Grant R. *The Hermeneutical Spiral: A Comprehensive Introduction to Biblical Interpretation.* Downers Grove: InterVarsity, 1991.

———. *The Resurrection Narratives: A Redactional Study.* Grand Rapids: Baker, 1984.

Ott, Craig, and Stephen J. Strauss. *Encountering Theology of Mission: Biblical Foundations, Historical Developments, and Contemporary Issues.* Grand Rapids: Baker, 2010.

Overman, A. Andrew. *Matthew's Gospel and Formative Judaism: The Social World of the Matthean Community.* Minneapolis: Fortress, 1990.

Packer, J. I. "The Work of the Holy Spirit in Conviction and Conversion." In Douglas, *Proclaim Christ until He Comes*, 100–104.

Padilla, C. René. "Evangelism and the World." In Douglas, *Let the Earth Hear His Voice*, 116–33.

———. "Integral Mission and Its Historical Development." In *Justice, Mercy and Humility: Integral Mission and the Poor*, edited by Tim Chester, 42–58. Carlisle: Paternoster, 2002.

———. "My Theological Pilgrimage." In *Shaping a Global Theological Mind*, edited by Darren Marks, 127–37. Hampshire, UK: Ashgate, 2008.

Pagin, Peter, and Francis Jeffry Pelletier. "Content, Context, and Composition." In *Context-Sensitivity and Semantic Minimalism: New Essays on Semantics and Pragmatics*, edited by Gerhard Preyer and Georg Peter, 25–62. Oxford: Oxford University Press, 2007.

Parks, R. Keith. "The Great Commission." In Douglas, *Let the Earth Hear His Voice*, 483–91.

Parsenios, George L. *Departure and Consolation: The Johannine Farewell Discourses in Light of Greco-Roman Literature.* Leiden: Brill, 2005.

Paschal, R. Wade. "Sacramental Symbolism and Physical Imagery in the Gospel of John." *Tyndale Bulletin* 32 (1981) 151–76.

Peterson, Brian Neil. *John's Use of Ezekiel: Understanding the Unique Perspective of the Fourth Gospel.* Minneapolis: Fortress, 2015.

Plöger, Otto. *Theocracy and Eschatology.* Oxford: Blackwell, 1968.

Quarles, Charles. "The New Perspective and Means of Atonement in Jewish Literature of the Second Temple Period." *Criswell Theological Review* 2 (2005) 39–56.

Redford, Shawn B. *Missiological Hermeneutics.* Eugene, OR: Wipf & Stock, 2012.

Rengstorf, K. H. "ἀποστέλλω, πέμπω, κτλ." In *TDNT* 1:403–6.
Ridderbos, Herman. *The Gospel of John*. Translated by John Vriend. Grand Rapids: Eerdmans, 1991.
Ro, Bong Rin. "The Perspectives of Church History from New Testament Times to 1960." In Nicholls, *In Word and Deed*, 11–40.
Robinson, John A. T. *The Priority of John*. Edited by J. F. Coakley. Eugene, OR: Wipf & Stock, 1985.
Rutayisire, Antonie. "The Church and the Message of Reconciliation." In *The Lausanne Movement: A Range of Perspectives*, edited by Lars Nilsen Dahle, 239–49. Oxford: Regnum, 2014.
Sanders, E. P. *Jewish Law from Jesus to the Mishnah*. London: SCM, 1990.
———. *Judaism: Practice and Belief, 63 BCE–66 CE*. London: SCM, 2005.
Saussure, F. de. *Course in General Linguistics*. Translated by W. Baskin. New York: Philosophical Library, 1959.
Scheuer, Blaženka. *The Return of YHWH: The Tension between Deliverance and Repentance in Isaiah 40–55*. Berlin: de Gruyter, 2008.
Schleiermacher, F. D. E. *Hermeneutics: The Handwritten Manuscripts*. Atlanta: Scholars, 1986.
———. *Hermeneutics and Criticism*. Cambridge: Cambridge University Press, 1998.
Schnackenburg, Rudolf. *The Gospel according to St John*. 3 vols. London: Burns & Oates, 1968, 1980, 1982.
Schneiders, Sandra M. "From Exegesis to Hermeneutics: The Problems of Contemporary Meaning in Scripture." *Horizons* 8 (1981) 23–39.
Schnelle, Undo. "Recent Views of John's Gospel." *Word and World* 21 (2001) 352–59.
Schreiter, Robert. "From the Lausanne Covenant to the Cape Town Commitment." In *The Lausanne Movement: A Range of Perspectives*, edited by Lars Nilsen Dahle, 411–18. Oxford: Regnum, 2014.
———. "From the Lausanne Covenant to the Cape Town Commitment: A Theological Assessment." *International Bulletin of Missionary Research* 35 (April 2011) 88–92.
———. *The Ministry of Reconciliation: Spirituality & Strategies*. Maryknoll: Orbis, 1998.
Schrenk, G. "δίκαιος." In *TDNT* 2:187–91.
Scott, John. "The Risks of Rapid Urbanization in Developing Countries." January 14, 2015. https://www.zurich.com/knowledge/topics/global-risks/the-risks-of-rapid-urbanization-in-developing-countries?page_url_input_url=https%3a%2f%2fwww.zurich.com%2fknowledge%2farticles%2f2015%2f01%2fthe-risks-of-rapid-urbanization-in-developing-countries.
Seland, Toreey. "Resident Aliens in Mission: Missional Practices in the Emerging Church of 1 Peter." *Bulletin for Biblical Research* 19 (2009) 565–89.
Senior, Donald, and Carroll Stuhlmueller. *The Biblical Foundations for Mission*. Maryknoll: Orbis, 1991.
Silva, Moisés. "Who Needs Hermeneutics Anyway?" In *Introduction to Biblical Hermeneutics*, 17–28. Grand Rapids: Zondervan, 1994.
Smith, D. M. *The Composition and Order of the Fourth Gospel: Bultmann's Literary Theory*. New Haven: Yale University Press, 1965.
Spevak, Olga. *Constituent Order in Classical Latin Prose*. Amsterdam: Benjamins, 2010.
Spinks, D. Christopher. *The Bible and the Crisis of Meaning: Debates on the Theological Interpretation of Scripture*. London: T. & T. Clark, 2007.

Stanley, Brian. *The World Missionary Conference, Edinburgh 1910*. Grand Rapids: Eerdmans, 2009.

Stanton, G. N. "Presuppositions in New Testament Criticism." In *New Testament Interpretation*, edited by I. Howard Marshall, 60–71. Grand Rapids: Eerdmans, 1977.

Stetzer, Ed. "An Evangelical Kingdom Community Approach." In *The Mission of the Church: Five Views in Conversation*, edited by Craig Ott, 91–116. Grand Rapids: Baker, 2016.

Steuernagel, Valdir R. "A Latin-American Evangelical Perspective on the Cape Town Congress." In *The Lausanne Movement: A Range of Perspectives*, edited by Lars Nilsen Dahle, 304–18. Oxford: Regnum, 2014.

———. "Social Concern and Evangelism: The Journey of the Lausanne Movement." *International Bulletin of Mission Research* April (1991) 53–56.

Stibbe, Mark W. G. *John's Gospel*. London: Routledge, 1994.

Stott, John R. W. "The Biblical Basis of Evangelism." In Douglas, *Let the Earth Hear His Voice*, 65–78.

———. *Christian Mission in the Modern World*. Downers Grove: InterVarsity, 2008.

———. *The Contemporary Christian: Applying God's Word to Today's World*. Downers Grove: InterVarsity, 1992.

———. "The Great Commission." In *One Race, One Gospel, One Task*, 37–44. Minneapolis: World Wide, 1967.

Stott, John R. W., and Christopher J. H. Wright. *Christian Mission in the Modern World*. Rev. ed. Downers Grove: InterVarsity, 2015.

Stroope, Michael W. *Transcending Mission: The Eclipse of a Modern Tradition*. Downers Grove: InterVarsity, 2017.

Sunquist, Scott. *Understanding Christian Mission: Participation in Suffering and Glory*. Grand Rapids: Baker, 2013.

Swanson, J. "Ὁράω." In *Dictionary of Biblical Languages with Semantic Domains: Greek (New Testament)*. Oak Harbor, WA: Logos, 1997.

———. "גָּבַשׁ." In *Dictionary of Biblical Languages with Semantic Domains: Hebrew (Old Testament)*. Oak Harbor, WA: Logos, 1997.

Talbert, Charles H. *Reading John: A Literary and Theological Commentary on the Fourth Gospel and the Johannine Epistles*. Macon, GA: Smyth & Helwys, 2005.

Tate, W. Randolph. *Biblical Interpretation: An Integrated Approach*. Grand Rapids: Baker, 2008.

Tennent, Timothy C. *Invitation to World Missions: A Trinitarian Missiology for the Twenty-First Century*. Grand Rapids: Kregel, 2010.

Tenney, Merrill C. *John: The Gospel of Belief; An Analytic Study of the Text*. Grand Rapids: Eerdmans, 1976.

Terranova, Carmelo B. "Living Holy." In Douglas, *Proclaim Christ until He Comes*, 116–18.

Tertullian. "The Chaplet, or De Corona." In *Latin Christianity: Its Founder, Tertullian*, edited by A. Roberts et al. Vol. 3. Buffalo: Christian Literature, 1885.

Thomas, John Christopher. *Footwashing in John 13 and the Johannine Community*. 2nd ed. Cleveland: CPT, 1991.

Thomaskutty, Johnson. "Glo[b/c]alization and Mission[s]: Reading John's Gospel." *New Life Theological Journal* 5 (2015) 56–77.

Thompson, Marianne Meye. *The God of the Gospel of John*. Grand Rapids: Eerdmans, 2001.

———. "The Gospel according to John." In *The Gospels*, edited by Stephen C. Barton, 182–200. Cambridge: Cambridge University Press, 2006.

———. "'His Own Received Him Not': Jesus Washes the Feet of His Disciples." In *The Art of Reading Scripture*, edited by Ellen F. Davis and Richard B. Hays, 258–73. Grand Rapids: Eerdmans, 2003.

———. *The Incarnate Word: Perspektives on Jesus in the Fourth Gospel*. Peabody: Hendrickson, 1993.

———. *John: A Commentary*. Louisville: Westminster John Knox, 2015.

Tizon, Al. "Evangelism and Social Responsibility: The Making of a Transformational Vision." In *The Lausanne Movement: A Range of Perspectives*, edited by Lars Nilsen Dahle, 170–81. Oxford: Regnum, 2014.

———. *Transformation after Lausanne: Radical Evangelical Mission in Global-Local Perspective*. Eugene, OR: Wipf and Stock, 2008.

Turner, David L. *Matthew*. Grand Rapids: Baker, 2008.

Um, Stephen T. *The Theme of Temple Christology in John's Gospel*. Library of New Testament Studies 312. London: T. & T. Clark, 2006.

Van Gelder, Craig. *The Missional Church in Context*. Grand Rapids: Eerdmans, 2007.

Van Engen, Charles E. *God's Missionary People: Rethinking the Purpose of the Local Church*. Grand Rapids: Baker, 1991.

———. *Mission on the Way: Issues in Mission Theology*. Grand Rapids: Baker, 1996.

Vanhoozer, Kevin J. *The Drama of Doctrine: A Canonical-Linguistic Approach to Christian Theology*. Louisville: Westminster John Knox, 2005.

———. "What Is Theological Interpretation of the Bible?" In *Theological Interpretation of the New Testament: A Book-by-Book Survey*, edited by Kevin J. Vanhoozer et al., 13–26. Grand Rapids: Baker, 2008.

Vicedom, Georg F. *The Mission of God: An Introduction to a Theology of Mission*. St. Louis: Concordia, 1965.

Voorwinde, Stephen. *Jesus' Emotions in the Fourth Gospel: Human or Divine?* Journal for the Study of the New Testament 284. London: T. & T. Clark, 2005.

Vos, Geerhardus. *Biblical Theology: Old and New Testaments*. Eugene, OR: Wipf and Stock, 2003.

Wallace, Daniel B. *Greek Grammar beyond the Basics*. Grand Rapids: Zondervan, 1996.

Wardle, Timothy. *The Jerusalem Temple and Early Christian Identity*. Wissenschaftliche Untersuchungen Zum Neuen Testament. 2. Reihe 291. Tübingen: Mohr Siebeck, 2010.

Warneck, Gustav. *Outline of a History of Protestant Missions*. Edited by George Robson. New York: Evangelical Literature, 1901.

Warren, Carter. *Matthew and the Margins*. Sheffield: Sheffield Academic, 2000.

Watson, Jude Tiersma. "What Does It Mean to Be Incarnational When We Are Not the Messiah?" In *God So Loves the City*, edited by Charles E. Van Engen and Jude Tiersma Watson, 7–26. Monrovia, CA: MARC, 1994.

Weiss, Herold. "Footwashing in the Johannine Community." *Novum Testament* 21 (1979) 298–325.

Wenham, David, and Steve Walton. *Exploring the New Testament*. Downers Grove: InterVarsity, 2001.

Whallon, William. "The Pascha in the Eucharist." *New Testament Studies* 40 (1994) 126–32.
Wolters, M. Albert. *Creation Regained*. Grand Rapids: Eerdmans, 2005.
Wright, Christopher J. H. "The Difference Jesus Made in His Context." In *Practicing Truth: Confident Witness in Our Pluralistic World*, edited by David W. Shenk and Linford Stutzman, 236–53. Scottdale: Herald, 1999.
———. "Mission as a Matrix." In *Out of Egypt: Biblical Theology and Biblical Interpretation*, edited by C. Bartholomew, 102–43. Grand Rapids: Zondervan, 2004.
———. *The Mission of God: Unlocking the Bible's Grand Narrative*. Downers Grove: InterVarsity, 2006.
———. *The Mission of God's People: A Biblical Theology of the Church's Mission*. Grand Rapids: Zondervan, 2010.
———. "Participatory Mission: The Mission of God's People Revealed in the Whole Bible Story." In *Four Views on the Church's Mission*, edited by Jason S. Sexton, 63–106. Grand Rapids: Zondervan, 2017.
———. "Response to John R. Franke." In *Four Views on the Church's Mission*, edited by Jason S. Sexton, 140–45. Grand Rapids: Zondervan, 2017.
———, ed. "The Third Lausanne Congress on World Evangelization: The Cape Town Commitment." *Evangelical Journal of Theology* 5 (2011) 166–224.
———. "Trinity." In *Living Witness*, 35–56. Eugene, OR: Wipf & Stock, 2012.
Wright, N. T. "Jesus and the Identity of God." *Ex Auditu* (1998) 42–56.
———. *Jesus and the Victory of God*. Minneapolis: Fortress, 1997.
———. *Justification: God's Plan & Paul's Vision*. Downers Grove: InterVarsity, 2009.
———. *The New Testament and the People of God*. Minneapolis: Fortress, 1992.
———. *Paul and the Faithfulness of God*. London: SPCK, 2013.
Yee, Gale A. *Jewish Feasts and the Gospel of John*. Edited by Mary Ann Gretty. Wilmington: Glazier, 1989.

Author Index

Adeyemo, Tokunboh, 153, 170
Akala, Adesola Joan, 53
Allen, R. Michael, 12
Allison, Cregg R., 21, 23
Allison, Dale C., 13
An, Keon-Sang, 26
Anderson, Bernhard W., x
Appold, Mark L., 54, 67
Arndt, William, 63
Ashton, John, 67

Baker, David L., 14
Ball, David Mark, 96
Barr, James, 20
Barram, Michael, 27
Barrett, C. K., 1, 49, 52, 54–55, 62, 67, 70, 76–78, 86, 98, 108, 121, 124, 128, 137
Barthes, Roland, 22
Barton, John, 17
Barus, Armand, 33, 86, 92, 181
Bauckham, Richard, x, 4, 11–12, 31, 61, 75, 114, 126, 129
Bauer, Walter, 63
Beale, G. K., 65, 67, 124
Beasley-Murray, 1, 38, 47, 75, 94, 116, 128
Bebbington, David William, 158–59
Bedford, Peter Ross, 64
Beker, J. Christiaan, 24, 26, 52
Belle, Gilbert van, 76, 86
Bennema, Cornelis, 32, 36

Bernard, J. H., 117
Bevans, Stephen B., 183
Beyerhaus, Peter, 169
Billings, J. Todd, 176–77, 182
Bird, Warren, 28
Bishop, E. F. F., 133
Black, David Alan, 23
Blauw, Johannes, x, 9
Blomberg, Craig L., 42
Blumhofer, Christopher Mark, 63, 66–67, 70, 81, 86
Bock, Darrell L., 67
Boer, Martinus C. de, 71, 78, 111, 113,
Booth, Steve, 96
Borgen, Peder, 53
Bornkamm, Gü["u" diaeresis]nther, 67
Bosch, David J., x, 6–8, 16, 26–27
Brown, Lindsay, 157
Brown, Raymond E., 1, 27, 33, 36, 38, 41–42, 55, 63, 67, 71–72, 77–78, 98, 103–4, 108, 116–17, 120–22, 125, 127, 130, 132, 134, 139, 144, 180, 184
Brown, Sherri, 71, 119
Brown, Tricia Gates, 87, 92–93
Brownson, James V., x, 8–9, 12, 24, 26
Bruce, F. F., 49, 93, 108, 111, 130, 184
Bultmann, Rudolf, 21, 23–24, 71, 87, 96, 117
Burge, Gary M., 91, 98, 107, 137
Bush, Luis, 153

Carey, W., 5-6
Carriker, Tim, 18
Carroll, Robert P., 64
Carson, D. A., 27, 64, 93, 103, 109, 124, 128, 139, 142, 144
Cartledge, Mark J., 180
Chennattu, Rekha M., 31, 36-37, 75, 126-27
Cho, Sukmin, 144
Clines, David J. A., 64
Collins, T., 67
Coloe, Mary L., 31, 36, 38, 65, 104, 108, 126
Corell, A., 75
Cory, Catherine, 119, 127
Costas, Orlando E., 39, 151-52, 175
Crowe, Brandon D., 49
Cullmann, Oscar, 10, 116
Culpepper, R. Alan, 34, 48, 70, 82, 86, 92, 108, 115, 117, 137-38, 141

Dahle, Lars., 153
Daly-Denton, Margaret, 67
Danby, Herbert, 82, 92, 137
Danker, Frederick W., 63
Davies, Margaret, 96
Davies, W. D., 13
Deborst, Ruth Padilla, 153, 158-59, 163, 166, 173, 180
Derrida, Jacques, 22
DeYoung, Kevin, 165, 169
Dodd, C. H., 1, 8, 27, 29, 41-42, 48, 77, 82, 86, 92, 137
Douglas, J. D., 160, 170
Dowsett, Rose, 162, 171-72
Dunn, James D. G., 88, 91
Dyrness, William A., 183

Emerton, J. A., 125
Enns, Peter, x, 25-26
Erwin, Fahlbusch, 33, 116
Escobar, Samuel, 151, 158, 169
Estrada, Rodolfo Galvan, 100, 115

Ferdinando, Keith, 19
Ferreira, Johan, 27
Flemming, Dean E., 16, 173, 176-77, 187-89

Flett, John G., 180
Ford, Leighton, 153, 171
Fowl, S. E., 180
Franke, John R., 154, 164, 166-67

Gammie, John G., 90
Gennari, Silvia P., 22
Gibson, David, 103
Gilbert, Greg., 165
Gilliland, Dean S., 176
Glasser, Arthur F., 14
Goheen, Michael W., 13-14, 16
Gombis, Timothy G., 86
Gorman, Michael J., 1, 15, 17, 30-33, 36-37, 85, 106-8, 182, 184
Graham, Billy, 150, 158, 168
Green, Joel B., 15-16, 18, 23-25, 27, 85
Guder, Darrell L., 28, 61, 175-79, 182, 185
Gundry, Robert H., 118
Gutierrez, Edna Lee de., 151

Hagner, Donald A., 13
Hahn, Ferdinand, 7, 124
Hall, Douglas, 180
Hamilton, James, 83, 119
Hammond, Pete, 171
Haran, Menahem, 63
Harrington, Daniel J., 36
Harris, R. Geoffery, 28, 30, 188
Harris, W. Hall, 37
Hastings, Ross, 31, 187-88
Hays, J. Daniel, 64
Hays, Richard B., 18, 118, 139
Hengel, Martin, 8
Hesselgrave, David J., 164-65, 175-76
Hestenes, Roberta, 152-53, 170
Higgins, A. J. B., 116-17, 124, 126
Hirsch, Eric D., 20
Hock, Ronald F., 92, 136
Hoskins, Paul M., 37
Houston, Tom, 151
Howell, David B., 13
Hultgren, Arland J., 1, 35, 129, 131
Hunsberger, George R., 12, 24, 155, 168
Hurtado, Larry W., 25, 54
Hutchinson, Mark, 161

Author Index

Jenny, T. P., 88
Jeremias, Joachim, 7, 116
Johnson, Andy, 164
Johnston, Arthur P., 170
Jones, Larry Paul, 75, 86, 124
Jonge, M. de, 67
Jørgensen, Knud, 156, 158, 161–62, 185

Kaiser Jr., Walter C., x, 21
Kampen, John, 74
Käsemann, Ernst, 117, 119
Keener, Craig S., 1, 33, 82, 120, 177–78, 180, 182
Kerr, Alan R., 65, 86
Kim, Young-Uk, 64
Kinzer, Mark, 37
Kirk, J. Andrew, 166, 173
Kitzberger, Ingrid Rosa, 34
Klein, William W., 22–23
Koester, Craig R., 34, 67, 71–72, 77, 82–83, 86–87, 98, 126, 132, 138
Köstenberger, Andreas J., xi, 1, 6, 19–20, 27–29, 32, 35, 49, 55, 65–66, 72, 79, 82–83, 89, 91–92, 94, 96–97, 105, 108, 118, 137–38, 141–42, 175–76, 184
Krentz, Edgar, 13
Kuzmic, Peter, 171
Kyle, Richard G., 179
Kysar, R., 144

Lacomara, Aelred, 94, 116
Ladd, George Eldon, 13
Lappenga, Benjamin J., 76, 135
Larson, Bruce, 179
Leeman, Jonathan, 163
Lenski, R. C. H. 82, 97
Leung, Mavis M., 67
Lightfoot, R. H., 42, 49 ,77
Lindars, Barnabas, 33, 37, 72, 104
Lieu, Judith, 37
Loader, William, 42, 49, 71, 103–4, 106, 109
Lombard, H. A., 108
Louw, J. P., 20, 121
Luz, Ulrich., 13

Malina, Bruce J., 120

Maling, Eduardo M., 171
Marinkovich, Peter, 65
Marsden, George M., 159
Marshall, I. Howard, 26, 85, 134
Martens, E. A., 85
Mathew, Bincy, 33, 35–36, 38, 92–93, 103–4, 113, 120, 128, 131, 133, 137–38
Maynard, Arthur, 1
McGavran, Donald A., 6, 179
McGrath, James F., 134
Meeks, Wayne Atherton, 143–44
Menken, M. J. J., 35, 116
Metzger, Bruce Manning, 128
Michaels, J. Ramsey, 38, 42, 48, 86
Miller, Paul, 61
Mlakuzhyil, George, 50, 124, 132
Moloney, Francis J., 71, 117, 119
Morris, Leon, 33, 79, 86, 104, 128, 139
Mott, John R., 6
Moule, H. C. G., 5–6
Myers, Bryant L., 157, 183

Netland, Harold, 158, 172
Newbigin, Lesslie, 139, 157, 189
Nida, Eugene A., 20, 121
Niemand, Christoph, 133
Nissen, Johannes, x, 8–9, 26, 92, 94, 180,
Noll, Mark A., 179

O'Brien, Peter Thomas, x
Okure, Teresa, 1, 104–6, 184
Oliver, W. H., 1, 104, 108
Olsson, Birger, 92, 180–81
Orchard, Helen C., 119, 126
Osborne, Grant R., 9, 12–13, 17–18, 20
Overman, A. Andrew, 13

Packer, J. I., 156
Padilla, C. René, 158–61, 169
Pagin, Peter, 20
Parks, R. Keith, 170
Parsenios, George L., 92, 180
Paschal, R. Wade, 1, 118, 127
Pelletier, Francis Jeffry, 20
Peterson, Brian Neil, 68
Plöger, Otto, 64

Quarles, Charles, 37

Redford, Shawn B., x
Rengstorf, K. H., 53
Ridderbos, Herman, 71, 88, 90, 98, 120, 125
Ro, Bong Rin, 153
Robinson, John A. T., 41, 98
Rutayisire, Antonie, 185

Sanders, E. P., 38, 74
Saussure, F. de, 22
Scheuer, Blaž[set hacek (caron) over z] enka, 66
Schleiermacher, F. D. E., 17
Schnackenburg, Rudolf, 1, 34, 39, 62-63, 70-71, 88, 103-5, 108, 117, 120, 128, 130-31, 141, 143-44, 176-77, 184
Schneiders, Sandra M., 21
Schnelle, Undo, 15, 49, 67, 114
Schreiter, Robert, 155-56, 171-72
Scott, John, 183
Seland, Toreey, 131
Senior, Donald, 8
Silva, Moisés, 17, 21
Smith, D. M., 34
Spevak, Olga, 20
Spinks, D. Christopher, 21, 23
Stanley, Brian, 6
Stanton, G. N., 13, 24
Stetzer, Ed., 158
Steuernagel, Valdir R., 150, 163,
Stibbe, Mark W. G., 53
Stott, John R. W., 39, 91, 149-50, 158, 168-69, 175-76
Strauss, Stephen J., 150, 169
Stroope, Michael W., 19
Stuhlmueller, Carroll, 8
Sunquist, Scott, 154
Swain, Scott R., 12, 53
Swanson, J., 66, 72, 89

Talbert, Charles H., 36
Tate, W. Randolph, 17, 22
Tennent, Timothy C., 165, 171, 186
Tenney, Merrill C., 42, 48
Terranova, Carmelo B., 152-53
Thomas, John Christopher, 1, 35, 117, 128, 131
Thomaskutty, Johnson, 183
Thompson, Marianne Meye, 1, 27, 31, 33-35, 38, 41-42, 46, 49, 53-54, 67, 69-71, 75, 79, 83, 85, 92, 94, 96-98, 102-4, 113, 121, 126, 133-36, 139, 142, 176-77, 188
Tizon, Al, 158-59, 160-61, 163, 181
Turner, David L., 13,
Turner, Max, 20

Um, Stephen T., 31, 65

Van Gelder, Craig, 5
Van Engen, Charles E., 17, 23, 181, 183
Vanhoozer, Kevin J., 13, 21, 24
Vicedom, Georg F., x, 9-10
Voorwinde, Stephen, 76
Vos, Geerhardus, 13

Wallace, Daniel B., 68, 128, 134
Walton, Steve, 17
Wardle, Timothy, 74
Warneck, Gustav, 5
Warren, Carter, 13
Weiss, Herold, 1, 34, 102
Wenham, David, 17
Whallon, William, 33, 116, 126
Wolffe, John, 161
Wolters, M. Albert, 184
Wright, Christopher J. H., x, 4, 11-15, 17, 85-86, 89, 155-58, 164-66, 183
Wright, N. T., 9, 12, 14, 18, 25, 37

Yee, Gale A., 82

Subject Index

abiding, 3, 31, 48, 85, 90, 102, 111, 123, 139, 181, 186
Abraham, Abrahamic, 15, 40, 72, 131
agent, 36, 53, 54, 58, 83
as . . ., so . . ., 2, 35, 36, 50, 55, 88, 89, 100, 109, 115, 136–38, 140–41, 143, 147, 174, 185
ascension, 36, 45, 47, 112, 118, 121, 172
authority, 13, 36, 47, 53–56, 60, 67, 78, 119–20, 125, 137, 140–41, 158, 168

baptism, 1, 33, 72, 91, 103, 116–17, 122–23
bath, bathing, 72, 113, 116, 127–28
belief, 25, 32, 42, 96, 137, 144, 150, 157, 170, 184
betray, betrayer, betrayal, 2, 38, 110, 113, 117, 119, 126–27, 132–33, 135–36, 143, 146, 188–89
biblical, x, xi, 2, 4, 6–14, 17, 19, 22–24, 26, 33, 39, 148–49, 153–58
  author(s), x, 13, 23, 25–27, 40
  foundation(s), 4, 5, 7–8, 39, 93, 149, 155, 167, 171, 187
  hermeneutics, 10, 17, 24, 26, 167, 180
  text(s), 13–16, 17–18, 20, 22–24, 2627, 39, 64, 152, 193
  theological, x, 8–10, 12–14, 16–17, 39

blood, 33, 42, 72–75, 77, 86, 102, 116–17, 122–25, 127
body, 33, 65, 71, 77, 86, 114, 116, 121, 124, 128, 149, 161–62, 176, 178, 191

canonical, 11–12, 14, 24
centrifugal, 8–9, 107–8, 145
centripetal, 8–10, 107–8, 145
ceremony, 33, 55, 74–75, 82, 86, 117, 122–23
Christian mission, 5–7, 9, 14 19, 20, 25, 149–50, 165–66, 168, 171, 176, 194
Christology, 42, 49, 65, 67, 184
Christological, 25, 32–33, 43, 49–50, 67
church, ix, xi, xiii, 5–12, 15, 19, 26–27, 33, 35, 39, 67, 94, 103, 116–17, 130–31, 143, 148–83, 185–88, 190–91, 193
clean, 38, 72, 76, 86, 102–03, 113, 123, 126, 129, 133–34, 178
cleanse, 66, 68, 73–74, 77, 90, 103, 116, 120, 122–25, 127, 131, 178,
cleanliness, 73, 102, 131
cleanness, 123, 126
cleansing, 55, 65, 66, 72, 74, 91, 102–03, 109, 116, 122–23, 125
come and see, 27, 29, 60, 93–97, 145, 192

215

Subject Index

command-obedience, command-obedience rationale, 15, 90, 98, 140, 155, 157, 167, 172, 186, 189
commandment(s), 13, 48, 55, 60, 88, 90–92, 106, 117, 133, 136, 139, 163
   Jesus's Great Commission, new Commandment, 31, 34, 59, 83, 85, 111, 113, 115, 127, 132, 139, 147, 158
community, x, 1, 7, 8, 16–17, 21, 23–27, 30–31, 35–38, 40–41, 47, 49, 65, 74, 92–94, 98, 101–2, 104–9, 115, 117, 124, 129–34, 136–37, 143–46, 150, 152, 163, 169, 174, 178, 180–83, 187–88, 190, 193
   Christian community, church, 155, 157, 173–74, 179, 183, 190
   consecrating community, consecrated, 125, 178–79
   eschatological community, 124
   faith community, of faith, 1, 2, 13, 21, 24, 26–27, 29, 31–34, 40, 45, 106–8, 110–12, 115, 117, 128–29, 133–34, 139, 146–47, 175, 179, 184, 187–90, 193
   hermeneutical community, 3, 27, 174, 180–81
   incarnational community, 174
   Johannine community, 32–35, 39, 65, 92–93, 98, 102, 104, 106–8, 110, 116–17, 129, 134, 136, 143–44, 146, 174, 180, 184, 193
   missional community, 2, 112, 188
   new community, 31, 115, 137, 140, 150
   purified community, 178
   sent community, 104, 170, 178, 180–81, 187–88, 190
   social community, 180
consecrate, 48, 54, 62, 67, 68, 73–75, 82–83, 88–89, 99, 101, 112, 114–15, 123, 125, 131, 137–38, 140, 146–47, 173, 178–79, 181, 185, 189, 190

consecration, 30, 75, 92, 122–23, 128, 132, 146, 178–79, 182
context(s), x, 5, 9, 16–17, 19–20, 22–27, 30, 32, 34–35, 37–40, 42, 45, 63, 66, 80, 82, 91–93, 95, 102–3, 105, 107–9, 112, 116–17, 122–24, 126, 135, 142, 150–51, 154, 156–60, 162, 169, 176–77, 180, 183–84, 187–88, 194
   cultural context, religious, 25, 149, 160
   historical context(s), 7, 8, 22–23, 26, 102, 134–35
   Johannine context, 36
   missional context(s), 13, 16, 133, 144, 187
   literary-theological context, 15, 23, 70
   literary context, 6, 10, 14, 18, 20–23, 40, 70, 101, 109–10, 122, 146, 192
   pluralistic context, 155, 162, 187
   theological context, 14
   semantic context, 16, 20
contextual, 6–7, 12–13–14, 22–28, 39, 92, 117, 156, 169, 174–76, 183
contextualize, contextualized, contextualization, 17, 25, 39, 176–77
conversion, ix, xi, 5, 10, 150, 153–54
covenant, covenantal, ix, 11, 14, 26, 31, 64–66, 68, 73, 76, 85, 89–90, 127, 136, 149–50, 153, 155, 160–61, 168, 170
cross, 2, 31, 47, 57, 71, 77, 79, 86–87, 95, 103, 109–10, 114–15, 118–21, 124, 129, 131, 135, 146, 150, 168, 172, 175, 189, 192
cross-cultural, 5, 7, 19, 91, 176–77
crucified, crucifixion, 34, 38, 49, 57, 72, 77–78, 95, 99, 104, 109–10, 114–15, 118, 120–21, 125, 129, 135, 138, 188

darkness, 44, 61, 77, 80–82, 96, 99, 103, 123, 125, 134, 138, 141, 147, 169, 171, 182

David, Davidic, 63, 66–67, 125, 154, 184
death, 1–2, 28, 30–34, 36–39, 42–44, 47–50, 59–62, 65, 70–72, 74–82, 85–86, 88, 94–95, 97, 99, 102–10, 112–27, 129–32, 134–36, 138–40, 143, 146, 150, 152, 169, 171–72, 175, 178, 181–82, 184, 187, 192
depart, departure, 34, 44, 47, 104, 115, 118, 125, 131
Derrida, Jacques, 22
dialogue, x, 45, 72, 113, 121, 139, 149–51, 156, 183
dichotomous, dichotomy, 3, 149–50, 156, 159, 167, 185–86, 190
disciples, ix, xi, 1–7, 13, 15, 17, 19–20, 27–51, 54–61, 63–64, 66–68, 70, 77–83, 85–118, 120–47, 152, 159, 162–66, 168–70, 172–93
discipleship, ix, xi, 27, 29, 31–33, 34, 36, 40, 102, 104–5, 108–9, 112, 115, 133, 138, 159, 163–64, 166, 170
discourse, 13, 17, 21, 23, 27, 30, 32–33, 36, 38, 42, 106, 110, 112, 122
diverse, diversity, ix–x, 13, 15–16, 19, 22, 25–26, 35, 39, 73, 102, 134, 150–51, 154–56, 158, 162, 183, 194
divine, 22, 25–26, 28, 31–32, 46, 67–68, 81–82, 87, 101, 131, 169, 176–77
doing, 15, 30, 37, 46, 56, 61, 69, 78, 85, 101, 104, 107–8, 113–14, 130, 135, 145–46, 151, 157–58, 161, 163, 165–66, 173, 177, 185–86, 190, 193
dwell, indwell, 1–3, 32, 37–38, 40, 43, 47, 56, 58–60, 62–70, 76, 85, 90–91, 95, 98–99, 102–8, 115, 123, 126–27, 129, 132–33, 138–39, 145–46, 158, 162, 173–74, 177, 181–82, 185–86, 188–92

ecclesial, 26, 33, 144, 151, 154

ego eimi, 56, 59
eschatological, 7–10, 13–14, 16, 25, 27–28, 33–34, 40, 52, 63–66, 70, 75–77, 79, 82, 86–88, 94, 97–98, 100, 105, 118, 124–25, 131, 151, 158, 178
eternal, eternal life, xi, 3, 27, 30, 33, 42, 44, 46–47, 56, 58–61, 65, 71, 77–80, 83–87, 90, 94–100, 115–19, 121–22, 131, 139–41, 143–45, 147, 158, 166, 169, 178, 184, 186–87, 189, 192
ethical, ethical life, 1, 11, 13, 33–34, 89, 104, 107, 117, 137, 164, 172
eucharist, 1, 33, 103, 116, 117
evangelicals, x–xi, xiii, 1, 3, 27, 39–40, 148–63, 165, 167–68, 171, 173–74, 179–81, 183, 185–86, 189–94
evangelistic, 59, 61, 86, 93, 96–97, 142–43, 153–54, 170–71
  evangelistic ministry, 60, 80, 95, 101
  evangelistic mission, 88
  evangelistic proclamation, 170
  evangelistic task, 80, 97, 140–41, 145, 147, 168
  evangelistic witness, 95, 98, 108, 170
evangelism, ix, xi, 1–3, 7, 27–29, 36, 40, 45, 47, 57–61, 79–81, 83–85, 88–89, 93–95, 97–101, 106, 108–9, 115, 129, 140–44, 146–51, 153–59, 161–74, 179–81, 183, 185–86, 189–91, 193
evangelization, 5–6, 100, 150, 153, 158, 160, 162–64, 167, 170–71
evil, Satan, 58, 60, 77, 80–82, 96, 103, 125–27, 134, 136–37, 141, 151, 155, 169, 172, 178–79, 182–83, 190
example, 1, 13, 26, 107, 131, 145
exegetical, x, 1–2, 8–9, 12, 16, 18–19, 21, 23–24, 27, 40, 192
Ezekiel, 37–38, 63–66, 68, 73–77, 86, 178

faith, x, 1–3, 6, 8, 11, 13–15, 21, 23–27, 29, 31–34, 36, 38–40, 42, 44–46, 48–49, 56, 58–60, 62, 65, 67, 77–79, 81–82, 85, 94–100, 103, 106–8, 110–12, 115, 117, 128–29, 133–34, 137, 139–40, 143–47, 150, 154, 156–58, 164–65, 168–71, 175–76, 179–80, 182, 184, 187–90, 192–93

feet, 32, 38–39, 59, 90, 102, 106–7, 111, 113–15, 117, 120, 122–24, 126–34, 136, 138, 140, 146, 179, 181–83, 187, 193

fellowship, 98, 116–17, 152, 156, 166–67, 170, 179–80, 183, 186

festival, 65, 74–76, 123

follow, following, 3, 26–27, 29, 44–46, 49–50, 59, 61, 77, 80, 83, 85, 93–97, 100, 102, 104, 111–18, 121, 123, 126, 129, 132–33, 137, 139–41, 168, 174, 179, 181, 184–85, 191, 193

follower(s), 46, 94–96, 123, 129, 175, 178, 183, 189, 193

foot-washing, foot washing, 1–4, 31–36, 38–40, 48, 100–103, 105–13, 115–22, 124–25, 127–29, 130–33, 135, 137, 140–41, 145–47, 178, 185, 188, 192

forgive, forgiven, 126, 134, 138–40, 152, 164, 171–72, 175, 178, 189

forgiveness, 1, 3, 28, 30–32, 34, 37–38, 43, 55–57, 60, 65, 68, 71–73, 79, 91, 94–95, 99–101, 103, 125, 131–32, 134–36, 138–41, 143, 147, 149, 151–55, 157, 163, 171–72, 179, 187–89, 192

fruit, 29, 43, 48, 5960, 83–86, 90, 92, 94, 97, 102–3, 105–6, 108, 111, 126–27, 129, 132, 138–139, 146–47, 170, 178–79, 181–82, 186

garment, 37, 114, 120, 130
gentiles, 7, 74, 77, 97–98, 134, 138, 145
glory, 33–34, 37, 42, 49, 53–54, 60, 63–65, 70, 74, 76–79, 81–82, 85, 110, 118, 121–22, 127, 149, 163–64, 172, 177–78

harvest, 7, 27–28, 40, 80, 84, 93–94, 97, 105, 192
harvesting, 27, 29, 80, 86, 93, 95, 97, 100, 105, 142, 145
harvester(s), 7, 55, 93, 145
hear, 46–47, 55–56, 61–62, 69, 79–80, 83, 87, 95, 127, 141, 165, 171
hermeneutic(s), 11, 13–17, 20–22, 24, 26, 156
    missional hermeneutics, x, 2, 4–5, 9, 10, 12–19, 21, 23–24, 27, 39–40, 192
    biblical hermeneutics, 10, 17, 26, 167
hermeneutical, 3–4, 9–10, 12–13, 15, 21, 23–24, 26–28, 35, 39–40, 174, 180–81, 190, 193–94
historical, x, 7–9, 12–14, 17–19, 23, 25, 102, 108, 134, 149, 165–66, 193
    historical criticism, 7
    historical critical methods, 9, 12
    historical critical approach, 12, 17–18, 39
holy, 11, 43, 47, 53, 63, 68, 72, 75, 82–83, 85, 89–91, 100, 103, 112, 115–16, 122–25, 127, 137–38, 152–53, 163, 178–79, 181–82, 190
holiness, 11, 62, 74, 88–90, 103, 111, 116, 123, 128, 137–38, 151–52, 156–57, 168, 179, 181–82, 184, 188, 190
holistic mission, 3, 11, 148, 150–51, 155, 159–64, 173–74, 190, 193
Holy Spirit, 2–4, 11, 23, 26, 41, 43, 45, 52, 56–57, 60–61, 65, 68, 74, 77, 85–88, 91–94, 98–99, 109, 111–12, 117, 122, 124, 126–27, 136–37, 141–42, 145–46, 150, 154, 168, 170, 172–73, 177–78, 180–82, 190
    Spirit-Paraclete, 87, 112
hospitality, 1, 130–31, 157
hour, 32, 34, 38, 42, 49, 104, 113, 117–18, 146

Subject Index 219

humble service, 2–3, 39, 59, 105, 108, 111, 120, 126, 129, 132, 135, 139–40, 146, 175, 178, 187, 190, 193
humble servant spirit, xi, 29
humility, 1, 34–35, 92, 100, 104, 130, 133, 142, 150, 157, 178, 183, 188

integrated witness, 1–3, 41, 61–62, 88, 99–101, 129, 146–47, 167, 185, 188, 190–93
identity, 2–3, 11–13, 24–25, 28, 33, 38–39, 42, 44, 46–48, 51, 53–57, 59, 61–62, 67–71, 74, 82, 84–87, 89–93, 98–99, 109, 129, 134, 136–37, 139, 143, 145–47, 159, 161, 164–65, 170, 173–74, 176–77, 179, 181–82, 185–86, 188–89, 192–93
imitate, 105, 156, 168–69, 175–76, 188
impurity, 68, 90, 125
in the midst of, 3, 38, 43, 58, 62–66, 68, 74, 76–77, 99, 106, 164, 178, 182, 186, 188
incarnate, incarnated, 3, 56, 62, 99, 115, 169, 174–75, 177, 182, 186, 189
incarnation, 28, 30, 43–44, 50, 62–66, 68–69, 85, 91, 169–70, 172–78, 182, 188, 192
incarnational, 3, 91, 169, 173–78, 182, 190, 193
ingathering, 27, 40, 77, 98
integral mission, 152–53, 155, 157, 159–60, 165, 169, 190, 193
invitation, 29, 33, 84–86, 94–96, 100, 122, 143, 165
invite, 30, 46, 84–85, 93, 95, 98, 100, 132, 139, 145, 152, 186, 192
Isaiah, 37, 71–72, 83, 86

jealous, jealousy, 75–76
Johannine mission, xi, 4, 28–29, 39–40 167, 174, 185, 193
Judas, Iscariot, 32, 38, 103, 110–11, 113, 115, 117, 119, 121, 127, 132–35, 146, 189

Judas, Maccabeus, 82
judgment, 44, 47, 55, 57–58, 60–61, 71, 77–81, 87, 94–96, 99, 122, 135, 141, 166, 171–72, 178, 182, 192

king, 7, 66–67, 73–74
Israel's king, king of Israel, 46, 64, 66–67, 75
Davidic king, 67
kingdom, God's kingdom, 7, 13–14, 61, 93, 98, 127, 137, 149, 151–52, 154, 158, 160, 163–164, 169–70, 172, 174, 188
know, 29, 39, 45–47, 49–50, 55, 58–59, 68–70, 76, 80–81, 83–85, 92–93, 99, 104, 111, 114, 118, 121, 130, 133, 137, 140–141, 143, 147, 154, 181, 183, 186
knowing, 80, 83, 85, 92–93, 123, 137, 141, 157, 187
known, 42–43, 45, 48, 51, 56, 58, 60, 62, 85, 88, 110, 118, 157, 191
knowledge, 82, 85, 93, 105, 157, 186

lamb, 71–73, 75–76, 96, 126, 140
sacrificial lamb, 49, 71–72, 77
Lamb of God, God's lamb, 46, 71–72, 75, 77, 123–24
paschal lamb, 33, 71–73, 86, 126
Lausanne, x, 3, 39, 149, 152–53, 161–62, 165, 167, 170, 172, 180, 190
Covenant, 1974, Lausanne I, ix, xi, 3, 148–49, 153, 157, 159–61, 167–68, 170, 189
Manila, 1989, Lausanne II, 148–50, 151–52, 157, 189
Cape Town, Lausanne III, 2010, 148, 157, 189
lead, leading, 36, 42, 46–47, 54, 58, 60, 74, 79, 80, 87, 92, 94, 96–99, 105, 137, 139, 145, 147, 159, 167, 169–70, 180–82, 185
life, x, xi, xiii, 1–2, 9, 13, 15–16, 23, 27–40, 42–49, 51, 53–59, 60–61, 65– 66, 70–71, 74–75, 77–101, 103–6, 108, 111–19, 121–24, 126–41, 143–47, 149–53, 155, 157–67, 169–73, 175–93

life (continued)
  daily life, 2, 38, 156, 185–86
  ethical life, 11, 13, 89,
  eternal life, xi, 3, 27, 30, 42, 44,
    46–47, 56, 58–61, 71, 77–80,
    83–87, 90, 94–100, 115–19,
    121–22, 131, 139–41, 143–45,
    147, 158, 169, 178, 184, 186–
    87, 189, 192
  life pattern, 34, 39, 56, 59, 65, 88,
    91, 104, 106, 108, 110, 112,
    115, 126, 129, 132–34, 137,
    140, 147, 172, 178–82, 186–89,
    191, 193
  lifestyle, 16, 36, 47–48, 92–92,
    110–11, 115, 130, 134, 143,
    146, 153, 157, 175–76, 188
  missional life, 31, 35, 104, 109, 112,
    133, 157, 181–82, 187–88
light, 3, 37, 44, 46, 58–61, 78, 80–83,
  85, 92, 96, 99, 124–25, 129,
  133, 135, 137–39, 147, 182,
  186–87, 189, 192–93
lift up, lifted up, 37, 57, 70–71, 78–79,
  116, 118, 133
literary, 2, 6, 13–18, 23, 32–35, 38–40,
  44, 103, 136
  literary context, world, 10, 14, 16,
    18, 20–23, 40, 70, 101, 109–10,
    122, 146, 192
  literary exegetical, x, 2, 18, 21, 24,
    27, 40, 192
  literary structure(s), 15–16, 20,
    28–29, 35, 41, 109, 170, 192
  literary theological, 13–15, 20, 23,
    39, 70
love, x–xi, 2–3, 13, 15, 28–32, 34, 36–
  38, 43–44, 48, 55, 50, 57–59,
  70, 78–81, 85, 89–92, 98–101,
  104–8, 111–16, 126–27, 129–
  35, 139–40, 142, 145–47, 149,
  151–59, 161–73, 178, 180–91,
  193
  mutual love, reciprocal, xi, 29, 85,
    90, 105, 132, 134, 136, 142
  loving service, 34–35, 37, 140, 151

sacrificial love, 2, 29, 32, 34–35,
  37–39, 107, 111, 132, 134–36,
  139, 146, 182, 184, 188, 191

make disciples, making disciples, ix, 5,
  13, 19, 163, 165–66, 172
martyrdom, 34, 102–3, 108–9, 145
metanarrative, x, 4, 10–12, 14, 16, 22,
  39
missio Dei, 4, 9, 15, 27–28, 31, 38, 42,
  48–51, 62, 64, 91, 135, 154–55,
  158–62, 165–67, 173–74, 180,
  186
missiological, ix, 6, 10, 14, 18–19, 28,
  159, 162, 165
missionary, ix–x, 5–9, 11–13, 26–27,
  39, 104–9, 144–45, 149, 160–
  61, 165, 168–69, 174
missional, x–xi, 1–7, 9–25, 27, 29–33,
  35–37, 39–41, 43–44, 47–51,
  55, 59, 68, 70, 87, 92–93, 97,
  99, 101–2, 104, 106–9, 111–12,
  129, 133, 136, 140, 143–45,
  148, 154–55, 157, 161–62,
  167, 173–75, 180–82, 184–85,
  187–88, 192–93
  missional implication(s), 1, 3, 27,
    39–40, 148, 173–74, 193
  missional language, 27, 133
  missional meaning, 14, 16, 18, 24,
    39–40, 70, 101–2, 108–9, 145,
    167, 192
  missional paradigm, 16
  missional perspective, x, 1, 4, 15,
    18, 36, 40, 49, 145, 148
  missional reading, x–xi, 10, 16, 39
  missional *theosis*, 30, 40
model, 8, 29, 34–35, 37–38, 55, 91,
  104, 107–8, 111–12, 114–15,
  127, 129, 131–32, 140, 143,
  145, 157, 165, 169, 174–77, 188
  incarnational model, 169, 175–76
  representational model, 29, 91, 175
monotheism, 25, 176,
mutual indwelling, 1–3, 32, 40, 43, 47,
  56, 58–60, 69–70, 85, 90–91,
  98–99, 103, 105–8, 115, 123,
  126–27, 129, 132, 138–39,

Subject Index   221

145–46, 162, 173, 181–82, 185–86, 189, 191–92

narrative, x, 1, 9–12, 15–16, 18, 21, 22–23, 27, 31, 33, 36, 38–39, 42, 49, 62, 66–68, 79, 101, 103–4, 106, 110, 112, 114, 117, 123, 125, 145–46
   foot-washing narrative, 1–4, 31, 33–36, 38–40, 100–104, 106–10, 113, 118–21, 125, 127, 129, 133, 137, 140–41, 145–47, 178, 185, 192
nation(s), 5–10, 13, 28, 46–47, 52, 64, 68, 70, 74–75, 77–78, 83, 85–86, 97–98, 110, 120, 132, 138, 145, 153, 164, 178

obey, ix, 6, 43, 60, 81, 85, 88, 107, 133, 157–58, 164, 171

part, 126–28, 137, 145–46, 156, 178, 189
participate, ix, 7, 17, 27–28, 30–32, 38–39, 47–48, 65, 74, 76, 84, 87, 93, 95–96, 101–3, 106–8, 110, 114–15, 117, 121, 130, 133, 135, 140, 145, 155, 158–59, 161–63, 165–66, 178–79, 181, 183, 187–88, 193
participation, 3, 12, 14–15, 21, 23, 30–31, 91, 102, 107–9, 123, 126, 145–46, 152, 154, 160, 174, 190, 193
Passover, 71–76, 104, 114, 117, 124, 126
persecution, 1, 47, 102, 108, 117, 168, 172
Peter, 26, 38, 68, 95, 110–13, 121, 130, 132, 139, 140, 171
Pilate, 67, 110, 119, 187
pluralistic, 156–57, 162, 187
portion, 126, 184
prejudice, 16, 21, 23
presupposition, 12, 24
proclamation, ix, xi, 2, 6–7 , 9, 16, 28, 45, 58–59, 67, 85, 88, 93–94, 99, 129, 141–45, 149–52, 155, 157, 159–60, 164, 167–69, 172, 177, 189
   verbal-proclamation, verbal proclamation, 32, 60, 84, 88, 94, 97, 98, 101, 109, 140, 145, 147, 153, 162–63, 166, 170, 172–73, 185, 191
   evangelistic proclamation, 170
promise, 9–10, 13–15, 25, 40, 63, 65–66, 68, 76–77, 79, 84, 86, 96, 122, 124, 178
proof-texting, ix, 5–6, 12–13, 23, 39, 167
pure, 25, 72, 74, 178
purification, 38–39, 70–72, 74–77, 82, 92, 102–3, 109, 116–17, 121–28 ,132, 134, 139, 146, 171, 178–79
purify, 72, 74–76, 122, 25, 127, 134, 138, 171–72, 179, 190

reader-centered, 21, 24, 40, 192
re-evangelization, 153
relationship, 1–3, 13–14, 27–29, 31–32, 35, 48–49, 53–54, 56–57, 59, 61–62, 70, 77, 83, 85–86, 88, 89–92, 98–100, 106–8, 115–16, 119, 121–22, 124–28, 130–32, 135–40, 146–47, 162, 166–67, 169, 172–75, 177, 179, 181–86, 188–93
release, 125–26, 138
repentance, 125, 135, 150, 154–55, 163–65, 168–72
reveal, 2, 4, 6–7, 25, 29, 35, 42, 44, 46, 48–49, 53, 58, 61, 63, 67, 69–70, 78–80, 82–83, 85, 87–92, 99, 101, 105–6, 115, 118, 129–30, 134, 136–38, 141, 144–45, 156–57, 168, 170, 173–74, 177–79, 182, 186–87, 189–90, 192–93
revelation, 6, 13, 26, 37, 42, 62, 79, 83, 85, 89, 99, 137, 142, 170, 176–77, 180, 187
return, 25, 38, 42, 44–48, 64, 66, 73–74, 76, 90, 108, 112–14, 118–19, 146, 168

Subject Index

restore, 38, 64, 66, 74, 76, 87, 90, 124, 132, 138, 140, 146, 155, 166, 172, 189
restoration, 38, 63–64, 66, 68, 86, 88, 98, 103, 110–11, 145, 153, 158, 165–67, 169, 184, 188
resurrect, 64, 87
resurrection, 30–32, 36–37, 42, 48–49, 50, 55, 59–60, 62–63, 65–66, 68, 78, 85, 99, 108–10, 112, 114, 118, 120–21, 123–24, 126, 140, 146, 150, 169, 172, 175, 178, 188, 192
ritual, 37, 71, 74–75, 116–17, 131, 176

sacramental, 33–34, 103, 117
sacrifice, 28, 36–38, 47, 58–59, 70–74, 76–79, 86, 89, 94, 100, 112, 117, 119, 121, 123–24, 126, 129, 132, 134, 136, 139–40, 146, 163, 178, 181–83, 188, 193
sacrificial, 2, 29, 32, 34–39, 43–44, 47, 49–50, 59, 61, 70–72, 75–79, 88, 99, 102–3, 107–8, 110–12, 114–16, 118–19, 121, 124, 126, 130–32, 134–36, 139–40, 146, 152, 168–69, 171, 175, 178, 181–82, 184, 187–89, 191–92
salvation, ix, 2, 4, 6, 8–10, 13–15, 30, 34, 37–38, 42, 44, 47, 49, 52, 57–61, 70–71, 73, 76–80, 83, 85–86, 88–89, 95–100, 105–6, 115, 125, 135, 138, 144–46, 149–53, 157, 160, 162–64, 167, 169–70, 172–75, 177, 187, 190
Samaritan, 29, 45, 80, 84, 86, 93–95, 98, 100, 115, 122, 134, 144–45, 184, 187
sanctify, 53, 72–74, 76, 89–90, 110
sanctification, 11, 73–74, 90, 102, 115, 123, 136, 138, 154, 182
semantic, xi, 2, 16, 19–23, 27–28, 40, 133
send, 2, 5–7, 13, 19–20, 27–28, 31, 36, 41, 44, 49, 52, 54–58, 61, 78–79, 83, 89–91, 93–95, 97–99, 110, 133, 136–41, 143–45, 158, 164, 166, 168–170, 173–74, 177–78, 182–83, 185–86
sending, x–xi, 3–4, 7, 13, 19–20, 29, 31, 33, 35–36, 40, 42–43, 48–49, 51–57, 62, 65–66, 69–70, 80, 82, 86–87, 90, 93, 97–99, 101, 107, 109–11, 115, 137–38, 142, 147, 154–55, 163–68, 171–72, 178, 185–89
sending language, xi, 1–2, 15, 18–21, 32, 38, 40–41, 48, 50–52, 57, 88, 99, 101, 118, 133, 136–37, 186–87, 192
sending formula(e), 7, 43, 50–51, 54–57, 78, 83, 99, 101, 168
sending structure, 42
Sender, 3, 20, 42, 44, 48, 52–57, 60, 69, 80–82, 84, 91, 97–99, 101, 106–7, 119, 121–22, 138, 141, 169, 175, 177, 186
sent one, the sent, 20, 43, 49, 51–57, 79, 81, 85, 94, 97, 99, 101, 106–7, 169, 177, 186
sentness, xi, 2–3, 31, 35, 37, 42–43, 46–49, 51–52, 55, 57, 62–64, 70, 79, 83, 85, 89–90, 92, 99–100, 104, 113, 118, 135, 137–38, 140–41, 173–75, 177, 182–83, 185
servant, xi, 7, 9, 29, 34, 59, 66, 71, 81–83, 107, 117, 120–21, 125, 131–32, 135–36, 175, 182
service(s), ix, xi, 2–3, 20, 32–35, 37–39, 48, 59, 70, 74, 78–79, 92, 100–101, 104–8, 111–12, 115, 117, 120–21, 123, 126, 129–32, 134–36, 139–40, 142, 145–46, 149–53, 156–59, 162, 165–71, 175, 178, 180–82, 184, 187–91, 193
share, 2, 6, 21, 27, 31, 33, 47, 56, 68, 77, 89–90, 98, 107, 122, 126–27, 145–46, ,153–55, 158, 173, 178, 182, 184, 188
sign(s), 28, 30, 36, 38, 41–44, 46, 48–49, 52, 57, 59–61, 63, 74, 77, 86, 97–98, 118, 138, 143–44, 150, 170

sin(s), 1, 5–6, 30–31, 37–38, 42, 46,
    50, 56–57, 59–60, 65– 66, 68,
    71–77, 79, 81–82, 85, 87, 91,
    94–96, 100, 102–3, 109–10,
    116–17, 121–28, 132, 134–41,
    147, 149–52, 154–55, 158,
    163–64, 166, 168– 69, 171–72,
    175, 178–80, 182, 188, 191–92
sinner, 28, 46, 71, 75, 91, 103, 122, 125,
    131, 137, 149, 152–53, 163–64,
    168, 171
slave, 35, 77, 81, 131, 133, 136, 184
slave(s) of sins, slavery of sin(s),
    servant of sin, 81–82, 110, 137,
    141, 180
social responsibility, 149–51, 155–57,
    167–68, 185–86, 190
story, x, 10–12, 14, 22–23, 27, 34, 38,
    44, 47–51, 55, 71–72, 110–11,
    119, 122, 124, 130–31, 145, 188
symbolic, 2, 8, 26, 35–36, 38–39, 68,
    82, 101, 103–4, 109–12, 115,
    120, 122, 129, 132, 146, 181,
    187
Synoptic, 6–7, 66, 93, 124, 127, 141

tabernacle, 43, 48, 62, 63–66, 68, 74,
    82, 90, 99, 174, 177, 178
task, 2, 13, 20–21, 24, 36, 44, 48, 51,
    57–58, 62–63, 80, 95, 97–98,
    104, 108–9, 140–41, 145, 147,
    149, 163, 165, 168, 171, 177
temple, 25, 32, 37–38, 62–67, 74–77,
    82–83, 86, 122–24, 136, 178,
    184, 186
tent, 62–63, 66, 123
    Tertullian, 117, 128
testify, 2, 27, 29, 43–44, 46–48, 55, 57,
    79, 88–89, 93, 96, 105, 129,
    141, 143–45, 147, 166, 173,
    181, 185, 191–92
testimony(ies), 2, 29, 42, 54–58, 61,
    68–70, 72, 79, 88, 94, 99, 111,
    145, 177
transform, 150, 160, 162, 180
transformative, transformational, 30,
    32, 107, 109, 166

transformation, ix, 3, 30, 93, 148, 153,
    156, 158–61, 163, 166–67, 172,
    174, 180–81, 188, 190, 193
truth, 3, 22, 26, 43, 48, 58–61, 69, 78,
    80, 82–89, 91–93, 96, 99–100,
    115, 125, 129, 135, 137–38,
    140–41, 145, 147, 150–59,
    161, 164–65, 168, 170–74,
    176, 180–84, 186–87, 189–90,
    192–93

unbelief, 77, 81, 96, 103, 138, 144
unbeliever(s), xi, 5, 11, 36, 45–46, 49,
    94–98, 119, 122, 125, 133, 138,
    141, 143–44, 149, 152, 154, 171
unbelieving, 1, 34, 45, 47, 96, 110,
    118–19, 134, 138
unclean, 73
uncleanness, 125
unconsecrated, 73
union, 47–48, 53, 57, 60, 85, 91, 98,
    104–5, 115, 123, 125, 141, 161,
    177–78, 182–83, 189–90
unique, x, 7–8, 16, 18, 25, 28, 31, 43,
    50, 56–57, 61, 70, 78–79, 109,
    124, 130, 133, 137, 156, 167,
    169, 175, 177–78, 193
uniqueness, 150, 156–57, 168, 170, 190
unity, xi, 15, 20, 26, 29, 32, 35, 43,
    52–53, 59, 61, 66, 69, 70, 83,
    85, 87, 89, 91–92, 94, 108, 111,
    121, 125–26, 129, 134, 145–46,
    150–57, 161–62, 168, 170, 172,
    177, 179–84, 186–87, 189–91
unity-relationship, 2–3, 32, 35, 48,
    53–54, 56–57, 61–62, 70, 77,
    85, 88–91, 98–100, 108, 122,
    126–28, 132, 138, 140, 146–47,
    162, 166, 173, 182, 185–86,
    188–89, 193

walk, 56, 81–83, 91, 96, 137, 139, 163,
    190
water, 38, 42, 46, 54, 61, 65, 68, 72,
    74, 76–77, 82, 84–88, 115–17,
    122–25, 160, 186

wash, 38, 59, 72, 77, 82, 91, 102–3, 111, 113–15, 120, 122–25, 128–33, 140, 146, 178–79, 182–83, 189
witness(es), xi, 2–4, 6–7, 11, 15–16, 25, 29, 31–32, 36, 38, 41–50, 54–63, 68–70, 77–78, 82, 87–103, 105–6, 108, 111–12, 118, 126, 129–30, 134, 137, 140–47, 149–53, 156–57, 160–61, 163–68, 170–73, 177–82, 185–93
witness in (daily) life, of life, life-witness, xi, 1–3, 16, 27–29, 36, 38, 40, 45, 47–48, 57–58, 61, 88–89, 91, 98–101, 108, 115, 129, 135, 140, 144–47, 150–53, 156–57, 161–62, 167, 169–73, 178, 184–86, 188–91, 193
evangelistic witness, 108, 170–71
worldly, 178–79
worship, 52, 61, 65–66, 73–74, 76, 80, 83–88, 99, 117, 122, 134, 145, 151, 157, 161, 164, 168, 174, 186, 192

Ancient Document Index

Genesis

1	25
1:28	163
2:3	90
18:4	35
18:1–18	131
19:2	35
22:13	72
22:7–8	76
22:13	72
24:32	35
28:12–22	65
43:24	35

Exodus

6:6	89
6:6–8	85
12	72
12:3	72–73
12:4	72
12:5	72
12:10	76
12:16	117
12:8–17	33
12:21	73
12:22	71–72
12:23	72
12:43	117
12:43–49	90
12:46	33, 71, 124, 126
13:13	72
13:21	82
19:5–6	89
19:6	90, 163
19:10	90
20:2–3	85
25:8	63
25:8–9	63, 90
25:9	66
28:40–43	90
29:4	128
29:42–44	90
29:43	90
30:17–21	123–24
30:18–20	122
31:13	90
33:11	47
34:6–7	85
40:12–13	128
40:31–32	124
43:24	131

Leviticus

1—7	74
11—15	74
10:3	103
10:10	103
11:44	103
11:44–45	89
14:4–6	71
14:49–52	71
15:8–13	128
15:10–12	128
15:11	128

Leviticus (continued)

15:13	128
15:16	128
15:31	66
16:1–24	90
16:4	128
16:24	122, 128
16:33	63
17:16	122
19:2	11, 89–90
20:3	90
20:24	125
20:26	90, 127
23:5	33
23:27	90
26:12	89

Numbers

9:12	73, 124, 126
9:14	73
10:21	63
15:5	76
15:11	76
18:20	126
18:29	63
19:9	125
19:13	125
19:18	71
19:20	125
19:21	125
21	135
21:4–9	135
21:7	135
28:16	33
28:16–25	73
33:3	73

Deuteronomy

4:6–8	164
4:32–34	85
4:34	85
5:6	85
5:12	90
16:1–6	73
18:15–22	184
21:6–8	128

26:17	89

Joshua

5:13	68

Judges

19:21	35

1 Samuel

25:41	35

2 Samuel

7:14	67
15:25	63

2 Kings

23:22–23	73

2 Chronicles

30:15	73
30:15–17	73
30:17	73
30:18–19	73
34:30–31	73
34:33	73
35:1–19	73
35:6	73

Ezra

6:19–21	73
6:20	73
9:11b	125

Nehemiah

9:12	82
9:19	82

Psalm

2:6–7	67
2:7	67
15:1	63
25:6	128

26:6	123	42:1	71
26:8	63	42:4	9
27:1	82	42:6	83
27:5–6	63	43:3	86
34:19–20	71	43:5	77
34:20	73	43:10	83
36:9	82	43:20	85–86
42:1–2	86	44:3	85–86
43:3	63	45:18–19	85
46:5	63	45:23	25
57:11	128	48:5	83
61:4	63	49:6	83
68:8	85	49:10	122
68:10	75	52:1–10	65
72:13	128	53:6–7	77
74:7	63	53:7	71–72
78:14	82	53:10	72
78:60	63	53:11	71, 77
80	127	55:1	86, 122
84:2	63	55:5	77
96:1–3	85	55:7	125
105:39	82	56:7	77
114:4	76	56:8	77
114:6	76	60:1	83
119:105	83	60:1–2	82
119:130	83	60:3	83
132:5	63	60:1–9	65
132:7	63	60:19–20	82
		60:6	77
		60:7	37
		63:18–19	65

Proverb

4:17–18	138
6:23	83
8:1–36	83
18:4	85
24:7–10	127

Isaiah

1:16	128
2:3	77
6:1–13	37
8:14	68
9:1	83
11:5	89
11:12	77
29:8	86
40—55	25

Jeremiah

7:23	89
17:12–13	122
23:2	77
23:3	77
31:31–34	66, 163
31:34	38
32:36–41	66

Ezekiel

3:18–19	127
5:11	75
5:13	75
5:13a	75

Ezekiel (continued)

5:13b	76
6:9	76
11:20	89
11:20b	66
11:23	65
16:4	128
16:9	128
16:42	76
16:63	38
23:25	76
34:12	77
34:16	77
34:17–19	76
34:25	68
35:11	76
36	52, 76
36:6	76
36:10	63, 74
36:22–28	74, 125
36:23	68
36:24–25	77
36:25	74, 76, 122
36:25–27	86
36:26	76
36:26–27	74
36:28	66, 76, 126
36:33	122
37	66, 68, 76
37:1–14	52, 68
37:5	66, 87
37:14	87
37:15–22	66
37:15–28	66, 68
37:21	63, 74, 77
37:23	66
37:23–28	38, 75
37:24–25	66
37:26	66, 68, 76
37:26–28	66
37:27	63, 66
37:28	63, 66, 74, 76
37:28a	68
38:19	76
39:12	76
39:16	76
39:19	76
39:28–29	76
41:1—47:12	76
43:5	76
43:7	63
43:18–27	76
43:26–27	131
43:2	64, 74
43:2–5	65
43:7	63–64
43:9	68
43:12–25	75
43:23	75
43:26–27	131
44:4	64–65
44:8	66
45:7–8	76
45:15	73–74
45:18–20	76
45:18–25	75
45:18–27	74, 76
45:21–25	73
45:22	73, 75
45:23	73, 75
46:4–7	76
46:4–13	75
46:5	75
46:6	75
46:11	76
47:1–9	65
47:1–12	68, 74, 76, 86, 122, 178
47:8–12	86
47:13–23	76
47:21–23	74
48	63
48:10	74
48:21	66, 74
48:35	64

Daniel

6:4	25
7	25
7:14	169

Hosea

2:15	85

12:9	85

Joel
2:28	87
3:18	85–86

Amos
3:1–2	85

Micah
2:12	77

Haggai
2:6–9	64
2:9	64

Zechariah
2:5	64
2:10–13	67
2:11	68
8:2	75
8:3	64–65
8:3–9	64
9:9	67
12:10	67, 124
13:1	68, 124–25
13:1–2	125
13:9	68, 125
14:7	82
14:8	65, 68, 85–86, 122
14:16	77

Malachi
3:1	64
3:7	64

Matthew
1:1	67
1:23	13
5—8	13
5:38–42	13
5:48	13
6:17	128
6:25–34	13
7:1	13
7:3–5	13
7:7–11	13
7:12	13
9:35	93
9:37–38	93
10:1	93
10:1–42	80
10:24	107
10:28–31	13
10:40	80, 93, 142
13:1–52	13
13:4	68
15:1–2	123
15:2	128
15:20	128
15:24	165
18—20	13
18:12–35	13
19:17	13
19:30	67
19:31	67
20:9	67
21:1–8	13
21:9	67
21:9–14	13
22:34–40	13
24:14	13
24:29—25:46	13
25:34–46	13
26:13	7
26:17–18	126
26:28	127
26:28–29	127
27:24	128
28:18	13
28:19	6
28:18–20	5, 7, 152, 164
28:19	6
28:19–20	ix, 5, 6, 31, 98, 149, 170
28:20	6, 13

Mark
1:11	67
4:29	93
7:2	128

Mark (continued)

7:3	128
9:37	141–42
10:45	34, 169
10:47	67
12:35–37	67
13:10	7, 165
14:9	7, 165
14:12	126
14:24	127
14:24–25	127
16:15	5–6, 13, 149, 170
16:20	6

Luke

1:27	67
1:69	67
1:71	67
3:21	68
3:40–41	131
7:36–50	34, 131
9:31	85
9:48	142
10:1–3	93
10:1–20	80
10:2	93, 142
10:10	93
10:16	80, 93, 142
11:38	123
12:37	132
19:5	169
22:18	127
22:20	127
22:27	34, 124, 131, 169
24:44–49	165
24:46–48	5, 149
24:46	6
24:47	6, 125, 170
24:47–48	6
24:47–49	13
26:17	6

John

1:1–4	43, 82, 92, 137, 141
1:1–18	30, 42–44, 48, 62, 83, 177
1:4	82, 92, 137
1:5	81
1:6	51, 54
1:6–8	57
1:7	58, 170
1:8	170
1:9	43, 80, 83, 92, 105, 137
1:10	50
1:10–11	96
1:10–12	124
1:11	44, 64, 76, 97, 111, 115, 133–35, 145
1:11–12	43
1:12	61, 66, 92, 115, 134, 136, 138
1:13	176
1:14	2, 4, 37, 42–43, 45, 49, 50, 53, 61–66, 68, 76, 177–78, 182, 189
1:14a	62
1:14b	62, 64
1:14–17	53
1:15	143
1:18	43–44, 49, 58, 62, 70, 91, 99, 171, 174, 178, 186
1:19	52, 54
1:19–51	46
1:19—2:11	42
1:19—4:53	46
1:19—4:54	42
1:19—12:43	44
1:19—12:50	30, 43, 46
1:22	52, 54
1:24	52, 54
1:25	54
1:26–36	60
1:29	31, 38, 46, 50, 57, 67, 70–73, 75–76, 79, 81, 95, 103, 110, 116, 123–24, 132, 140, 175, 178
1:29–34	58
1:30	45
1:31	45
1:32	27
1:33	4, 45–46, 51, 54

1:34	43, 45–46, 83	3:3	87, 93, 115, 124, 168
1:36–50	134	3:4–11	4, 72, 77
1:37	139, 141, 189	3:5	61, 86–87, 116, 168
1:37–38	83, 91, 96, 137	3:6	87, 124
1:38	139, 141, 189	3:6–8	168
1:39	27, 46, 60, 93–96	3:11	45–46, 55, 58, 60, 70
1:39–41	98	3:12	45
1:40	91, 96, 137, 139, 141, 189	3:12–15	49
		3:13	70
1:41	83	3:13–14	53, 59, 70
1:43	27, 43, 46, 83, 91, 96, 137, 139, 141, 189	3:14	44, 123
		3:14–15	57, 70–71, 77–79, 116, 178
1:46	27, 46, 60, 93–97		
1:47	135	3:14–16	133
1:49	46, 66–67, 75, 83, 143	3:14–17	70
		3:14–18	135
1:50	49, 94, 96	3:14–21	56, 131
1:51	37, 45–46, 65	3:15	46, 78, 116, 134
2:1–11	49, 75, 123	3:15–18	61
2:1—11:57	42	3:15–21	83
2:1—21:25	109	3:16	xi, 15, 31, 35, 38, 44, 50, 57, 59, 61–62, 70, 78–79, 92, 101, 108, 110–11, 115–16, 131–32, 135, 139–40, 171–72, 186, 188–89
2:3	123		
2:5	121, 189		
2:6	38, 72, 74–75, 123		
2:7	38, 123		
2:8–11	76		
2:9	38, 46, 64, 121, 189	3:16a	78
2:11	49, 68, 70	3:16b	78
2:13–17	75	3:16–17	42, 48, 78, 85, 99, 105, 167, 173, 175
2:13–18	77		
2:13–22	65	3:16–18	47, 70, 121
2:14–22	65	3:16–19	168
2:16	76, 83	3:16–21	4, 46, 178
2:17	76	3:17	43, 50–51, 56, 61, 70, 78, 141, 169
2:18	49, 168		
2:18–22	37	3:17a	50, 78
2:19	45, 117	3:17b	50, 78
2:20–21	49	3:17–18	60, 96
2:21	37, 65, 76, 86, 124, 178, 186	3:17–21	80
		3:18	42–43, 81, 85
2:21–22	123	3:18–19	77
2:22	37, 49, 74, 76, 114	3:18–20	103
2:22–25	49	3:19	78, 80–81, 169
2:23	42, 46, 49, 115, 130	3:19–20	60
3	52	3:20	134–35, 141
3:1	134	3:20a	81
3:1–22	93	3:21	61, 78, 83, 85, 87, 89, 93, 135, 137, 186
3:2	45–46, 49, 70, 83		

John (continued)

3:22–23	38
3:22–26	72, 77, 123
3:22–30	60
3:23	117, 123
3:23–24	85, 133
3:23–25	54–55
3:25	72, 74–75, 122–23
3:26	58, 123
3:28	45, 57–58, 70
3:28–36	97
3:31	70
3:31–32	61, 70
3:31–36	58, 61, 83, 176, 178
3:32	46, 47, 58, 61
3:32–33	15, 58, 70
3:32–33	62
3:33	58
3:34	137
3:35	53, 59, 119, 136, 140, 146
3:36	58
4:1–2	77, 123
4:1–3	168
4:1–26	65
4:1—12:43	42
4:4	134
4:4–42	184
4:6	123, 134
4:6–14	123
4:9	105, 134
4:10	86
4:10–14	65, 93
4:11	61, 86
4:12	45
4:14	84, 86–87, 105, 116, 122–23
4:14–15	84
4:15	84
4:15–18	38
4:19–24	65
4:20–22	83
4:20–24	37
4:20–25	134
4:21	59, 84
4:21–26	65
4:22	45
4:23	84
4:23–24	83, 85, 112, 172
4:24	52, 80, 88, 145, 174, 186
4:28	145
4:29	46, 60, 93–94, 96, 98, 145
4:29–30	145
4:31–38	105
4:32	45
4:34	49, 51–52, 54–55, 70–71, 78, 94, 96–97, 107
4:34–38	57, 95, 139
4:34–42	145
4:35	45, 71, 93
4:35–38	86, 93–94, 98, 134, 142, 145
4:36	27, 49, 80, 97
4:36–38	29, 88
4:38	33, 51–52, 54–55, 60, 89, 93, 97
4:39	27, 42, 58, 60, 93–94, 134, 145
4:39–42	80, 86, 98, 134, 145
4:41	93
4:42	45–47, 50, 59, 84, 88, 94, 96, 115, 168–69, 172
4:44	58–59
4:45	86, 115, 134, 145
4:46	123
4:47	123
4:48	48
4:50	59, 123
4:51	121, 189
4:52–53	46
4:53	46, 59, 61, 84, 115, 123
5:1	130
5:1–8	46
5:1–14	38
5:1—6:71	42
5:1—12:50	46
5:2–9	123
5:3	123
5:16	42
5:17	53–54

5:17–18	46, 48, 141	6:2	91, 96, 139, 141, 189
5:18	42, 49, 53–54, 90, 118	6:5	45
		6:14	50
5:18–19	56	6:17	45, 81
5:18–29	53	6:20	80
5:19	45–46, 53, 61, 164	6:25–29	33
5:19–32	42	6:26	45
5:20	45, 101, 136	6:27	45, 54
5:21–30	123	6:28	80
5:22	53	6:28–29	50
5:22–39	62	6:29	51, 54, 59, 95
5:23	51, 53–54, 56, 90, 134, 173	6:29–30	95
		6:30	45, 48, 116
5:24	42, 51, 53, 56, 61, 78, 79, 95, 138	6:31	
		6:31–35	78
5:25	45, 79, 118	6:32	45, 78
5:25–26	85	6:33	42, 50
5:25–27	54	6:35	56, 59, 78, 80, 87, 95–96
5:26	53, 140		
5:27	53, 60, 119, 141	6:36	46, 170
5:28	118	6:37	35, 134
5:29	81, 141	6:37–38	49, 59
5:30	45–46, 51–54, 141, 164, 173	6:38	51, 54–55
		6:38–39	141
5:31	45	6:39	35, 38, 44, 46, 51, 54, 56, 59, 79, 119, 134, 174
5:31–38	61		
5:32	88		
5:33	54, 58, 60, 137	6:40	49, 61, 95, 134
5:34	61, 88	6:41	80
5:36	51–52, 54–55, 70–71, 78, 88–89, 173	6:43	46
		6:42	45–46
5:36–37	61	6:44	51, 54, 61, 79
5:37	51–52, 54, 56, 88–90	6:45	134
5:38	42, 51, 54–55	6:46	43, 61–62, 90
5:39	79, 170	6:47	42, 61
5:40	45, 97	6:48	80
5:41	70	6:50–51	90
5:42	101, 134	6:51	45, 50, 71, 80, 96, 134, 176, 182
5:42–45	45		
5:43	52	6:51–54	61, 119
5:44	54, 70	6:51c–58	116
5:44–47	115	6:52	45, 116
5:46–51	62	6:53–58	175
5:47	46, 79	6:54	123, 126
5:54	123	6:56	126
5:56	123	6:57	51, 54, 56
5:57	62	6:57–58	169
6:1	130	6:58	45, 61

John (continued)

6:60–71	135
6:61–63	45
6:61–64	45
6:63	87
6:64	119, 135
6:66–69	45
6:67	45
6:68	46, 60, 79
6:69	43, 62, 138
6:70	45, 135
6:70–71	119, 133, 135
6:71	42, 119
7:1	118–19, 127, 130
7:1—8:59	65
7:1—11:53	42
7:2	76, 119
7:3–5	170
7:4	134
7:5	46
7:6	118
7:7	50, 54, 58, 81, 134–35
7:7–8	45
7:8	118
7:11	118
7:14	80
7:15	46
7:16	46, 51–52, 54, 59, 61, 80, 177
7:17	80
7:18	51–52, 70
7:19	45–46, 118, 123
7:19–20	127
7:20	118
7:22–23	45
7:25	118, 123
7:27	46
7:28	45, 48, 51–52, 56, 80, 143
7:28–29	62
7:29	51, 54–55, 92
7:30	118, 127
7:31	185
7:32	52, 54
7:33	45, 51–52, 54
7:34–36	121
7:35	45, 80, 98, 145
7:37	84, 87, 143
7:37–38	84–85, 168
7:37–39	4, 59, 65, 76–77, 86, 95, 122–23, 178
7:38	61, 84–87, 123–24, 185
7:38–39	65, 86, 116, 122
7:39	49, 86, 92–93, 96
7:40–44	67
7:42	67
7:45–46	59
7:45—52	46
7:47	45
7:50	134
7:52	46
8:1–11	38, 134
8:12	27, 50, 52, 56, 59, 61, 80–83, 91–92, 96, 122, 124, 137, 139, 141, 186–87, 189
8:12–13	46
8:12–20	81
8:12–51	81
8:13	58, 79–80, 96
8:13–14	70
8:14	45, 58–59, 79
8:15	45, 176
8:16	51, 52
8:17	45, 79
8:18	51–52, 58, 89
8:19	45, 52, 138
8:20	123
8:21	45, 81, 138, 141
8:21–22	127
8:21–24	123
8:21–25	81
8:21–26	45
8:22	45
8:24	81, 83, 127, 138
8:25	82
8:26	61, 141
8:27–28	138
8:28	4, 45, 57, 70–71, 78, 80, 83, 92, 118, 137, 164
8:28–29	48, 95, 141
8:28–30	80

Ancient Document Index   235

8:29	49, 51–52	9:4	4, 51–52, 54–55, 69, 82, 96, 168
8:30	42	9:4–5	60
8:31	42, 61, 64, 80–81, 85, 125, 135, 137, 181–82	9:5	45–46, 50, 82–83
		9:6–7	123
8:31–32	45, 61, 83, 85, 125, 180, 184	9:7	51, 54, 103, 122–23, 128
8:31–34	81, 126, 138	9:7–11	123
8:31–36	122	9:11	103, 122–23, 128
8:32	77, 82–83, 85, 92, 125, 137, 141, 171, 173, 176	9:12	123
		9:15	12819
		9:16	45–46, 122
8:32–34	179	9:24	45, 70
8:33	45, 121, 125	9:25	122
8:34	77, 81, 103, 121, 123, 135, 137, 169, 189	9:27	45–46, 125
		9:27–30	47
8:34–44	82, 103	9:28–31	47
8:34–35	60, 121, 180	9:29	47
8:34–36	110	9:30	47, 138
8:35	82, 121, 189	9:31	45, 81
8:36	125, 141, 171	9:31–34	122
8:36–39	45	9:34	81, 127
8:37	118, 127	9:35–36	83
8:38	43, 60–61, 69, 92, 103, 135, 137	9:35–37	81
		9:35–38	103
8:40	43, 118, 127, 137	9:35–41	59, 61, 96, 103
8:41	45	9:36–37	125
8:41–44	77, 180	9:37–38	124
8:42	45, 51, 62, 69, 118	9:38	46
8:43	135	9:39	50, 60, 81
8:43–44	82	9:39–41	77
8:44	60, 81, 103, 127, 135, 137	9:40–41	103, 123
		9:41	60, 81, 96, 122, 125, 127, 138
8:45	135, 137, 141, 176		
8:46	81, 137, 141	10:1	71
8:47	79, 82, 127	10:1–6	83
8:48	45	10:2	71
8:50	70	10:3	79–80, 124
8:51	80	10:4	80, 83, 91, 96, 124, 134, 137, 139, 141, 189
8:54	70		
8:55	45		
8:58–59	82	10:5	83, 91, 96, 137, 139, 141, 189
8:59	65		
9:1–12	122	10:6	45, 79
9:1–41	61, 125	10:7	59, 71, 80
9:2–3	123	10:7–18	44, 78, 112
9:3	49, 54, 60–61, 69, 70, 95–96, 174	10:9	45, 56, 59, 80
		10:10	61, 131, 175

John (continued)

10:10–11	116, 178
10:11	36, 42, 45–47, 57, 59–60, 70–71, 75, 80, 110, 118, 120, 123–24, 132, 135, 182
10:11–15	79, 140
10:11–17	62, 70
10:11–18	140
10:13	71
10:14	45, 59, 80
10:15	36, 71, 110, 114, 120, 123–24, 139, 182
10:15a	139
10:15b	79
10:16	77, 80, 83, 97–98, 115
10:17	36, 47, 57, 77, 119–20, 123–24, 136, 178
10:17–18	79, 139, 182
10:18	36, 43, 71, 119–20, 123
10:22	75
10:22–39	65
10:24	134
10:25	48, 52, 59, 89–90
10:26	71
10:26–28	116
10:27	27, 45, 61, 79–80, 83, 91, 96, 137, 139, 141, 170, 189
10:27–28	94, 96
10:28	60, 178
10:28–29	35, 118
10:28–30	90
10:30	46, 53, 62, 90, 98
10:32	53, 61, 70, 90
10:35	168
10:36	46, 54, 60, 62, 72, 75, 83, 85, 88–89, 103, 123, 138, 181
10:36–38	53, 90
10:37	52, 90
10:37–38	48, 70, 82, 92, 137, 141
10:38	35, 45, 47–48, 54, 60, 62, 88–90, 111, 123, 129–30, 181
10:41	124
10:41–42	134
10:42	94
11:1	134
11:2	120
11:3	52, 54
11:4	60
11:9	60, 82
11:9–10	83, 96
11:15	45, 48, 50
11:24–25	123
11:25	45, 49, 56, 60, 80, 96
11:25–27	79
11:26	94, 96
11:31	139, 141, 189
11:34	120
11:39–40	79
11:40	49, 60, 70, 76, 78–79
11:42	45, 50–53, 79, 134
11:43	143
11:44	103
11:45	60, 79, 170
11:46	170
11:47	45
11:47–48	45
11:48	135
11:49	45
11:49–50	49
11:49–53	124
11:50	71, 78
11:50–52	42, 46–47, 57, 59, 62, 70, 77–78, 86, 110, 112, 120, 132, 135, 139
11:51	70, 138
11:51–52	75–77, 110, 118, 124, 178
11:52	49, 70, 94, 97, 124, 138
11:53	42, 124
11:54	42
11:55	72, 74–75, 123
11:56	45
11:57	42, 124
12:1	76, 124

Ancient Document Index   237

12:1—20:31	42	12:33b–34c	71
12:1–8	34, 120, 131, 187	12:34	57, 78
12:2	101, 121, 123, 189	12:35	45, 81–82, 96, 124
12:3	120	12:35–36	83
12:4	119, 135	12:36	45, 61, 79–80, 83, 85, 91, 96, 124–25, 137–38, 140, 182
12:6	133, 135		
12:7	119–20, 123, 131, 134		
		12:36a	42
12:8	45, 120	12:36b	42
12:9	44	12:37	44, 49, 132
12:11	60, 79, 86	12:37–44	44
12:12	62	12:37–50	44, 178
12:13	46, 66–67, 75, 143	12:41	70, 77
12:13b	64	12:42	44–45
12:15a	64	12:43	42, 44, 70
12:16	37, 70, 114, 120, 130	12:44	42, 48, 51–55, 91, 173
12:17	58, 71		
12:17–19	79	12:44a	143
12:19	45–46	12:44–45	42, 62, 143
12:20	115, 145	12:44b-45	143
12:20–22	98	12:44–46	97, 137
12:20–23	86, 134	12:44–47	78, 82
12:20–25	47, 94	12:44–50	44, 45, 48, 106, 139
12:20–33	47	12:45	44, 51–55, 129, 144, 178
12:21	145		
12:23	49, 71, 78, 110, 118	12:46	44, 50, 61, 80–81, 124, 134–35, 137, 140, 143, 185–86
12:23–24	118		
12:23–26	59		
12:24	29, 42, 49, 57, 59, 75, 77, 105, 110, 115, 118, 124, 178	12:46–50	61
		12:47	50, 82, 169
		12:47c	44
12:24–25	119, 135	12:47–48	47, 60–61, 96
12:24–26	62, 70, 78–79, 115, 120–21, 131, 139, 168	12:47–50	79
		12:48	55, 57, 71, 78, 81
		12:49	44, 51–52, 54–55, 164, 173
12:25	86, 134		
12:25–26	32	12:49–50	85, 107, 144
12:26	61, 83, 91, 94, 96, 101, 121, 132, 137, 139, 141, 178, 189	12:50	30, 42–43, 46, 59, 61, 83, 116, 137, 141, 184
12:28	49, 52	13—15	103
12:31	50, 81, 169	13—17	32–33, 36, 47, 91, 104, 106, 109, 111–12, 127
12:32	97, 178		
12:32–33	70, 118		
12:32–34	95, 118–19	13—21	29, 38, 41, 45, 48, 50, 99, 109–10, 112, 129, 146
12:32–43	110		
12:33	47		
12:33–34	178		

Ancient Document Index

John (continued)

13:1	2, 32–33, 35, 38, 43–44, 47, 59, 75–76, 79, 108, 110–15, 117–19, 121, 124–25, 133, 135, 139, 146, 171, 188
13:1a	113
13:1b	113
13:1–3	32
13:1–8	104
13:1–11	33, 104, 109–11, 114–15, 129, 146, 192
13:1–14	123
13:1–15	xi, 29, 140
13:1–17	104
13:1–20	34–35, 67, 92, 131
13:1–30	103–4, 109, 115
13:1–35	136
13:1–38	1, 36, 65, 100–101, 109–10, 113, 145–46, 173, 178, 192
13:1—16:33	42
13:1—17:26	30, 44, 109
13:1—19:42	30, 106, 109
13:1—20:31	42–43, 103
13:1—21:22	42
13:2	38, 45, 110–11, 113, 119, 121, 126, 133, 135
13:2–5	33
13:3	45, 53, 110, 118–20, 137, 140, 146
13:3–5	113
13:3–11	181
13:4	34, 114, 120–21, 123
13:4–11	72, 77
13:5	38, 48, 90, 113, 120, 123, 128
13:5–10	75
13:6	62, 72, 128
13:6–9	121
13:6–10	113
13:6–11	34, 109
13:7	33, 37, 48, 110, 112, 114, 118, 130
13:8	36, 38, 103, 107, 110, 114, 118, 120, 122, 125–26, 128, 131, 140, 146, 178, 184–85, 189, 191
13:8c	81
13:8–9	38
13:10	38, 72, 75, 82, 110, 116, 120, 122–23, 127–29, 133, 171, 185, 189, 191
13:10–11	178
13:10b–11	113
13:11	45, 72, 110, 113, 117, 135
13:11b	103
13:12	37, 48, 113–14, 120, 125, 128–30, 132
13:12–15	49, 182
13:12–17	104, 109
13:12a	113
13:12b–17	113
13:12–18	34
13:12–20	33, 109
13:12–38	104, 111, 114–15, 129, 146, 193
13:13	72, 112
13:14	38, 78, 111, 114, 127–28, 130–32, 134, 183, 185
13:14b	114
13:14–15	36, 48, 59, 79, 129, 134, 137
13:14–16	184
13:15	4, 29, 35, 37, 47, 49, 56, 89, 104, 107–8, 110–12, 114–15, 127, 130–34, 136, 143, 178, 181, 185, 187, 191
13:15–16	36
13:15–17	101
13:16	2–3, 35, 38, 51, 56, 88, 90, 100, 105, 107, 111, 115, 121, 129, 133–34, 137, 141–43, 147, 178, 185, 187, 189, 191

13:16–17	141		129–30, 133–35, 137,
13:16–21	57		139, 145, 170–71,
13:17	29, 50, 114, 130–31,		181, 184, 186, 189,
	138, 143		191
13:18	45, 110, 113, 116,	13:35–36	185
	121, 126, 133, 141	13:36	2, 27, 45, 57, 88,
13:18–19	143		94, 112, 114–15,
13:19	50, 83, 108, 112, 114,		121, 129, 139, 141,
	117–18, 121, 135,		184–85, 189, 191
	146,	13:36b	139
13:19–20	45, 113, 124, 137	13:36–37	83, 91, 96, 118, 123,
13:20	2, 15, 35–36, 38, 43,		137, 178
	47, 49, 53–54, 56–57,	13:36–38	38, 110, 111, 121,
	80, 88–89, 93–94,		132, 141
	100–101, 106, 108,	13:37	110, 139, 141, 189
	111–12, 115, 129–30,	13:37–38	78, 114
	134, 136–38, 140–43,	13:38	121, 139
	146, 171, 178, 184–	14:1	42, 45, 62, 112
	85, 187, 191	14:2	65, 112
13:20a	51	14:3	45
13:20b	33, 51	14:4	45
13:21	45, 82, 110, 121, 137	14:5	45
13:21–30	45, 113, 121	14:5–6	60
13:23	136	14:6	56, 60, 80, 99, 137,
13:24	121		141, 170–72, 186
13:26	110, 119	14:7	99, 144
13:26–27	119, 126	14:7–10	61, 90, 130, 182, 186
13:26–30	121, 127	14:7–11	62, 111, 177
13:27	119, 133, 135	14:7–12	49
13:29	133, 135	14:8	99
13:30	119, 135	14:8–9	70
13:31–32	49, 71, 79, 110, 121	14:8–10	62
13:31–38	113, 115, 127	14:9	xi, 88
13:31—17:26	103–4, 109	14:9–10	174
13:33	45, 112, 115, 121	14:9–11	58, 129
13:34	32, 35, 45, 92, 114–	14:10	4, 49, 70, 79, 89–90,
	15, 132–33, 135–37,		98–99, 139, 141, 144,
	139–70, 189		164, 181
13:34b	114, 139	14:10a	91
13:34–35	4, 35, 38, 47–48,	14:10–11	35, 44, 58, 70, 144
	56–57, 59, 78, 81, 85,	14:10–12	61, 112, 173, 187
	91, 111–12, 115, 127,	14:11	42, 90, 99, 174, 181
	129–30, 132, 178,	14:12	29, 32, 43, 47, 49,
	189		56–57, 69, 88–90, 94,
13:34–36	36, 49, 146		107, 178
13:35	xi, 2, 29, 34, 48,	14:12–21	126
	58–59, 81, 83, 88, 90,	14:13	45
	92, 105–6, 115, 125,		

Ancient Document Index

John (continued)

14:15	60, 81, 85, 88, 91, 115, 136, 139, 189
14:15–17	111
14:15–21	45
14:15–26	92
14:16	57, 78, 87, 94, 122, 170
14:16–17	98, 126, 172
14:16–18	112, 177
14:17	50, 86–88, 92, 111, 137, 181
14:20	35, 59, 61, 86, 91, 103, 111, 123, 126, 130–31, 138–39
14:20a	61
14:20–21	48
14:21	35, 59, 92, 126, 136, 171, 189
14:21–24	182
14:23	65, 136, 139
14:23–24	112
14:24	51–52, 54–55, 59, 69, 79–80, 93, 189
14:24–30	45
14:25	87, 92
14:25–26	88, 172
14:26	51–54, 56–57, 69, 85, 87–88, 92–93, 112, 122, 127, 137, 180
14:26–27	136
14:28	45, 54, 69, 136, 189
14:29	49–50, 59, 93, 112, 114, 117, 143
14:30	81, 169
14:30c	81
14:30–31	117
14:31	29, 58, 60–62, 71, 93, 98, 107, 132, 135–36, 174, 189
15:1	56, 60, 80
15:1–5	59
15:1–8	105, 181
15:1–10	92
15:1–14	138
15:1–15	92, 136
15:1–17	60, 83, 92, 111
15:1–27	127
15:2	127, 129, 138
15:2–3	178
15:2–4	111
15:2–17	90
15:3	72, 75, 82, 102–4, 113, 115–17, 123, 125, 131–32, 138, 140, 189
15:3–4	103, 134
15:3–5	45, 107, 185
15:3–6	123
15:3–8	56, 127
15:3–12	181
15:4	86, 111, 132, 139, 186
15:4–5	90, 129, 131, 182
15:4–7	111, 127
15:4–17	48
15:5	80, 96, 105, 139
15:6	81
15:7	64, 79, 86, 90, 103, 189
15:7–8	107
15:7–12	45
15:8	29, 48, 59, 61, 85, 90, 105, 111, 139, 181, 186
15:9	35, 136, 138
15:9–10	90
15:9–17	105, 152
15:10	59, 86, 92, 139
15:11	136
15:12	35, 90, 92, 111, 115, 136, 138, 170, 172, 189
15:13	xi, 29, 71, 78, 101, 131, 136, 182
15:14	98, 135
15:14–20	45
15:15	43, 85, 121, 133, 184, 189
15:15a	90
15:15b	90
15:16	29, 32, 92, 105, 139, 181
15:17	59, 90, 111, 136, 189
15:18	50, 60, 74, 134

15:18–19	134	16:13	87, 92, 94, 137, 141, 180–82
15:18–21	168	16:13–14	92
15:18–25	135	16:13–15	87
15:18–27	112	16:14	87, 112
15:19	50, 106, 111, 134	16:14–15	93
15:20	90, 96, 107–8, 142, 185	16:15	177
15:21	51, 54, 56, 60	16:17	45
15:21–23	81	16:20	50
15:21–24	96	16:20–27	45
15:22	81, 138	16:27	43–44, 62, 112, 136
15:22–24	142, 187	16:27–28	45
15:23	134	16:27b–28	118
15:24	60, 79, 81, 127, 134, 138	16:27c–28	69
		16:28	43, 62, 69, 105, 112
15:25	134–35	16:30	45, 112
15:26	33, 51–54, 57, 69, 87, 98, 111, 115, 137, 142, 144, 168, 180–81	16:31–33	45
		16:32	4, 69, 110, 132
		16:33	42, 50, 112
		17	111
15:26a	87	17:1	47
15:26–27	4, 15, 29, 41, 43, 47–48, 56–57, 60, 89, 99, 112, 145–46, 170, 177, 189	17:1–26	47, 92, 136
		17:2	35, 53, 61, 78, 85, 105, 125, 137, 140, 175–76
15:27	3, 32, 46, 48–49, 57–58, 60, 87–88, 94–96, 98, 105, 130, 140, 142, 144, 168	17:2–3	42, 95
		17:2–4	78
		17:3	51–52, 54–56, 80–81, 85–86, 89, 112, 137, 141, 143
16:1	45, 185	17:4	71, 78, 94, 141
16:2	34, 94, 102, 134	17:6	35, 85, 88, 93, 98, 111, 125, 140, 168
16:3	60, 117		
16:4	34, 117	17:6–8	81, 85
16:4a	102, 180	17:7	50, 98, 134
16:4–7	45	17:7–9	85
16:5	45, 51, 54, 69, 121	17:8	31, 43, 51, 54–55, 62, 69, 70, 93, 98, 111–12, 141, 182
16:7	33, 52, 54, 56, 69, 87, 137		
16:7–11	4, 57, 87	17:8b	118
16:7–15	98	17:8–26	45
16:8	50, 81, 87	17:9	50, 112, 117, 181
16:8–11	89, 94, 170	17:9–10	86
16:8–12	94	17:9–19	35
16:9	81, 127, 138	17:11	32, 45, 83, 92, 98, 103, 111, 123, 125, 128, 181
16:10	45		
16:10–15	45		
16:11	50, 81, 169		
16:12–15	170, 172	17:11–18	169

Ancient Document Index 241

John (continued)

17:11–23	168
17:12	59, 82, 111–12, 117, 127
17:14	50, 82, 127, 134, 137–38
17:14–16	112
17:14–19	125
17:14–20	184
17:14–26	43, 182
17:15	50, 117, 125, 168, 182
17:16	50, 82, 86, 111
17:16–17	181
17:16–19	85
17:17	72, 75, 85, 103, 116, 124, 127, 137, 144, 176, 188
17:17–18	88–90, 181
17:17–19	83, 88, 115, 173
17:18	xi, 2, 4, 15, 20, 27–28, 32–33, 35, 38, 42, 47, 49–57, 86, 88–89, 90, 93, 98, 104, 108–9, 112, 115, 133, 137–38, 140–41, 144, 165, 168–69, 174–75, 181, 185
17:18b	55
17:18–19	53, 137–38
17:18–20	139, 178
17:19	62, 67, 71, 75, 83, 85, 113, 116, 123, 127–28, 137, 188
17:19–22	138
17:19–26	125
17:20	3, 28–29, 42–43, 55, 57–58, 60, 86, 88, 90, 93–94, 96, 98, 100, 105, 130, 140–41, 177
17:20–21	50, 140
17:21	xi, 29, 31, 51, 53–54, 59, 61, 69, 82, 85, 88–90, 111–12, 115, 127, 129, 131, 133, 138, 170
17:21–22	49
17:21–23	35, 92, 182
17:22	70, 98
17:22–23	32
17:22–26	177
17:23	xi, 2, 29, 48, 50–51, 54, 57–59, 83, 85–86, 90–92, 103–4, 108, 111–12, 123, 125, 127, 129–30, 132, 135–37, 141, 144, 146, 170–71, 174, 181, 184–86, 189, 191
17:24	49, 53, 136
17:24–26	70
17:25	xi, 29, 70
17:25–26	59
17:26	30, 32, 42, 44, 50, 103–4, 109, 133, 136
17:26b	111
18—21	112
18:1—19:42	30, 44
18:1—20:31	42
18:1—21:25	42
18:2	119, 127, 133
18:2–5	119, 126
18:3–5	110
18:5	45, 119, 127
18:6	45, 120
18:8–9	111, 124
18:9	35, 44, 112
18:10	121, 189
18:11	71
18:14	77, 112, 120, 132
18:15	139, 141, 189
18:15–18	110, 132
18:18	121, 132
18:19	59, 112, 124
18:19–24	111
18:21–30	113
18:24	52, 54
18:25–27	38, 110, 132
18:26	121
18:28	71, 73, 75, 124
18:28—19:16	67
18:30	119
18:32	112, 123

18:33	66–67	20:9	42, 67
18:35	119	20:11	134
18:36	119, 137, 169	20:17	45, 54, 64, 75–76, 124
18:37	29, 57–59, 67, 79, 82, 85, 96, 130, 134, 137, 140–41, 170, 173, 176–77, 189	20:17c	68
		20:17–23	66
		20:19	58, 64, 68, 76–77, 94, 125, 178
18:37–38	171		
18:38	137	20:19b	68
18:39	66–67, 124	20:19c	68
19:1–3	67	20:19–23	31, 35, 62–63, 87, 137, 168
19:3	67		
19:7	67	20:19–29	66, 99
19:9	119	20:19–31	48, 113
19:10	120	20:20–21	172, 188
19:11	81, 110, 119–20	20:21	x–xi, 2, 4–6, 13, 15, 20, 27–28, 31–33, 35, 38, 41–45, 47, 49, 31, 50–57, 62, 68, 88–89, 91, 94, 100, 104, 108–9, 112, 115, 137–39, 141, 144, 162–63, 165, 168–71, 174–175, 177, 182–83, 185–86, 190
19:14	124		
19:16	67, 119		
19:19	67		
19:20	137		
19:21	66–67		
19:23	34, 37, 114, 120		
19:28	33, 109, 118		
19:29	71		
19:30	47, 71, 77, 86, 88, 95, 109–10, 113, 118–20, 141, 178		
		20:21a	51
		20:21b	51–52, 55
19:30–37	123	20:21–22	65, 180
19:31–36	71	20:21–23	112, 167, 186
19:31–37	49, 71	20:22	13, 57, 60, 65, 68, 75–77, 86, 92, 94, 116, 122, 124, 126, 177–78, 180
19:32	124		
19:33	33, 76		
19:34	38, 42, 75–77, 86, 93, 123–25		
		20:22–23	4
19:35	42–43, 50, 58–60, 77, 95, 109, 112, 141, 178	20:23	3, 28, 31, 43, 45, 55–57, 60, 70, 81, 91, 94–95, 100–101, 103, 110, 125–26, 134, 137–41, 143, 171, 175, 179, 189
19:36	71, 76, 124, 126–27		
19:37	57, 59, 77, 124, 127, 178		
19:38–42	93, 134	20:23b	125
19:40	114	20:24–29	49, 59
19:42	30, 44, 106, 109	20:24–31	49
20	127	20:26	58, 68, 77
20:1	81	20:27	112
20:1—21:25	30, 44	20:28	48, 54, 67–68, 70, 172
20:6	139, 141, 189		
20:8	42, 61	20:29	44, 94, 96, 112

Ancient Document Index   243

Ancient Document Index

John (continued)

20:29–31	48
20:30	44, 49
20:30–31	6, 41, 43–44, 50, 55, 61, 85, 94, 105, 140, 143, 144
20:31	42–43, 50, 56, 58, 64, 95–96, 103, 112, 121, 130, 137, 143–44, 189
21	66, 110
21:1	130
21:1–23	111
21:1–25	41–44
21:3	38, 62
21:5–23	59
21:9	132
21:9–13	132
21:11–12	123
21:15	71, 111, 136, 189
21:15–17	44, 79, 110, 118, 132, 140
21:15–18	111–12
21:15–19	57, 112
21:15–22	112
21:15–23	110
21:16	136, 189
21:17	136, 189
21:18	111, 121
21:18–19	27, 114, 140, 189
21:18–21	118, 126
21:18–22	96, 123
21:18–23	127, 132
21:19	49, 83, 91, 96, 102, 111–13, 137, 139
21:19–20	121
21:20	44, 119, 139, 141, 189
21:22	42, 44, 61, 83, 91, 96, 112, 137
21:22–23	126
21:22–25	49
21:23	79
21:23–25	42
21:24	27, 43–44, 50, 55, 58, 95, 105, 112, 130, 141
21:24–25	41, 48, 144
21:25	30, 42, 44, 109

Acts

1:1–4	152
1:6	67
1:8	5–6, 1659:37
2:1–4	152
4:15	5
9:37	116, 128
10:1—11:18	7
11:20	7
13:26	6
16:33	116, 128
19:31	6
22:16	116, 128
22:21	5
26:16–18	5
28:28	6

Romans

1:1	6
1:1–3	13
1:3	67
1:15	6
12:13	35
14:11	25
15:7–13	164

1 Corinthians

1:10–17	26
1:17	6
1:30	89
3:16	163
5—15	26
6:11	116, 128
6:17	163
8:6	25
11:23	117
12	152
12:3	26

2 Corinthians

4:5	152
4:6	85

5:16–21	152
6:3–10	152

Galatians

1:8	26
1:9	26
1:13	25
2:4–5	25
2:5	26
2:7	7
2:9	7
2:11–14	25
2:14	26
4:19	124
5:13	35
6:2	35
6:10	152

Ephesians

3:8–11	164
4:15–16	124
5:26	116, 128

Philippians

1:27	26
2:5–8	169
2:6–8	35
2:11	25
2:19	6

Colossians

2:15	85

1 Thessalonians

4:3	89
4:4	89
4:7	89
5:11	164

2 Thessalonians

1:8	26
2:2	26
2:13	89

1 Timothy

1:15	164
3:2	35, 131
3:16	7
5:10	128, 130–31
6:3	7

2 Timothy

1:10	7

Titus

1:8	35, 131
2:15	89
3:5	116, 128

Hebrews

2:8	68
10:22	116, 128
12:14	89
13:2	35, 131

1 Peter

1:2	89
1:12	6, 89
1:15–16	89
2:5	163
2:9	163
4:9	35, 131

2 Peter

2:22	116, 128
3:15–16	26

1 John

1:1–3	105
1:2	133
1:7	134
1:9	122, 128, 133–34
1:9—2:2	134
2:1	87, 128
2:1–6	134
2:2	128
2:3	133
2:3–5	92

1 John (continued)

2:5–6	133
2:6	133
2:9–10	134
2:22–23	117
2:24	133
3:13	134
3:14–16	133
3:16	131
3:18	133
4.2–3	26
4:9	105, 169
4:10	169
4:10–11	134
4:12	133
4:14	105, 133, 169
5:4–6	117

3 John

7–8	164

Revelation

1:9	6
5:6	71
7:9–10	164
7:15	62
12:12	62
13:6	62
13:11	71
14:6–7	7
21:3	6

The History of Herodotus (Erato)

6.19.2	120
1QS iii	138

Sirach

22:4	63

4Q174

	67

4Q285

	67

m. Sukkah

5:1–4	82

Berakhot

15a	123
53b	123

1 Maccabees

2:12	74
4:36–51	82
4:52–59	82
14:36	74

2 Maccabees

2:18	74
2:18–36	82
10:1–4	82
10:5–8	82
14:36	74
15:18	74

T. Abr

3:7–9	35

Jos. Asen

7:1	35

1 Enoch

48:4	83
105:2	67
105:4	67

Yoma

3:3	123

Esd A

1:1	73
1:6	73
1:8	73
7:12	73

Ancient Document Index   247

4 Ezra
7:28–29   67
13:26–27   67
13:52   67
14:9   67

Philo's *Moses*
2.71–75   74

Moses II
74   74
2.72, 73   74

V. Mos. II
174   74

Philo's the Similitudes of Enoch
            25

Spec. Leg.
I 66   74

Leg. Ad Gaium
156   74

Ebr.
66   74

Tob
5:10   124
14:10   124

Josephus, Wars
4:2   74
4:3   74
4:5   74
4:6   74

Mishnah Ber
5:5   53

De somniis
1.148   128

www.ingramcontent.com/pod-product-compliance
Lightning Source LLC
Chambersburg PA
CBHW050846230426
43667CB00012B/2168